SOVEREIGNTY'S ENTAILMENTS

First Nation State Formation in the Yukon

In recent decades, Indigenous peoples in the Yukon have signed land claim and self-government agreements that spell out the nature of government-to-government relations and grant individual First Nations significant, albeit limited, powers of governance over their peoples, lands, and resources. Those agreements, however, are predicated on the assumption that if First Nations are to qualify as governments at all, they must be fundamentally state-like, and they frame First Nation powers in the culturally contingent idiom of sovereignty.

Based on over five years of ethnographic research conducted in the southwest Yukon, *Sovereignty's Entailments* is a close ethnographic analysis of everyday practices of state formation in a society whose members do not take for granted the cultural entailments of sovereignty. Paul Nadasdy illustrates the full scope and magnitude of the "cultural revolution" that is state formation and exposes the culturally specific assumptions about space, time, and sociality that lie at the heart of sovereign politics.

This timely and insightful work illuminates how the process of state formation is transforming Yukon Indian people's relationships with one another, animals, and the land.

PAUL NADASDY is an associate professor in the Department of Anthropology at Cornell University.

PAUL NADASDY

Sovereignty's Entailments

First Nation State Formation in the Yukon

UNIVERSITY OF TORONTO PRESS
Toronto Buffalo London

Toronto Buffalo London
www.utorontopress.com

ISBN 978-1-4875-0264-5 (cloth) ISBN 978-1-4875-2207-0 (paper)

Library and Archives Canada Cataloguing in Publication

Nadasdy, Paul, author
Sovereignty's entailments : First Nation state formation in the Yukon/ Paul Nadasdy.

Includes bibliographical references and index.
ISBN 978-1-4875-0264-5 (cloth). – ISBN 978-1-4875-2207-0 (paper)

1. Native peoples – Yukon – Politics and government.
2. Native peoples – Government relations – Yukon. I. Title.

E78.Y8N33 2017 971.9'100497 C2017-904298-X

This book has been published with the help of a grant from the Federation for the Humanities and Social Sciences, through the Awards to Scholarly Publications Program, using funds provided by the Social Sciences and Humanities Research Council of Canada.

University of Toronto Press acknowledges the financial assistance to its publishing program of the Canada Council for the Arts and the Ontario Arts Council, an agency of the Government of Ontario.

Canada Council for the Arts Conseil des Arts du Canada

Funded by the Government of Canada Financé par le gouvernement du Canada

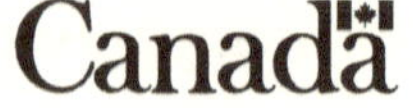

In memory of Joseph Johnson

Contents

Maps

Photos

Acknowledgments

I have been working on this book for a very long time and have benefited from the kindness, help, and insights of many people over the years. First and foremost, I could not even have conceived of – much less written – this book without the people of Burwash Landing. Over twenty years ago, they welcomed me into their community and allowed me take part in their lives. I will be forever grateful for their kindness, hospitality, and friendship. Although everyone in Burwash made me feel welcome and taught me valuable lessons about life in the Yukon, there were some who played particularly important roles in shaping the arguments I make in this book (which is not to say they all necessarily agree with me). They include Math'ieya Alatini, Robin Bradasch, Joe Bruneau, Bob Dickson, Dennis Dickson, Dick Dickson, Gerald Dickson, Janice Dickson, Donalda Easterson, Mark Eikland, Agnes Johnson, Bernie Johnson, Kathleen Johnson, Katie Johnson, Lena Johnson, Luke Johnson, Mary Jane Johnson, Sandy Johnson, Simon Johnson, Geraldine Pope, Josie Sias, Pauly Sias, and Grace Southwick. I owe a special debt of thanks to the late Joe Johnson, who, though he dedicated much of his life to negotiating Kluane First Nation's land claim and self-government agreements, was not at all averse to criticizing them. I miss him more than I can say.

I learned a great deal about Kluane First Nation's final and self-government agreements from all those who took part in negotiating them, including Shawn Allen, Karen Armour, Jim Bishop, Robin Bradasch, Patricia Eels, Gary Hall, Karen Hougen-Bell, Dave Jennings, Dave Joe, Joe Johnson, Alexandre Martel, Leslie McCullough, and Ron Sumanik. Robin Bradasch, in particular, has always been willing to answer my questions and help me understand the arcana of land claims. Many of those who were involved, in one way or another, with the Implementation Review Group, the PSTA table, and/or the Senior Financial Affairs Committee, too, gave me invaluable insights into complexities of these agreements and what it takes to actually implement them, including especially Roger Alfred, Fran Asp, William Asp, Gail Barnaby, Greg Charlie, Cathy Constable, Tim Gerberding, Fred Green, Elizabeth Hanson, Lisa Hutton, Dave Janoff, Ross Knox, Lori Leduc, Hal Mehaffy, Matthew Mehaffy, Skeeter Miller-Wright, Hugh Monaghan, Viola Mullett, Sharon Peter, Kim Smarch, Crystal Trudeau, Mike Vance, Angie Wabisca, and Pat Wiens. There were others, too, both in and out of government who helped me to understand some of the processes I discuss in this book, including Will Jones, Dave Neufeld, and Barney Smith.

This book emerged in part out of a long and ongoing conversation with Norman Easton on the nature and importance of boundaries in the southwest Yukon, and I look forward to continuing that conversation (and others) with him in the years to come. My orientation to the subject matter of this book also owes a great deal to Katherine Verdery, whose influence is evident throughout. Many people read various parts of this book (or what later became parts of it) and provided me with valuable feedback. Among them are Michael Asch, Robin Bradasch, Jessica Cattelino, Cathy Constable, Ray Craib, Julie Cruikshank, Norman Easton, Terry Fenge, Chris Garces, Chuck Geisler, Luke Johnson, Sandy Johnson, Ed Labenski, Stacey Langwick, Hirokazu Miyazaki, Adam Moore, Sara Pritchard, Aaron Sachs, Marina Welker, Steven Wolf, Wendy Wolford, and two anonymous reviewers. I presented different parts of what would eventually become chapters of this book at meetings of the Alaska Anthropological Association, the American Anthropological Association, and Ilàà Katì: A Festival of Traditional Knowledge in Yellowknife, NWT, as well as to audiences at the University of Aberdeen, the University of Alberta, Binghamton University, Charles Darwin University, the University of Chicago, Cornell University, the University of Uppsala, the University of Victoria, and the University of Wisconsin–Madison. I am grateful to the organizers of those events and to all those who provided questions and comments that helped shape my thinking in important ways. Earlier versions of some of the sections now in chapters 2, 3, and 4 appeared in the *Canadian Journal of Political Science* (Nadasdy 2016) and *Comparative Studies in Society and History* (Nadasdy 2012), so this book benefited indirectly from feedback provided by anonymous reviewers of those articles and from the oversight and suggestions of the journal editors, Graham White and Andrew Shryock. Similarly, parts of chapters 2 and 5 appeared in edited volumes published by the University of Calgary Press (Nadasdy 2017) and SAR Press (Nadasdy 2008), respectively. The former benefited from comments provided by participants at an authors' meeting at Trent University and especially from the ministrations of volume editors Stephen Bocking and Brad Martin. The latter benefited immensely from intense and enjoyable discussions at an advanced seminar at the School of Advanced Research in Santa Fe, and especially from comments provided by Karen Strassler, and volume editors Elizabeth Ferry and Mandana Limbert.

This book could not have been written without generous support from the National Science Foundation and the Wenner-Gren Foundation for Anthropological Research, which funded the research on which it is based. It was during a sabbatical leave supported by the American Philosophical Society and the University of Wisconsin–Madison that this book first began to take shape in my mind. The Institute for Social Sciences at Cornell University provided me with time and space to write much of chapter 3. I wrote the bulk of the book in Malang, Indonesia, while on sabbatical leave from Cornell. Although it sometimes felt odd writing about the Yukon while sweltering in the tropical heat, my time in Malang was wonderfully productive. Thanks, too, to my colleagues in Anthropology and American Indian and Indigenous Studies at Cornell for providing a supportive and stimulating community.

I am grateful to the University of Toronto Press for helping make this book a reality, particularly Daniel Quinlan for his uncanny timing in reaching out to me and for his interest in and enthusiasm for the manuscript, and to John St James for his copy-edits. For the maps, I owe thanks to Gerry Perrier at the Yukon government's Information Management and Technology Branch and to Tracy Sallaway at the Maps, Data and Government Information Centre, Trent University.

Finally, I must acknowledge my own kinship relations. Gabor and Phyllis Nadasdy; Beth, Billy, Emily, and Matt Karpowic; Scott, Denise, Julia, and Joseph Newman; and John, Anna, and Evelyn Nadasdy have all provided me with love and support over the years. I am especially grateful to Marina Welker for her help and companionship; our conversations have shaped the book in ways too numerous and subtle to describe. Perhaps even more important, she, Andor, and Zoli help keep me grounded and fill my life with joy.

A Note on Terminology

First Nation is the preferred term in Canada for those indigenous people (and their governments) who are neither Inuit nor Métis. In use since the early 1980s, this term has the virtue of acknowledging indigenous peoples' place – alongside the immigrant English and French nations – among the founding peoples of Canada. As I take pains to argue in this book, however, the concept of *nation* is culturally loaded. Along with concepts like *sovereignty, territory,* and *citizenship,* its use reflects and helps naturalize a set of state-derived assumptions about the nature of "human" society whose application badly mischaracterizes indigenous Yukon society. For this reason, I avoid the common practice of using *First Nation* as a synonym for "indigenous" or "Indian" – particularly in relation to those indigenous beliefs, practices, and social relations that I argue are actually being undercut by the process of First Nation state formation. I limit my use of *First Nation* to those occasions when I want to refer to the actual state-like polities enshrined in land claim and self-government agreements (or earlier treaties), and I use terms such as *First Nation people* or *First Nation citizen* only insofar as I want to index peoples' relationship with one of those polities. Otherwise, I use terms such as *indigenous people* or *indigenous beliefs and practices.* Such terms carry their own cultural baggage, of course. After all, *indigeneity,* too, implies the existence of a state. But it at least has the virtue of being an oppositional term; and, as we will see, many of the beliefs and practices that I refer to as "indigenous" in this book do indeed stand in stark opposition to those sanctioned by the First Nation state. Another term I use regularly is *Yukon Indian people.* It is likely that no term carries more baggage than "Indian," which has all manner of troubling legal and cultural connotations (and is a defined term in both the Indian Act and the Yukon agreements), but it is also an everyday term of self-designation and, as we shall see, an important marker of identity. In everyday contexts, indigenous people in the Yukon regularly think of and refer to themselves as "Indians" (in contrast to "indigenous," which one almost never hears). And crucially, as I discuss in chapter 3, they often use the term specifically to refer to those beliefs, practices, and social relations they see as distinguishing them culturally from Euro-Canadians. For these reasons, despite its many problems, I generally prefer the term to others.

SOVEREIGNTY'S ENTAILMENTS

First Nation State Formation in the Yukon

First Nation State Formation

State formation ... is cultural revolution.

Philip Corrigan and Derek Sayer (1985: 3)

Since the seventeenth century, the European concept of *sovereignty* has played a key, if sometimes implicit, role in nearly all theories of political life. Although sovereignty entails a host of culturally specific assumptions about the nature of space, time, knowledge, and sociality that once seemed bizarre and radical, those assumptions have long since faded into the background of received wisdom (and legal convention) and so are rarely questioned today. In a world dominated by nation states, sovereignty shapes political arrangements everywhere; indeed, some theorists have argued that sovereignty has come to serve as the precondition for politics, that it has become nearly impossible for us to conceive of politics (or, indeed, of society) outside the relationship of sovereignty. Yet, because initial efforts to theorize sovereignty went hand-in-hand with broader efforts to delegitimize the political systems of colonized peoples, the concept's application in non-European contexts has always been particularly problematic. Nowhere is this more apparent than in relation to indigenous peoples within settler states.

Ever since Chief Justice John Marshall simultaneously acknowledged and qualified American Indian tribes' sovereign status by declaring them to be "domestic dependent nations," the nature and scope of that sovereignty has been the source of endless contestation and debate. Yet, because sovereignty today serves as the precondition for politics, any effort by indigenous people to engage with settler state officials in the political arena requires them to conform to the cultural entailments of sovereignty – a set of assumptions about the nature of space, time, knowledge, and sociality that is intimately bound up with the state form – or risk not being heard at all. The result is a process of state formation that is transforming in profound ways indigenous peoples' ways of thinking, acting, and being in the world.

The process of indigenous state formation also has a powerful effect on how we can understand indigenous politics, because scholars in indigenous studies, anthropology, and related disciplines have been compelled to use what in many ways is a set of culturally inappropriate concepts to describe and analyse indigenous political systems and their complex relationship to the settler states that encompass them. In their efforts to grapple with this problem, they have developed theoretical approaches to sovereignty that are attentive to history and cultural difference – generating in the process a unique literature on the nature and utility of the sovereignty concept. Unfortunately, their insights have not generally informed broader debates on the topic among political theorists and legal scholars, but their work does resonate powerfully with recent thinking by some scholars in those "mainstream" disciplines who have also come to see sovereignty as the product of culture and history rather than as a timeless and universal principle.

I draw on and extend both these strands of literature on sovereignty (and link them to that on state formation) by conceptualizing sovereignty not simply as a *product* of culture and history but also as a powerful engine for sociocultural and environmental change in its own right. It can, however, be hard to appreciate the full scope and magnitude of the changes wrought by sovereignty and attendant processes of state formation, because many of sovereignty's cultural entailments (e.g., assumptions about the nature of space, time, knowledge, and sociality) seem so basic that most of us mistake them for universally valid principles that reflect the realities not only of *human* sociality (in non-state as well as state settings), but of nature as well. In fact, they are nothing of the kind. By examining a particular process of indigenous state formation in a context where not everyone takes for granted the (seemingly "natural and "universal") cultural entailments of sovereignty, it is possible to illustrate in a particularly powerful way the full extent of the "cultural revolution" that is required to speak and act in accordance with the assumptions of sovereignty. This book, which is based on over five years of ethnographic fieldwork carried out in Canada's Yukon Territory over the past twenty years, is an attempt to do just that. In the pages that follow, I provide a close ethnographic analysis of a process of indigenous state formation that is still in its early stages. I pay particular attention to the far-reaching social and environmental transformations involved and expose in the process the culturally contingent nature of some of our most basic assumptions about the nature of time, space, knowledge, and sociality.

State Formation in the Yukon

Yukon Indian people are among the many indigenous peoples across the Canadian north who have recently signed and ratified comprehensive land claim and self-government agreements with federal and territorial (or, in some cases, provincial) governments. These modern treaties create state-like indigenous political entities where there were none before. I use the term "state-like" advisedly. Because they remain embedded within the Canadian state and lack many of the powers associated with independent states (especially but not solely in the domain of international relations), the new First Nations resulting from these agreements cannot be considered independent sovereign states. Yet, the agreements do establish First Nations as a new order of government in Canada with jurisdiction over clearly defined territories. They spell out the nature of government-to-government relations among the signatory governments, and grant northern First Nations real, albeit limited, powers of self-government, including a role in the management of lands and resources upon which their people have long depended. As a result, First Nation governments across the Canadian north have emerged as significant players in regional politics.[1] This is very different from the days, not so long ago, when they lived under the colonialist dictates of the federal Indian Act and had virtually no say either in their own governance or in the management of their lands and resources. Land claim and self-government agreements, then, have clearly empowered the indigenous peoples of northern Canada and helped foster a significant shift in indigenous–state relations there.

1 Some, like the Grand Council of the Cree, have become prominent – and sometimes effective – players on the national and international stage as well (see Carlson 2017). Even First Nations who have not yet signed such agreements are sometimes able to invoke their sovereign (state-like) status to play a significant role in international relations (Montsion 2015).

Empowerment, however, is never simply a matter of "giving power" to formerly disempowered people, as if power were a substance that one could possess only in varying amounts. To the extent that it requires formerly disempowered peoples to alter themselves and their society as a prerequisite for the exercise of that power, "empowerment" must *also* be viewed as a form of subjection (Henkel and Stirrat 2001: 182).[2] Because treaties are generally taken to be "agreement[s] between two or more fully sovereign and recognized states operating in an international forum, negotiated by officially designated commissioners and ratified by the signatory powers" (Prucha 1994), Canada's modern treaty-making process necessarily projects onto northern indigenous societies some very particular assumptions about the kinds of political entities they must be in order to participate in such a process at all. To the extent they have participated, northern indigenous peoples have had to accept – in practice if not in theory – a host of Euro-Canadian assumptions about the nature of power and governance that are implicit in the notion of a treaty between sovereign (or semi-sovereign) entities.

To avail themselves of the powers afforded by the new land claim and self-government agreements (in fact, just to gain a seat at the negotiating table), northern indigenous peoples have had to change their ways of life dramatically (Nadasdy 2003). For over a generation now many have spent the bulk of their lives in offices using computers, phones, and fax machines rather than out in the bush hunting, fishing, and trapping as their parents or grandparents had done. And they have had to learn to speak the language of Euro-Canadian lawyers, scientists, and other agents of the Canadian state; to be heard at all, they have had to express their interests and needs in distinctly Euro-Canadian terms – terms such as *sovereignty, self-government, jurisdiction, property, citizenship, knowledge, nation,* and *history* (to name just a few) that together form the conceptual framework for Canada's modern treaties with First Nations. None of these are indigenous terms, and few of them were of much relevance to northern indigenous people's lives as few as fifty years ago. Significantly, all of these terms take "the state" for granted as the locus of politics.

2 Anthropologists have long recognized that it can at times be impossible to distinguish analytically between subjection and resistance (Abu-Lughod 1990; Mitchell 1990).

To function in a universe of states and state-like political entities (other "state-like" entities include Canadian territories and provinces), First Nations have themselves had to assume the trappings of the state. Like states, the new First Nations that have emerged from the modern treaty-making process are composed of citizens, and their governments exercise significant – if limited – jurisdiction over clearly defined territories and peoples. All of this is clearly laid out in the new agreements. Indeed, no government-to-government relationship would be possible among First Nations, Canada, and territorial or provincial governments without a clear statement of First Nations' powers and responsibilities vis-à-vis those of other governments (whose powers and responsibilities are also clearly laid out in the agreements). Not surprisingly, one of the principal functions of the new land claim and self-government agreements in this regard is to carve out jurisdictional space for the new First Nation governments by delineating precisely which government has jurisdiction over what and where.[3] And if the new First Nations hope to actually implement the new government-to-government relationship laid out in the agreements, then First Nation government officials must be able to interact with their bureaucratic counterparts in other governments. This means First Nation governments must organize themselves into bureaucratic departments that correspond at least roughly with those in the federal and territorial governments. Thus, although the powers and responsibilities created by indigenous land claim and self-government agreements are real enough, they are predicated on the assumption that if First Nations governments are to qualify as governments at all, they must be fundamentally state-like. Since there were no indigenous polities in the Canadian north that could in any way be construed as state-like prior to Canada's assertion of colonial authority,[4] the negotiation and implementation of northern land

3 First Nation self-government agreements do not generally present an exhaustive accounting of which government has jurisdiction over what; rather, they list those domains of governance over which First Nation governments may assume control if they choose and lay out a process for negotiating the transfer of self-government powers in the event a First Nation decides to do so. For overviews of the range of First Nation self-government arrangements in Canada, see Coates and Morrison (2008) and Morse (2008).

4 I will back up this assertion with evidence in the chapters to come.

claim and self-government agreements must be viewed as key moments in an ongoing process of First Nation state formation.

In their celebrated history of the rise of the English territorial state, Philip Corrigan and Derek Sayer (1985) famously argue that the process of "state formation is … cultural revolution" (3). Perhaps more important than the centralization and consolidation of political power, state formation entails dramatic and far-reaching changes in how people can even think about their relations with one another: "out of the vast range of human social capacities – possible ways in which social life could be lived – state activities more or less forcibly 'encourage' some whilst suppressing, marginalizing, eroding, undermining others." The state, they show, is not merely a form of social organization; it is also a new way of seeing the world. State formation is a totalizing project that entails "normalizing, rendering natural, taken for granted, in a word 'obvious,' what are in fact ontological and epistemological premises of a particular and historical form of social order" (ibid.: 4). And it is precisely these totalizing and naturalizing tendencies of state formation that render the process – particularly its cultural dimensions – largely invisible to those of us who happen to live in states. Indeed, for those who embrace the state as the natural order of things, it becomes hard to imagine society organized in any other way (see also Elias 2000: 311).

From such a perspective, non-state societies appear as "primitive" societies that have "not yet" developed into states, and the state itself appears as a natural and obligatory stage in universal human history. This evolutionary framework, still so prevalent in the study of non-state societies, makes it easy to view such societies as somehow deficient, lacking something essential that state societies possess; and, indeed, scholars have tended to characterize such societies negatively by what they lack rather than positively according to the practices and institutions they possess (Clastres 1987). State formation is not, however, an inevitable stage in human history. On the contrary, states' apparent historical inevitability is itself a product of the cultural revolution of state formation.[5] Yet this evolutionary framework has a profound

5 As political theorist Karena Shaw (2008: 39) puts it, "We do not have sovereign states because they are inevitable or necessary, but because their inevitability and necessity have been produced."

effect on how we understand both state and non-state societies. Among other things, it authorizes scholars and activists to treat historically and culturally contingent categories derived from the state – concepts such as *sovereignty, self-government, citizenship, nation, history,* and *territorial jurisdiction* (to name a few that will occupy us in this book) – as human universals that are therefore just as pertinent to the analysis of non-state societies as to states. Although it is not hard to find social practices in non-state societies that can be characterized as "embryonic" forms of state territoriality, citizenship, nationalism, and so on,[6] framing them in this way necessarily reinforces an evolutionary view of society and burnishes the concepts themselves with a false patina of universality, thus hindering our efforts to understand state and non-state societies alike.[7]

While it is certainly not wrong to find cultural continuities between state (or state-like) societies and those that preceded them,[8] it is, I believe, a fundamental error to treat state-derived concepts as universal. Although these concepts are all flexible and contested, they are not infinitely so; using them inevitably entails making historically and culturally specific assumptions about the nature of society – and about the world. These assumptions enable some sorts of politics and foreclose others. To treat state-derived concepts as universal by projecting them onto non-state societies is to naturalize those assumptions and the politics they enable while suppressing (even rendering unthinkable) the alternative forms of social life and politics they helped eclipse.[9]

6 The classic example of this in the anthropological literature is Lowie (1927), who locates the origins of state institutions in the social relations of the "simplest" hunting and horticultural societies.

7 Along these lines, see Segal and Handler (1992) for a well-articulated critique of the tendency among scholars – sometimes despite their conscious efforts to the contrary – to project the cultural assumptions of nationalism "back" onto prior social forms and so universalize them.

8 Indeed, Corrigan and Sayer (1985: esp. 17–18) themselves admit that from some historical perspectives state formation can appear more as "evolution" than as "revolution."

9 Corrigan and Sayer (1985: 7) lament that "state forms have been understood within state formation's own universalizing vocabularies, without reference to what they are formed against," thus obstructing our efforts at analysis. See also Segal and Handler (1992) for a discussion of this problem in relation to nationalism in particular.

For the most part, those who have analysed and evaluated comprehensive land claim and self-government agreements in Canada have taken for granted an array of state-derived concepts. They tend to frame their investigations around such questions as: do the agreements go far enough (or too far) in recognizing the inherent *sovereignty* of First Nations? What are the implications for governance/management of the fact that the agreements divvy up *jurisdiction* in the way they do? How do the agreements define First Nation *citizenship*, and is this justified and/or adequate for *self-government*? How well are various governments actually implementing the agreements as ratified? Because the new agreements are in fact built upon state-derived concepts, it is vital that we ask such questions. To the extent they take these concepts for granted, however, such studies ignore – and in so doing help to render invisible – the cultural transformation that northern indigenous societies had to undergo before such questions could even be asked. Comprehensive land claim and self-government agreements do not merely recognize pre-existing state-like First Nation polities and make room for them within the federal system of Canada. Rather, as we shall see, they are mechanisms for *creating* the legal and administrative systems that bring those polities into being, and the resulting process of First Nation state formation is transforming in profound ways how the indigenous people of northern Canada relate to one another, the land, and animals.

I should say at the outset that I try to remain neutral about these changes. Some Yukon Indian people I know think they are on the whole beneficial and that the trade-offs they entail are necessary if Yukon Indian people are to assume some measure of control over their lives and lands. Others are horrified by what they see happening. It is not my place to judge. All societies are constantly changing, after all; and there are always those who oppose change as well as those who embrace it. But I do think it is important to try to understand the nature of these changes. How exactly are Canada's modern treaties helping to transform northern indigenous peoples' way of life and why? It is my contention that scholars – and many indigenous people too – have dramatically underestimated the magnitude and extent of the sociocultural transformation involved in the implementation of comprehensive land claim and self-government agreements. In this book, I explore that transformation through a close ethnographic analysis of the agreements in Canada's Yukon Territory, in particular those of the Kluane

First Nation and its neighbours in the southwest Yukon, where I have carried out research since 1995.

Although my arguments about First Nation state formation necessarily attend closely to the particularities of the Yukon situation, they are directly relevant all across the Canadian north where structurally similar agreements have been signed or are currently under negotiation. They are also clearly relevant to the US context, which served in some important ways as the template for the agreements in Canada. Because the concept of indigeneity implies the existence of the state – and so tends to orient theorists and activists alike towards the creation of state-like indigenous polities as the means for championing indigenous peoples' interests vis-à-vis the states that encompass them – the process of indigenous state formation I analyse in this book has analogues around the world, not only in the settler states of North and South America but also throughout Africa, Asia, and Australia – wherever marginalized people are making claims in the language of indigeneity. By focusing on the initial stages of state formation in a social context where not everyone takes for granted the cultural entailments of sovereignty, this book highlights just how dependent most of us are, in our efforts to understand "human" society, upon a set of culturally and historically specific assumptions about the nature of the world, and it suggests some of the sociocultural and political consequences of imposing those assumptions upon people who do not share them.

The Cultural Entailments of Sovereignty

I focus in this book upon a constellation of state-derived concepts that serve as the philosophical bedrock upon which the Yukon agreements have been built: *sovereignty*, *territory/jurisdiction*, *citizenship*, *nation*, and *history/time*. Together, these concepts frame and constrain the universe of possibilities for indigenous–state relations (as they do contemporary politics more generally). Although all these concepts are inextricable from the process of state formation, *sovereignty* stands out among them because of the structuring role it plays. Having a concept of *sovereignty* necessarily entails also having a concept of *territory*, of *citizenship*, of *nation*, of *history*, and so on. Thus, sovereignty serves as the implicit precondition for all the other state-derived concepts I examine in this book; and they, in turn, derive their meanings from it. This is why I refer to these other concepts – along with the world view and practices associated with them – as sovereignty's entailments.[10]

That the concept of sovereignty is central to my analysis of Yukon First Nation state formation should hardly be surprising, since the idea of sovereignty is inextricable from that of the state. As R.B.J. Walker (1993: 165) puts it: "The modern principle of sovereignty has emerged historically as the legal expression of the character and legitimacy of the state." If this is so, and if state formation really does entail a cultural revolution, then the concept of *sovereignty* must express – and so help legitimize – the historically and culturally specific assumptions upon which the modern territorial state is built – and, by extension, also the state-like First Nations modelled upon them.

This is consistent with recent scholarship that views sovereignty not as a timeless principle but rather as socially constructed; that is, as a historically contingent "ideal" or "effect" arising out of – and informing – the actual practices of state officials (Biersteker and Weber 1996; Walker 1993).[11] Central to the analysis of sovereignty as socially constructed are practices of recognition. A state is recognized as sovereign only if it acts in ways expected of a sovereign state. As Weber and Biersteker (1996: 12, 13) put it, "Sovereignty provides the textual and/or contextual prescriptions for what a state must do to be recognized as sovereign,"

10 Alternatively, various scholars have described this constellation of concepts as characteristic of "modernity" (see, for example, Lyons 2010; Sayer 1991: esp. 49; Tully 1995; Tully 2014). I am resistant to follow their lead on this for two reasons. First, I find modernity to be too vague a concept to be of much use. I simply do not see the analytic value in wrapping *sovereignty, citizenship, territory, nation, history,* and other concepts discussed here in the vague blanket of modernity. Second, it seems to me that such a strategy poses a danger. Modernity is, after all, a temporal category, and its use implies a "pre-modernity" (which it supposedly displaced). Any use of the term, then, threatens to smuggle a social evolutionary perspective on indigeneity back into the analysis, a tendency that is especially insidious when it comes to hunting peoples. By starting with *sovereignty* rather than *modernity,* I can explore more precisely the social and epistemological relations among *citizenship, territory, nation, history,* and related concepts while avoiding the evolutionary implications of *modernity* (*capitalism* might serve equally well as the central structuring concept, as Coulthard [2014] has shown, though this would lead to a somewhat different analysis than I offer here).

11 These studies are also very much in line with recent treatments of the concept of the state itself (e.g., Mitchell 1991).

and "as the prescriptions for sovereign recognition change, so does the meaning of sovereignty." Geographer Alexander Murphy (1996) has shown that the prescriptions for sovereign recognition have, in fact, evolved significantly over the past few centuries, with corresponding changes in the meaning of the term (see also Tully 1995: 193–8).[12] Rather than possessing sovereignty by definition, then, states must constantly negotiate their sovereignty, that is, their legitimacy as states, according to ever-changing ideals of what a state is and how it should behave, a process that entails considerable effort on the part of state officials, intellectuals, and others.[13] Thus, practices of recognition do not merely serve to acknowledge (or not) states' prior status as sovereign entities, they actually produce the normative requirements of sovereignty along with the very states that (seek to) conform to them. In such a view, "statecraft is not primarily about relations between different state units, but about the construction and reconstruction of the units themselves. By granting and withholding recognition, international society participates in the construction of sovereign states" (ibid.: 5–6).

This resonates powerfully with recent critical scholarship on the "politics of recognition" in Canada and elsewhere throughout the settler colonial world. Political theorist Glen Coulthard (2014: 21) defines the "politics of recognition" in Canada as a

> range of recognition-based models of liberal pluralism that seek to "reconcile" Indigenous assertions of nationhood with settler-state sovereignty via the accommodation of Indigenous identity claims in some form of renewed legal and political relationship with the Canadian state. Although

12 Murphy (1996) points out, for example, that at times in the past one state could legitimately act within another state's sovereign territory – or even annex it – without necessarily violating contemporary understandings of the principle of sovereignty. Gradually, however, and particularly in the post-Second World War era, sovereign territory has come to be regarded as sacrosanct.

13 Weber and Biersteker (1996: 3) note that "attempting to realize this ideal [of sovereignty] entails a great deal of hard work on the part of statespersons, diplomats, and intellectuals: to establish and police practices consistent with the ideal, its components, and the links between them; to delegitimate or quash challenges or threats; and to paper over persistent anomalies to make them appear to be consistent with the ideal or temporary divergences from the diachronic trajectory toward a pristine Westphalian ideal."

> these models tend to vary in both theory and practice, most call for the delegation of land, capital, and political power from the state to Indigenous communities through a combination of land claim settlements, economic development initiatives, and self-government agreements.

Many indigenous studies scholars (Alfred 2005a; Coulthard 2014; Eisenberg et al. 2014; Povinelli 2002; Simpson 2014) have criticized these politics of recognition because of the way they take for granted the authority of the settler state (which can choose whether and how to recognize indigenous polities) and, perhaps even more importantly, because of the way such politics transform the indigenous societies seeking recognition. Eisenberg (2014: 295) describes the latter concern thus: "Indigenous minorities often realize that they must frame their interests in terms the state is willing to recognize and doing this often distorts their identities in ways that can further entrench the disadvantage of the group." Thus, the politics of recognition involve much more than the mere recognition of that which already exists; rather, they are constitutive of the recognized self. Building on Hegel's master/slave narrative, numerous scholars have argued that recognition is "'constitutive of subjectivity: one becomes an individual subject only in virtue of recognizing, and being recognized by another subject.' Our senses of self are thus dependent on and shaped through our complex relations with others" (Coulthard 2014: 27–8, citing Fraser and Honneth 2003). Thus, recognition entails – ideally mutual – social transformation. In the context of colonial domination, however, the transformation process is seldom if ever mutual. As Coulthard notes (drawing on Fanon), "When delegated exchanges of recognition occur in real world contexts of domination the terms of accommodation usually end up being determined by and in the interests of the hegemonic partner in the relationship" (ibid.: 17). To be recognized, then, indigenous people must assume the political guise mandated by the settler state, thus leading indigenous people to replicate the "worst manifestations of the state's power within the intensified context of our own communities and governance structures" (Coulthard 2014: 159, paraphrasing Alfred).

This is an important critique. What these critics of recognition have largely overlooked, however, is the degree to which the politics of recognition are a necessary corollary to any sovereign claim. Indeed, one recent edited collection even goes so far as to frame "recognition" and "self-determination" as two distinct, even antithetical, strategies for addressing the ongoing problem of colonial domination in indigenous–state relations.[14] There is a widespread tendency on the part of many of these critics to portray the politics of recognition as the result of efforts on the part of settler state governments to *deny, ignore,* or *subvert* indigenous claims to sovereignty. Such a view leads Coulthard (2014) and others to reject the politics of recognition as a form of "colonial politics" and advocate instead for a politics of "self-recognition," which would enable indigenous peoples to develop their own culturally appropriate ways of life and institutions of governance without any need to have them validated by the settler state. I contend that while such politics might indeed have positive effects, they are not at all consistent with the politics of sovereignty. As we have already seen, recognition is an essential aspect of sovereignty; there can be no such thing as sovereignty without recognition by other – recognizably similar (i.e., sovereign) – political entities.[15] Far from being an alternative to (or the antithesis of) sovereignty, the politics of recognition are a logical and necessary consequence of indigenous peoples' claims to sovereign status. A brief return to the international relations literature may help us see why.

When they write about the role of recognition in the social construction of sovereignty, international relations scholars such as Biersteker and Weber have in mind primarily formal diplomatic processes of state

14 To be sure, some of these critics do acknowledge that the politics of recognition emerged in direct response to indigenous peoples' struggles for self-determination (Coulthard 2014: 1–6), while others note that strategies of "recognition and self-determination often co-exist and are mutually reinforcing" (Eisenberg 2014: 299). Nevertheless, most tend to maintain a clear distinction between the politics of self-determination/sovereignty on one hand and the "liberal" politics of recognition on the other, and to view the latter as in large part the negation of the former. For a clear statement of such a position, see Simpson (2014: 11).

15 This point has been acknowledged by a few indigenous studies scholars (e.g., Den Ouden and O'Brien 2013), leading them to view recognition as fundamentally ambivalent in indigenous contexts. On the one hand, the need for external (i.e., settler state) recognition is essential to the exercise of indigenous sovereignty, yet on the other it entails a (partial) surrender of that very sovereignty. This ambivalence is real, but it is hardly unique to the indigenous context. As we have seen, negotiating the terms of recognition is an essential aspect of sovereignty in the international arena as well, and such negotiations regularly take place on an extremely uneven playing field (see Grovogui 2002). No state has complete control over the terms of its own recognition, and if weaker states wish to be recognized as sovereign, they must conform to the normative requirements of sovereignty as dictated (largely) by more powerful states.

recognition. While these are certainly important, the full implications of viewing sovereignty as socially constructed become apparent only if we expand the notion of recognition beyond the formal diplomatic realm. After all, for "international relations" to exist at all, nation-state governments must first be recognizable to one another *as governments*. Only then can the question of formal diplomatic recognition even arise. As a practical matter, government-to-government relations (whether they entail treaty negotiations, collaboration on a scientific initiative, educational exchange, or what have you) require representatives from one government to interact with functionally equivalent representatives from another. Government officials have to have some confidence that their counterparts in the other government have the authority to work with them on the matter in question. This is only possible if the governments share broadly similar structures of authority. Considerable institutional variation is possible, of course, but some forms of socio-political organization – those found in non-state societies, for example – are simply too different; they do not possess recognizable (to state officials) structures of authority that would enable government-to-government relations (Corrigan and Sayer 1985: 5). It goes without saying that such societies by definition fail to meet the historically and culturally constituted prescriptions of sovereignty.

This failure to recognize the sovereignty of non-state societies is not the same as explicitly refusing diplomatic recognition for political reasons (often in an effort to initiate political change) to an entity that is obviously state-like (Taiwan or Israel, for example). State officials' failure to recognize non-state political forms as legitimate is less the result of their conscious refusal to do so than of their inability to perceive such forms as political in the first place. State officials often view non-state peoples' "lack of government" (we will see in chapter 1 that the assumptions of sovereignty render "politics" and "government" largely synonymous) as evidence of primitive backwardness, even savagery, and subject them to a range of coercive processes to "civilize" them and render them politically "legible" (Scott 1998). In a world dominated by powerful states, the need to become "recognizable" to states serves as an almost irresistible incentive for non-state peoples to develop political institutions that conform to the basic prescriptions of sovereignty. For indigenous peoples embedded in settler states, this is usually a prerequisite for any effort to wrest from settler state governments some measure of control over their own lives. It is indigenous peoples' practical need to become recognizable to settler states for the purpose of engaging with them politically – more than any desire to gain formal acknowledgment of their sovereign status – that serves as the primary motivation for achieving recognition, with all the socio-political transformation that entails.

The social constructivist approach has the virtue of explicitly linking sovereignty to a specific set of cultural practices. Although the precise practices associated with state sovereignty (and hence the meaning of the term itself) have undergone important changes over the centuries, they are now and have always been linked to the key components of the state: territory, population, authority/power, and time/history. To be recognized as sovereign, states must have – or at least be able to maintain the fiction that they have – a territorial basis, a clearly defined population (composed of citizens and other kinds of residents), a monopoly on the legitimate use of force within their borders, and so on.[16] All these components of state sovereignty, it turns out, "are intimately tied up with the construction, reconstruction, and maintenance of boundaries" (Biersteker and Weber 1996: 13). Indeed, one might plausibly claim that sovereignty is fundamentally an exercise in boundary making. State sovereignty requires – and emerges from – a set of interrelated processes and day-to-day material practices that establish and maintain distinctions between those people, lands, and processes that are *inside* the state (geographically, socially, temporally, epistemologically) and those that are *outside* (Agnew 1994; Shaw 2008; Walker 1993).[17]

16 Although contiguous non-overlapping territories, clearly demarcated boundaries, and uniform sovereignty may be the territorial nation-state ideal, reality is, of course, a good deal messier. Political scientists, legal scholars, and others have long drawn a distinction between de facto and de jure sovereignty, pointing out that some states are able to exercise their sovereign power well beyond their territorial borders, while others are unable to do so even within their own borders (Agnew 2005; Grovogui 2002; Jackson 1992; Raustiala 2009). Although they may have been formally recognized, states that are unable to meet the practical requirements of sovereignty in the eyes of the international community are often referred to – and, indeed, treated – in ways that that suggest otherwise. Whatever their formal de jure status in international law, these "failed" or "quasi" states, it is said, lack de facto sovereignty.

17 Although Kevin Bruyneel (2007) seeks to trouble this binary inside/outside distinction – particularly in regards to US tribes' relation to the United States – he clearly recognizes the central importance of boundary-making practices to the social construction of sovereignty; indeed, it is his recognition that the binary nature of sovereignty lies at the root of so many of the political difficulties faced by indigenous people in settler states that leads him to try to transcend it by articulating a "third space" of sovereignty.

To be recognized as sovereign in the broad sense I outlined above, then, people in non-state societies – who generally do not make categorical distinctions of this sort – must begin drawing and maintaining clear boundaries between their territory and that of "foreign" sovereigns (indigenous as well as settler), between citizens and non-citizens, between their nation and others. As we shall see, sovereign recognition is also based on a host of less overtly political distinctions, including those between history and stasis, between human and non-human, between knowledge and superstition. Taken together, these boundary-making practices produce not only new forms of governance, but also new ways of perceiving the world and of situating oneself and acting within it. These are the cultural entailments of sovereignty, the engines of state formation's cultural revolution, and powerful mechanisms for social and environmental change.

Today, the cultural entailments of sovereignty appear obvious, even natural, to many of us living in states; but this was not always the case. Indeed, they once seemed "bizarre and radical, even nonsense" (Walker 1993: 167). Gradually, however, as "the claims of state sovereignty itself recede[d] into the background, into the silence of received wisdom and legal convention" (ibid.: 170), it has become more and more difficult even to imagine politics that do not take for granted the cultural assumptions of sovereignty. Over the past few hundred years, our conception of the world as a system of sovereign states – themselves often composed of smaller, hierarchically nested, state-like political entities – has become so naturalized as to be virtually hegemonic (Agnew 1994; Anderson 1991; Malkki 1992; Murphy 1996). The global proliferation of the sovereign state model has been neither accidental nor innocent. As a wide range of scholars has argued (Anaya 2004; Grovogui 1996: chap. 2; Kuehls 2003; Strang 1996; Tully 2014: esp. 59–61), our current international system of sovereign states was – at least in part – the result of a conscious effort by European political theorists to delegitimize the political systems of those they colonized. Indeed, the legitimating role of sovereignty became so central a component of the colonial project that it came to structure even the possibilities for anti-colonial struggle, a state of affairs that has spawned "derivative" states and state-like polities around the world (Anderson 1991: 156; Chatterjee 1993). I view the rise of state-like First Nations as very much fitting this mould. For, although indigenous people (like other marginalized peoples) have found the language of sovereignty quite useful in their quest for an end to colonial oppression, its use has also been to a large extent obligatory.

To make political claims against the settler state, indigenous people must first become recognizable to settler colonial governments; and this means portraying themselves as long-standing, discrete, and culturally unified human political communities (i.e., "tribes" or "nations") that have a long and continuous history of governing themselves upon and in relation to particular territories.

Just because the language of sovereignty is of European origin, of course, does not mean that it has no resonance for indigenous people, who long governed themselves in accordance with their own (quite varied) political ideas and institutions and who, by and large, wish to continue doing so. To express their ideas and practices of governance and human–land relations in the historically and culturally contingent language of sovereignty, however, requires a process of translation. Given the diversity of indigenous political systems, it is impossible to generalize about this process; for some indigenous peoples, the cultural entailments of sovereignty are no doubt a better fit than for others. Even when the fit is reasonably good, however, cultural translation of this sort is fraught with peril, despite the best efforts of scholars and activists to indigenize *sovereignty* and related concepts (see chapter 1).[18] After all, terms associated with the sovereign state system have very specific – if contested – meanings in Euro-American legal and political discourse, and it is these meanings that tend to inform the actions of negotiators, politicians, and other agents of settler states (who are for the most part either ignorant of or opposed to the implications of indigenous political theory). It could hardly be otherwise, since these meanings are both created by and reflected in the complex legal and political institutions of the sovereign state system.

Yukon Indian people, like indigenous people everywhere, have made effective use of statist concepts such as *sovereignty*, *territory*, *citizenship*, *nation*, and *history* in their efforts to regain some measure of control over their own lives and lands. In the Yukon case, however, the translation of indigenous Yukon beliefs and practices into the language of sovereignty is particularly fraught because of the complete absence of state-like institutions and boundary-making practices there prior to the onset of colonialism. The Yukon final and self-government agreements

18 On the perils of translating indigenous ideas into the "universal" terms of the modern state, see Chakrabarty (2000).

are the latest and by far the most powerful mechanisms for drawing and maintaining the boundaries (territorial, demographic, national, temporal, epistemological) of sovereignty. Enacting these boundaries, which are all essential to the structure of the agreements and to the associated constitution of self-governing Yukon First Nations, entails a dramatic reworking of indigenous Yukon society that has profound social and environmental consequences.

Before embarking on my analysis of the sometimes subtle but far-reaching consequences of Yukon First Nation state formation, however, a few words about the Yukon agreements themselves are in order, as is a brief discussion of the research upon which the book is based.

The Yukon Agreements

In contrast to the situation in much of southern Canada, the Canadian government never negotiated any land cession treaties in the Yukon.[19] Even so, it claimed to control all lands in the Yukon and maintained the position that Yukon Indian people had no legal entitlement to the land, except to those few small parcels the government had explicitly set aside for them.[20] Yukon Indian people made no unified effort to assert their rights to land until the early 1970s. In 1973, Elijah Smith, president and co-founder of the newly formed Yukon Native Brotherhood, a political organization representing status Indians[21] throughout the Yukon, presented the federal government with a document entitled *Together Today for Our Children Tomorrow* (1973), which laid out their

---

19 The only potential exception is a small part of the southeast Yukon, which was included in Treaty 11, signed in 1921. Even there, however, it is doubtful that Yukon Indians willingly ceded their lands. Although the Canadian government regards Treaty 11 as a land cession treaty, there is ample ethno-historical evidence to show that the Indians who signed it did not view it that way at all, believing instead that they were signing a treaty of peace and friendship (Asch 2013). The same, of course, can be said of many – though by no means all – Indian treaties in other parts of Canada and the United States (see, e.g., Hildebrandt, First Rider, and Carter 1996; Price 1999).

20 It was estimated in 1962 that only 4800 acres of land in the entire Yukon had been allocated for Indian use. This included a few very small reserves. Most Indian villages in the territory, however, were not legally designated reserves but were set aside for Indian use by Orders in Council (Coates 1991: 235).

21 The term *status Indians* refers to those people who are legally designated Indians under the federal Indian Act.

vision for a more just relationship with the federal government and Yukon settler population. Canada accepted the document as a basis for negotiations. Despite early hopes for a quick settlement, however, negotiations dragged on for two decades.[22] Finally, in 1993, representatives of the federal and Yukon governments along with the Council for Yukon Indians, the Yukon Native Brotherhood's successor organization, signed the Yukon Umbrella Final Agreement (UFA).

The UFA is not in itself a land claim agreement; rather, it is a framework for the negotiation of specific tripartite "final agreements" between each of the 14 individual Yukon First Nations and the federal and Yukon governments (Council for Yukon Indians 1993). It is a complex document consisting of twenty-eight chapters that deal not only with land and financial compensation, but also with the ownership and management of both renewable and non-renewable resources, land use planning, taxation, heritage, economic development, and more. The UFA contains many general provisions that apply to the entire Yukon and also identifies the areas in which individual First Nations may negotiate provisions specific to their own needs. Each individual Yukon First Nation (as noted above, there are fourteen in the territory, though not all have signed onto the UFA) was to negotiate its own specific final agreement within the framework of the UFA. The complex structure of the Yukon agreement was the result of compromise between Yukon First Nations, who were generally wary of a single Yukon-wide agreement, preferring instead multiple agreements that would be more sensitive to local needs, and the federal government, which preferred a Yukon-wide agreement so as to avoid the administrative nightmare of having fourteen completely distinct treaties in the Yukon.

Alongside their final agreements, Yukon First Nations also negotiated self-government agreements. These agreements formally dissolve the Indian Act bands that were parties to the negotiations and in their place create First Nations possessing a broad – yet limited – range of powers to govern themselves and their lands.[23] In addition, each Yukon

22 For a good overview of the comprehensive land claim process in Canada, and the evolving federal policy environment in which it took place, see Fenge (2015).

23 For discussions of the Yukon self-government agreements, the range of powers they grant to First Nations, and some early issues surrounding their implementation, see Dacks (2004) and Hogg and Turpel (1995). For discussions of these agreements in a comparative Canadian perspective, see Coates and Morrison (2008) and Morse (2008).

First Nation was required to produce and ratify a constitution, which came into effect at the same moment as its final and self-government agreements. The self-government agreements specify the form and essential elements of these new First Nation constitutions – thus subjecting them to approval, albeit indirectly, by federal and Yukon negotiators (Kluane First Nation 2003a: 9–10). One of these specifications is that the new First Nation constitutions must include a citizenship code explicitly laying out the requirements for First Nation citizenship, a term to which the self-government agreements give form and structure (see chapter 3).[24]

Fundamental to the new final and self-government agreements is the statist assumption that political power is territorially organized. That is, governments – if they are to qualify as governments at all – must have jurisdiction over clearly bounded territories, within which they exercise their power and authority. The creation of new First Nations, then, required the creation of corresponding territories. To this end, the final agreements create two new forms of political territory in the Yukon: First Nation "traditional territories" and First Nation "settlement lands," both of which are precisely mapped and jurisdictionally significant.[25] I will provide a detailed analysis of these two new forms of territory/jurisdiction in chapter 2; for now I simply note that both are essential to the new political regime in the Yukon because they structure the mechanisms of First Nation governance and management. They also make intergovernmental relations with Canada and

24 It is important to note here that the status of First Nation *citizenship* is exclusive to self-government agreements. It is distinct from the category of *beneficiary*, which includes all those eligible for rights and benefits under a land claims agreement. It is possible for someone to be a citizen of a First Nation but not a beneficiary of its land claim agreement. In the case of Kluane First Nation, the central focus of this study, however, the two categories are nearly isomorphic (though that could change). There are presently only a handful of KFN citizens (all of whom gained their citizenship through adoption) who are not also beneficiaries. In some parts of Canada, however, the categories are much more distinct. In some places, for example, such as in the Inuvialuit settlement region, where there is a land claim agreement in place but as yet no self-government agreement, (indigenous) citizenship is not a relevant legal category at all.

25 The maps of these territories are formally included in each Yukon First Nation final agreement as an appendix and published as a separate volume. In addition, final agreements also provide detailed descriptions of settlement lands (see, e.g., Kluane First Nation 2003b: 421–84).

the Yukon possible. As noted above, one of the key functions of the new agreements is to clearly delineate First Nations' jurisdiction vis-à-vis the jurisdiction of other governments in the Yukon, including other First Nations, Canada, and the Yukon (all of which are also territorially organized); and the new territories created by the agreements are of central importance in this regard.

In addition to introducing new geographical boundaries, the agreements also create new social boundaries by allocating the indigenous people of the Yukon among the different First Nation states. The new laws and institutions of First Nation citizenship are key here, because they create and define "the people" in whose name the new First Nations govern. At the same time, these laws and institutions exclude as "non-citizens" not only Euro-Canadians but also many Yukon Indians – to say nothing of animals and other beings regarded by many Yukon Indian people as sentient and powerful persons and kin. Like the geographical boundaries created by the agreements, these social boundaries are essential to the new regime of governance and management. Citizens have special rights and responsibilities vis-à-vis the emerging First Nation state and its newly defined territories; while non-citizens lack those rights and responsibilities, having no say in a First Nation's governance nor in the management of its lands and resources. Thus, the new agreements are boundary-making mechanisms. They create First Nations that, like states, take for granted the social distinction between citizen and non-citizen and wield territorially constituted authority over geographically bounded areas.

As treaties, Yukon First Nation final agreements are protected by section 35 of Canada's Constitution Act (1982), which "recognizes and affirms" existing aboriginal and treaty rights, including those spelled out in comprehensive land claim agreements. Although the Yukon self-government agreements are not similarly protected,[26] the two sets of

26 Because the framework for Yukon self-government agreements was negotiated prior to the Canadian government's 1995 acknowledgment of First Nations' inherent right to self-government (see chapter 1 for a discussion of the inherent right), the Yukon final agreements expressly state that the accompanying self-government agreements are *not* to be construed as treaties under section 35 of the Constitution Act (and thus are presumably not constitutionally protected), though they do explicitly provide for the possibility that the parties might subsequently amend the agreements to grant them constitutional protection (see, e.g., Kluane First Nation 2003a: 395–6). Many of the post-1995 First Nation self-government agreements negotiated elsewhere in

agreements were negotiated simultaneously and are completely interdependent. Indeed, the self-government agreements would be largely meaningless without the final agreements, precisely because of the way the new self-governing First Nations' authority is territorially constituted; the territories within which First Nations exercise their self-government authorities are created by the final agreements (see chapter 2). Similarly, the force and scope of the final agreements would be vastly diminished without the self-government agreements, which create (some would say "recognize") many of the powers that the new First Nations exercise within their newly defined territories. In combination with one another, the final and self-government agreements create Yukon First Nations

---

Canada (e.g., the Tłįcho, Nisga'a, and Inuit of Labrador final agreements) *are* constitutionally protected by virtue of the fact that, unlike the Yukon self-government agreements, they are not stand-alone agreements but rather form part of the comprehensive land claim agreements (which, we saw, are explicitly recognized as treaties by section 35 of the Constitution Act). Negotiations to extend similar constitutional protections to the Yukon self-government agreements took place in the late 1990s, but stalled in the early 2000s. According to one First Nation negotiator, the main sticking point during those negotiations was the issue of legal paramountcy. Federal negotiators insisted on a clause stating that federal laws were paramount in the case of any inconsistency, but First Nations would not agree to this. She said that there has been little appetite among First Nation officials to reopen negotiations on this matter in recent years because neither side is likely to have changed their views on it and because the Yukon agreements actually give First Nation law higher standing versus provincial/territorial law than do many of those self-government agreements that *are* entrenched. At least two prominent scholars of Canadian aboriginal law, however, suggest that an amendment explicitly enshrining the Yukon self-government agreements in the Canadian constitution is unnecessary. They point out that although the Yukon final agreements explicitly state that rights spelled out under the self-government agreements are not to be construed as "treaty rights" under section 35, they are silent on whether they can be regarded as "aboriginal rights," which are also recognized and affirmed by section 35. If First Nations have an *inherent* right to self-government (a fact recognized by the federal government itself in its 1995 policy), then that right is by definition an aboriginal right, meaning that the "the self-government agreements can be regarded as giving form and structure to the Aboriginal right of self-government" and so would automatically be protected under section 35 (Hogg and Turpel 1995: 211–12). According to the same First Nation negotiator mentioned above, Dave Joe, one of the architects of the Yukon agreements and KFN's legal counsel during its negotiations, shares this opinion. This, she said, is another reason Yukon First Nations have not bothered to pressure the federal government to reopen negotiations on constitutional entrenchment. In practice, she said, it just does not seem to matter very much.

as politico-territorial organizations that function in many respects like (small, weak) states.

Rather than attempt to negotiate fourteen sets of agreements at once, the governments in the Yukon initially focused on four: those of the Champagne and Aishihik First Nations, the Vuntut Gwich'in First Nation, the Nacho Nyak Dun First Nation, and the Teslin Tlingit Council. The first four agreements were finalized along with the UFA in 1993, and all of them came into effect in 1995. Over the next ten years, seven more Yukon First Nations followed suit, negotiating, signing, and ratifying their own final and self-government agreements. Three Yukon First Nations, the Liard First Nation, the Ross River Dena Council, and the White River First Nation, ultimately rejected the terms of the UFA and opted out of the land claim and self-government process altogether. One result of this piecemeal approach to negotiations is that the three First Nations in the southwestern Yukon that feature most prominently in this book (see map 1) all occupy structurally different positions with respect to the land claim process. Champagne and Aishihik First Nations (CAFN), headquartered in the village of Haines Junction, is one of the largest First Nations in the Yukon. As noted above, it was one of the first four to sign and ratify its land claim and self-government agreements. As a result, the CAFN government, which has been up and running since 1995, is in the vanguard of self-governing Yukon First Nations, with relatively well-developed structures for governance and management by now firmly in place. The Kluane First Nation (KFN) in Burwash Landing negotiated its final and self-government agreements during the period from 1995 to 2002. These were signed and ratified in 2003 and came into effect on 1 February 2004. Because it is a much smaller First Nation than CAFN and located further from Whitehorse, the Yukon's capital, KFN faces a considerably bigger challenge in recruiting and retaining staff qualified to serve as government bureaucrats, thus slowing the implementation of KFN's agreements. As a result, KFN's government structures are much more rudimentary than are those of CAFN. Finally, the White River First Nation (WRFN) in Beaver Creek was engaged in negotiations during the same period as KFN, but its leadership declined to bring the agreement-in-principle (initialled in 2002) before the First Nation membership for a ratification vote. As a result, WRFN has no land claim or self-government agreements, and its members – unlike those of self-governing Yukon First Nations like CAFN and KFN – are still subject to the provisions of the federal Indian Act.

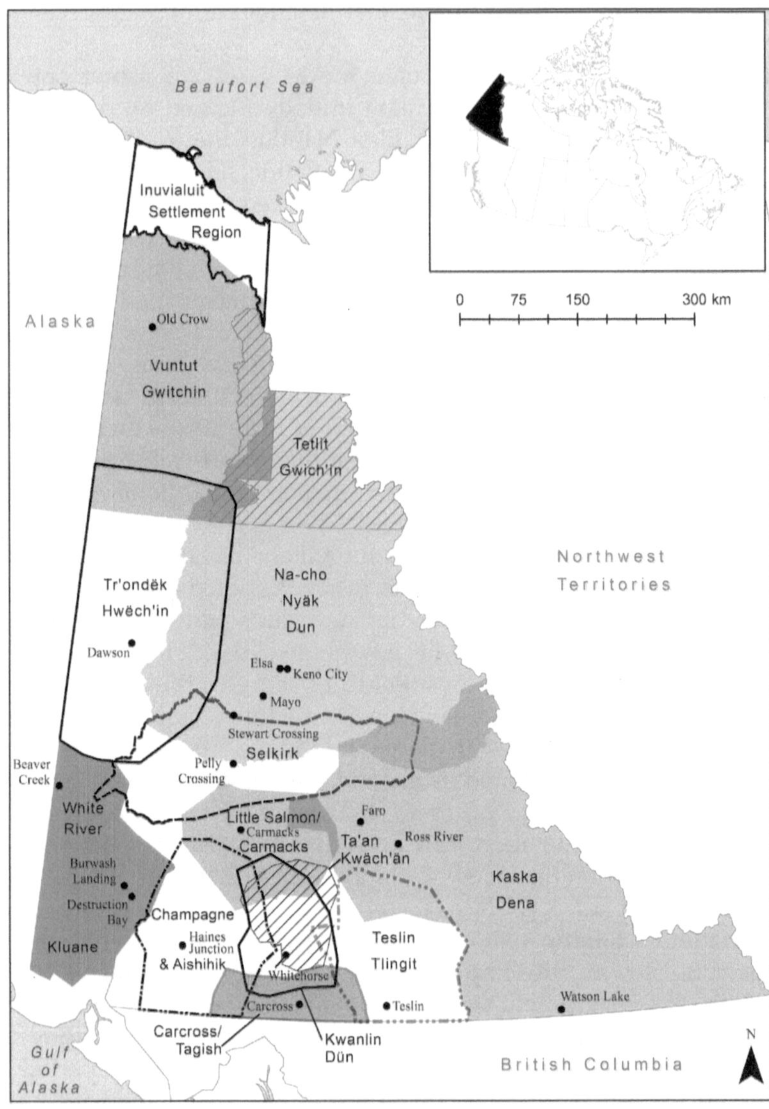

Map 1 Yukon First Nation traditional territories by Tracy Sallaway (Maps, Data and Government Information Centre, Trent University). Contains information licensed under the Open Government Licence – Canada (http://open.canada.ca/en/open-government-licence-canada); all other data – Geomatics, Department of Environment, Government of Yukon.

Figure 1 Village of Burwash Landing, Yukon, seat of the Kluane First Nation government, as seen from Kluane Lake in winter (photo by author)

The Research

In 1995, when I first arrived in the village of Burwash Landing to begin my dissertation research, Kluane First Nation was just beginning to negotiate the specific provisions of its final and self-government agreements.[27] As part of my participation in the daily life of the village, I began attending the meetings that KFN negotiators held to inform the community about the status of negotiations. Before long, I was given permission to observe the negotiations themselves and to attend and participate in meetings of KFN's land claim caucus, which I did throughout the main period of negotiations from 1996 through 1998. In the spring of 1997, KFN's then chief negotiator asked me to research, draft, and then

27 Certain KFN citizens, however, had been involved in the land claim process in various capacities since 1973, and some played important roles in the negotiation of the UFA.

negotiate the specific provisions for a chapter of KFN's final agreement (chapter 13 – Heritage). This gave me the opportunity to interact with and get to know the other negotiators (from all three governments) as a negotiator myself. By working closely with them in this way, I not only gained an understanding of the technical aspects of the land claim, I was also able to observe and participate in the social dynamics of the negotiations and get a sense of both KFN and government negotiators' respective approaches to and understandings of the agreements.

After my departure from Burwash Landing in 1998, I kept in contact with KFN's negotiators. My ongoing conversations with them, along with return visits to the village each summer, enabled me to follow the progress of the negotiations fairly closely. Then, in 2003, I returned to the Yukon for another full year of fieldwork – this time focusing more squarely on the land claim process than I had during my dissertation fieldwork. Originally, I had intended to resume my participation in the negotiations; but, as it happened, KFN ratified their agreements in August 2003, shortly before my arrival. So in addition to attending the signing ceremony (a symbolically charged event attended by dignitaries from all over Canada and the Yukon), I worked part-time in KFN's land claim department throughout the following year, observing and assisting with the transition from negotiations to implementation. I was present on 2 February 2004 when the agreements formally came into effect, and was able to observe and participate in KFN's transition from an Indian Act band into a fully self-governing First Nation. I continued talking with people informally during the course of my daily life in the village. Since the agreements were – and remain – a topic of general interest, I had many conversations with people who supported the agreements as well as with those who were critical of or indifferent to them. Some of the insights I gained from these conversations – along with some of the conversations themselves – figure prominently in this book.

An important part of my work that year involved serving as KFN's official representative on an intergovernmental body known as the Implementation Review Group (IRG). The IRG included representatives from all the self-governing Yukon First Nations, the Council for Yukon First Nations, and the federal and Yukon governments. Their task was to conduct a comprehensive nine-year review[28] of the signatory

28 The review was required by the agreements themselves (some of which were then entering their tenth year).

Figure 2 Kluane First Nation signing ceremony, Burwash Landing, 18 October 2003. Yukon Government Leader Dennis Fentie, Federal Minister of Indian Affairs Robert Nault, and Chief of Kluane First Nation Robert Dickson holding aloft just-signed copy of KFN's final agreement (photo by author)

Figure 3 Kluane First Nation signing ceremony, Burwash Landing, 18 October 2003. Kluane First Nation elders Dorothy Johnson and Lena Johnson signing as witnesses (photo by author)

Figure 4 Kluane First Nation signing ceremony, Burwash Landing, 18 October 2003. Kluane First Nation's Chief Negotiator Robin Bradasch and Luke Johnson signing as witnesses (photo by author)

governments' efforts to implement the Umbrella Final Agreement and First Nation final and self-government agreements, along with related program and service transfer agreements and financial transfer agreements (see below for a description of these). Because KFN had no agreements in place until 2 February 2004 – and so had no history of implementation to review – they only had observer status on the IRG. Observing the process, however, was valuable to KFN because of the structure of the land claim agreements in the Yukon. Since the Umbrella Final Agreement serves as a template for all the individual First Nation final agreements, KFN's final and self-government agreements are very similar to those of the First Nations that were actively engaged in the review process. Indeed, many of the provisions discussed by the IRG were identical to those contained in KFN's agreement, so observation of the review process provided advanced warning of many of the issues and difficulties KFN officials, too, would soon be confronting. Much of the discussion at the IRG table was necessarily interpretive, as the parties attempted to characterize the intended meaning of specific provisions in the agreements in an effort to determine whether or not those intentions had been fulfilled. Since many of those involved in the review – especially on the First Nation and Yukon sides – had also been involved in negotiating the agreements, these discussions provided me with a window onto various negotiators' understandings of what it was they thought they had agreed to.

I also attended, again as KFN's official representative, ongoing monthly negotiating sessions at which federal, Yukon, and First Nation representatives met to hammer out agreements for the transfer of federal and Yukon government programs and services to self-governing First Nations. Known as Program and Service Transfer Agreements (PSTAs), these agreements are anticipated in and authorized by the self-government agreements. While attending these negotiations, I watched the parties work together (and/or struggle with one another) to develop what would become key mechanisms for intergovernmental relations in the Yukon. Finally, I served as KFN's representative on the Senior Financial Arrangements Committee (SFAC), an inter-governmental body established under the Yukon self-government financial transfer agreements to monitor and periodically renegotiate these agreements (which must be renewed/renegotiated every five years). The financial transfer agreements are the fiscal mechanisms for transferring funds from the federal to First Nation governments for the implementation of final and self-government agreements and for the administration of programs and services. In 2003–4, SFAC discussions took on an added dimension as a result of the nine-year review process discussed above, because SFAC members (many of whom also served on the Implementation Review Group) took it upon themselves to consider the adequacy of self-government funding.[29] Discussions at the SFAC table were often

29 The SFAC took on this role for a couple of reasons. First, its members' familiarity with the FTAs made them by far the most knowledgeable about self-government funding. Second, the IRG's mandate did not originally include an assessment of self-government funding adequacy. Throughout the year I spent on the IRG, federal representatives were extremely reluctant to even discuss the adequacy of self-government funding, and they justified their reluctance by noting that, in contrast to the First Nation final agreement implementation plans, the self-government agreement implementation plans do not explicitly mention funding adequacy as subject to the nine-year review (contrast, for example, Kluane First Nation 2003c: 5 with Kluane First Nation 2003d: 3, 11). Although they eventually agreed to include the adequacy of self-government funding as part of the review, federal representatives

extremely technical, but implicit in the complex talk about gross expenditure base, own source revenue, and tax room were fundamental assumptions about the nature of First Nation governments and their proper relationship to federal authority.

Indeed, my experience on the SFAC helped inspire me to write this book. In their discussions over how to go about assessing the adequacy of self-government funding, SFAC members considered the use of two different possible methodologies. The first was to review the self-government agreements and associated program and service transfer agreements provision by provision and decide what if any costs might be associated with implementing each. Given the uncertainties involved, nearly everyone taking part in the review acknowledged that this method was practically unworkable. The other option was to take what SFAC members at the time referred to as a "model government" approach. Starting from the premise that self-governing First Nations need to receive enough funding to deliver essential services to their citizens at levels comparable to those of other governments in the Yukon,[30] proponents of the model government strategy argued that the best way to estimate the amount of funding necessary for self-government is actually to design a government capable of delivering the necessary

---

on the IRG refused ever to formally acknowledge that self-government funding was inadequate, despite overwhelming evidence to that effect (Implementation Review Group 2007). Yukon and First Nation officials found the federal position on self-government infuriating, arguing that adequate funding is obviously essential for self-government. Without that, even the best self-government agreements are worthless (see also Dacks 2004; Hogg and Turpel 1995). And, it turns out, inadequate funding for self-government has been a problem for self-governing First Nations across Canada (e.g., Dacks 2004; Rynard 2001; White 2009). Indeed, this was one of the major factors prompting self-governing First Nations across the country to form the Land Claims Agreements Coalition (LCAC), an organization intended to present a united front to the federal government in addressing implementation grievances (see Fenge 2015 for an account of the LCAC and its history).

30 This "comparability" requirement is contained in the self-government agreements themselves, which commit the parties to ensuring that self-governing First Nations can "provid[e] essential public services of reasonable quality to all [First Nation] Citizens" (Kluane First Nation 2003a: 3) and impose a requirement that any program or service drawn down by a First Nation government be funded at "a level or quality equivalent to the Government program or service and existing program or service quality is not diminished" (ibid.: 28).

programs and services at the appropriate quality and then estimate how much it would cost to run such a government. In practice, this entailed drawing up an organizational chart that showed the necessary government offices and departments (e.g., governance, finance, lands, health and social programs, etc.) – each endowed with an adequate staff and operating budget – for them to deliver the programs and services for which they are responsible. All of these figures would, of course, have been subject to negotiation.[31] Estimating the costs to run such a government would then be relatively straightforward (at least in theory), because negotiators could invoke the comparability clause of the self-government agreements to justify the use of Yukon government figures (salaries, as well as basic program and capital costs) as the basis for estimating the costs associated with running the model government.[32] The resulting total cost could then be compared to existing funding levels to assess their adequacy.

First Nation and Yukon government representatives on the IRG and SFAC championed the model government approach as the only workable strategy – and, not coincidentally, one virtually guaranteed to highlight just how inadequate federal funding of self-government actually was (and, as it turns out, remains). Federal representatives, for their part, largely agreed that a provision-by-provision strategy was unworkable, but they refused to sign on to the model government approach (during that year at least). Many First Nation and Yukon SFAC members suspected that federal officials' refusal to embrace the model government approach grew out of concerns that the model would generate an estimated cost of self-government that was much higher than

31 Given the significant range in population sizes among the Yukon First Nations, SFAC participants at the time considered generating three different models: small, medium, and large.

32 In practice, of course, such a process is far from straightforward, because of the lack of some relevant data as well as the need to compensate for a range of factors undermining the supposed comparability of Yukon government figures. Such factors include differences in the cost of living between Whitehorse and the more remote villages, the high transportation costs associated with regularly having to move people and materials between Whitehorse and First Nation offices in the villages, the scarcity – and sometimes complete lack – of available housing for new government employees in the villages, and so on.

the federal government was willing to pay.[33] Despite federal officials' reluctance to agree to the model government approach, however, they never proposed any alternative methods of assessing self-government funding adequacy (aside from a few half-hearted and quickly abandoned attempts to get SFAC members to go through the agreements provision by provision). In the absence of any viable alternative methodologies, First Nation representatives on SFAC (myself included) expended a great deal of time and effort that year producing position

33 In light of all this, one might legitimately ask what methodology the parties used to arrive at the original – and grossly inadequate – funding levels back in 1993. I was able to piece together an account of the process by which negotiators arrived at those funding levels in interviews with several Yukon and First Nation government officials who took part in it. They painted a very unflattering picture of the federal government, claiming that federal officials at the time had been completely uninterested in trying to determine the actual costs of self-government. The federal Treasury Board had approved Yukon land claim implementation funding levels in 1988. Significantly, that was before the self-government agreements had even been contemplated, much less negotiated, so the federal funding mandate did not include any money at all for self-government. It was also before *R. v. Sparrow* (1990), a Supreme Court decision that had significant implications for the funding of chapter 16 (wildlife) of the Yukon First Nation final agreements. During negotiations, federal negotiators had assured their Yukon and First Nation counterparts that they would go back to the Treasury Board for an updated funding mandate once the agreements were finalized. When that finally happened (in the early 1990s), however, the federal government was in the midst of a financial crisis. During that time of budget cutting, federal negotiators refused to approach the Treasury Board to ask for more money. First Nation and Yukon representatives both described the federal position on funding at the time as "take it or leave it." Despite repeated attempts to get federal officials to justify funding levels by relating them to the obligations and responsibilities created by the agreements, federal officials never complied with these requests. One Yukon official told me that a federal official had even confessed to him in confidence that the federal government never even made any internal effort to determine the actual cost of implementing the agreements. By contrast, the Yukon government did do extensive research to determine the costs (to the Yukon government) of First Nation self-government, and they tried to present the results of this research to the federal government during negotiations. Yukon officials who had participated in the process, however, unanimously reported that the federal negotiators had refused to even look at their figures. In the end, funding for Yukon First Nation self-government was based directly on bands' historic spending levels. Given the fact that First Nations have a much broader scope of responsibilities than Indian Act bands ever did, this funding strategy virtually ensured inadequate funding for self-government. It was, however, fully in keeping with federal policy on self-government, released in 1995, subsequent to the finalization of the first four Yukon agreements. Although that policy acknowledges that there will be new costs associated with self-government, it states clearly that no new funds will be made available for self-government:

papers, conducting research we hoped would eventually feed into the model, and otherwise attempting to demonstrate the utility and feasibility of the model government approach.[34] We argued passionately and relentlessly for adoption of the approach, and I have no doubt that under the circumstances it was far and away the best strategy for convincing the federal government to provide additional – and desperately needed – funding for self-government.[35]

"All federal costs associated with the implementation of self-government agreements will have to be accommodated within existing expenditures" (Minister of Indian Affairs and Northern Development 1995: 16). It thus appears to be official Canadian government policy to underfund First Nation self-government.

34 Some of the documents they produced (or later revised versions of them) are cited in Implementation Review Group (2007).

35 The federal government eventually relented and agreed to consider the adequacy of self-government funding using the model government method. In 2006 they began a pilot project (dubbed the "GEB project") to develop and test the methodology. The project was still ongoing in 2007 when the rest of the IRG's nine-year review report was ready for release, so the IRG released the report, noting simply that upon completion of the GEB project the parties would go on to assess the adequacy of self-government funding:

"Canada representatives indicated that they would be unable to comment on the adequacy of SGA [self-government agreement] funding until the composition of the Gross Expenditure Base (GEB) has been examined in detail. However, all representatives acknowledged that Self-Government Financial Transfer Agreement (SGFTA) funding was negotiated without addressing all of the factors set out in SGA 16.1–4 [the provisions requiring comparability of programs and services] and agreed that work is required to develop a measurement tool against which to assess this funding. To that end, the Parties have undertaken work to develop a methodology for estimating YFN expenditure needs for 'general governance' responsibilities. Assuming a viable methodology can be developed, it is anticipated that work will proceed to complete construction of GEBs that address the full scope of YFN expenditure needs. The results would enable completion of the funding adequacy review required as part of the reviews and inform mandates for renegotiation of IPs [implementation plans] and SGFTAs" (IRG 2007: 6).

The "general governance" segment of the GEB review was completed and presented to senior federal officials in 2007, but no similar study of "the full scope of YFN expenditure needs" (e.g., programs and services and land claim implementation) was ever carried out. In 2010 new FTAs finally came into effect. These did include a significant increase in funding for First Nation governance, an increase one First Nation official attributed directly to the GEB project; but they did not include any additional funds for other aspects of self-government (e.g., program and service delivery), which remain underfunded. Along with the increase in funding for general governance, however, federal officials also insisted on decreasing the annual funding escalators. Existing escalators had resulted in a rate of increase that was rapidly outpacing the growth of First Nation populations, so they were reduced to bring them in back in line with the population growth rate.

At times, however, as I looked around a table full of career bureaucrats (First Nation representatives included) discussing arcane financial topics,[36] I was struck by the incongruity of the argument we were making. Underlying all our efforts – and questioned by no one at the table – was a culturally and historically specific vision of government. Indeed, the model government approach took it entirely for granted that First Nation governments should be miniature versions of the federal and Yukon governments, that is, that they should be bureaucratic organizations subdivided into a number of different departments, each with its own staff and operating budgets. They should be passing laws, administering justice, and delivering essentially the same kinds of programs and services as the governments of the Yukon and Canada. The vision of "self-government" underlying the model government approach, then, actually entails the imposition of foreign ideas and practices of governance. And, ironically, the better funded such a government, the less space it would leave for indigenous forms of politics and sociality. As one Yukon government official who had some misgivings about the whole process perceptively put it:

> The self-government agreements … try to cram First Nations into the existing container we have for what governance looks like. We give them heads of power; we give them legislative powers; we frame it as though they're going to pass laws in the model we're familiar with. We talk about, you know, taxation powers; we talk about administration of justice powers. So, in other words, we've defined self-government as what we think government looks like. And in some ways, I think history may show that the self-government agreements were the most effective assimilation policy that governments ever came up with.

And it is not simply that the final and self-government agreements require the creation of bureaucratic governments where there were none before. More fundamentally, they take for granted the "self" of self-government, the notion that each First Nation is composed of a

36 SFAC representatives were all lawyers, accountants, or bureaucrats/consultants with decades of experience dealing with financial matters, and they spoke in a language that was, to put it mildly, rarefied. It was only after attending their meetings for a few months, engaging in extensive conversations with other SFAC representatives, and reading the documents they were producing that I gradually began to get a handle on what they were talking about.

distinct and pre-existing group of people who share – and have long shared – a political identity, a culture, a homeland, and a set of interests that set them apart from those of its neighbours (see chapter 4). In this view, each First Nation, as a distinct "people," requires its own territory and separate (bureaucratic) government. As we shall see in this book, however, the idea that indigenous people in the Yukon are divided up in this way is a relatively new one, stemming in large part from the legacy of Canada's colonial administration in the region. By treating colonial administrative divisions as if they were pre-existing political and cultural ones, the final and self-government agreements reify, extend, and perpetuate them. Insofar as government officials (First Nation officials included) attempt to implement the provisions of these agreements, they enact – and so actually help bring into being – the "traditional" territories and culturally distinct peoples that served as the supposed raison d'être for the creation of the various Yukon First Nation states. Just by using the model government approach to argue for increased funding for their respective self-governing First Nations, for example, SFAC representatives participated in this process and so helped naturalize the division of Yukon Indian people into distinct collective First Nation "selves."

Repeatedly over the course of this book, I will show that efforts to implement the Yukon agreements enact – and so help bring into being – First Nations as state-like social entities, thus authorizing and naturalizing a statist vision of Yukon indigenous politics and society.[37] I am

37 Also taken for granted by SFAC representatives – along with nearly everyone else attempting to implement the agreements – is the socio-economic context within which these new discrete First Nation polities must operate. In discussions of "own source revenue" (the self-government agreements require First Nations to contribute funding for self-government from their own sources of revenue), for example, SFAC members discussed whether it was realistic to expect First Nations to generate revenue by issuing government bonds. In these discussions, everyone seemed to share the assumption that First Nations must eventually become (or at least strive to become) "integrated into private capital markets," to use one federal official's phrase at the time. First Nation representatives never questioned the goal of capitalist integration; they merely took exception to federal characterizations of the speed and ease with which such a goal might be achieved. Given the close relationship between state formation and capitalism (Corrigan and Sayer 1985: 200), this should not be surprising, but it does lend weight to recent criticisms (e.g., Coulthard 2014; Samson and Cassell 2013) that condemn comprehensive land claim and self-government agreements as merely the latest chapter in an ongoing story of capitalist exploitation of settler colonial lands and resources.

interested in examining the sociocultural consequences of this process of First Nation state formation, especially in how the rise of state-like First Nations is transforming Yukon Indian peoples' ways of relating to one another, the land, and animals.

Outline of the Book

This book is divided into five chapters. In each, I focus upon a particular concept, beginning with *sovereignty* itself and moving on to consider a handful of others – *territory, citizenship, nation,* and *history/time* – that are themselves cultural and historical entailments of sovereignty. Claims to indigenous sovereignty and the government-to-government relations resulting from such claims (such as those ushered in by the Yukon agreements) have accelerated a process of indigenous state formation begun under the colonial regime; and the resulting state-like indigenous polities take sovereignty and its entailments as the structuring principles of indigenous–state relations. *Sovereignty, territory, citizenship, nation,* and *history/time* all play key boundary-making roles in the creation and maintenance of the new First Nation states. What is more, sovereignty and its entailments not only come to structure relations between indigenous people and the state, but also relations among indigenous people and between them, the land, and animals. The entailments of sovereignty constrain the possibilities for indigenous politics by fostering state-sanctioned ways of thinking and interacting while rendering indigenous knowledge, practices, and sociality increasingly unthinkable and impractical. By implementing their agreements, Yukon Indian people help create and continuously enact Yukon First Nations as state-like political organizations whose very existence is transforming Yukon Indian peoples' beliefs, practices, and social relations. Although all the various boundary-making processes set in motion by the agreements are intimately interconnected, it is necessary to separate them for analytic purposes.

I begin in chapter 1 by taking a close look at sovereignty. There are some theorists (hailing from all sides of the debate over indigenous sovereignty) who reject the idea that there can be such a thing as "indigenous sovereignty" (there are conservative thinkers who still reject the idea because they believe indigenous people were too primitive to have exercised sovereignty before the arrival of Europeans, while some indigenous scholars reject it as incompatible with indigenous culture). A brief account of the theory and practice of indigenous sovereignty in

North America, however, suggests that, like it or not, the concept of sovereignty underlies nearly all theories of indigenous–state relations – even where settler governments (e.g., Canada) are loath to invoke the term. This is because sovereignty has come to serve in contemporary political thought as the theoretical precondition for politics (Shaw 2008). If indigenous peoples have politics, then it follows that those politics must be playing out within a sovereign community, whether that sovereign is First Nation or Canadian. This is why rejections of settler state sovereignty are nearly always followed by assertions of indigenous sovereignty, despite sovereignty's culturally specific origins. It also explains why, despite many indigenous theorists' discomfort with the cultural baggage that accompanies the notion of sovereignty, most feel compelled to salvage it by "indigenizing" it, cleansing it of its inappropriate cultural connotations. In this chapter, I show that although the literature on indigenizing sovereignty provides useful insights into the use of *sovereignty* in indigenous contexts (and, indeed, into sovereignty more generally), invocations of "indigenous sovereignty" do not transcend sovereignty's statist assumptions; indeed, indigenous scholars' insights about the cultural dimensions of sovereignty resonate powerfully with those of recent theorists in "mainstream" disciplines who also view sovereignty as the product of culture and history rather than as a timeless politico-legal principle. This means that indigenous claims to sovereign status, like all sovereign claims, necessarily imply that indigenous polities must be fundamentally state-like; and it is the cultural entailments of this fact that I examine in subsequent chapters.

First and most obviously, sovereign states and state-like political organizations are geographically bounded. More than that, sovereign power is fundamentally territorial. That is, authority within sovereign entities is territorially ordered, a fact that informs common-sense notions of the world as divided up among political entities, each exercising jurisdiction over discrete mutually exclusive territories separated by linear borders (Biolsi 2005; Malkki 1992). Such a vision of political space implies that to qualify as a government in the first place, a political entity must have jurisdiction over a clearly defined territory, and its agents must claim legitimate authority within that territory. This vision of the political clearly informs the Yukon agreements, which create new jurisdictional boundaries in the Yukon and use them to structure the authority of the new First Nation governments. This is the subject of chapter 2. After discussing pre-contact (non-state, non-territorial) social organization in the Yukon, I recount the Canadian government's gradual imposition of territorially ordered politics in the Yukon, culminating in the comprehensive land claim and self-government agreements. I examine the agreements' territorial dimensions and show that insofar as Yukon Indian people abide by them (and even sometimes when they do not), they necessarily help enact the new First Nation states as politico-territorial entities. I pay particular attention to how the new territories – and the territorial practices associated with them – are transforming the ways in which Yukon Indian people can relate to the land and resources and to one another with respect to those resources.

Sovereignty implies social boundaries as well as geographical ones. Today, sovereign power emanates from "the people," a clearly delineated subset of humanity with a special relationship to the state's geographical territory; and states ostensibly exercise their power on behalf of their people (a legitimizing claim made even by dictatorships). The Yukon agreements create state-like social entities not only by drawing geographical boundaries around First Nation territories, but also by erecting and maintaining new boundaries among Yukon Indian people who are otherwise connected to one another by dense relations of kinship and reciprocity that cross-cut territorial boundaries and extend throughout the Yukon and beyond. The agreements do this by formally distinguishing between First Nation citizens and non-citizens (who may simultaneously be citizens of other First Nations and close kin). In chapter 3, I explore the legal and cultural dynamics of First Nation citizenship and their implications for indigenous social organization and conceptions of personhood. I show that the boundaries of citizenship create categorical legal and administrative differences among people who not so long ago viewed themselves in relational rather than categorical terms. At the same time, the homogenizing effects of citizenship (even in its differentiated guise) erase important forms of social-cultural difference *within* the new First Nations. Finally, and perhaps most significantly, I show that the institutions of First Nation citizenship erect boundaries not only among the citizens of different Yukon First Nations, but also between humans and non-humans – in stark contrast to many Yukon Indian peoples' ongoing belief that animals and other non-human persons play an important – and overtly political – role in Yukon society.

In chapter 4, I shift from an analysis of citizenship as a legal and political category to the concomitant emergence of ethno-nationalist sentiments and identities. The laws and bureaucratic practices that differentiate between citizens and non-citizens vis-à-vis territory have begun to produce significant lived distinctions between "us" (citizens of the same First Nation) and "them" (citizens of other First Nations). As a result, what were initially merely political/administrative distinctions have begun taking on an ethno-nationalist flavour. Increasingly, Yukon Indian people (and others) view the new institutions of territoriality and citizenship analysed in chapters 2 and 3 as resulting from – rather than causing – the supposedly pre-existing differences in language, culture, and history that frame the citizens of one First Nation as different *kinds* of people than those of another. Given the close and essential relationship between state formation and nationalism, it should not be surprising that the Yukon agreements, as engines of First Nation state formation, are rooted in and lend force to the assumption that each First Nation, as distinct from other First Nations, is a culturally homogeneous social entity (the "self" of self-government) with primordial ties to a particular homeland. In chapter 4, I examine the day-to-day processes of internal cultural homogenization and external differentiation authorized by the agreements and show how they foster the rise of ethno-nationalist attachments to the new First Nation states. By implementing and abiding by the provisions of the new agreements, Yukon Indian people (and others) breathe life into the territorial and social boundaries drawn by the agreements and so enact First Nation states as the containers of their own ethno-territorial nations. And, like *citizenship*, the concept of *nation* almost by definition excludes animals.

Nationalism, a "people's" drive for a state of its own, is a fundamentally territorial ideology, but it is also associated with a distinctive temporality. Despite continual changes in the demographic composition of all states and in the institutions, laws, and practices that together constitute them, states themselves – or at least the nations that aspire to them – endure. They move steadily through what Anderson (1991) has referred to as "homogeneous empty time" as they progress inexorably from the distant past into the far future. As numerous historians have pointed out (e.g., Chakrabarty 2000; Duara 1995), history itself, both the concept and the discipline, emerged and continue to draw their meaning from a nationalist perspective on the world. In the latter part of chapter 4, I examine efforts – intimately bound up with the Yukon land claims process – to reframe Yukon Indian people's relationship to their ancestors and to the land in explicitly nationalist terms; that is, in ways that construct and take for granted the First Nation as historical social entity.

In chapter 5, I build on the observations about national history made in chapter 4 to explore the question of time more generally. Although state sovereignty is not associated with any single temporal framework, the process of state formation nevertheless entails a revolution in how people think about and relate to time. Not surprisingly, the Yukon agreements have imposed a new temporal order in the Yukon. This is not to suggest that some unitary "agreement time" has replaced "indigenous time" in a straightforward manner. Rather, the agreements have introduced a whole range of new temporal frameworks for the management and governance of both people and resources. Just as they are rooted in a set of spatial/territorial assumptions, the Yukon agreements are also built upon a set of temporal assumptions. They take it for granted that the various processes of management and governance unfold in particular kinds of time (though not always the same one!); and that these processes stand in particular temporal relationship to one another and to the First Nation state as a whole. To the extent, then, that First Nation people engage in and/or abide by the practices of management and governance as spelled out in the agreements, they must adopt – or at least adapt to – those new temporal frameworks. This is not simply a matter of altering the *timing* of their activities; it also often involves substantive change in the nature of the activities themselves. A focus on the temporal politics of these agreements, then, can provide new insights into the nature of the social and environmental changes they bring.

A case in point involves the agreements' provisions for the management of "renewable resources." Although everyone in the Yukon – wildlife biologists and Yukon Indian hunters alike – can agree that fish and wildlife populations are a "renewable resource," this masks a fundamental disagreement over the meaning of renewability itself and the spatio-temporal order it implies. Wildlife biologists view animal populations (and the humans who hunt them) as embedded in cyclical time, characterized by the periodic recurrence of similar events of the same type. Yukon Indian people, by contrast, are more likely to view them as embedded in circular time, a spatio-temporal framework within which the same event occurs over and over again. This difference has significant implications for how each group conceives of animals as resources, the proper role of human agency vis-à-vis animals, and what constitutes appropriate management. Although First Nations can and do exert some control over space and time within the state bureaucratic context of wildlife co-management, that very context takes for granted the cyclical topology of bureaucratic space-time and is therefore incompatible in many ways with their views of proper human–animal relations. To the extent Yukon Indian people exercise the co-management powers granted them under the new agreements, then, it becomes increasingly difficult for them to challenge dominant Euro-Canadian views of wildlife management and human–animal relations.

One central objective of this book as a whole is to explore the social and environmental consequences of framing indigenous struggles for autonomy within the settler state as efforts to assert *sovereignty*. Because the sovereignty concept requires an inside and an outside, its use necessarily entails the production and maintenance of boundaries of all sorts – territorial, sociocultural, temporal, and epistemological. In the Yukon, this boundary making is manifest in myriad ways: in the creation of territorial boundaries both between and within First Nations, in the division of Yukon Indian people into various distinct First Nation citizenries – along with accompanying processes of cultural and historical differentiation (and internal homogenization), and in the adoption of knowledge production practices that draw a clear distinction between state-authorized "knowledge" and "superstition." Taken together, these new boundaries are having a profound effect on how Yukon Indian people think about and interact with one another, and their creation has precipitated a dramatic reorganization of indigenous society in the Yukon.

This has important implications for the study of indigenous–state relations. For, while scholars studying land claims in Canada have examined the intricacies of indigenous–state relations under specific agreements, few have concerned themselves much with how these agreements affect relations across claims area boundaries – between the beneficiaries of one agreement and those of another other. Yet, the boundaries between First Nations (and their claims areas) cannot be taken for granted, since they are themselves a key product of the land claims process and the sovereign assumptions upon which it is based. This suggests that a full understanding of indigenous–state relations in Canada (and wherever else indigenous–state relations are framed by sovereignty) requires close attention to the *constitution* of First Nations as distinct political entities and how this process has affected social relations across the boundaries between First Nations and from one claims area to the next.

Framing indigenous–state relations in the language of sovereignty, however, does more than simply create and maintain new boundaries among indigenous people. It also narrows the field of politics – and, indeed, of sociality more generally – to the realm of the human. Most political theorists, along with nearly everyone else thinking and writing from the vantage of the state, take it for granted that only humans can be political actors. Although plants, animals, and other elements of "the environment" can be the objects of politics, they cannot be its subjects. From the perspective of sovereignty, they are not "citizens" but "resources."[38] The situation was – and in some contexts still is – quite different in indigenous Yukon society. Yukon Indian people, like many other indigenous peoples around the world, view animals, plants, and some abiotic parts of the environment as sentient and spiritually powerful persons with whom they can interact and to whom they are bound through ongoing relations of kinship and reciprocity (Nadasdy 2007b). Not only are these other-than-human persons[39] entangled in a complex web of social relations with human persons (as well as with other kinds of non-human persons), they also play an explicitly political role in Yukon indigenous society. Indeed, it was animal-people who handed down many of the laws that continue to govern not only relations between human and non-human persons, but also relations among humans. These laws are contained in a body of Long Time Ago stories that continue to serve Yukon Indian people as guides for proper behaviour towards the human and non-human world (chapter 3).

It is hard to imagine how any arrangement that excludes these politically powerful beings from participation in the political realm could legitimately be called Yukon Indian "self-government"; yet there is no more room for animals in the (semi-)sovereign communities of the new Yukon First Nations than there is in any other sovereign state. Hobbes himself was clear about the need to exclude animals and inanimate objects from the realm of the political. Not only did he explicitly reject them as potential members of the sovereign community (on the grounds that, lacking language, they do not have the rational capacity to enter into

38 For an apparent exception, see Donaldson and Kymlicka (2011). Elsewhere, however, I show that the exception is only partial and that Donaldson and Kymlicka's conception of animal citizenship/sovereignty is in any case incompatible with indigenous Yukon conceptions of animals and human–animal relations (Nadasdy 2016).

39 This term was suggested by Hallowell (1960) and has since been widely adopted in the ethnographic literature to refer to the belief that animals and other elements of the environment are sentient social beings who, though they differ superficially from humans, share with them the fundamental attribute of personhood: the capacity to be social actors.

the social contract),[40] he also marked as illegitimate many of the ways of knowing and being in the world (dreams, visions, traditional stories, nonlinear temporal frameworks) that together frame Yukon Indian people's interactions with the other-than-human persons that inhabit their world (see chapter 1). Political theorist Karena Shaw (2008) shows that Hobbes's views on sovereignty still largely shape Euro-Canadian views of indigenous–state relations and of politics more broadly (see also Asch 2014); and this is certainly evident in the exclusion of other-than-human persons (and ways of knowing them) from the political regime established by the Yukon agreements.

40 "To make covenants with brute beasts is impossible, because not understanding our speech, they understand not, nor accept of any translation of right, nor can translate any right to another: and without mutual acceptation, there is no covenant" (Hobbes 1998: 85).

Chapter One

Sovereignty

Few people have questioned how a European term and idea – sovereignty is certainly not Sioux, Salish, or Iroquoian in origin – came to be so embedded and important to cultures that had their own systems of government since the time before the term *sovereignty* was invented in Europe. Fewer still have questioned the implication of adopting the European notion of power and governance and using it to structure the postcolonial systems that are being negotiated and implemented within indigenous communities today.

Taiaiake Alfred (2005b: 39)

The very attempt to treat sovereignty as a matter of definition and legal principle encourages a certain amnesia about its historical and culturally specific character.

R.B.J. Walker (1993: 166)

As political theorist Taiaiake Alfred notes in the epigraph above, the European concept of *sovereignty* has long played – and continues to play – a key role in shaping not only indigenous–state relations but also many indigenous peoples' visions of and aspirations for a decolonized future. It is not simply sovereignty's foreign origins that are so troubling to Alfred, but more particularly its rootedness in a set of cultural assumptions that he sees as incompatible with – even contrary to – indigenous ways of being in the world. Building on previous work by Boldt and Long (1984), he argues that "the simple act of framing the goal in terms of sovereignty is harmful in itself. 'Sovereignty' implies a set of values and objectives in direct opposition to those found in traditional indigenous philosophies" (Alfred 1999: 57). The political and cultural implications that he finds so objectionable, it turns out, are precisely those associated with the modern territorial state. "In making claims to sovereignty," he argues, indigenous leaders "are making a choice to accept the state as their model and to allow indigenous political goals to be framed and evaluated according to a statist pattern. Thus the common criteria of statehood – coercive force, control of territory, population numbers, international recognition – come to dominate discussion of indigenous peoples' political goals" (1999: 56). The statist framework imposed by the concept of sovereignty, Alfred believes, inappropriately constrains the universe of possibilities for indigenous politics. For this reason, he (at times) advocates a total rejection of the sovereignty concept.

Although scholars writing from a wide range of political perspectives acknowledge Alfred's work in exposing sovereignty's imperialist roots, few are as willing as he is to jettison the notion entirely (but see Boldt and Long 1984). On the contrary, many maintain that, despite its flaws, the concept of sovereignty is essential to the struggles of indigenous peoples. Because sovereignty is not some timeless principle, but is instead a "historically contingent" notion "with no fixed meaning" that "must be situated within the historical and cultural relationships in which it is articulated," Joanne Barker (2005a: 21) and others argue, it can and should be rehabilitated and/or indigenized for use in the struggle against colonial domination.[1] And, as it turns out, even Alfred himself takes a more ambivalent stance towards sovereignty than that with which he is generally credited. Although at times he does seem to reject sovereignty altogether, at other times he argues instead that indigenous people must reject not the term itself but only the Euro-American *meanings* assigned to it. In effect, he too argues for its indigenization:

> "Sovereignty" *as it is currently understood and applied* in indigenous–state relations cannot be seen as an appropriate goal or framework, because it has no relevance to indigenous values. The challenge before us is to detach the notion of sovereignty from its current legal meaning and use in the context of the Western understanding of power and relationships. We need to create a meaning for "sovereignty" that respects the understanding of

1 For a selection of articulate but quite different arguments opposing Alfred's call for the total rejection of the sovereignty concept, see Cobb (2005), Donaldson and Kymlicka (2011: 171–3), Lyons (2010: 133–8), Rifkin (2009: 108–10).

> power in indigenous cultures ... (Alfred 1999: 54, emphasis added; see also Alfred 2005b: 42)

I shall have more to say about efforts to indigenize sovereignty later in this chapter. For now, I simply point out that although the concept of sovereignty is indeed flexible, it is not infinitely so. The term cannot plausibly be made to mean absolutely anything. Indeed, to invent a *completely* new meaning for the term is tantamount to rejecting it altogether. Why, after all, would one want to refer to something that is *completely* different from the standard meaning of sovereignty as "sovereignty" at all, when one could avoid a good deal of confusion by simply inventing a new term to go with that completely new meaning? Nor would such "conceptual separatism" (Lyons 2010: 136) necessarily be in the interests of indigenous people. As a self-avowed Anishinabe nationalist, Scott Lyons points out that *sovereignty*

> is a modern and universal political concept indissolubly associated with the idea of the nation. To reject this conceptual language out of hand risks getting out of the national game altogether and ending up with something that might be "ethnic," or "racial," or even a "community," but it won't be a nation unless it is willing to speak the language of nations. That language is by definition a modern, universal lingua franca. (2010: 135–6)[2]

By this he does not mean that *sovereignty* (or *nation*) has some fixed and agreed upon meaning, but only that if the concept is to be at all useful to indigenous people in their dealings with settler states, its meaning must bear at least a family resemblance to those generally ascribed to it in the nation-state context. As he puts it, "We must be careful not to accentuate our differences to the point of incommensurability lest we drop out of political conversations altogether" (Lyons 2010: 136).

---

2 Lyons is explicitly critical of Alfred here, noting that his conceptual separatism with regard to sovereignty is inconsistent with his nationalism. There is some merit to this critique, but Alfred's position on nationalism is complex and has changed over time. In later works, such as *Wasase* (2005a: 224–5), he draws a distinction between "Native Nationalism" (a derivative ideology that "has resulted in the transformation of our local governments into bureaucracy-mimicking shadows of true Onkwehonwe governance") and "indigenous nationhood" ("an authentic sense of Onkwehonwe collective being") and grapples with the possibility of a truly post-sovereign (and therefore post-nationalist) politics.

If indigenous political discourse is to remain commensurable with political discourse more broadly, the concept of *indigenous sovereignty*[3] must remain linked to that of the state. This is not the same as asserting, as some critics still do (e.g., Flanagan 1985), that only independent states can be sovereign.[4] It is, rather, simply to acknowledge the fact that the sovereign state form – along with the concepts that are inextricably bound up with it, such as *citizenship, nation,* and *history* – have become central to our very conception of politics – and indigenous politics is no exception to this rule.[5] Consider, for example, Kevin Bruyneel's very broad definition of sovereignty (which he based on a similar formulation by Robert Yazzie): "the ability of a group of people to make their own decisions and control their own lives in relation to the space where they reside and/or that they envision as their own,"[6] and he notes that, "according to this definition, sovereignty expresses the relationship between people, power, and space over time" (Bruyneel 2007: 23). This definition has the virtue of remaining broad enough to allow for ongoing contestation/negotiation over who or what might qualify as

3 I use "indigenous sovereignty" as a catch-all term, including what American Indian and indigenous studies scholars have variously referred to as "Indian sovereignty," "tribal sovereignty," "native sovereignty," "First Nation sovereignty," and the like. Occasionally I use one of these terms as well when engaging with a particular scholar's work, but generally I try to stick with "indigenous."

4 International legal scholar Hurst Hannum (1996: 15) notes: "One principle upon which there seems to be universal agreement is that sovereignty is an attribute of statehood, and that only states can be sovereign." This is a presumption that indigenous studies scholars must continuously counter, despite growing acknowledgment in some quarters of political theory that sovereignty does not map unproblematically or solely onto independent states. Audra Simpson's recent book (2014) can be read (in part and among other things) as a refutation of this standard presumption and a justification for applying the language of sovereignty to Indian Nations. I do not read her as attempting to indigenize sovereignty, however, but rather as arguing that Mohawk sovereignty is essentially similar to US and Canadian sovereignty (which it disrupts). As she puts it, "sovereignty may exist within sovereignty. One does not entirely negate the other, but they necessarily stand in terrific tension and pose serious jurisdictional and normative challenges to each other" (ibid.: 10). On this notion of "nested sovereignties," see also Biolsi (2005).

5 Indeed, it should be borne in mind that *indigeneity* is itself a statist concept. In the absence of states, there can be no "indigenous people," nor can there be "indigenous politics."

6 Robert Porter (2002: 10) suggests a definition of Indian sovereignty that, though more bluntly stated, amounts to more or less the same thing: "We retain the right to do whatever we want in our own territory without limitations."

sovereign (i.e., it makes theoretical space for state-like organizations, such as First Nations, to claim recognition as sovereign political entities) while capturing all the basic historical and cultural entailments of sovereignty (territory, people, power, time).[7] Insofar as indigenous studies scholars and activists ascribe their notion of sovereignty to indigenous "nations" composed of culturally distinct "peoples" each with its own distinct homeland, history, and corresponding right of "self-government," they take for granted the cultural entailments of sovereignty, which themselves derive from a statist logic. Thus, although indigenous studies scholars have largely succeeded in disassociating

7 Because Bruyneel is interested in tribal sovereignty in the United States, he necessarily has in mind the kind of sovereignty characteristic of what has variously been referred to as the modern state, the nation state, the Westphalian state, or the territorial state – a curious beast that did not appear on the scene until relatively recently in the long history of state formation. Historically, other kinds of states were organized along principles that differ markedly from those governing the modern territorial state. In such states, sovereignty must be conceptualized somewhat differently, but it is worth pointing out that Bruyneel's definition is flexible enough to characterize sovereignty in historical states of all kinds, provided one adjusts the meanings of its key concepts – *territory*, *people*, and *time* – to reflect the power dynamics at play in each. Political geographers, archaeologists, and others (Jones 1959; Scott 2009; Smith 2003; Thongchai 1994), for example, have argued that states of the past seldom if ever had contiguous and non-overlapping territories separated by clearly demarcated boundaries; nor were they elements in a system of states whose combined territories encompassed the globe. Thus, until relatively recently, there were significant "zones of no sovereignty" (Scott 2009: 60). What is more, in many pre-modern states, sovereign power was rooted in control over people (who could be taxed and conscripted) rather than over territory per se. Despite these important differences, states have always had an important spatial dimension, and the exercise of state sovereignty has always been to some extent an exercise in territoriality. Even in those states that sought to control people rather than territory, the exercise of sovereignty (e.g., taxation and conscription) was shaped in critical ways by territorial considerations. In the "mandala" states of Southeast Asia described by Thongchai (1994) and Scott (2009), for example, state power gradually faded the further one got from the centre. Thus, for these states sovereignty was not an all-or-nothing affair. Multiple states might exert overlapping sovereignties – of varying intensity – over any particular locale; and the reach of a state's sovereign power varied not only with distance, but also by the type of terrain and the season. Walker (1993: 167–8), however, warns against presentist readings of history that project "sovereignty" back in time to other types of states. In any case, like Bruyneel, my focus in this book is on the modern territorial state and self-governing First Nations, those state-like political entities made in its image.

sovereignty from the independent state – thus opening up a space for assertions of indigenous sovereignty – they have not generally succeeded in (nor, indeed, have many even sought to) completely dissociate it from the territorial state form.

But if, as Alfred suggests, the problems with sovereignty lie in its statist implications, then why not abandon it entirely and start afresh? Why not develop new concepts that are more suited to the indigenous context? What is it about the sovereignty concept that – despite its statist baggage – indigenous studies scholars and activists find so indispensable? I have already suggested some general answers to these questions in the introduction to this book. These have to do with sovereignty's powerful legitimating role. A state that lacks sovereignty cannot really be said to be a state at all; a government without some measure of sovereignty (whether inherent or delegated) is – in the eyes of most of those who live in state societies – no government at all. Indeed, as Karena Shaw (2008) points out (I will discuss her work in more detail below), sovereignty has become the precondition for politics today. That is, "politics" only happens within sovereign states or state-like social organizations, where it has become largely synonymous with "governance." The absence of sovereignty, then, implies the absence of government. So any claims to legitimate governance – by indigenous people or anyone else – must be accompanied by claims to sovereignty. As we saw in the introduction, however, it is never enough for a state to merely assert its sovereignty. Because it is not a timeless principle but rather a constantly changing ideal and effect of statecraft, sovereignty must constantly be produced and negotiated. To be recognized as a sovereign state with a legitimate government, a political organization must look like a state and it must act the way a state is supposed to act; that is, it must conform to the evolving prescriptions for statehood conveyed by the ever-changing ideal of sovereignty.

The same can be said for state-like social organizations. Indigenous people who desire some measure of autonomy within the settler state (or, indeed, outside of it) must assert a desire for self-determination and demonstrate (to the satisfaction of settler state officials) a capacity for self-government. Since settler state officials – along with most everyone else – only recognize as governments those organizations that are sufficiently state-like, indigenous people must back up their claims to sovereignty by developing state-like institutions and practices. First Nations must resemble states if they hope to be recognized as sovereign. That is, they must conform to the prescriptions of sovereignty.

This is why First Nation land claims in the Yukon – and the agreements that flow from them – are conceived and written in the language of sovereignty. Indeed, sovereignty serves as the conceptual precondition not only for the Yukon land claim and self-government agreements, but also for indigenous–state relations more generally. Some will no doubt disagree with this assertion and argue (with some justification) that comprehensive land claim and self-government agreements in Canada – to say nothing of other even darker chapters in the history of indigenous–state relations in North America – are not about indigenous sovereignty at all but rather are simply the latest stage in the colonial process. So I need to clarify what I mean. This will require a (brief) account of the role sovereignty has played in the history of indigenous–state relations in North America.

Sovereignty as the Conceptual Basis for Indigenous–State Relations

From the first days of European settlement in North America, European governments were eager to establish their own sovereignty over newly discovered lands. Although Europeans varied considerably in how they perceived the peoples they encountered here, European governments treated indigenous polities as sovereign – at least implicitly – insofar as they entered into treaty relations with them and otherwise treated them as foreign powers. Until it discontinued the practice in 1871, the United States (like Britain and France before it) regularly entered into treaty relations with Indian nations and otherwise treated them as sovereign political entities. The framers of the US constitution regarded Indian nations, like the foreign nations of Europe, to be extra-constitutional political entities (Clinton 2002: 248; Wilkins and Lomawaima 2001: 20), as did much of the federal legislation that framed US–Indian relations in the early years of the republic (as, e.g., in the Trade and Intercourse Acts, see Clinton 2002: 133–4; Johnson 1973: 976–89; McNeil 1998: 297–8). It is also telling that it was the Department of War, that administrative unit charged with defending the country from *external* threats, which initially assumed responsibility for Indian affairs. It was not until 1849 that that responsibility was transferred to the Department of the Interior. Canada, for its part, is still negotiating treaties with First Nations, though there was a hiatus of fifty-four years between the signing of Treaty 11, the last of the numbered treaties, in 1921 and signing of the James Bay and Northern Quebec Agreement, the first of the modern treaties, in 1975.

Chief Justice John Marshall, who is generally credited with first articulating the principle of tribal sovereignty in US Indian law, explicitly argued that by entering into treaties with Indian tribes, the United States had implicitly recognized them as sovereign states. In *Cherokee v. Georgia*, he characterized the Cherokee as a state (and not as merely state-like) for precisely this reason:

> [The Cherokee] have been uniformly treated as a state from the settlement of our country. The numerous treaties made with them by the United States recognize them as a people capable of maintaining the relations of peace and war, of being responsible in their political character for any violation of their engagements, or for any aggression committed on the citizens of the United States by any individual of their community. Laws have been enacted in the spirit of these treaties. The acts of our government plainly recognize the Cherokee Nation as a State, and the courts are bound by these acts. (Cited in Lyons 2010: 126)

By the time Marshall was writing, however, the US settler state had expanded to encompass many indigenous lands and peoples (including the Cherokee), making it harder to construe its relationship with them as one between independent sovereign states. Indeed, it was in an attempt to elucidate the nature of the relationship between the United States and the indigenous polities within its borders that Marshall explicitly recognized their prior sovereignty.[8] Referring to them as "domestic dependent nations,"[9] he ruled that they retained a measure of sovereignty despite their incorporation into the United States. This, he believed, was consistent with principles of international law that allow "a weak state ... [to] place itself under the protection of one more powerful, without stripping itself of the right of government, and ceasing to be a state" (cited in Wilkinson 1987: 56). Thus, though tribes internal to the United States may have surrendered their external sovereignty,

8 In another oft-cited passage from his majority opinion in *Worcester v. Georgia* (1832), Marshall affirmed the prior sovereignty of Indian tribes in the following way: "America, separated from Europe by a wide ocean, was inhabited by a distinct people, divided into separate nations, independent of each other and of the rest of the world, having institutions of their own, and governing themselves by their own laws" (cited in Macklem 1993: 1334).

9 Marshall coined this phrase in the second of three landmark cases, *Cherokee v. Georgia* (1828).

they retained powers of self-government on their own lands. In this view, tribes' powers of self-governance are *inherent*; they derive from Indian people's prior sovereignty rather than from having been delegated to them by the US government.[10]

To be sure, the United States has not always honoured the sovereign status of tribal governments; indeed, federal legislation and court decisions – particularly in the latter part of the nineteenth and early twentieth centuries but continuing today – have so eroded tribes' powers of self-government that it is sometimes hard to recognize them as "sovereign" at all (see Aleinikoff 2002). Yet, the doctrine of tribal sovereignty never completely disappeared from US Indian law, even in the darkest days of the late nineteenth century; and legal scholar Felix Cohen breathed new life into it when he wrote in his authoritative *Handbook of Federal Indian Law* (1942) that, "perhaps the most basic principle of all Indian law ... is the principle that those powers which are lawfully invested in an Indian tribe are not, in general, delegated powers granted by express acts of Congress, but rather inherent powers of a limited sovereignty which has never been extinguished" (cited in Wilkinson 1987: 58).[11]

Although US tribes are no longer regarded as independent sovereign states, in the Marshall-Cohen formulation they retain all the powers of a sovereign state except those *explicitly* terminated or limited by treaty or congressional legislation.[12] Of course, many are critical of the

10 Coffey and Tsosie (2001: 195), however, argue that in a string of important Indian law cases over the past few decades the US Supreme Court seems to be moving toward a notion of tribal sovereignty as delegated rather than inherent.

11 Legal scholar Charles Wilkinson notes that the courts (including the US Supreme Court) have by now cited what he calls the "Marshall-Cohen formulation" of tribal sovereignty so often by that it has "attained something of the weight of a Supreme Court opinion" (1987: 58). Numerous scholars have traced the ebb and flow of tribal sovereignty in US Indian law; see, for example, Aleinikoff (2002), Barsh and Henderson (1980), Wilkins (1997), Wilkins and Lomawaima (2001), and Wilkinson (1987).

12 It is worth citing Cohen more extensively in this regard: "Each Indian tribe begins its relationship with the Federal Government as a sovereign power, recognized as such in treaty and legislation. The powers of sovereignty have been limited from time to time by special treaties and laws designed to take from the Indian tribes control of matters which, in the judgment of Congress, these tribes could no longer be safely permitted to handle. The statutes of Congress, then, must be examined to determine the limitations of tribal sovereignty rather than to determine its sources or its

notion – taken for granted by both Marshall and Cohen – that Congress can/should have the authority to unilaterally limit tribal sovereignty, authority rooted in what has come to be known as the plenary power doctrine.[13] Not only does the plenary power doctrine assert that the US Congress has unlimited authority over tribes, it also holds that the exercise of such power is political (rather than legal) and so stands outside the jurisdiction of the courts. Thus, tribes have no legal recourse when Congress strips them of their sovereign powers. Clearly, such a reading of the plenary power doctrine is theoretically incompatible with any substantive notion of tribal sovereignty. Shorn of the plenary power doctrine, however, the Marshall-Cohen view of inherent tribal sovereignty has wide appeal precisely because it provides a rationale – consistent with US and international law – for tribes' ongoing sovereignty even after they have been geographically incorporated into the settler state (cf. Clinton 2002).[14] In practice, however, the US government has continued to recognize tribes' inherent sovereignty while steadily chipping away at their sovereign powers through legislation authorized by the plenary power doctrine.

These legal considerations aside, US tribes are "state-like" political entities insofar as they retain (limited) powers of self-government and exercise quite broad jurisdiction over their own peoples, lands,

positive content. What is not expressly limited remains within the domain of tribal sovereignty" (cited in Wilkinson 1987: 58). See also Wilkins and Lomawaima (2001: chap. 4) for an extended discussion of the doctrine of reserved rights associated with this view.

13 According to Wilkins and Lomawaima (2001: chap. 3), the plenary power doctrine – as applied to tribes – derives in part from a particularly self-serving interpretation of the Commerce Clause in the US constitution. The doctrine was then elaborated in a series of notorious decisions handed down by the Supreme Court towards the end of the nineteenth century, including *United States v. Kagama* (1886) and *Lone Wolf v. Hitchcock* (1903). Alexander Aleinikoff (2002) has argued that a full understanding of the plenary power doctrine must also take into account developments in the law regarding US overseas possessions and immigration – the two other legal domains in which the doctrine is invoked. For good legal histories – and powerful critiques – of the plenary power doctrine and the fundamentally racist assumptions upon which it is based, see Aleinikoff (2002), Clinton (2002), Wilkins and Lomawaima (2001), and Williams (2005).

14 Although recent decades have witnessed various attempts to indigenize the term *sovereignty* (see below), many efforts along these lines retain at least a family resemblance to the Marshall-Cohen formulation minus the plenary power doctrine.

and resources within their (now diminished) territories. Tribes today have their own court systems, police departments, and legislatures. They have law-making authority over a wide range of civil (and some criminal) matters on tribal lands, including those relating to family law, child welfare, inheritance, economic development, natural resources, taxation, corporations, traffic, and property, among others.[15] They collect taxes and royalties. They issue licence plates, land-use permits, and hunting licences. They conduct environmental reviews. They negotiate and enter into agreements with other sovereign governments (most prominent of late are the high-profile gaming compacts some tribes have signed with states), and federal courts have been fairly consistent in upholding tribal sovereign immunity.[16] The increasing exercise of these state-like powers has led some to comment on the emergence of "tribal states" (Nesper 2007). Today, *tribal sovereignty* has become a standard, if contested, term in the discourse on indigenous–state relations in the United States. Many contemporary scholars and activists explicitly see themselves as engaged in a struggle for *tribal sovereignty*.[17] There is plenty of disagreement about what the term means, but nearly everyone – including US presidents and Supreme Court justices – takes

---

15 Although Congress has stripped tribes of their jurisdiction over most criminal matters, they retain some criminal and considerable civil jurisdiction on reservation lands – especially as regards tribal members. See Richland and Deer (2016: chaps. 12, 13) for a discussion of tribal jurisdiction in the United States.

16 For a discussion of tribal sovereign immunity in the United States, see Wilkins and Lomawaima (2001: chap. 7).

17 Although Indian people have always struggled to preserve control over their own lands and peoples, and the explicit language of "tribal sovereignty" has been around at least since the 1820s (and references to Indian "Nations" are far older than that), Nancy Lurie (1999) notes that before the 1960s talk about "tribal sovereignty" was relatively rare (and was perceived by many Indian people as dangerously radical). Instead, she says, Indian people in the first half of the twentieth century tended to frame their grievances against the US government in terms of its failure to honour treaty obligations. The term "tribal sovereignty," she suggests, did not assume its current importance the Indian-English lexicon until the late 1960s and early 1970s, which is roughly coincident with its re-emergence as an important legal principle in US Indian law. Kevin Bruyneel (2007: chap. 5) argues that the florescence of "tribal sovereignty" as a key element in contemporary US Indian discourse owes a great deal to the writings of Vine Deloria and other members of the Red Power movement, who viewed the situation of Indian tribes as "almost the same, but not quite" as that of newly de-colonizing nations in Africa and Asia. For a good account of the rise of post-1960s tribal sovereignty discourse, see also Carlson (2016).

it for granted that *sovereignty* is a relevant and important concept for thinking about tribes' relationship to the United States.

This is less obviously the case in Canada, which historically theorized its legal and political relationship with First Nations very differently. Indeed, despite the Royal Proclamation of 1763,[18] the Canadian government for a long time explicitly rejected the notion that First Nations are – or perhaps ever were – sovereign entities. For much of the country's history, Canadian law viewed First Nation sovereignty – if it ever existed at all – as having been completely extinguished by the mere assertion of British sovereignty, thus implying that any powers of self-government that a First Nation might possess in the present could not be residual sovereign powers that survived incorporation into the settler state (as they have long been regarded in the United States), but must instead have been delegated by the federal government (see, e.g., discussions in Macklem 1993: 1320–2; Morse 1999). This formal position, however, belies the fact that both the British government – and, after Confederation, the Canadian government, too – regularly entered into treaties (military agreements, peace and friendship treaties, land cession treaties) with indigenous polities, a practice that continued into the twentieth century and that would have been entirely unnecessary if indigenous sovereignty had, indeed, somehow vanished with the mere assertion of British sovereignty.[19]

Notwithstanding Canada's historical reluctance to refer to First Nations as sovereign, sovereignty has become a key term in Canadian debates over indigenous–state relations.[20] As in the United States, indigenous people in Canada have begun to formulate their claims explicitly in terms of sovereignty. A relatively early example of this was the *Dene Declaration* of 1975 (Watkins 1977; see also Coulthard 2014: chap. 2).

18 Referred to as the "Magna Carta of Aboriginal Rights in Canada," although it applied to the thirteen colonies as well (Morse 1999: 16), the Royal Proclamation of 1763 clearly identifies Indian nations as "nations" with legal possession of their lands that could only be appropriated by the Crown via a formal land cession treaty.

19 As Bradford Morse (1999: 18) puts it: "The intense period of treaty negotiations from 1871 to 1910 suggests that the recognition of Indian nationhood, including the capacity of Indian nations to make treaties, was alive and well." For an excellent history of treaty making in Canada, see Miller (2009).

20 Canada's reluctance to apply the word "sovereignty" to First Nations within its borders likely reflects, at least in part, long-standing concerns about the political status of Quebec.

Even when they have not explicitly used the language of sovereignty, however, they have always demanded the right to govern themselves and their lands.[21] And the Canadian government's official position on First Nation sovereignty has begun to change in recent decades. Indeed, adoption of "First Nation," the official Canadian term for indigenous peoples and their governments (which, significantly, entered the lexicon in the early 1980s – in the context of struggles over Quebec nationalism), is symbolic of the Canadian government's increasing willingness to acknowledge – on some level at least – indigenous peoples' claims to ongoing sovereign status. The landmark Supreme Court decision *Calder v. Attorney General of British Columbia* (1973) indirectly acknowledged that indigenous people had been self-governing before the arrival of Europeans (and, in a dissenting opinion that explicitly cited John Marshall, three justices acknowledged it directly). Canadian legal scholar Bradford Morse (2008: 43) suggests that this planted the seed for subsequent legal debates over the ongoing status of First Nation sovereignty and, perhaps more importantly, caused many Canadian scholars and activists to look for inspiration south of the border, where tribes were daily exercising their state-like powers of self-government. Subsequently, the Canadian Supreme Court did explicitly acknowledge First Nations' prior sovereignty (in *R. v. Sioui*, which also cited Marshall; see Morse 1999: 17), but it has yet to acknowledge First Nations' ongoing sovereignty,[22] despite clear and compelling arguments by numerous legal scholars (Asch 2014; McNeil 1998; Morse 1999; Slattery 1992) and the high-profile Royal Commission on Aboriginal Peoples (1992)[23] for adopting the notion of inherent First Nation sovereignty as the organizing principle for indigenous–state relations in Canada (Morse 2008: 62). Instead, the court ruled in *R. v. Van der Peet* (1996) that section 35 of the Constitution Act (which recognizes and affirms aboriginal rights) did not so much recognize First Nation sovereignty as "provide the

---

21 A good example of this is *Together Today for Our Children Tomorrow*. Explicit references to First Nation *sovereignty* are entirely absent from the Yukon's foundational land claim document; yet, its authors were clear in their demand that the Canadian government recognize their right to govern themselves and their lands.

22 According to Morse (2008), the only clear acceptance by a Canadian court of a First Nations' ongoing inherent right to self-government was in a decision by the Supreme Court of British Columbia that was never appealed.

23 The royal commission recommended adoption of some sort of "shared" or "merged" sovereignty.

means by which [First Nations'] prior occupation is reconciled with the assertion of Crown sovereignty over Canadian territory" (cited in Asch 2002: 29), and the high court has subsequently maintained – and elaborated on – this position in high-profile aboriginal law decisions such as *Delgamuukw v. British Columbia* (1997) and *Tsilhqot'in Nation v. British Columbia* (2014). As a result, the goal of reconciling First Nations' prior existence with Canadian sovereignty has by now come to serve as one of the pillars of aboriginal law and policy in Canada. As Asch (2014: chap. 1) points out, however, this notion of reconciliation elides the question of how – and, indeed, whether – Canada itself ever legitimately acquired sovereignty. If First Nations had prior sovereignty, as the Canadian Supreme Court has admitted, then, Asch argues, it is not the pre-existence of First Nation society that needs to be reconciled with Canadian sovereignty; rather it is the other way around: it is Canadian sovereignty that needs to be reconciled with the prior and ongoing sovereignty of First Nations.[24]

In the realm of policy, the Canadian government has adopted a broadly similar approach. In 1995, the federal government released its policy on Aboriginal self-government, widely known as the "Inherent Right Policy," in which it explicitly acknowledged "the *inherent* right of self-government as an existing Aboriginal right within section 35 of the Constitution Act, 1982" (Minister of Indian Affairs and Northern Development 1995: 1, emphasis added). Because section 35 of the Constitution Act does not create but merely "recognizes and affirms" existing aboriginal rights (which, by definition, are rights possessed by First Nations before their incorporation into Canada), the policy does represent a formal admission by Canada that First Nations' "inherent" rights to self-government are not delegated from the Crown, but are instead residual rights that stem from First Nations' prior status as sovereign (Dacks 2004; Morse 1999).

24 See also Tully (2008: 234). Asch sees a glimmer of hope in the Supreme Court's unanimous ruling in *Taku River Tlingit First Nation v. British Columbia* (2004), which reformulated the notion of reconciliation in the following way: "the purpose of s. 35(1) of the *Constitution Act*, 1982 is to facilitate the ultimate reconciliation of prior Aboriginal occupation with *de facto* Crown sovereignty." Insertion of the term *de facto*, he notes, leaves open the possibility that Canadian sovereignty may not be entirely legal/legitimate (Asch 2014: 32).

Beyond that, however, the 1995 policy places fairly severe restrictions on just how much First Nation sovereignty Canada is willing to recognize. The policy states, for example, that "the inherent right of self-government does not include a right of sovereignty in the international law sense, and will not result in sovereign independent Aboriginal nation states" (Minister of Indian Affairs and Northern Development 1995: 4), and that "aboriginal governments and institutions exercising the inherent right of self-government will operate within the framework of the Canadian Constitution" (ibid.: 3). The first of these clauses is clearly designed to foreclose the possibility of First Nation secession from Canada (a fear that Canadian officials associated closely with the term "inherent," see Morse 1999: 23), and together, the clauses set "as a precondition [to negotiating self-government] the principle that indigenous political rights exist only to the extent that they can be reconciled with *Crown* sovereignty" (Asch 2014: 24).[25] What is more, the policy unilaterally limits First Nation self-government to those "matters that are internal to the group, integral to its distinct Aboriginal culture, and essential to its operation as a government or institution" (Minister of Indian Affairs and Northern Development 1995: 3). Such wording leads Coulthard to argue that "instead of proceeding with negotiations based on the principle of Indigenous self-determination, Canada's policy framework is grounded in the assumption that Aboriginal rights are subordinately positioned within the ultimate sovereign authority of the Crown" (Coulthard 2014: 123). Such observations have led him, along with numerous other scholars (see, e.g., Alfred 1999; Asch 2014: 23–7; Biolsi 2005: 243) to argue that the policy's supposed recognition of First

25 The second of these clauses is also clearly intended to affirm the Canadian government's policy of "extinguishing" aboriginal rights through the negotiation of land claim and self-government agreements. As we saw in the introduction, section 35 of the Constitution Act recognizes and affirms both aboriginal and treaty rights. Aboriginal rights, however, remain largely undefined. As a result, Canada has sought to achieve "certainty" by insisting that First Nations must exchange their prior (residual) aboriginal rights – which from the state's perspective are legally vague and poorly understood – for an exhaustive list of treaty rights spelled out in land claim and self-government agreements and entrenched in the constitution. Although Canada has backed off from the language of "extinguishment," the new language that has replaced it – requiring Yukon Indian people to "cede, release and surrender" their aboriginal rights in exchange for their new treaty rights (see, e.g., Kluane First Nation 2003b: 18) – is functionally equivalent (on extinguishment and certainty, see Blackburn 2005; Woolford 2005).

Nations' inherent right to self-government is a sham and that any self-government agreements negotiated in accordance with the policy[26] are therefore incompatible with First Nation sovereignty.

The problem, of course, runs much deeper than the wording of Canada's 1995 self-government policy. Anthropologist Michael Asch, an influential critic of aboriginal law in Canada, has convincingly argued that the Canadian government's claim to sovereign jurisdiction over Canadian territory is itself illegitimate because it was – and continues to be – rooted firmly in the now discredited doctrine of *terra nullius* (Asch 1999; Asch 2002). Since there is no question that Canadian territory was occupied before the arrival of Europeans, any claim to the effect that it was *terra nullius* depends entirely on the racist assumption that indigenous peoples at the time of contact were too primitive to assert sovereignty over their own lands and peoples.[27] Because comprehensive land claim and self-government agreements presuppose the underlying sovereignty of the Canadian state (and, indeed, purport to "reconcile" First Nation political rights with that sovereignty), it follows that these agreements are actually predicated not on the recognition of First Nation sovereignty, but on its *denial*. And, indeed, critics taking this approach have argued that modern land claim and self-government agreements are less about recognizing First Nation sovereignty than they are about facilitating corporate access to First Nation lands (Alfred 1999; Asch 2014; Coulthard 2014). They view the new agreements as merely perpetuating the colonial relationship of exploitation between Canada and First Nations. What is more, insofar as these agreements *do* provide First Nations with some limited means to govern themselves and safeguard their lands, their efforts to do so have been stymied in

26 Because the Yukon self-government agreements were negotiated before the policy's release, they obviously could not have been negotiated under its auspices. Yet, the Yukon agreements are so consistent with the policy that they look as though they could have been, and for good reason: several of those who had been involved in negotiating the first four Yukon agreements told me that the Canadian government used their mandate for negotiating the Yukon agreements as a template for developing the 1995 policy.

27 In fact, there are still some scholars and government officials who reject the idea of indigenous sovereignty on these very grounds (see, for example, Flanagan 2000; McEachern 1991). Other scholars have discussed the racist reasoning underlying settler state sovereignty; see, for example, Rifkin (2009) and Williams (2005).

large part by federal and provincial governments' marked failure to actually implement the agreements as ratified.[28]

These critiques are all well taken. Certainly, Canada has made it clear that it is willing to entertain the notion of First Nation sovereignty in only a very limited sense. But this does not mean that the Inherent Right Policy is completely incompatible with the idea or practice of First Nation sovereignty. After all, sovereign power is always to some extent limited and dependent upon internal and external power relations (Murphy 1996; Tully 1995: 193–4; Wilkinson 1987: 54). As Jessica Cattelino (2008: 162) puts it, "No modern sovereign exercises absolute sovereignty, and in this, indigenous peoples are no exception" (see also

28 The literature on governments' failure to adequately implement comprehensive land claim and self-government agreements is large and growing. Significantly, some of the most damning reports have come from the Canadian government itself. Canada's auditor general, for example, audited Canada's implementation of particular northern agreements in both 2004 and 2007. The AG's reports found Canada's implementation efforts to be largely inadequate, and they expressed their criticisms in hard-hitting language. The 2003 report, for example, claimed that "INAC [Indian and Northern Affairs Canada] seems focused on fulfilling the letter of the land claims' implementation plans, but not the spirit" (Auditor General of Canada 2003: 1), while the 2007 report characterized Canada's efforts to implement the Inuvialuit Final Agreement thus: "Twenty-three years after the Agreement came into effect, INAC still has not developed a strategy for implementing it" (Auditor General of Canada 2007: 2). Widespread recognition of the Canadian governments' failure to adequately implement land claim and self-government agreements led newly self-governing First Nations to unite under the banner of the Land Claims Agreements Coalition (LCAC) to address common concerns about implementation (Fenge 2015). Critical scholarly analyses of these issues tend to focus not only on governments' failure to adequately implement northern agreements as ratified but also on the extremely problematic (indeed coercive) nature of the negotiations themselves, in particular some of their key provisions (e.g., the extinguishment clause, which many see as a symptom of Canada's absolute refusal to recognize First Nation sovereignty). For a sample of critical studies along these lines across Canada, see Blackburn (2005), Feit and Beaulieu (2001), Rynard (2000), and Samson and Cassell (2013). The federal government's record of implementing the Yukon agreements is no better than it is anywhere else in Canada. In fact, when I observed the nine-year review of the Yukon Agreements in 2003–4 (see introduction), I was shocked at times by Canada's blatant refusal to take its implementation responsibilities seriously. Not only was the government failing to implement many provisions of the agreements, but federal implementation officials also routinely refused to justify their failure to do so. Their behaviour was so egregious that one senior Yukon official told me point blank (after a particularly frustrating session), "Those guys [the federal officials] make me embarrassed to be a Canadian." The Yukon negotiations were also plainly coercive, since,

Deloria 2002; Warrior 1995: 124). For all its limitations, Canada's Inherent Right Policy does not preclude a Marshall-Cohen style formulation of sovereignty for First Nations as domestic dependent nations with significant rights of self-government within Canada.[29] Indeed, it seems to me that the policy is precisely about enabling First Nations in Canada to negotiate and exercise powers of self-government that are equal to, and in some ways even exceed, those exercised by tribal governments in the United States.[30] Certainly, there is one very important way in which self-governing First Nations in Canada are in a stronger position than their counterparts in the United States. Because self-government agreements are supposed to be (and most are) entrenched

---

as elsewhere, federal loans provided to fund First Nation's participation in the negotiation process were debited against the compensation payments they would receive upon signing, thus penalizing First Nations who held out for better terms. The federal government did eventually agree to forgive some of the loans for those First Nations who signed latest, but without this concession there would have been no agreements at all. By 2003, for example, Kluane First Nation's loans were so great that KFN leadership refused to put the agreements to KFN members for a ratification vote unless the federal government agreed to forgive part of their debt. Also, the federal government continued to alienate lands and permit mining, grazing, and other activities within First Nations' traditional territories throughout the negotiations (though there were some restrictions and "interim protection" was granted to a small selection of lands First Nations identified as likely to become settlement lands – though even these were vulnerable to development and exploitation). Because any other interests in the land trumped First Nation interests at the negotiating table (see Nadasdy 2008), there was enormous pressure on First Nations to settle quickly before more lands were lost.

29 By way of comparison, the US government, too, has often striven to ensure that tribal self-government "operates within the framework" of the US constitution, as when Congress passed the 1968 Indian Civil Rights Act (ICRA), which extended many protections of the Bill of Rights to individuals under the jurisdiction of tribal governments. Although this act certainly placed limits on tribal sovereignty, it did not negate the principle of tribal sovereignty. This is evident, for example, in the post-ICRA Supreme Court decision in *Santa Clara Pueblo v. Martinez* (1978), which barred Julia Martinez's civil rights claim against the tribe on the grounds that it possessed sovereign immunity (for a discussion of the case, see Wilkins and Lomawaima 2001: 228–9).

30 For example, while courts in the United States have stripped tribes of most of their powers to enforce their laws over non-tribal members on tribal lands (leading scholars such as Aleinikoff [2002] and Dussias [1993] to view tribal sovereignty today as membership- rather than territory-based), Yukon First Nation final and self-government agreements provide First Nations with (potentially) much more extensive power to govern non-citizens on First Nation lands.

in the constitution, Canadian First Nations' sovereign powers are explicitly protected from the kinds of arbitrary and unilateral assaults sanctioned by the plenary power doctrine in the United States.[31] To be sure, the domestic dependent nation model of sovereignty, like Canada's 1995 policy on self-government, also draws on racist assumptions about indigenous "primitives" to justify the limitations placed on indigenous sovereignty, and it takes the questionable legitimacy of settler state sovereignty entirely for granted. So, my goal here is not to dispute scholars and activists who criticize the Inherent Right Policy on these grounds. Rather, I simply want to make the point, often at least implicitly denied by those critics, that modern self-government agreements in Canada are rooted in the model of state sovereignty, however limited First Nations' sovereignty may be under them. That is, to the extent First Nations are believed to have any powers of governance at all, it is assumed that they must be fundamentally state-like. Like tribes in the United States, self-governing First Nation governments exercise (limited) jurisdiction over specific and clearly defined territories in the name of the – also clearly defined – "people" they represent. Whether or not the agreements explicitly recognize First Nation sovereignty is irrelevant. Indeed, the word "sovereignty" appears only twice in Kluane First Nation's final agreement, and then only in reference to Canadian sovereignty; and the word does not appear at all in KFN's self-government agreement. Nevertheless, these agreements grant the new self-governing First Nation extensive state-like powers (or the right to assume them) equal to or exceeding those exercised by tribes in the United States. (For a full list of these powers, see Kluane First Nation 2003a.)

For these reasons, I contend that *sovereignty* is as essential a concept for thinking about indigenous–state relations in Canada as it is in the United States – despite the government of Canada's reluctance to use the word. Even those who reject entirely the idea that indigenous polities might themselves be sovereign take *sovereignty* for granted as

31 Even if the agreements were not constitutionally protected, there is nothing resembling the plenary power doctrine in Canada – though recent bills proposed (though never passed) by Stephen Harper's Conservative government (S-6 and C-15) did raise the spectre of arbitrary and unilateral assaults by the federal government on the powers accorded to First Nation governments under land claim and self-government agreements.

the theoretical ground from which to reject indigenous rights. Indeed, opponents of indigenous sovereignty tend to argue that such a thing is impossible precisely because it would be inconsistent with the sovereignty of the settler state (e.g., see Flanagan 2000; McEachern 1991).[32] Thus, although there are plenty of disagreements over who possesses sovereignty and how it is distributed within the settler state, nearly everyone agrees that the question of indigenous–state relations is fundamentally about sovereignty. In this way, *sovereignty* must be seen as the unexamined precondition of nearly all theories of indigenous–state relations in North America. Indeed, one might reasonably argue that the concept of indigeneity itself is unthinkable without some notion of sovereignty and the state. But, as we have already seen, sovereignty is hardly a natural – or neutral – category. On the contrary, it arose within a specific historical and cultural milieu, and it takes for granted a set of culturally specific ideas about the nature of human society and of the world more generally. Thus, as Taiaiake Alfred suggests, its application in an indigenous context is potentially problematic. For this reason, it is essential that we take a closer look at the concept of sovereignty itself and cultural assumptions upon which it is based.

Sovereignty: The "Enabling Ground of Politics"

So, to echo Alfred's question from the opening epigraph, how and why is it that a concept rooted in a set of historically and culturally specific assumptions about the world has become, in R.B.J. Walker's (1993: 166) words, the "crucial constitutive principle of modern political life" – for indigenous people as much as it is for Euro-Americans? In her important book *Indigeneity and Political Theory*, political theorist Karena Shaw explores this question in considerable detail. She traces the production and practice of sovereignty across a wide range of contexts, from Hobbes's *Leviathan*, through early Canadian Indian policy, to Canadian court rulings in the landmark case *Delgamuukw v. B.C.*, and in so doing shows that the Hobbesian notion of sovereignty has become so deeply

32 See Asch (2014: chap. 2) and Culhane (1998) for detailed refutations of Flanagan's and McEachern's arguments, respectively. Both show that it is the presumption of Canadian sovereignty (and its contrast to the supposed lack of government among indigenous "primitives") that serves as the basis for these authors' rejection of First Nation sovereignty.

entrenched – and constitutive of common sense – in contemporary Canadian political thought (as elsewhere) that we are hardly able to conceive of politics without it. Indeed, she argues that sovereignty has become "the enabling ground of politics" (2008: 10)[33] and explores how it is that the particular cultural assumptions upon which it is based have come to be regarded as universal human truths. More than that, she shows how the concept and practice of sovereignty have naturalized a whole set of epistemological and ontological assumptions that are not themselves overtly "political."

The naturalization of the sovereign world view follows from the boundary-making practices that are so central to the sovereignty concept. As we saw in the introduction, sovereignty entails making distinctions between inside and outside (see also Walker 1993). Those who are inside the relation of sovereignty, that is, those who have voluntarily relinquished some of their individual authority in exchange for the security provided by the sovereign, become part of a political community; relations among them and with their sovereign are political in nature. By contrast, outside the umbrella of sovereignty, where there is no legitimate authority above the level of the individual, the enabling conditions for politics simply do not exist. Life there (as Hobbes so famously characterized it) is "solitary, poor, nasty, brutish, and short"; it is a war of all against all. Outside of sovereignty is a realm of *savagery* (and, indeed, Hobbes himself used "the savage people in many places of America" as the epitome of life outside the relation of sovereignty, see Shaw 2008: 18–19) and *anarchy* (as it is frequently characterized in the study of international relations).[34] Although excluded from the realm of the political, this realm of external savagery/anarchy is essential to the conceptualization of sovereignty because it serves as the oppositional category against which sovereignty is produced. Hobbes "produce[s] an 'outside' that is so awful ... as to coerce those 'inside' to bind together, to produce a common 'sovereign' identity" (Shaw 2008: 30; see

33 Similarly, Jens Bartelson (1995: 3–5) refers to sovereignty as "the unthought foundation of political knowledge."

34 Walker (1993) remarks that we speak of "international relations" rather than "international politics" for precisely this reason. In the absence of an overarching global sovereign, relations among sovereign states cannot be characterized as "political." They can have "relations" with one another; but in the anarchic realm between states, politics are not possible.

also Rifkin 2009, Walker 1993: 174). Thus, for Hobbes, sovereignty itself is not a political matter; rather, it is the *precondition* for politics; it is presupposed in the constitution of "the political." Since there can be no politics outside of sovereignty, "the political" becomes synonymous with "relations of government"; it is that which takes place within already-constituted sovereign political communities (Shaw 2008: 35, 203).[35] By consigning the production and maintenance of sovereignty – processes that necessarily entail both physical and symbolic violence – to the realm of the "pre-political," Hobbes renders sovereignty "apolitical, and uncontestable, necessary and inevitable" (ibid.: 9).

Sovereignty, then, entails the production of a political community, a group of people who relinquish some of their authority for the common good and engage one another in the realm of politics. Complete homogeneity is neither possible nor necessary (indeed, that would negate the need for politics altogether), but in Hobbes's view sovereignty does require that members of the sovereign community have enough in common that they can communicate and engage productively with one another in the political realm. Shaw shows that, for Hobbes, the common ground of the political is built from some fundamental assumptions about the nature of the world and how we can know it, and he spends the first few chapters of *Leviathan* laying out sovereignty's ontological and epistemological foundations. To begin with, individual humans can only know the world through their "conscious senses." The privileging of our conscious senses was of central importance to Hobbes, since his project was to construct a purely secular source of political authority (i.e., without recourse to the legitimizing role of God or divine revelation; see Shaw 2008: 28–30). Shared understanding, then, is only possible within a bounded space where individuals have common points of reference. And if humans are to make collective sense of those perceptions (by applying, say, the principle of cause and effect), they must be situated within a linear temporal framework. As Shaw puts it: "In order even to think (to make sense), we must think *in a place*, a bounded and located space mediated by sense, moving through an ordered linear time … What and how one can know are thus ordered" (ibid.: 22; emphasis original). So, the sovereign community must be

35 As Shaw (2008: 35) puts it, "'Politics' [for Hobbes] is confined to and defined as the negotiation of rights and duties between already-constituted 'subjects' and their 'sovereign.'"

spatially bounded and move through time in a linear progressive fashion. And, again, this is explicitly *in opposition* to that which exists outside the relation of sovereignty, a space characterized not only by violence, but also by a *lack* of spatial and temporal order:

> The political ground we – supposedly – share (in fact that we must share in order to communicate) ... consists of a very specific ordering of time and space, one that functions to enable and privilege a certain form of reason, providing the basis for an identity differentiated by these very specific forms of difference. Those who do not share this resolution of time and space (and that which follows from it) will come to inhabit – and mark – the "outside" of Hobbes' neatly delineated space, their "difference" enabling the recognition of something "we" share. (Shaw 2008: 23)

Once he has established the spatial and temporal dimensions of sovereignty, Hobbes must specify the nature of social interaction among individuals who live inside the boundaries of the sovereign community. Shared language is essential here because it enables communication and "the right use of reason," which in turn are the bases for scientific knowledge (Shaw 2008: 22–4). But reason alone is not enough, for while "all men by nature reason alike, and well, when they have good principles" (Hobbes, cited ibid.: 23), they do not always start from good principles. Indeed, Hobbes takes great pains to warn his readers about the dangers of rational thought based upon anything other than the "facts" derived from our conscious senses. Neither imagination/memory (which he views as "decaying senses") nor dreams/visions (which he dismisses as absurd and irrational) are suitable bases for "the right use of reason" (ibid.: 19–21), because, in the absence of a higher divine or religious authority, they cannot be legitimated; they stem from – and are authorized by – individuals alone. Any knowledge produced from such first principles therefore cannot form the (shared) basis for a sovereign community. Only reasoning built upon our conscious senses can result in the production of shared knowledge, or science; and it is precisely science, knowledge shared by the sovereign community, that enables collaboration and thus scientific and historical "progress" over time. It also serves as the basis for a common political identity. This, of course, means that scientific knowledge is contingent on the authority of the sovereign, as Hobbes himself explicitly recognized. Indeed, Shaw points out that in Hobbes's account, (scientific) knowledge and sovereignty co-constitute one another:

> Rather than existing "outside" of the state, knowledge is an expression of how sovereignty "works" to produce a common identity, the possibility of order, communication. This suggests the importance of knowledge and knowledge production in the reproduction of sovereignty. All knowledge exists in reference to and reproduces the resolutions [temporal and spatial] of sovereignty. Sovereignty exists in as much as things "make sense," as there is a way in which, a basis upon which, disputes can be arbitrated (science, objectivity). In the absence of this guarantee of meaning, of security, knowledge loses its capacity to make sense, and thus there is no basis for an assertion of legitimate authority ... Sovereignty in this way becomes the principle that structures the intellectual, as well as physical, world, as it reinforces the ontological and epistemological principles that guide our own activities and practices as knowledge producers, as "subjects" who apprehend the world as Hobbes describes. His production of "man" as a "knowing subject" thus provides the basis for a reorientation of authority along two parallel axes: the subject (who knows with authority) and the sovereign state (who embodies/guarantees this authority). Knowledge, subjectivity, and sovereignty are intimately interwoven, yet "politics" is confined to the realm in which they are already constituted. (Shaw 2008: 36–7)

Thus, sovereignty not only enables politics, but also knowledge, science, identity, and history: "The sovereign state take[s] on the task of providing not only security but meaning for its citizens ... To be part of a sovereign unit is not only to be secure from harm, but to be part of a larger identity, spatially bounded, progressing through time, achieving feats of science, technology, advancing knowledge, and so on" (ibid.: 30).

By contrast, then, the space outside sovereignty is characterized not only by anarchy and the lack of security, but also by the absence of knowledge, identity, and history. It is a timeless realm of ignorance and senseless brutality where progress (scientific, political, or otherwise) is not only impossible but also inconceivable. For such an account of sovereignty to be convincing (i.e., for sovereignty to "work"), however, "the conditions of its production must be forgotten, naturalized, excluded from the study (and practices) of 'politics'" (ibid.: 35). The historically and culturally specific assumptions – about the nature of space, time, knowledge, and subjectivity – which sovereignty both depends upon and enables (and which were not, in Hobbes's time at least, self-evident), must come to be seen as universal, as the product of *human nature* rather than of any particular society.[36] This equation of sovereignty and human nature not only universalizes a particular set of culturally and historically specific assumptions about the world, it also produces a culturally specific definition of humanity. By drawing a sharp distinction between humans (those beings capable of entering sovereign relations) and non-humans (those who are not), sovereignty serves as an "anthropological machine," a "device for producing the recognition of the human" (Agamben 2004: 26). This function of sovereignty has had two principal effects. Most obviously, sovereignty has come to circumscribe the realm of the human; only those who live – or are perceived to live – in sovereign communities can be fully human. Those outside are necessarily animal-like. This has serious implications for indigenous people – particularly hunters and other obviously stateless peoples – who have historically been viewed as standing outside the relation of sovereignty. Perceived as lacking government, knowledge, identity, history, and the other trappings of sovereignty, such peoples come to seem more like animals than humans. And, indeed, indigenous peoples – particularly hunting peoples – have often been regarded as animal-like.[37] After all, how could they be fully human when they lack sovereignty, a natural "human" social response to the violence and insecurity of the "natural" world? The relegation of such peoples to the realm of animal-like savagery is no accident. Because sovereignty is viewed as a product of human nature and because it requires an oppositional and coercive "outside," representations of indigenous people as animal-like savages cannot be written off as simply the result of racism and ignorance; rather, they are *essential* to the maintenance of sovereignty itself (Shaw 2008: 34; see also Rifkin 2009).

The second effect flowing from the equation of sovereignty and human nature is somewhat subtler, because it is even more deeply

36 According to Hobbes, it is "because of our nature *as humans*" that we "must come together to create an overarching authority to enable us to move through time, attain our desires, progress. All of these, of course, require a bounded space, the precondition for thought, the production of knowledge, the account of time, identity" (Shaw 2008: 32, emphasis added; see Hobbes 1998: 76–9).

37 The assumption that hunting peoples are somehow animal-like can be remarkably subtle. Ingold (2000: 27–39), for example, shows that such an assumption underlies many anthropological analyses of hunting societies despite anthropologists' conscious efforts to avoid such pernicious stereotypes.

embedded in statist "common sense." This is the exclusion of animals (and other non-human elements of the environment) from the realm of the political. These days, while the exclusion of "animal-like" humans from politics seems problematic to many (at least when stated so baldly), the same cannot be said for the exclusion of animals, plants, and landforms. Humans engage in politics; moose, spruce trees, and rocks do not. This seems like simple common sense to most of us. This is because the sovereignty concept (and its attribution to human nature) entails an implicit distinction between humans and the rest of the "natural" world (Goldberg-Hiller and Silva 2011). But this is a distinction that many indigenous peoples simply do not make. As we shall see in subsequent chapters, Yukon Indian people have long regarded animals, plants, and other aspects of the environment as sentient and powerful actors enmeshed along with themselves in relations of kinship and reciprocity; and these powerful non-human actors have long played an explicitly political role in indigenous Yukon society (see Nadasdy 2007b; Nadasdy 2016). Because the idea that moose, spruce trees, and rocks might be political actors is utterly inconsistent with the concept of sovereignty, its use necessarily consigns many Yukon Indian people's beliefs about the world to the realm of irrational superstition – and anyone who believes such "superstitious nonsense" to the realm of ignorant savagery.

As we shall see over the course of this book, sovereign assumptions about the nature of space, time, and the beings who inhabit the world (and how we can know them) are often incompatible with many northern indigenous peoples' understandings of the world. Sovereignty, far from being a neutral and necessary precondition for politics, is deeply implicated in "the production of an ontological ground that renders the difference expressed by Indigenous peoples as uncivilized and barbaric" (Shaw 2008: 35). The exclusion of dreams and visions as a sound basis for knowledge, the concept of time as linear-progressive, or even the assumption that only humans can be political subjects, for example, all work to delegitimize northern indigenous peoples' ways of being in and knowing the world. More precisely, because such beliefs – and the practices based upon them – by definition stand "outside" the relation of sovereignty, indigenous people who claim knowledge based on dreams, whose hunting practices, say, are rooted in a different temporal order, or who view animal people as powerful political actors, necessarily place themselves "outside" the Hobbesian relation of sovereignty. They construct themselves (in the eyes of those "inside") as backward, irrational, even animal-like savages who are clearly "not yet ready" for self-government. How could they be when they still subscribe to such "primitive and irrational superstitions"?

Sovereign Strategies

Because sovereignty has become the enabling ground of politics – and, indeed, a device for recognizing humanity – any effort to conceive of an alternative *non-sovereign* politics is exceedingly difficult and fraught with perils. As a result, those who would advocate for the rights of indigenous people are seemingly constrained to one of two very general – and, as we shall see, overlapping – strategies, both of which necessarily involve drawing indigenous people into (or denying that they were ever outside of) the relation of sovereignty. The first strategy is to seek an equitable place for indigenous people under the sovereign umbrella of the settler state. Those who follow this first strategy are a heterogeneous lot who back a host of different forms of governance (and invoke a variety of different theoretical positions) that differ significantly from one another with respect to how exactly sovereignty is distributed within the settler state (Macklem 1993). These range from the incorporation of indigenous people into the state as a minority population (with no indigenous sovereignty at all) to the recognition of tribes/First Nations as partially sovereign "domestic dependent nations" that exercise perhaps significant rights of self-government but that are ultimately subject to the overriding sovereignty of the settler state. To the extent that a First Nation possesses any "legitimate authority," it is necessarily grounded – at least implicitly – in the sovereign status of the First Nation (which can be either inherent or delegated) and instantiated through the exercise of limited state-like powers of governance (over a bounded territory and people located within the settler state). The newly emergent self-governing First Nations of the Yukon and elsewhere in northern Canada can reasonably be viewed as products of this general strategy, since they possess significant state-like powers; but, according to the agreements that constituted them, they are still subject to the overriding sovereignty of the Crown.

The second possible strategy is to reject the settler state's sovereignty over indigenous people altogether. But because sovereignty has come to be the only basis for legitimate political authority (not to mention the basis for knowledge, identity, history, and humanity), the rejection of settler state sovereignty must be (and almost always is) accompanied by an assertion of First Nation sovereignty in its place. In effect, the only legitimate grounds on which to reject settler state sovereignty over indigenous peoples and lands is the prior and ongoing sovereignty of First Nations themselves. In its pure form, this strategy is relatively rare, because few scholars or activists argue that First Nations are or should become completely independent sovereign states (Niezen 2000; Porter 2002: 99); but some scholars and activists, especially those (and there are many) who take the position that First Nation sovereignty is inherent rather than delegated, argue that independent statehood should at least be a theoretical possibility.[38] Those who pursue some version of this strategy – even that of total independence – still face the task of theorizing and/or negotiating the relationship between First Nation and settler state sovereignties, which, because First Nations are enclaves within the settler state, is particularly complex.[39] Given Canada's recognition of First Nations' inherent right to self-government and the very real state-like powers of self-government provided by northern First Nation land claim and self-government agreements, one might also plausibly view the new self-governing First Nations of the Yukon as products of a (weak) version of this second strategy.

The very fact that it is difficult to decide how to categorize the new self-governing First Nations in relation to these two strategies suggests that they are not quite so distinct as one might initially imagine. In fact, both strategies take sovereignty itself for granted; they differ only with respect to how that sovereignty is distributed among First Nations and the settler state. Indeed, one might view the vast majority

38 If indigenous polities possess *inherent* sovereignty, this implies at least a potential for (legitimate) separatism, regardless of their political aspirations at the moment (which is why Canada so long refused to recognize First Nations' inherent sovereignty – see Morse 1999: 23). Political theorist Burke Hendrix (2008: chaps. 7, 8) shows that even from the perspective of liberal political theory it is possible to present a reasoned argument for the legitimate secession – and/or partial separation – of indigenous polities. And Scott Lyons (2010: 113) argues that indigenous movements in North America are increasingly separatist, despite claims to the contrary (as, for example, in Niezen 2000).

39 Such a situation, however, is not unprecedented among independent sovereign states. Think, for example, of Vatican City and Lesotho, two independent sovereign states that are enclaves within another nation state. Neither of these micro-states is remotely independent in an economic sense, and their political and economic relations with Italy and South Africa, respectively, are also particularly complex. See Hendrix (2008: 141–4) for a theoretical discussion of enclaves.

of the theories about the nature of indigenous–state relations as existing on a spectrum. At one extreme, theorists presume that the settler state is the sole sovereign, and indigenous peoples are merely minority populations within the body politic; at the other end, they assume that the settler state and First Nations are each completely independent sovereigns. In fact, not only do most scholars and activists take a position somewhere between these extremes, but in actual practice most operate from different positions on the spectrum depending upon the social and political context.[40]

The fact that nearly all arguments about indigenous–state relations take sovereignty for granted is significant because, as we have seen, sovereignty is based on a set of culturally and historically specific assumptions about the nature of the world and how we can know it, assumptions that are often incompatible with those to which many indigenous people themselves subscribe. Invocations of First Nation sovereignty, then, inevitably run the risk of authorizing Euro-American assumptions about the world and the practices that derive from them while simultaneously consigning many indigenous beliefs and practices to the realm of superstition. At the very least, this calls into question the utility of sovereignty as an objective for indigenous politics. Might it not be better, given the culturally and historically particular assumptions undergirding sovereignty, for indigenous people to discard the concept altogether?

In recent decades, scholars of indigenous–state relations have become increasingly wary of the concept of sovereignty for precisely this reason. This has led many to adopt one of two basic (but, again, interrelated) strategies. A few have urged a total *rejection* of the concept of sovereignty in the indigenous context. The majority, however, prefer instead to retain the term and *indigenize* it, attempting to free it from its Euro-American

40 Recent influential discussions of indigenous politics in the United States, I think, illustrate this point nicely. Anthropologist Thomas Biolsi (2005) identifies multiple – if not always mutually consistent – political "spaces" within which indigenous activism occurs. As it turns out, all the political spaces he identifies – different as they are from one another – can be ranged along the sovereignty spectrum I outline here. Similarly, Bruyneel's (2007) discussion of the "third space of sovereignty" reflects the politically ambiguous status of First Nations insofar as they sometimes locate themselves (or are located by others) as "inside" and sometimes as "outside" the political space of settler state sovereignty, with a corresponding shift in the degree to which they are located "outside" or "inside" the space of their own tribal sovereignty.

cultural baggage, and render it fit for use in an indigenous context.[41] As we shall see, however, neither the sovereignty concept itself nor its principal cultural entailments are easily dispensed with.

Indigenizing Sovereignty and the Tribal State

Mohawk political theorist Taiaiake Alfred (1999: 55–69) is perhaps the scholar most closely associated with the strategy of total rejection (but see also Boldt and Long 1984). As we saw above, he not only rejects the idea that settler states are sovereign over First Nations (a common enough position), but he refuses to base this rejection on the "fact" of First Nations' prior and ongoing sovereignty. "Sovereignty," he argues, is simply "inappropriate as a political goal for indigenous peoples" (Alfred 2005b: 38). Sovereignty, along with associated statist concepts such as *taxation*, *citizenship*, and *executive authority*, "should be eradicated from politics in Native communities," because they inappropriately constrain the possibilities for indigenous politics. Indeed, he suggests that sovereignty is incompatible with "the essence of indigenous North Americans," and "to remain Native ... our politics must shift to give primacy to concepts grounded in our own cultures" (1999: xiv). To make claims in the Euro-American language of sovereignty, then, is for him tantamount to a rejection of indigenous culture.

Crucially, according to Alfred, the cultural entailments of sovereignty are not merely the obviously "political" ones, such as a hierarchical political structure and the bounding of territory and population; he also

41 The project of "indigenizing" sovereignty is not always viewed as one of radical redefinition. Indeed, many scholars view the Euro-American notion of sovereignty as flexible enough for use by indigenous people, despite its less than savoury history. All who would theorize about indigenous sovereignty, however, must address counter-arguments to the effect that indigenous people cannot be sovereign because they are no longer members of independent polities. Such arguments assume that sovereigns must be autonomous, and sovereign power must be unlimited. Though characteristic of early sovereignty theorists like Bodin, Hobbes, and Pufendorf (who were writing about the absolutist state), these assumptions are no longer widely held by legal and political theorists, most of whom recognize that all sovereign power is to some extent limited and dependent upon internal and external power relations (Tully 1995: 193–4; Wilkinson 1987: 54). To some extent, then, to "indigenize" sovereignty may simply involve insisting that more nuanced contemporary theoretical understandings of the term be applied in indigenous contexts too. I will elaborate further on this below.

draws attention to the way sovereignty entails a particular relationship to the natural world. The hierarchical relationship sovereignty establishes among humans is extended also to the land and animals, because the sovereign presides not only over the humans within its territory, but also over the land itself and all its non-human inhabitants, which come to be viewed as the "resources" of the nation state (Alfred 1999: 60–2; Alfred 2005b: 45–6). As we have seen, this implies that only humans can be political actors and that, as a result, it is they alone who get to decide on the use and disposition of "their" resources. This anthropocentric approach to politics, Alfred argues, is at odds with the view of many indigenous people, who commonly believe "that people, communities, and the other elements of creation coexist as equals – [and that] human beings as either individuals or collectives do not have a special priority in deciding the justice of a situation" (Alfred 2005b: 48; Alfred 1999: 60–2).[42] As we shall see in chapters 2 and 3, the denial of political subjectivity to animals, plants, and other elements of the environment (i.e., their exclusion from the body politic) lies at the heart of some of the most profound cultural transformations associated with First Nation state formation across the Canadian north. The rejection of non-human persons as potential political subjects also implies a set of assumptions about the nature of non-human beings and how we can – or cannot – know them and their interests. To accept these assumptions is necessarily to frame many indigenous peoples' understandings of animals and the natural world as irrational superstition.

Alfred's complete rejection of sovereignty as a basis for indigenous politics, however, poses some potential dangers. If sovereignty is indeed the enabling ground of politics, then Alfred's strategy risks ejecting indigenous people from the realm of the political altogether. For those who take sovereignty for granted as the foundation of politics (most everyone), Alfred's strategy may appear to relegate indigenous peoples to a position "outside" of sovereignty, that timeless realm of irrational savagery to which many opponents of indigenous sovereignty

42 Alfred is not alone in pointing out the anthropocentric implications of sovereignty. In his analysis of the works of Osage writer John Joseph Mathews, Robert Warrior (1995: 101) argues that "the terms self-determination and sovereignty connote in their most immediate sense much of the human arrogance that Mathews believed was at the root of twentieth-century problems. They do not convey any sense of how limited human power and action are when they are part of, rather than against, biological processes." See also Goldberg-Hiller and Silva (2011).

would be only too happy to consign them. Although Alfred himself is clearly engaged in an effort to reconstitute "the political" in the absence of sovereignty,[43] the practical efficacy of any "sovereignty-free politics" that result from such theorizing are open to question. For one thing, they will likely not seem much like politics at all to anyone who views them from the perspective of sovereignty. What is more, those who take sovereignty for granted are likely to write off as so much irrational nonsense any claims to "legitimate" knowledge or authority that are not underwritten by sovereignty (and we will see numerous instances of this throughout this book). So, practically speaking, efforts to promote a sovereignty-free politics in the context of the sovereign settler state may get nowhere and even runs the risk of undermining the modest gains First Nations have made using the discourse of sovereignty. One of the central justifications for colonialism, after all, has always been that those espousing such "irrational" views obviously cannot be ready for "sovereignty."

It is for such reasons, I suspect, that few scholars and activists are willing to reject the discourse of sovereignty as completely as Alfred at times seems to do. Indeed, as we saw in the introduction to this chapter, Alfred himself takes a more ambivalent position on sovereignty than is commonly supposed, at times arguing not so much for its rejection as for its indigenization. Here, he is in much better company. Many scholars agree that in its Euro-American guise, sovereignty is an inappropriate framework for indigenous politics, and they have sought to rethink it in terms more compatible with an indigenous context. Many, including Alfred, take their cue from Vine Deloria and Clifford Lytle's (1984: 15) assertion that the Euro-American concept of sovereignty, although at times useful, is ultimately incompatible with the "intangible, spiritual, and emotional aspirations of American Indians." Rather than rejecting sovereignty altogether, however, Deloria, perhaps the most

43 Alfred is quite explicit about his project of building a post-sovereign politics: "Before their near destruction by Europeans, many indigenous societies achieved sovereignty-free regimes of conscience and justice that allowed for the harmonious coexistence of humans and nature for hundreds of generations. As our world emerges into a post-imperial age, the philosophical and governmental alternative to sovereignty and the central values contained within their traditional cultures are the North American Indian's contribution to the reconstruction of a just and harmonious world" (Alfred 2005b: 49). Shaw, for her part, characterizes Alfred's work in just this way (2007: 182–8).

influential theorist of Indian sovereignty in recent decades, argues for its indigenization. But what does this look like? Does Deloria's indigenized conception of sovereignty avoid the statist assumptions that make Alfred so leery of the term?

Here, I think, a distinction needs to be made between the project of liberating the concept of indigenous sovereignty from the political and legal constraints of the settler colonial state (e.g., assertions to the effect that tribes cannot be sovereign because that would contradict settler state sovereignty), on one hand, and that of constructing a non-statist concept of indigenous sovereignty, on the other. In his formulation of tribal sovereignty, Deloria certainly does the former, but he never even attempts the latter. Indeed, he begins his widely cited article on "Self-Determination and the Concept of Sovereignty" (1979) by arguing that prior to contact tribes were sovereign political entities and that Europeans long recognized this by treating them as independent foreign states. He then draws on a standard notion of popular sovereignty (with an ethno-nationalist inflection) to argue that the fact of ongoing Indian cultural difference (and hence, nationhood) means that, despite their subsequent incorporation into settler states, tribes retain their sovereign status: "Numerous references to sovereignty cite the notion of a distinct people, separate from others, as the chief characteristic of Indian sovereignty indicating that so long as the cultural identity of Indians remains intact no specific political act undertaken by the United States government can permanently extinguish Indian peoples as sovereign entities" (ibid.: 25–6).

Cultural identity/integrity is the key to Deloria's vision of tribal sovereignty. Reacting to excessively legalistic constructions of sovereignty (not a surprising stance given that it is US Indian law, a colonial body of law if there ever was one, that frames legal expressions of tribal sovereignty), he argues that "the idea of Indian sovereignty is not simply a legal concept" (ibid.: 25). Nor, he argues, can tribal sovereignty be equated in a straightforward manner with a tribe's possession of political power, since for him the proper exercise of power is as important as its source or quantity (ibid.: 26). For tribes to be sovereign, they must not only wield power, but that power must be constituted in culturally appropriate ways and its exercise must support rather than undermine a tribe's cultural integrity:

> Although sovereignty originated as a means of locating the seat of political power in European nations, it has assumed the aspect of continuing

> cultural and communal integrity when transferred to the North American setting … Sovereignty, in the final instance, can be said to consist more of continued cultural integrity than of political powers and to the degree that a nation loses its sense of cultural identity, to that degree it suffers a loss of sovereignty. When we view sovereignty in this broadly expanded light, new possibilities for constructive action arise. Cultural integrity involves a commitment to a central and easily understood purpose that motivates a group of people, enables them to form efficient, albeit informal social institutions, and provides for them a clear identity which cannot be eroded by the passage of events. Sovereignty then revolves around the manner in which traditions are developed, sustained, and transformed to confront new conditions. (Deloria 1979: 26–7)

Deloria's formulation of sovereignty here is dynamic. It does not bind indigenous nations to some hidebound notion of "tradition," but instead allows for – indeed, demands – continual adaptation and transformation in response to changing historical circumstances (see also Warrior 1995: 93–8). The essential thing is that sovereign tribal power be constituted and exercised in culturally appropriate ways. Culture, then, serves Deloria as tribal sovereignty's principal boundary-making mechanism. By providing "a unified vision" and "a commitment to a larger whole" that leads to "a strong sense of community discipline and a degree of self-containment and pride that transcends all objective codes, rules and regulations" (1979: 27), culture produces a sovereign political community, a nation. Those who share in the culture of the nation are part of that sovereign community, while everyone else necessarily stands outside the nation and outside the relation of tribal sovereignty.

Deloria's stress on the importance of cultural integrity/identity also has important territorial implications. Although he does not explicitly elaborate on them in his 1979 article, he maintains elsewhere that tribal cultural identities and religious practices are inextricably linked to particular lands. As he put it in *Custer Died for Your Sins*, "Culture, if any exists, is a function of the homeland" (Deloria 1988: 178), and "No movement can sustain itself, no people can continue, no government can function, and no religion can become a reality except it be bound to a land area of its own" (179). Key to this connection between "a people" and its homeland is the fusing of history and geography into what he refers to as "sacred geography": "Every location within [a tribal nation's] original homeland has a multitude of stories that recount the migrations, revelations, and particular historical incidents that cumulatively produced the tribe in its current condition" (Deloria 1992: 121). These sacred geographies and the cultural practices with which they are entangled are fundamental to the formation of Indian cultural and national identities (ibid.: 142) and therefore to the constitution and exercise of tribal sovereignty. "Peoplehood," he says, "is impossible without cultural independence, which in turn is impossible without a land base" (Deloria 1988: 180). For Deloria, then, culture serves not only to demarcate the social boundaries of the sovereign community but also to bind it to a particular territory. Sacred geographies and the cultural practices associated with them link Indian nations to their homelands, those territories to which they have a special claim because of historical connections that give meaning to their peoples' lives, religion, and politics. As we shall see in chapter 4, such rhetoric is a staple of nationalist discourse, and it derives its force and meaning from the boundary-making practices of sovereignty.[44]

Many indigenous studies scholars have embraced Deloria's cultural approach to tribal sovereignty. Indeed, the claim that indigenous sovereignty is more about the maintenance of cultural integrity and continuity in the face of historical change and colonialism than it is about political and legal power per se has become standard in indigenous studies (e.g., Cobb 2005: 121; Coffey and Tsosie 2001; Porter 2002; Rickard 2011; Wilkins 1997: 21). Although some have warned of the dangers of using "culture" as a justification for sovereignty (Barsh 1993; Cattelino 2010; Coulthard 2014; S. Deloria 2002), most agree with Coffey and Tsosie (2001) that to achieve and maintain sovereignty, indigenous people must build systems of governance, law, and ways of being in the contemporary world (including government-to-government relations with settler states) based upon their own distinct beliefs and cultural

44 I want to be clear here that I am not suggesting that tribal nationalists like Deloria fabricated the human–land relationship in the interests of nation building. The centrality of land to indigenous knowledge and practice is indisputable. What I want to point out is the explicitly nationalist framing that Deloria uses to describe that relationship, which might otherwise be cast in more relational and less categorical terms (such as, for example, kinship): "As we look for the origins of religions, we must discover nations of people, and whichever way we look, it is to the lands on which the people reside and in which the religions arise that is important" (Deloria 1992: 142). In subsequent chapters, we will see that the Yukon agreements lead to a reframing of human–land relations (which have always been central to Yukon Indian cultural practice) in similarly nationalistic terms.

practices. This requires that they "revitalize and reaffirm the values and norms embedded within Native belief systems" (2001: 203). Only then will true "self-government" be possible. This cultural view of sovereignty and concomitant need to "revitalize and reaffirm" indigenous cultural practices has led many indigenous studies scholars to view the deployment of culture and "tradition" in tribal law and politics – as well as in a broad range of economic, intellectual, artistic, and literary endeavours – as quintessential examples of indigenous sovereignty in practice.[45] Their focus on the cultural dimensions of sovereignty-in-practice has led to a productive debate about the nature, scope, and meaning of indigenous sovereignty. But it raises an important question: just how compatible are indigenous beliefs and practices with assertions of (indigenous) sovereignty?

Before addressing this question, it is necessary to point out that indigenous studies scholars' insights about the cultural dimensions of indigenous sovereignty, productive though they have been, do not serve to radically differentiate between two different "kinds" of sovereignty: "indigenous" and "Euro-American." As it turns out, "Euro-American" sovereignty, too, is very much a product of culture. We saw in the introduction to this book that recent critics from "mainstream" disciplines such as international relations and political theory, especially those who take a social constructivist approach, have critiqued the *sovereignty* concept in ways that are quite reminiscent of Deloria's treatment of tribal sovereignty. R.B.J. Walker, for instance, refers to the "myth" that sovereignty is a purely legal concept and notes that "the very attempt to treat sovereignty as a matter of definition and legal principle encourages a certain amnesia about its historical and culturally specific character" (Walker 1993: 166); and, as we saw earlier in this chapter, this amnesia is itself a product of sovereignty, which can only "work" if the historical and culturally specific assumptions upon which it is based are naturalized. Like Deloria's concept of tribal sovereignty, then, Hobbesian sovereignty, too, is primarily a cultural – rather than a purely legal or political – concept. Indeed, we saw that Hobbes himself viewed sovereignty principally as a mechanism for producing a political identity rooted in a set of shared assumptions about the nature of the world and

45 This literature is large and growing. For a selection of scholars taking this approach to the indigenization of sovereignty, see Barker (2005b), Cattelino (2008), Cobb (2005), Lyons (2000), Richland (2011), Rickard (2011), Simpson (2014), and Warrior (1995).

how we can know it, assumptions that in today's terms would have to be characterized as "cultural." So long as we hold sovereignty to be a set of historical and culturally specific assumptions that enable a certain kind of politics – rather than, as the "myth" of sovereignty would have it, a universal principle that serves as the precondition for any politics at all – then Deloria and others' characterization of sovereignty as a cultural and not (just) political or legal concept is not peculiar to "indigenous" sovereignty at all but is equally applicable in Euro-American and international contexts. In fact, given the culturally and historically contingent meaning of *sovereignty* everywhere, most scholars' invocations of *indigenous sovereignty* fall well within the already broad and contested range of meanings for sovereignty more generally.[46]

This has an important implication for our purposes here. For while Deloria and other theorists of cultural sovereignty have clearly opened a space for distinctly indigenous forms of sovereign politics (and polities) within the settler state, it means that their formulations of indigenous sovereignty continue to take for granted the sovereign state form itself as a vehicle for indigenous emancipation. This is evident in the fact that indigenous studies scholars and activists continue almost without exception to employ terms such as *citizen, nation, history,* and *self-determination,* all of which are themselves statist notions and direct entailments of the sovereignty concept.[47] In the coming chapters,

46 This is a point also made by Bruyneel (2007: 24, 222). While a detailed comparison of Deloria and other indigenous studies scholars' writings with recent critiques of sovereignty from mainstream disciplines would no doubt be fruitful, it is unfortunately beyond the scope of this book. I offer but a single additional example here. Deloria's claim that indigenous sovereignty involves a "commitment to a larger whole" that "provides [for indigenous people] a clear identity which cannot be eroded by the passage of events" resonates powerfully with Walker's claim that sovereignty imparts a sense of "permanence" associated with a "relatively unchanging territorial space to be occupied by a state characterized by temporal change; or a spatial-cum-institutional container to be filled by the cultural or ethnic aspirations of a people" (Walker 1993: 166; on this point, see also Coffey and Tsosie 2001: 202).

47 In their influential article on cultural sovereignty, for example, Coffey and Tsosie (2001: 191) see tribal sovereignty as rooted in "the cultural existence of an Indian nation with its own territory, identity, and history." Even Taiaiake Alfred continues to adhere to some of the entailments of sovereignty. Although he rejects the sovereignty concept itself along with some of the key concepts associated with it, he continues to invoke the idea of Indian "nations" and, indeed, considers himself a Mohawk nationalist. Lyons (2010: 135–6) points out the inconsistency in this position.

I will show how these and a handful of other concepts (and the practices associated with them) flow directly from the territorial, social, and temporal boundary-making practices of sovereignty. One simply cannot talk about indigenous *nations* or *nationalism,* for instance, without invoking – at least implicitly – the concepts of the state and state sovereignty, unless one is willing to so completely redefine them that they become unintelligible to others (Lyons 2010: 136). As long as scholars and activists invoke the idea of indigenous "nations" composed of culturally distinct "peoples," each with its own distinct homeland, history, and corresponding right of "self-government," they necessarily take for granted some of the key cultural entailments of sovereignty, all of which derive from a statist logic.

Deloria's vision of sovereignty as a mechanism for drawing boundaries among culturally distinct tribal nations (and between them and the settler state), each with its own homeland and history, suggests he does not so much reject the state form as seek to indigenize it. That is, he and the scholars following his lead retain the state form but seek to develop alternative practices of governance that are more consistent with indigenous beliefs and practices. In his recent analysis of Deloria's writings, David Carlson (2016: 58) similarly concludes that Deloria "adopt[s] the Western view of the sovereign state as a source of authority legitimized by an integrated people but ... then employ[s] culturally specific definitions of that people to fundamentally alter the way that the state is understood to function ... A broad concept of popular sovereignty ... is deployed in order to produce an alternative vision of how to organize the government of the state."

This is a powerful vision and clearly one that motivates much contemporary scholarship on indigenous sovereignty. Even the fiercest critics of the tribal state seem to view its indigenization – the project of rendering it compatible with indigenous beliefs and practices – as a worthy, if perhaps unattainable, objective (Alfred 2005b; Barsh 1993; S. Deloria 2002). But just how compatible is the sovereign state form with indigenous cultural practices? Is a truly indigenized tribal state even possible? Or does the very form of the state impose a structure that is somehow fundamentally incompatible with key indigenous beliefs and practices? Taiaiake Alfred clearly thinks so. For him, the adoption of the state form requires a transformation in world view and social practice so dramatic as to threaten all he believes worth preserving of indigenous culture and society. But not everyone agrees. Scott Lyons, for example, acknowledges the non-indigenous status of concepts such as *sovereignty*, *nation*, and *citizenship*; and he freely admits that their adoption by indigenous people is culturally transformative (2010: chap. 3, 4). Rather than viewing this as necessarily negative, however (particularly given the problematic nature of all appeals to pre-contact cultural purity), he embraces the political possibilities they engender (e.g., tribal nationalism) as the best options for protecting indigenous lands and cultures. For him, this necessarily entails, among other things, the creation of a tribal state: "The [Indian] nation doesn't need to have absolute sovereignty or a fully independent state to exist, but it should have enough 'statehood' to move away from culture towards more discourse on rights, duties, and responsibilities – in order to care for the citizens who make up the nation" (Lyons 2010: 146–7).

So, is the adoption of state-like forms of governance evidence of cultural contamination and inherently destructive of indigenous culture? Or is it the best hope for the preservation of those cultures and the lands on which they are based? It seems to me that this question has no single – or simple – answer. Given the high degree of cultural variation among indigenous peoples, the answer necessarily depends on the particularities: the state form is more of a "foreign" imposition in some indigenous contexts than it is in others. And given the value-laden-ness of the question (what one person views as cultural contamination/loss another sees as successful adaptation), the answer also clearly depends on who is doing the answering. Regardless of the cultural context or standards of evaluation, however, it is clear that indigenizing the tribal state is never easy or straightforward. Given the colonial history of all tribal institutions and ongoing political realities in settler states, tribal state institutions are necessarily profoundly ambivalent. This ambivalence is in large part due to the inherently dual character of sovereign recognition.

Claims to indigenous sovereignty, like all sovereign claims, must be justified both externally (to foreign states and, in the case of First Nations, also to agents of federal and provincial governments and non-native residents) as well as internally (to the First Nation's own citizens). As Larry Nesper shows in his fine-grained ethnographic analysis of a tribal court at Lac du Flambeau in northern Wisconsin, these two legitimizing projects are often incompatible with one another (Nesper 2007; see also Barsh 1993: 303). As key sites of tribal state formation, tribal courts are caught between the internal and external imperatives of sovereignty. The very legal and bureaucratic forms that are essential if tribal state institutions are to be recognized as legitimate by external governments often serve to undermine the tribal state's legitimacy in the eyes of its own citizens. Nesper highlights the tension between these largely incompatible legitimizing projects in the day-to-day practices of the court and shows that the results are variable, multilayered, and highly ambivalent. At times, the tribal court sanctions – and even itself engages in – culturally inappropriate practices, thus confirming Alfred's fears about the imposition of sovereignty as a model for governance. At other times, however, the court looks more like an agent of properly indigenized sovereignty, with court officials manipulating the legal apparatus to conform to Ojibwe cultural norms and deploying the law to strengthen rather than erode indigenous beliefs and practices. Either way, though, the court constantly enacts the tribal state's sovereign authority "over" its "subjects." Given the inescapable tension between the need for internal legitimacy and external recognition, it is likely that such multilayered ambivalence pervades the workings of all First Nation government institutions.[48]

It certainly pervades the institutions of self-government in the Yukon. As I will show in the remainder of this book, *sovereignty* as a way of conceiving of politics – and, indeed, of the world – is in many ways incompatible with pre-contact Yukon society and with many Yukon Indian peoples' ongoing beliefs, practices, and ways of being in the world. To harness it in defence of Yukon Indian peoples' rights requires a dramatic shift in world view and social practice. Insofar as Yukon land claim and self-government agreements are rooted in the assumptions of sovereignty, their implementation entails just such a shift. The processes of state formation they initiate are transforming social and environmental relations in the Yukon in profound ways. But there is no consensus about how to evaluate these changes. To some, they look like the loss of "Yukon Indian culture." To others, they look more like successful adaptation to the realities of life and politics in the Canadian settler state. Both positions, it seems to me, are defensible.

The authors of *Together Today for Our Children Tomorrow*, the original claim put forward by the Yukon Native Brotherhood in 1973, assert that "the objective of the Yukon Indian people is to obtain a Settlement in place of a treaty that will help us and our children learn to live in a

48 For discussion of a similarly ambivalent sovereign practice, see Anna Willow's (2013) analysis of indigenous counter-mapping strategies in northern Ontario.

changing world. We want to take part in the development of the Yukon and Canada, not stop it. But we can only participate *as Indians*" (Yukon Native Brotherhood 1973: 18, emphasis added).[49] There can be no doubt that the Yukon agreements give Yukon Indian people a role in the ongoing development of the Yukon and Canada. The question is whether the agreements allow them to do so *as Indians*; that is, whether this role is consistent with "the core elements of [their] cultural existence" which are "the essence of cultural sovereignty" (Coffey and Tsosie 2001: 202). Since there is no agreement on what exactly those core elements are, nor on what kinds of changes are consistent with continued "Indianness," it follows that there can be no agreement on how to evaluate the cultural appropriateness of the Yukon agreements. And, in fact, scholarly opinions differ dramatically on this question.

Most sanguine are those, like political scientist Gurston Dacks, who, despite the many problems he identifies with the Yukon agreements and their implementation, believes that it is "possible under the agreements to create governments that embody traditional practices." He bases this assertion on the fact that the agreements allow Yukon First Nations to tweak their practices of governance to bring them more in line with "traditional" practices. For example, he points out that some Yukon First Nations diverge from the one-person-one-vote system of electing office holders and instead allow clans to appoint them, while others allow for hereditary chiefs (Dacks 2004: 677).[50] In contrast, political scientist

49 Compare this to the Kluane First Nation final agreement, which lists first among its objectives the following: "Kluane People have traditional decision-making bodies and practices, based on a moiety system, and wish to maintain those bodies and practices, integrated with a contemporary form of government" (Kluane First Nation 2003a: first "whereas" clause).

50 To be sure, Dacks recognizes that "it is too early to tell how well these institutions will fare in handling issues that bring contemporary and traditional values into conflict"; yet, he is confident that "the cultural authenticity that underlies [the agreements] should assist in the resolution of such issues" (Dacks 2004: 677). Central to his assessment of the self-government agreements is his assumption that the institutions they create are "culturally authentic." Elsewhere in the same article, for example, he claims that "the new First Nation governments in the Yukon are more culturally authentic and their policies promise to be more sensitive to their traditional values than was the case with their *Indian Act*-based predecessors" (690). Considering how low he sets the authenticity bar here (the Indian Act band structure, after all, was unilaterally imposed on Yukon Indian people who had no say in the matter at all), most everyone would probably agree with this statement; but Dacks neglects

Graham White (2009), evaluating the Nunavut agreement, is far less confident about the long-term prospects for efforts to establish "a government that would not only be numerically dominated by Inuit but also would operate by Inuit cultural principles." Identifying many of the same problems Dacks did in the Yukon agreements, he nevertheless expresses doubts about "just how deeply any government system resting on a large Euro-Canadian bureaucracy can accommodate itself to a set of values so fundamentally contradictory to Weberian bureaucratic norms" (White 2009: 58, 78). Finally, there are those, such as Taiaiake Alfred (2005a) and Glen Coulthard (2014), who not only view comprehensive land claim and self-government agreements as fundamentally inconsistent with northern indigenous peoples' beliefs and practices but also as actively facilitating the ongoing (and, indeed, intensifying) exploitation of indigenous peoples and their lands.

There is certainly plenty of room for legitimate disagreement over how to evaluate the agreements and their effects, but in my view no fair evaluation is possible without first acknowledging the agreements for what they are: key mechanisms in a process of First Nation state formation that is ushering in a revolutionary transformation in social, cultural, and environmental relations. Such an acknowledgment will hardly end the disagreement; people can and no doubt will evaluate this transformation very differently. I suspect there will always be those who view the agreements as engines for the destruction of indigenous cultures, just as there will always be others who see them as essential adaptive mechanisms for protecting those cultures. It seems to me, however, that any informed contribution to the debate must first take into account the magnitude and nature of the sociocultural transformation itself. The remaining chapters of this book represent my effort to do just that. I begin by looking at the agreements' territorial dimensions through a focus on the production of sovereign jurisdiction.

---

to consider just how constrained Yukon Indian people were in negotiating their agreements. Yes, they had some say in the specifics of self-governance, but only so long as they agreed to the creation of a thoroughly Euro-American model of government. What is more, the new self-governing First Nation governments – precisely because they have so much more power and legitimacy than band governments ever had – possess far greater power to transform Yukon peoples' beliefs and practices than the Indian Act bands ever did.

Chapter Two

Territory

In the modern conception, state sovereignty is fully, flatly, and evenly operative over each square centimetre of a legally demarcated territory.

Benedict Anderson (1991: 19)

Territoriality is settler colonialism's specific, irreducible element.

Patrick Wolfe (2006: 388)

Land is not territory, except in a colonial way of looking at the landscape ... Home is everywhere and we are all related. Territorial boundaries are an assault on this indigenous sense of place and being.

Taiaiake Alfred (2005a: 206–7)

Geographer Robert Sack famously defined territoriality as "the attempt by an individual or group to affect, influence, or control people, phenomena, and relationships, by delimiting and asserting control over a geographic area" (1986: 19). Territoriality is thus a particular kind of political strategy, one that focuses on controlling people and processes through the demarcation and control of space. Sack concedes that while there are many other, non-territorial, ways of exercising power, "territoriality is the primary spatial form power takes" within the modern state (ibid.: 26).[1] Indeed, Sack (along with others) views the modern

1 Although Sack and others view the modern state as the quintessentially territorial macro-political form, territorial strategies are utilized in all societies and at all scales. According to Sack, the appeal of territoriality lies in its efficiency. If a parent wants

state as a fundamentally territorial form of political organization, and he suggests that two state territorial strategies in particular have played a central role in the transformation of indigenous people's relationship to land: the establishment of political jurisdiction and the delimitation of property rights in land (ibid.: 15).

Anthropologists, environmental historians, and others have focused a great deal of attention upon the latter, arguing that the imposition of Euro-American property regimes has dramatically altered how indigenous peoples can relate to the land, animals, and one another (Biolsi 1995; Cheyfitz 1991; Cronon 1983; Merchant 1989; Tully 1993; Williams 1986). Along these lines, I previously argued (Nadasdy 2002; Nadasdy 2003, chap. 5) that comprehensive land claim and self-government agreements in Canada, insofar as they are "written in the language of property," entail the imposition of a culturally inappropriate (in the Yukon at least) set of ideas about how humans should relate to one another and animals with respect to the land. Scholars of indigenous–state relations, however, have paid considerably less attention to the imposition of jurisdiction, a concept that is every bit as culturally specific as property.[2]

Territorial jurisdiction, a government's exclusive right to exercise power and authority within a clearly demarcated territory, is a fundamental premise of nearly all contemporary understandings of politics,[3]

---

to prevent his or her very young children from playing with dangerous items in the kitchen, for example, it is more efficient to simply exclude them from the kitchen (a territorial strategy) than to try to explain and enforce a distinction between those items with which they may and may not play. Similarly, it is more efficient to supervise convicts by confining them in a prison (a territorial strategy) than it would be to allow them to roam freely accompanied by guards (1986: 22).

2 Of course, property and jurisdiction are not completely distinct concepts; indeed, they are so deeply implicated in one another that we might better view them as different aspects of state territoriality than as distinct territorial strategies in themselves (Asch 2000). Assertions of state jurisdiction, after all, are premised upon an assumption that the sovereign state possesses "underlying title" to all the land within its territorial boundaries, while "property" relations are guaranteed by the state within whose jurisdiction they lie; and it is from that state context that they derive their force and meaning. This means that focusing on either property or jurisdiction alone is inadequate if we hope to understand how practices of state territoriality have affected indigenous peoples.

3 This stands to reason since, as we saw in the previous chapter, the concept of sovereignty, which has become the precondition for politics, takes for granted its own geographical boundedness.

a fact that informs commonsense notions of the world as divided up among political entities, each exercising jurisdiction over discrete mutually exclusive territories separated by linear borders (Anderson 1991; Malkki 1992; Murphy 1996). Such a vision of political space implies that to qualify as a government at all, a political entity must have jurisdiction over a clearly defined territory. This vision clearly informs the Yukon land claim and self-government agreements, which carve the Yukon into fourteen distinct First Nation "traditional territories." But what are the cultural and political consequences of using territorial jurisdiction as the framework for building First Nation states in the Yukon?

In this chapter, I expand the purview of my inquiry into the comprehensive land claims process in Canada beyond my previous focus on *property* and consider the imposition of state territoriality more generally – with particular attention to the notion of territorial jurisdiction.[4] To this end, I focus on the territorial (and territorializing) aspects of the Yukon land claim and self-government agreements. These agreements are fundamentally territorial; that is, it is primarily (though not solely) by demarcating space and assigning various governments control over the resulting territories that the agreements constitute First Nations authority in relation to other governments and their own citizens. The agreements create two distinct types of First Nation territory (in Sack's sense of the term). First, as noted above, they carve the Yukon into fourteen distinct First Nation *traditional territories* (see map 1). Second, within each traditional territory the agreements also demarcate smaller areas of First Nation *settlement land* (see map 2). As we shall see, traditional territories and settlement lands are both integral to the structure of Yukon final and self-government agreements. It is tempting to view settlement lands as a form of property (which, in fact, they are) and traditional territories as being more about jurisdiction. There is some truth to this characterization, but in reality things are considerably more complex. In fact, each of these territorial

4 In part as a result of helpful discussions with Michael Asch, I now believe I previously overstated the degree to which land claim and self-government agreements are "written in the language of *property*." I view my much broader focus on territoriality in this chapter – and indeed the entire book – as in some sense a corrective to my overly narrow focus on property in earlier works.

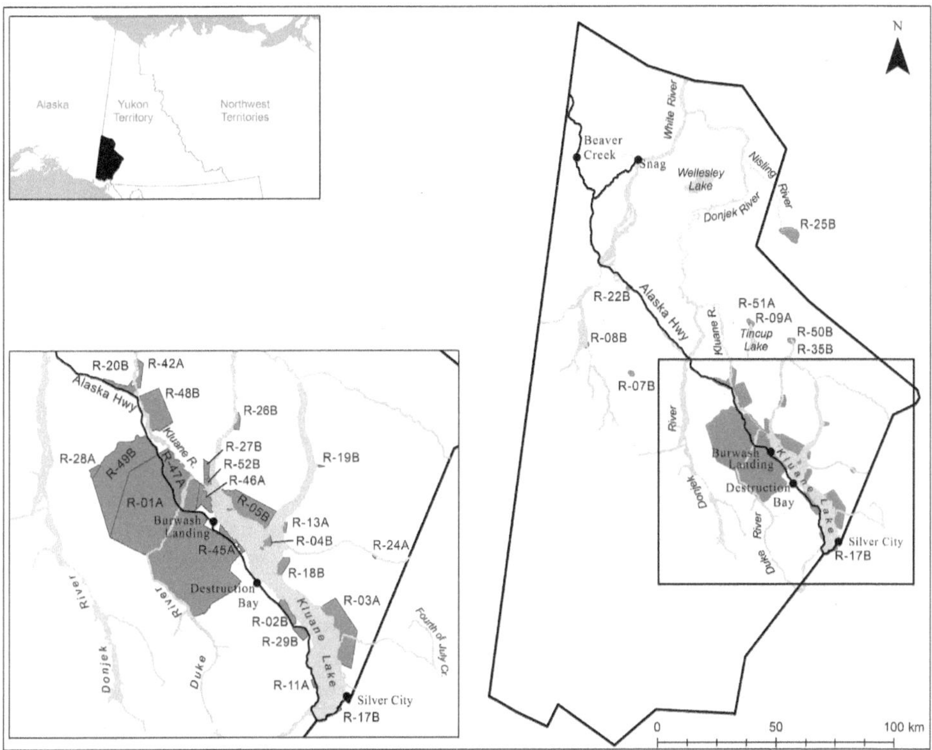

Map 2 Kluane First Nation traditional territory and settlement lands by Tracy Sallaway (Maps, Data and Government Information Centre, Trent University). All data – Geomatics, Department of Environment, Government of Yukon.

forms has both proprietary and jurisdictional aspects. Having considered the proprietary aspects of the Yukon agreements elsewhere (Nadasdy 2002), however, I focus in this chapter primarily on their jurisdictional dimensions.

Although many people – Indian and Euro-Canadian alike – assume that traditional territories reflect "traditional" patterns of land use and occupancy, indigenous society in the Yukon was not, in fact, composed of distinct political entities each with jurisdiction over its own territory; such entities are actually a recent phenomenon in the Yukon. The new agreements, then, are not simply formalizing jurisdictional boundaries among pre-existing First Nation polities; they are mechanisms for *creating* the legal and administrative systems that bring those polities into being. In fact, the agreements are premised on the assumption that First Nation governments – if they are to qualify as governments at all – must be discrete politico-territorial entities.

Thus, although the Yukon agreements do grant First Nations some very real powers of governance, those powers come in the peculiarly territorial currency of the modern state. Not only does this implicitly devalue indigenous forms of socio-political organization (which, as we shall see, were not primarily territorial), it is also helping transform First Nation society in radical and often unintended ways. Throughout this book I will examine the many interconnected ways in which the territorial order imposed by the Yukon land claim and self-government agreements is transforming how Yukon Indian people (particularly those of the Kluane First Nation and its neighbours in the southwest Yukon) can relate to one another and to the land and animals. My focus in this chapter is on how, through the creation of fish and wildlife management bureaucracies, these new agreements are recasting social relations in explicitly territorial terms. This process of territorialization is not only transforming how Yukon Indian people can relate to the land and animals, it is also changing how they can relate to one another with respect to the land and animals. Before embarking on this analysis, however, it is necessary to say a bit more about what I mean by territoriality and about the territorial assumptions underlying the Yukon agreements.

Territoriality and the State

The Territorial State

Over the past two decades, political geographers, anthropologists, and others have analysed the territorial dimensions of the modern state. Rather than simply taking for granted its territorial boundedness, as scholars had previously done, they have begun systematically examining the role of territory – and of territoriality – in constituting the state as a particular socio-historical phenomenon. Building on Sack's political conception of territoriality, contemporary political geographers now agree that modern state power is largely – though by no means exclusively – an exercise in territoriality; that is, states seek to control people and resources principally through the demarcation and control of space.[5] The demarcation and control over territory, within which the state supposedly exercises exclusive sovereign power, has long been viewed as an essential aspect of the modern state. Max Weber's famous definition of the state as "a human community that (successfully) claims a monopoly of the legitimate use of physical force *within a given territory*" (Weber 1946a: 78, emphasis added), for example, recognizes its fundamentally territorial character. More recently, Anthony Giddens (1987: 20) reformulated Weber's definition in even more explicitly territorial terms. For him, the state is "a political organization whose rule is territorially ordered and which is able to mobilize the means of violence to sustain that rule." The establishment and maintenance of clear boundaries both among and within states is essential to the concept of the modern state and to the exercise of state power. Though specific boundaries (both external and internal) may change over time, the fact that such boundaries exist is so fundamental to the state form that it is generally taken completely for granted.[6] Indeed, political geographers now view territoriality as such an intrinsic aspect of the modern state that many have taken to referring to it as the *territorial state*, to distinguish it from other kinds of historical states (Agnew 1994; Agnew 2005).[7]

---

5 Sack explicitly argues that because human territoriality is a political strategy, it has little in common with territoriality among animals, long the subject of research among zoologists and ethologists. In the process he also disavows earlier anthropological approaches to human territoriality (Ardrey 1966) that drew heavily on the zoological literature and treated territoriality among humans as biological instinct rather than political strategy. By contrast, Edward Soja (1971), who outlined a political concept of territoriality in many ways similar to Sack's, views the literature on animal territoriality as potentially useful in that it provides important analogies for the study of human territoriality. For a review of the many meanings of territoriality among humans, see Malmberg (1980).

6 As Agnew (1994: 54) puts it: "A state is territorial much like life on earth is terrestrial." Adopting the same terrestrial metaphor, Ruggie (1993: 174) observes that "it is truly astonishing that the concept of territoriality has been so little studied by students of international politics; its neglect is akin to never looking at the ground one is walking on."

7 There are many forms of non-territorial political organization. This is not to say that territorial strategies are never used in such societies, but only that territoriality is not their organizing principle, as it is in the territorial state. European feudalism and the "postmodern" global economic system are the two non-territorial political systems most frequently discussed in the critical literature on the territorial state system (e.g., Agnew 2005; Anderson 1996; Appadurai 2003; Ruggie 1993), but many others

The boundaries of the territorial state delimit – at least in theory – the spatial extent of its legal and administrative jurisdiction, its authority to levy taxes, and the extent of its control over people and resources.[8] Not surprisingly, maps have played a particularly important role in creation and consolidation of state power. As historian Thongchai Winichakul (1994) shows in his study of the birth of the Thai nation, early government-generated maps of the country were not simply abstract representations of political reality. Rather, "a map anticipated spatial reality, not vice versa. In other words, a map was a model for, rather than a model of, what it purported to represent." He shows that maps served as models *for* the construction of Siam as a modern territorial state: "All the requisites of a map of a nation had not been given in pre-modern Siam and thus had to be created to meet the demands of a map ... The regime of mapping did not passively reflect Siam. Rather, it has actively structured 'Siam' in our minds as well as on earth" (ibid.: 130). Thus, maps are a crucial technology for constructing the territories within which states supposedly exercise their sovereignty.[9] Like early government maps of Siam, the official maps attached to the Yukon First Nation land claim and self-government agreements delineate the territorial boundaries of the new First Nations and, in so doing, serve as models for the creation of state-like First Nations.

---

can be found in anthropological and related literatures (e.g., Anderson 1990; Evans-Pritchard 1940a; Fortes and Evans-Pritchard 1940; Thongchai 1994). Not surprisingly, it is impossible to specify a precise date for the emergence of the modern territorial state. For convenience, political theorists often refer to the Treaty of Westphalia in 1648 as marking the birth of the territorially sovereign state system, but this origin myth belies the fact that key elements of the territorial state system developed gradually over a period of centuries, beginning as far back as 1000 AD (Strayer 1970; Corrigan and Sayer 1985), and that the nature of the sovereign territorial state has continued to evolve in significant ways since 1648 (Osiander 2001; Murphy 1996; Teschke 2003). Peter Sahlins (1989: 6, see also 28–9) provides a nuanced account of the long transition in France and Spain from what he calls "jurisdictional sovereignty," a system of rule premised on the Crown's jurisdiction over subjects, to "territorial sovereignty," with its focus on control over a clearly delimited territory.

8 By contrast, Peter Sahlins (1989: esp. chaps. 1 and 2) shows that in early modern France and Spain – neither of which had yet fully undergone the "territorialization of sovereignty" – jurisdiction over military affairs, justice, taxation, commercial affairs, and the like often failed to coincide either with one another or with the nascent political boundaries ostensibly separating French from Spanish territory.

9 For more on the way in which maps construct rather than merely represent the world, see Harley (1989), Wood (1992).

It turns out that First Nations' territorial jurisdiction is not quite so geographically clear-cut as I have just suggested. As we shall see, there is considerable overlap of First Nation traditional territories in the Yukon (and elsewhere); thus, the relationship between a First Nation's territory and its power/authority is actually quite complex. Even among territorial states, however, the link between state territory and sovereign power is far from clear-cut *in practice* (see, e.g., Anderson 1996; Agnew 2005; Appadurai 2003; Biersteker and Weber 1996; Raustiala 2009; Ong 1999). Although territorial sovereignty is the *ideal* basis for state power and perceptions of its legitimacy (Murphy 1996), the exercise of that power – like the territorial claims upon which it is based – is always contingent and open to contestation. In the context of indigenous struggles against settler colonialism, however, the distinction between de facto and de jure sovereignty can obscure the cultural hegemony of sovereign territoriality as the only legitimate form for the expression of political authority. As I suggested in the introduction, the territorial state has become virtually the only template available to indigenous peoples seeking a measure of self-determination, even if that template is culturally inappropriate. Thus, because they represent a tacit admission to play by the rules of the political game as formulated by the colonizer, even those indigenous assertions of sovereign territoriality that are successful can *in practice* be viewed as part of the legacy of colonial domination.

Internal Territoriality

Following Benedict Anderson (1991), scholars have pointed out the homogenizing tendencies of the modern state, arguing that its creation entails – at least ideally – the melding of previously distinct populations into a single territorially constituted "imagined community" (for more on this in the Yukon, see chapter 4). At the same time, however, ongoing processes within territorial states produce administrative differences among citizens and carve the landscape into different geographical subunits. Indeed, Sack (1986: 53) observes that the modern state is not only externally territorial (i.e., vis-à-vis other states), but also internally territorial: it produces a hierarchy of nested territories right down to the level of individual factories and households, which are themselves internally territorialized. This internal territoriality involves not only the creation of jurisdictional boundaries within states but also the formalization and protection of property rights in land.

These processes of internal territorialization produce administrative differences among citizens and carve the landscape into different geographical subunits. This is essential because, although the creation of a unified state requires the erasure of certain kinds of difference, other kinds of differences among people and places are essential for the practice of governance. Internal boundaries (whether jurisdictional or proprietary) allow for the delegation of authority and the rationalization of jurisdiction among different levels of government, aid in the coordination and delivery of government services, facilitate the management of people and resources, and so on. Maps play a crucial role in these processes of internal territorialization as well. To return once more to the birth of the Thai state, Thongchai (1994: 130) shows that government maps not only helped constitute Thailand as a territorial state vis-à-vis other such states; they were also essential for developing *internal* administrative mechanisms: "Not only was mapping a necessary device for new administrative mechanisms and military purposes ... but indeed the discourse of mapping was the paradigm within which both administrative and military operations worked and served."

Boundary making within the territorial state is far from politically neutral. Malcolm Anderson points out that boundaries within states, though "often presented as technical adjustments to promote efficiency of administration, are never independent of changes in power relationships" (1997: 107). Indeed, as Vandergeest and Peluso (1995) show, processes of internal territorialization have played a key role in efforts to expand and consolidate state control over peoples and resources, particularly (but not exclusively) in colonial and post-colonial contexts. In settler states, such processes have resulted in the (often violent) reworking of indigenous social relations, transforming in fundamental ways how certain kinds of people can relate to one another as well as to the land and resources (Cronon 1983). Internal territorialization, however, is not always a top-down process, nor are its socio-political consequences always those intended by either state officials or those who would resist them. "Like international boundaries," Anderson (1997: 106–7) asserts, "some sub-state boundaries are the outcome of long historical processes of conflict and adjustment between competing interests."

Although the distinction between internal and external state territoriality can at times be analytically useful, it can be difficult to distinguish between them in practice. Indeed, Anderson (1997: 106–7) points out that from a historical perspective the distinction between internal and external boundaries is not at all an easy one to maintain, since internal boundaries have a tendency to become external ones and vice versa. Similarly, Agnew (1994: 59, 65–8) argues that the domestic/foreign dichotomy is theoretically problematic because it obscures the interaction of political and economic processes across such boundaries and at different scales. Whether one views the territorializing processes I analyse in this book as either internal or external is very much a matter of one's analytic perspective. To the extent that the Yukon agreements establish boundaries between different state-like political organizations (i.e., other First Nations), they can be viewed as initiating a process of external territorialization. And this is largely how I view them in chapters 3 and 4. In the present chapter, however, I consider how the agreements create new regional and administrative boundaries *within* the Canadian state; that is, as initiating a process of internal territorialization. Before proceeding with this analysis, however, it will be necessary to provide a brief historical overview of territoriality and political authority in the Yukon.

Territoriality, Political Authority, and Socio-environmental Relations in the Yukon

The Pre- and Early Contact Yukon

Up until the middle of the twentieth century, Yukon Indian people were nomadic, covering large distances in the course of their annual subsistence round. For much of the year they lived in small hunting groups. These groups were extremely flexible; there were no formal rules for membership, and their composition was constantly changing as the result of seasonal and longer-term variations in the availability of resources, social tensions among group members, marriage, long-distance trading, and so on.[10] Anthropologist Catharine McClellan, who conducted ethnographic research in the southern Yukon between 1948 and 1951, characterized nineteenth-century Yukon socio-political organization thus:

10 See McClellan (1975: 95–105) and McClellan and Denniston (1981) for a description of the annual subsistence round in the southern Yukon and the entire subarctic Cordillera, respectively. For rich descriptions of the social dynamics in northern Athapaskan hunting groups, see Sharp (1988) and McDonnell (1975).

> A very sparse population was spread over a vast area, making a loosely linked social network with very few sharply defined linguistic and cultural boundaries ... Cohesive political units did not exist – just widely scattered clusters of living groups whose composition and size changed throughout the year as people moved about in quest of food. Large social gatherings were sporadic and brief. They were either for trading or potlatch purposes, and they were structured along either sib or moiety lines.[[11]] Only during the present [twentieth] century have the Indians become attached in numbers to permanent settlements, which are the nodal points of the [Indian Act] bands now recognized by the federal government. (1975: 14)

McClellan reports that, like many small-scale hunting and horticultural societies, the contact era Indians of the southern Yukon "had 'political organization' in only the very broadest sense ... [There was no] aboriginal institution or office that was unequivocally political, if we imply by that term an administrative or judicial unit that was the commonly recognized locus of coercive power. No officials or councils existed whose primary function was to administer either inter-tribal or extra-tribal civil affairs" (ibid.: 481).[12] In short, there was no locus of sovereign authority. To be sure, there were local headmen, sometimes referred to in English as "chiefs," who wielded considerable authority in certain contexts, but

> unlike the modern elected "chief," the aboriginal chief was never part of an institutionalized civil hierarchy. While his opinion often carried great weight with those most closely associated with him, he certainly never had clearly defined judicial or punitive powers over all persons living in a delimited territorial unit. Among the more northern bands of the Southern Tutchone, the chief was simply the outstanding man of a labile, kin-structured social group. In the southern bands, where lineage and sib were

11 A moiety is one of two unilineal descent groups into which a society is divided for marriage and other ritual purposes. Athapaskan people of the southern and central Yukon are divided into the Crow and Wolf moieties, which are matrilineal and exogamous (i.e., one must marry a member of the opposite moiety). Among Tlingitized groups of the southern Yukon, these moieties are further subdivided into several sibs (or clans), unilineal groups descended from a common (often mythic) ancestor.

12 Indeed, as we shall see shortly, the term "tribal" itself is inappropriate in the indigenous context.

> more fully developed, he was the ranking male representative of his lineage, so that in groups comprising more than one lineage there was, of course, more than one "chief." (ibid.: 481–2)

Local headmen did not have the power to make or enforce decisions for the local group (which, as we have just seen, might include more than one headman). McClellan stresses that "in no case did the 'chief' have absolute power. Much depended on the forcefulness of his character and on his ability to acquire and manipulate wealth" (ibid.: 482). Although there are ethnographic accounts of headmen using or attempting to use force to coerce people into doing their bidding, people in this highly nomadic society nearly always had the option of voting with their feet rather than submitting to the authority of someone with whom they disagreed. Rather than exercising authority over their "followers," then, headmen instead relied on the strength of their personalities to harangue, cajole, or otherwise convince people to go along with their plans. In standard anthropological parlance, they would more accurately be classified as "big men" than as "chiefs." In the absence of any hierarchical political institutions or means of coercion, people generally arrived at collective decisions via a slow process of consensus building (with headmen playing the role of influential shapers of opinion rather than decision makers). As in many other stateless societies, dissenters were generally free to leave or to simply refrain from taking part in any action eventually decided upon.[13]

Social relations among Yukon Indian people were ordered by principles of kinship and reciprocity rather than territoriality. Although indigenous kinship networks certainly existed in space, they were not defined by – nor did they define – specific territories, in Sack's sense of the term. This is not to say that Yukon Indian people never used territorial strategies of the sort described by Sack. It seems clear, for example, that moieties "owned" particular fishing sites and wildlife-rich river valleys, and local headmen regulated access to these important

13 Anthropologists working with stateless peoples all around the world have described non-coercive consensus-based decision-making processes of this sort; see, for example, Rappaport (1984: 30–1). Even today, Yukon Indian people continue to make many collective decisions – about, e.g., when and where to hunt, when to hold a potlatch – in this way. See Brody (1982: 35–8) for a nice description of such a process in contemporary Athapaskan village life.

areas.[14] Even in such cases, however, kinship tended to be more important than territory in the regulation of access. Indeed, McClellan observed that "all ideas of territorial 'ownership' were structured along either moiety or sib lines, and exclusive rights of exploitation were not vested in an entire local group nor in a private individual" (1975: 481). As she explains:

> In the past all three groups [Southern Tutchone, Tagish, and Inland Tlingit] seem to have recognized that some parts of the territory which they exploited were "owned," while other parts of it were "free" ... In these groups the localized sib segments provided a social reality with respect to territorial claims, but there was never, so far as I can tell, any individual or "family" ownership of land ... I believe that it was always possible in the past for a man to manipulate his kin ties so that in effect he could exploit almost any area which attracted him. (483)

Because moieties in the Yukon are matrilineal and exogamous, any request to hunt or fish in a particular locale could always be framed in

---

14 Frederick Johnson and Hugh Raup, who were the first to inquire about property rights in the Kluane region during their 1944 and 1948 expeditions there, paint a somewhat different picture of property rights in the region: "The testimony we have is to the effect that there are no claims to the land; anyone can travel and hunt where he pleases. There is some evidence that hunters habitually hunted in certain general areas, but the camps might be moved, and even the cabins built since 1900 could be used by anyone if they were empty. Whether or not the fur industry had resulted in some rules we do not know, but in 1948 the fur trade was at a minimum and appeared to have little effect on the economy, at least at Burwash" (Johnson and Raup 1964: 196).

Practically speaking, their characterization may be largely correct, especially for the area around Burwash at the time (and I have little doubt that they received testimony to this effect). Their failure to note the role of moieties and headmen in regulating access to fishing sites and prime hunting lands is probably an artefact of their relatively brief visit to the region (especially in contrast to McClellan's much longer fieldwork) at a time when the role of moieties and headmen in this regard was already declining (for reasons discussed by McClellan 1975: 485–7). Moiety ownership of certain important fishing sites in particular is well remembered by Yukon Indian people across the southern Yukon today. Somewhat less well remembered are the roles moieties and headmen played in regulating access to particular hunting areas. As we shall see in chapter 3, however, some Kluane people do still recall this and explicitly contrast First Nation citizens' universal rights (under the new land claim agreements) to hunt anywhere within their traditional territory with the "traditional" requirement that they obtain permission from the headman to hunt in moiety "owned" areas.

kinship terms, addressed either to one's "mother's people," members of one's own moiety, or one's "father's people," members of the opposite moiety. It was important that permission be sought, but once kinship relations had been established and acknowledged, it would have been difficult for the local headman to deny access (ibid.: 483–4). "So far as I know," McClellan noted, "a lineage head never tried to exploit the entire area himself ... All lineage members and anyone with paternal or affinal ties could ask permission to hunt or trap there, and consent was usually freely given" (485). In McClellan's view, then, indigenous people in the southern Yukon drew on far-flung networks of bilateral kin to travel widely and exploit resources more or less where they pleased.[15]

Dominique Legros (1985) paints a very different picture of indigenous social relations in the central Yukon during the nineteenth century. In his account, family control over critical fishing sites led to the emergence of mafia-like corporate kin groups and extreme social inequality. Despite their very different interpretations of the admittedly scant historical data, however, neither Legros nor McClellan ever suggests the existence of distinct polities with jurisdiction over their own bounded territories.[16] Recall McClellan's assertion, cited above, that local headmen "never had clearly defined judicial or punitive powers

15 Similarly, in her land use and occupancy study of the neighbouring White River region, Helene Dobrowolsky (1997: 2–3) states: "Family and travel groups were not fixed in number or membership. People joined other groups through marriage. Upon marriage, a man would often spend time hunting for his wife's family. A band might split into smaller family groupings in times when the land's resources were in short supply. If there were deaths, two smaller groups might decide to join forces. Likewise, travel and use of the land was fairly fluid. There were no fixed boundaries and various groups might make use of the same land and resources. People moved on to different areas depending on the season and the availability of game."

16 Perhaps not surprisingly, Legros also paints a very different picture of chiefly authority than that outlined above. In his view, headmen did indeed wield authority that was backed up by coercive force. While their power had a territorial component (control over access to specific fishing sites, in particular), it was nevertheless constituted entirely through their manipulation of kin ties. Although I am inclined to think that Legros overstates the degree to which violence and coercion characterized pre-contact social relations, there is nothing in his account that contradicts my assertion that kinship and reciprocity – rather than territoriality – were the central organizing principles of social and political life in the Yukon before the advent of colonialism. Indeed, I will draw heavily on his work, particularly in chapter 4, to back up my argument about the lack of distinct tribes or ethno-territorial groups in the pre-contact Yukon. See Ives (1990: 233–42) for further reflections on Legros's work and an effort to reconcile his description of pre-contact Tutchone social organization with McClellan's.

over all persons living in a delimited territorial unit." Prior to contact, it seems clear, Yukon Indian people were not organized into distinct "tribes" or "nations" with control over fixed territories. In her ethnographic survey of the southern Yukon, McClellan did divide up Yukon Indians geographically on the basis of language and referred to these divisions as "tribes," but she insisted that this was purely for the convenience of the ethnographer and warned that "it is not the kind of classification which the Indians themselves are likely to stress, or perhaps even recognize" (see also Legros 2007: esp. 100–4; McClellan and Denniston 1981: 384). In fact, it is questionable whether Yukon Indian people recognized "tribal" categories at all.[17] "Tribe" was a particularly problematic term, McClellan warned, because "usually it implies a sense of political unity which the Yukon natives ... never had" (ibid.: 13).[18] Nor did tribal categories organize Yukon Indian kinship practices, trade, or political relations. I will explore the emergence of tribal/national identity in considerable detail in chapters 3 and 4, but for now it is enough to note that while social boundaries did exist in the Yukon before European contact, those boundaries did not mark off the territories of distinct political units (McClellan 1992), nor were they used to regulate people's access to resources.[19] Yukon Indian people

---

17 McClellan reports that "the natives have always been baffled by government officials and others who have wanted to know their overall 'tribal name.' My Southern Tutchone friends laughed as they recalled a census taker who insisted that they *must* have a tribal name. They explained to him, as they did to me, that Indians are just dAn' (persons) [rendered elsewhere in this book as *dän*] – they have no tribal name" (McClellan 1975:14).

18 In the Yukon today there are several "Tribal Councils," mid-level cultural/political organization situated between individual First Nation governments and the Council for Yukon First Nations. These are recent constructions that correspond roughly to cultural and linguistic boundaries laid out by anthropologist Cornelius Osgood, the author of the original Athapaskan "tribal distributions map" which, with some minor revisions, forms the basis of nearly all subsequent ethnographic maps of the western subarctic (Osgood 1936: 4; see also Meek 2010: 128–30).

19 This is not to say that Yukon Indian people had no way of distinguishing legitimate from illegitimate land use. It is simply to say that that their criteria of legitimacy were derived from interpersonal rather than territorial relations. As Colin Scott (1988: 40) put it for the Cree, "This system [of human–animal–land relations] entails specific criteria for inclusion within the network of human beings who practise it. Cree, in their own view, legitimately exercise and maintain their rights as against alien claimants who fail to conform to criteria of sharing and stewardship. Historically, when white men have apparently conformed to tenets of reciprocity, and contributed

did not organize themselves into distinct politico-territorial units until well after European contact; indeed, as we shall see, it was as a result of their contact with the Canadian state that they first began to think and act in such terms.

Before turning to the rise of territorially ordered political organization in the Yukon, it is worth noting that despite McClellan's (tentative and qualified) use of the term "ownership" to refer to moieties' special relationship with particular hunting areas and fishing sites, moieties' relationship to "their" lands and resources differed fundamentally from states' assertion of property relations and jurisdiction. Moieties had an obligation to "care" for their lands. This is not to say that local headmen were expected to be wise stewards of the land and resources in an environmentalist sense (an obligation some would argue nation states have with respect to "their" lands); rather, they had a responsibility to manage social relations between humans and the powerful other-than-human beings who inhabit the boreal forest (a responsibility that might or might not coincide with the expectations of environmental stewardship; see Nadasdy 2005a for a detailed discussion of this distinction). This not only meant ensuring that human people in the region interacted in appropriate ways with animal-people (Nadasdy 2005a; Nadasdy 2007b); it also involved communicating with, honouring, and sometimes placating rivers, mountains, and other powerful and sentient landforms by holding potlatches in their honour and performing other ritual practices (McClellan 1975: 483–5). Far from being "resources" to be "managed" by humans exercising jurisdiction/ownership over them, these other-than-human persons were important political actors in their own right. Indeed, as we shall see in chapter 3, Yukon Indian people regarded themselves as among the least powerful inhabitants of the boreal forest; and it was animal- rather than human-people who initially laid down many of the laws that still govern not only human–animal but also human–human relations in the Yukon. Thus, what on the surface may appear analogous to a form of state territoriality (e.g., moiety "ownership" of hunting and fishing

---

to stewardship of resources, they have been accorded a measure of legitimate participation in the Cree system. Thus, when white men fail these standards, evasion or opposition is deemed legitimate by Cree." See also Carlson (2008) for a detailed historical account of European efforts to conform to – and later reject and undermine – these Cree social standards.

areas) was in fact part of a fundamentally different way of relating to the land and animals.

The Expanding State, Territoriality, and First Nation Land Claims

Although indigenous Yukon political organization did change in response to the fur trade (which began to affect the region by the middle of the nineteenth century), the pace of change accelerated markedly in the 1940s and 1950s, when federal officials began asserting control over the lands and peoples of the Canadian north. To this end, they divided the nomadic indigenous population into distinct administrative "bands," each with its own elected chief and council. These bands, created under the federal Indian Act, had no relation to any existing indigenous politico-territorial units (which, as we have seen, did not exist); rather, they were composed of different families who had in many cases very different patterns of seasonal movement and who had settled in a number of central locations. This is not to say that Indian Act bands had no relationship whatsoever to the geographical distribution of Yukon Indian peoples at the time of their creation; it is simply to suggest that the situation was too complex to allow for any straightforward 1 to 1 mapping along those lines. McClellan (1975: 481) characterizes the situation as follows: "Most of the modern government 'bands' have probably been organized on the basis of aboriginal territorial groupings, in the sense that those individuals who most often came together in the past probably segregated into the particular local groups that first built their cabins around a particular trading post, mining centre, church or school. Yet each such centre also attracted other families whose ties to the nuclear group were loose or non-existent." What is more, families that came together at the same trading post at certain times of the year – and so ended up in the same band – often ranged over very different country at other times of the year.[20] Julie Cruikshank (1985: 176–7, personal communication) suggests that band composition was shaped in large part by the construction of the Alaska and Klondike highways. Within several decades of their construction, most Yukon Indian people

20 Some families that ended up in the Burwash band, for example, spent much of their year along the Donjek and White Rivers, while others were oriented more in the direction of Kloo Lake and the Alsek drainage.

had relocated (sometimes having been coerced to do so) to highway settlements, many of which were eventually designated as bands.

The enforced settlement of nomadic populations in easily accessible locations is a strategy that has been used by expanding states the world over; it enables officials to assert control over these peoples and to provide them with government programs and services. The bands themselves, despite having elected chiefs and councils, had little real self-government authority and acted instead as bureaucratic intermediaries between the federal government and local populations, helping to administer government programs such as the provision of social assistance, medical care, and housing (Coates 1991: 233). Thus, the geographical division of the indigenous Yukon population into separate administrative bands had more to do with federal administrative objectives than with any cultural or linguistic factors. In fact, as we shall see, the federal government occasionally amalgamated and otherwise reorganized previously distinct bands for purely administrative reasons, principally to streamline and decrease the cost of service delivery (Nadasdy 2012).

With the signing of land claim and self-government agreements, self-governing First Nations have replaced Indian Act bands throughout much of the Yukon. Although the transformation from band to First Nation has led to some important changes in their demographic composition, there is a great deal of continuity between these new self-governing First Nations and their Indian Act predecessors. To some extent, this was probably inevitable. As we saw in the introduction, Yukon Indian people were loath to enter into a Yukon-wide agreement, preferring instead a series of individual First Nation final agreements that would allow them to address local issues and concerns. Since popularly elected band governments already existed throughout the territory when land claims negotiations began in the 1970s, these intermediaries between the federal government and Yukon Indian people naturally played an important role in the process. It was individual bands that entered into negotiations with the federal and territorial governments and ultimately became signatories to the agreements. In fact, in everyday conversation, people regularly referred to "band final agreements" (rather than the official "First Nation final agreements") through the mid-1990s.

The political continuity between Indian Act bands and self-governing First Nations is also evident in the fact that First Nations inherited responsibility for the delivery of programs and services that had previously been administered by bands (and, as we saw in the introduction, funding levels for First Nation self-government were based directly on the bands' historical spending levels). Although First Nations have also assumed responsibility for additional programs and services that were not administered by bands, there is nevertheless an important sense in which self-governing First Nations evolved from the Indian Act bands that preceded them. The current configuration of First Nations in the Yukon, then, reflects quite closely the legacy of the Canadian Department of Indian Affairs' administration of Indian people in the territory.

The Territorial Dimensions of the Yukon Land Claims Agreements

Despite the continuities, there are some very important differences between Indian Act bands and the self-governing First Nations that have succeeded them. Primary among these is the fact that, unlike bands, First Nations are political entities whose powers and authorities are territorially constituted. As noted above, the two principal forms of First Nation territory created by the agreements are traditional territories and settlement lands. Both are defined and mapped in First Nation final agreements, and, as we shall see, they are integral to the structure of both final and self-government agreements. They play a particularly important role in the new regime for managing wildlife and other natural resources.

Traditional Territories

First Nations do not "own" their traditional territories; but they do retain some rights on these lands that can be viewed as proprietary, including the right to hunt and fish throughout the entire traditional territory.[21] When they ratified their agreements, Yukon Indian people exchanged their aboriginal right to hunt anywhere in Canada for the

21 The right to hunt can be viewed as residual usufructuary right (see Nadasdy 2002). The agreements also provide First Nations and their citizens with some opportunities for preferential employment and other forms of economic development within their traditional territories.

more limited treaty rights spelled out in their agreements (e.g., Kluane First Nation 2003b: 236). In addition to granting Yukon Indian people residual use-rights of this sort, the agreements also grant First Nations a prominent role in the management of wildlife, heritage, and other resources throughout their traditional territories – primarily through participation in formal co-management processes created under the agreements. Of central importance to First Nations, whose citizens are still heavily dependent upon hunting for their subsistence, is the process for co-managing fish, wildlife, timber, and other renewable resources. Each agreement establishes a Renewable Resources Council (RRC) as the "principal instrument for renewable resource management" throughout a First Nation's traditional territory (ibid.: 241). Composed of members appointed by the Yukon and First Nation governments, RRCs make management recommendations directly to the relevant Yukon minister (usually the minister of the environment) and/or First Nation.[22] Thus, traditional territories have become significant administrative units for the management of renewable resources throughout the Yukon.

The federal and Yukon governments did not play a major role in the original creation of First Nation traditional territorial boundaries; instead, they left it up to the bands to work these out among themselves, presumably based on patterns of historic land use. Several officials (both federal and territorial) told me their governments had been loath to get involved in disputes over territory among the different bands and so had left it to them to draw up their own traditional territory boundaries. Yet, as we have seen, administrative bands were themselves recent and fairly arbitrary amalgamations of different families and individuals, each with their own historically distinct patterns of land use and residency. In some cases, members of the same immediate family – with very similar land-use practices – became members of different administrative bands. Intermarriage among members of different bands was also common. These factors, along with increased individual mobility, rendered extremely problematic any attempt to map a band's traditional territory based on the historical use and occupancy

22 Who gets the recommendation depends on which government (First Nation or Yukon) and which department within a government has jurisdiction over the matter in question.

Figure 5 Entering Kluane First Nation Territory (photo by author)

of its members and their ancestors.[23] What is more, there was little coordination among First Nations in mapping their territorial boundaries, and First Nations seem to have pursued different strategies when confronted with the task. Some took an inclusive approach, drawing their boundaries as widely as possible to capture the historic land use of all their members; others were more conservative, giving up their claim to certain areas in an apparent effort to minimize potential overlap with other First Nations. The amalgamated Kluane Tribal Council (see below) seems to have taken the latter approach, since a number of areas used by Kluane people and/or their ancestors now fall well outside their traditional territory.[24]

---

23 See Thom (2009) for discussion of a similar situation among the Coast Salish on Vancouver Island.

24 These include the region around Kloo Lake and McKinley Creek as well as the Ladue and Nisling valleys, all of which were used by various members of KTC and/or their ancestors.

There are three direct results of this ad hoc and uncoordinated process for drawing up First Nation traditional territory boundaries. First, there is a great deal of overlap among First Nation traditional territories in the Yukon (see map 3). Some First Nations are in a situation where well over half their traditional territories overlap with those of their neighbours. Second, there are a few areas in the Yukon that do not fall within any First Nation's traditional territory. The largest of these is located in the southwest Yukon. Dubbed "the black hole," it includes a large portion of the Nisling River valley northeast of Kluane First Nation territory (see map 3).[25] Third, some Yukon Indian people feel that they have been cheated, because they have lost all say in the management of – and, in the case of the black hole, the right to hunt as Indian people in – certain areas of special importance to them personally and to their families. As a result, the issue of traditional territory boundaries has become quite contentious in some parts of the Yukon.

Although the federal and Yukon governments played a minimal role in the creation of traditional territory boundaries per se, they were adamant about the need to minimize and even eliminate overlap. Because traditional territories are primarily administrative units that determine the jurisdiction of various management boards and councils set up under the land claim agreements, any territorial overlap necessarily creates jurisdictional conflict. In anticipation of this problem, First Nation final agreements require First Nations to "resolve" any overlap by negotiating an "Overlap Resolution Boundary," a contiguous line that in effect eliminates the conflict by specifying where one board's jurisdiction begins and another's ends (e.g., Kluane First Nation 2003b: 37). Until overlap is resolved in this way, overlap areas exist in a jurisdictional void, and several very important provisions of the final agreements do not apply within them. This poses a particularly acute problem in the arena of resource management, because Renewable Resources Councils have no jurisdiction at all in overlap areas. Although this way of handling overlap does prevent jurisdictional conflicts between Renewable Resources Councils, it also means that Yukon Indian people have virtually no say over the management of

---

25 The only other sizeable area in the Yukon not included within any First Nation traditional territory lies between the Kluane and Champagne/Aishihik territories. It poses less of a problem for First Nations, however, because it is composed of uninhabited and virtually inaccessible mountains and ice fields.

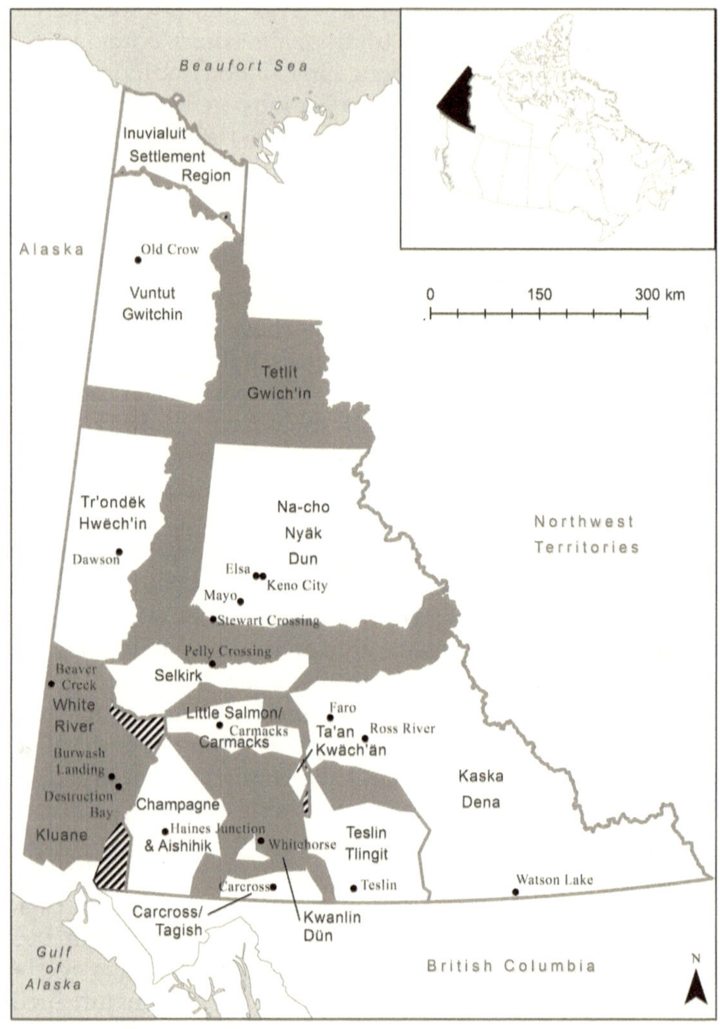

Map 3 First Nation traditional territory overlap in the Yukon by Tracy Sallaway (Maps, Data and Government Information Centre, Trent University). Shading denotes overlap; cross-hatching indicates areas not included in any First Nation traditional territory. Contains information licensed under the Open Government License – Canada (http://open.canada.ca/en/open-government-licence-canada); all other data – Geomatics, Department of Environment, Government of Yukon.

fish, wildlife, and timber in overlap areas (except on settlement lands in those areas, to be discussed below).[26]

In theory, overlap resolution boundaries would be used only to establish the jurisdiction of a few co-management boards and to bring a handful of other provisions (mostly regarding economic development) into effect in the overlap areas. For most other things, including the exercise of hunting rights, the First Nations could continue to "share" the overlap areas (i.e., citizens of both First Nations could hunt there); and, in fact, there has been some interest in and activity around the negotiation of "sharing accords" among neighbouring First Nations. These are reciprocal agreements that go beyond the shared use of overlap areas by extending to one another's citizens certain rights, particularly hunting rights, throughout the signatory First Nations' *entire* traditional territories.[27] In practice, however, the negotiation of overlap resolution boundaries has often been contentious and difficult. This is not surprising, since it requires Yukon Indian people to do something they have never done before: construct firm political boundaries between themselves and their neighbours (who are, often enough, close kin). The notion of a contiguous line separating "us" from "them" flies in the face of important cultural values of kinship and reciprocity, which continue to structure social relations among Yukon Indians people (Nadasdy 2003: chap. 2; see also Easton 2007; Thom 2009).[28]

Technically, First Nations could continue to share most everything in the overlap area, since an overlap resolution boundary applies only to certain jurisdictional issues, but in my experience this is often poorly understood. The very term "traditional territory," with its invocation of

26 In KFN's agreement, the Kluane Park Management Board is the other important co-management board that has no jurisdiction in overlap areas. Indeed, the Kluane Park Agreement (attached to chapter 10 of KFN's final agreement), which not only establishes the board but also spells out KFN hunting and fishing rights within the park, does not apply in overlap areas. There are other provisions as well that do not come into effect in overlap areas, including some regarding heritage, forestry, and economic development. For a complete list of provisions not in effect in overlap areas, see Kluane First Nation (2003b: 35, 39–40, 44).

27 The three Northern Tutchone First Nations of the central Yukon signed and ratified a Sharing Accord in 1995. The three Southern Tutchone First Nations, including KFN and CAFN, also signed such an accord, but KFN never ratified it for reasons discussed below.

28 Hans Carlson (2008: 215–16), too, vividly describes Cree hunters' discomfort with drawing territorial boundaries among themselves.

"tradition," seems to imply a link to historical use and occupancy, and Yukon Indian people (along with government negotiators) by and large think of them in this way. Yet, any well-defined territorial boundary between First Nations must necessarily be cross-cut by kinship relations and inconsistent with both historical and contemporary patterns of use and occupancy. What is more, for many Yukon Indian people, traditional territories have become emblematic of what they see as their special connection to the land and their long history upon it, a phenomenon closely bound up with emerging attachments to national "homelands," to be discussed in chapter 4. As a result, there is often great reluctance to "give up" land to neighbouring First Nations through the "resolution" of overlap, because to many this seems tantamount to denying their affective ties to the land derived from historical and contemporary use. As we will see in chapter 4, this is precisely what happened in failed efforts to resolve overlap between the Kluane and White River First Nation territories.

Those areas, such as the black hole, that fall outside the bounds of any traditional territory present First Nations with a different set of issues. Although such lands constitute but a tiny percentage of the total area of the Yukon, their exceptional status illustrates just how important traditional territories are for structuring First Nation hunting and management rights in the post–land claims Yukon. Falling as they do outside all First Nation traditional territories, areas like the black hole do not come under the jurisdiction of any Renewable Resources Council at all – in effect giving the Yukon government a disproportionate role in wildlife management there.[29] The issues posed by these administrative anomalies are even more significant with respect to hunting rights. By ratifying their agreements, citizens of self-governing First Nations have lost their aboriginal right to hunt in the black hole, without having gained any treaty-based hunting right to replace it.[30] If they wish to hunt on such lands legally, they now have no choice but to obtain

29 These areas do still fall under the jurisdiction of the Yukon Fish and Wildlife Management Board, a co-management board established under the Yukon Umbrella Final Agreement with jurisdiction over the entire Yukon. Given the much broader scope of the board's authority, however, it is unlikely its members could devote as much focused attention to issues in the black hole as could more "local" members of an RRC.

30 The members of First Nations that have not ratified a final agreement, such as WRFN, retain their aboriginal right to hunt in the black hole.

a Yukon hunting licence and abide by Yukon hunting regulations like any non-Indian resident hunter.[31]

In practical terms, obtaining a Yukon hunting licence is not a problem for Yukon Indian people, but to do so is to submit to the authority of the Yukon Fish and Wildlife Branch. As I have detailed elsewhere (Nadasdy 2003: 38–41), fish and game laws were among the principal mechanisms used by federal and territorial officials to establish and maintain control over Yukon Indian people, and the consequences of their imposition were especially dire in the southwest Yukon, where in the 1940s they threatened Yukon Indian peoples' very survival. Indeed, opposition to Yukon fish and game laws was one of the prime factors motivating Yukon Indian people to organize politically and push for the settlement of land claims in the 1970s. They had been staunch defenders of what they saw as their aboriginal hunting rights and would never have agreed to a treaty that subjected them to Yukon hunting regulations (ibid.: 55). That they must now do so in the black hole and a few other such areas not only highlights how important traditional territories are for structuring contemporary Yukon Indian hunting rights, it also shows just how unanticipated and problematic anomalous areas of this sort are for the territorial regime established by the agreements.[32]

31 First Nation citizens, however, do have a treaty right to hunt on settlement lands within the black hole. Kluane First Nation, for example, has an 18.9 km^2 parcel of settlement land at the junction of Onion Creek and the Nisling River, well inside the black hole (see Kluane First Nation 2003b: 238).

32 That no First Nation of the central or southwest Yukon claimed the black hole as part of its traditional territory does not mean it was historically unimportant to them. On the contrary, the Nisling River valley has long been a vital hunting and (especially) fishing area for people throughout the region (Easton, Kennedy, and Bouchard 2013: 51, 104, 132, 155–60, 172; Hayes 1892: 122; McClellan 1975: 30–1, 483). See also 1977 interview with Sophie Watt (translated by Billy Joe); Yukon Archives, Kluane First Nation Collection, accession number SR234-(1). Several KFN citizens regularly hunted and trapped in the valley (mostly in winter) throughout the period of my fieldwork and continue to do so into the present. Before the construction of the Alaska Highway, the Nisling valley was also at the nexus of a set of important trade and travel routes. It was on the "Carmacks trail" that linked the Yukon River to the upper White River, with branches connecting to Kluane Lake, Aishihik, and the Donjek/White River country (Easton, Kennedy, and Bouchard 2013: 112; Johnson and Raup 1964: 196). A couple of kilometres above the Nisling's confluence with the Donjek River lie the remains of Lynx City, a key settlement in the region until its abandonment about 1940 (see map 8). The historical use and occupancy of Lynx City epitomizes the cosmopolitanism of pre-1950s Yukon Indian society. It was a

Settlement Lands

In contrast to traditional territories, where First Nations retain only some residual use and management rights, settlement land is clearly a form of property. Much smaller than the traditional territories within which they are located, the parcels that comprise settlement land are owned by First Nations, who are deemed to possess in them "the rights, obligations and liabilities equivalent to fee simple"[33] (Kluane First Nation 2003b: 67) (see map 2).

But settlement lands are not simply a form of First Nation property; they also define the territorial limits of a self-governing First Nation's full political, legal, and administrative jurisdiction. It is on their settlement lands – and only on their settlement lands – that Yukon First

---

meeting place for Southern Tutchone speakers from Kluane, Aishihik, and Kloo Lakes; Upper Tanana people from the Yukon/Alaska borderlands; and Northern Tutchone people from along the Yukon River – all of whom were connected to one another by ties of marriage and kinship. Gotthardt et al. (2004: 6) note that "at one time, many large potlatches were held [at Lynx City] and it was said that approximately 16 people were buried [there]. Many people lived [there] year round, and when they left, they dispersed to Snag, Burwash or Beaver Creek." The well-known Copper family, whose descendants are now citizens of half a dozen First Nations in the central and southwest Yukon, was based in the Nisling and lower Donjek valleys (Gotthardt, Robinson, and Skuce 2004; Easton, Kennedy, and Bouchard 2013: 161–2; McClellan et al. 1987: 301), and there are still elders alive today – in various contemporary First Nations – who were born at Lynx City and/or spent many of their younger years in and around the Nisling valley. Although Lynx City itself falls just within several First Nations' traditional territories (Kluane and White River First Nations of the southwest Yukon and the Selkirk First Nation of the central Yukon), the fact that most of the Nisling valley is not part of any traditional territory at all must be attributed to the ad hoc and uncoordinated nature of the boundary-making process. Prior to ratification of its final agreement, Kluane First Nation attempted to rectify this problem by amending its traditional territory to include the black hole, but it was unable to obtain the required consent of all Yukon First Nations. The chief stumbling block was territorial overlap with White River First Nation (see chapter 4 and Nadasdy 2012).

33 The reason for this somewhat strange phrasing is that under their final agreements First Nations retain aboriginal rights and title to most of their settlement lands (Kluane First Nation 2003b: 18, 65). The exact nature of aboriginal title remains undefined, but it is deemed for purposes of the agreements to be at least equivalent to fee simple. To further complicate matters, the agreements actually define three different categories of settlement land – category A, category B, and fee simple – and the exact nature of First Nation rights differs for each. Chapter 5 of the Yukon agreements (e.g., Kluane First Nation 2003b: 65–79) lays out these rights in detail.

Figure 6 Entering Kluane First Nation settlement land (photo by author)

Nations exercise full self-government authority, including significant powers of governance, taxation, management, regulation, and administration (Kluane First Nation 2003b: 68; Kluane First Nation 2003a).[34] It is for this reason that the federal government was reluctant to agree to a First Nation's selection of settlement land[35] outside its traditional territory – and then only with the consent of the First Nation within whose traditional territory the selection lies.[36] Consent was deemed necessary

34 It should be noted that First Nations also have a set of powers, particularly relating to governance and the delivery of services to their own citizens, that are not confined to settlement land (Kluane First Nation 2003a: 13–14).

35 For a discussion of the settlement-land selection process, see Nadasdy (2008).

36 Kluane First Nation, for example, has five parcels of settlement land that lie outside its traditional territory. By far the largest of these (at 18.9 km^2) is located in the black hole (see note 31). The other four are small site-specific selections within CAFN's territory. The largest of these is a 15-hectare parcel near the village of Haines Junction, approximately 120 km south of Burwash Landing. Since there is no high school in

Figure 7 Kluane First Nation signing ceremony, Burwash Landing, 18 October 2003. Kluane First Nation's chief negotiator Robin Bradasch signing settlement lands maps, which form an appendix to KFN's final agreement (photo by author)

because these parcels of settlement land become embassy-like pockets of jurisdictional exception within another First Nation's traditional territory. Consent from another First Nation was also generally required when a First Nation chose a parcel of settlement land in an overlap area *within* its own traditional territory, because, depending on the location of any overlap resolution boundary, jurisdictional issues might be nearly as complex in overlap areas as outside the traditional territory altogether.

Especially significant for the purposes of this chapter is the fact that First Nations have full jurisdiction over hunting and many other forms of land use on settlement lands, category A settlement lands in

Burwash, KFN students (along with their parents) often relocate to Haines Junction for several years so they can attend school there. KFN selected land in Haines Junction so it could provide housing for its citizens residing there.

particular (Kluane First Nation 2003a: 14). First Nation jurisdiction on these lands interacts in complex ways with the Yukon government's jurisdiction over wildlife on non-settlement land. While a Yukon First Nation has the power to regulate its own citizens' hunting throughout its traditional territory,[37] the Yukon government has final jurisdiction over non-Indian hunting on non-settlement lands. All non–First Nation citizens must obtain a Yukon hunting licence to hunt in the Yukon. This entitles them to hunt anywhere in the Yukon except on First Nation Category A Settlement lands, which are owned and exclusively managed by First Nations. Hunting on all lands is subject to regulation by the government that has jurisdiction over wildlife management on the land in question – First Nation governments on settlement land, the Yukon government on non-settlement land. First Nation governments may permit non–First Nation citizens to hunt on their lands, and may charge them a fee to do so, but those hunters are then subject to First Nation wildlife laws as well as general Yukon hunting laws (see, e.g., Kluane First Nation 2003b: provisions 16.5.0 and 16.12.0).

Imposing Territoriality in the Southwest Yukon

The new territorial divisions created by the Yukon agreements were initially devoid of social meaning for most Yukon Indian people. Over time, however, this has begun to change. Like Thongchai's maps of Siam, the maps attached to the Yukon land claim agreements were created as models for a new territorially ordered form of governance, as mechanisms for the creation of a particular system of legal, administrative, and jurisdictional relations. To the extent that they now undergird a complex system of political and legal relations, these maps and the territories they create have gradually assumed significance not only in the realm of indigenous–state relations, but among Yukon Indian people as well. As we shall see in chapter 4, one of the most

37 First Nations also have the power to regulate the hunting of other First Nation's citizens in areas that lie "within the geographical jurisdiction of the [Renewable Resources] Council established for that First Nation's Traditional Territory" (Kluane First Nation 2003b:238–239). This means that in overlap areas where there is no overlap resolution boundary, First Nations can only regulate hunting by their own citizens; citizens of another First Nation may be subject to different regulations on the same land (see also Kluane First Nation 2003b:35, 40, 44).

important manifestations of this is the rise of ethno-territorial nationalism among First Nations. Closely associated with this, however, is what Vandergeest and Peluso (1995: 389) refer to as the "territorialization of resource control," upon which I will focus for the remainder of this chapter.

Vandergeest and Peluso note that "all modern states divide their territories into complex and overlapping political and economic zones, rearrange people and resources within these units, and create regulations delineating how and by whom these areas can be used. These zones are administered by agencies whose jurisdictions are territorial as well as functional." And they argue further that the maps created by these bureaucratic agencies play "a central role in the implementation and legitimation of territorial rule" (ibid.: 387). In Canada, as elsewhere, the imposition of state regimes for the management of wildlife and other renewable resources has played an important role in this territorializing process, which has taken place on multiple scales. The federal government long ago devolved the management of fish and wildlife to the provinces and territories, which generally have jurisdiction over these matters within their respective borders.[38] But the provinces/territories are also themselves internally territorialized. The Yukon government, for example, has subdivided the entire Yukon into game management zones and subzones (see map 4). At the same time, other government maps subdivide the Yukon into conservation officer districts, outfitting concessions, and/or trapping concessions (see maps 5–7). Although they overlap and otherwise fail to correspond to one another, each

38 In fact, however, provincial/territorial jurisdiction over wildlife is complicated by several factors. First, the federal government retains jurisdiction over some species, such as salmon and other anadromous fish, which fall under the purview of the federal Department of Fisheries and Oceans. Second, the federal government can pass legislation, such as the Species at Risk Act, and enter into international agreements, such as the Migratory Bird Treaty of 1916 and the 1973 International Agreement on the Conservation of Polar Bears, which impinge upon provincial/territorial jurisdiction over fish and wildlife. Third, because animals do not respect political boundaries, their effective management often requires provinces/territories to work collaboratively with other jurisdictions (a prominent example of this kind of inter-jurisdictional cooperation in the Yukon is the co-management of the Porcupine Caribou herd, which involves cooperation with governments in Alaska and the Northwest Territories).

Map 4 Yukon game management zones and subzones. © Yukon Department of Environment, Information Management & Technology Branch 2016.

of these internally territorializing maps is essential for administering some aspect of human–wildlife (and human–human) relations in the Yukon. As models *for* wildlife management, they (or some earlier version of them) were crucial for developing the administrative mechanisms of the Yukon government's Fish and Wildlife Branch, and they remain vital tools for implementing and enforcing hunting, fishing, and trapping regulations.

Arbitrary as they are, the internal territories created by these maps have come to structure people's actual experiences on the land. Wildlife biologists, for example, tend to bound their wildlife surveys by management subzone; and outfitters and trappers, because they are only legally permitted to guide hunters or trap within their respective

Map 5 Yukon conservation officer districts. © Yukon Department of Environment, Information Management & Technology Branch 2016.

concessions, tend to focus their activities there. As a result, these maps now play a critical role in shaping how wildlife biologists, outfitters, trappers, and others come to know and think about the land and animals. In this way, the arbitrarily drawn internal territories of wildlife management serve to structure the kinds of management interventions that are possible and even *thinkable* by various actors (for analysis of a specific case, see Nadasdy 2003: 193–6).

Yukon First Nation final agreements do not disrupt the territorial order of state wildlife management; on the contrary, they reinforce it by superimposing a new layer of internal management-relevant territories upon the old. Maps of First Nation traditional territories and settlement lands have now joined those showing game management zones and

Map 6 Yukon outfitting concessions. © Yukon Department of Environment, Information Management & Technology Branch 2016.

trapping concessions as important tools for delineating how and by whom Yukon lands and resources can be used.[39] Just as the older administrative maps were models *for* the complex of human–environment relations they helped bring into being, so too the new First Nation final agreement maps envision a new set of relations among humans, the land, and animals; and they take for granted a set of far-reaching social

39 It is perhaps worth noting that maps 1 and 2, which depict First Nation traditional territories and settlement lands, are simplified versions of maps produced by Environment Yukon, the same government agency that produced maps 4–7, and all are available on the same government website, http://www.env.gov.yk.ca/maps.

Map 7 Yukon trapping concessions. © Yukon Department of Environment, Information Management & Technology Branch 2016.

and institutional changes whose intent is to transform that vision into reality. Principal among these changes has been the institutionalization of First Nation "management" through the creation of First Nation bureaucracies modelled on those of the Yukon government.

Because they now have legal jurisdiction over fish and wildlife (and other renewable resources) on their settlement lands and over First Nation hunting throughout their entire traditional territories, self-governing Yukon First Nation governments have had to create their own bureaucratic mechanisms for managing these resources. As in the Yukon government, First Nation resource officers are generally housed within departments that manage all aspects of land and resource use. Kluane First Nation's resource officer, for example, is in charge of managing all renewable resources and answers to the director of KFN's department of lands, resources, and heritage (hereafter, lands department). The creation of First Nation management bureaucracies is having a significant effect on how Yukon Indian people can relate to one another and to the land and animals. One of these effects, predicted by Sack (1986: 33), is that "by classifying at least in part by area rather than by kind or type, territoriality helps make relationships *impersonal*." As the following story illustrates, the replacement of personal by impersonal social relations is an important aspect of the territorialization of resource control in the Yukon.

In the summer of 2006, as we were about to depart for several days of moose hunting around Fourth of July Creek just across the KFN-CAFN border, Joe Johnson surprised me when he told me that in preparation for the hunt he had obtained a Yukon hunting licence. Recall that under the terms of KFN's final agreement, Joe, a KFN citizen, was free to hunt anywhere in KFN's traditional territory without a Yukon hunting licence. To hunt within another First Nation's territory (such as along Fourth of July Creek), however, he had a choice: he could either get permission to hunt there from that First Nation (in this case, CAFN), or he could obtain a Yukon hunting licence in the same fashion as any non-Indian Yukon resident and be subject to Yukon – rather than First Nation – hunting regulations. I was completely taken aback to learn that Joe had chosen the latter option. As noted above, it was no more difficult for him to obtain a Yukon hunting licence than to get permission to hunt from CAFN, but to do so was politically and culturally unpalatable, because it required him to submit to the authority of the Yukon Fish and Wildlife Branch. Indeed, years before, Joe himself had flouted Yukon hunting regulations and risked imprisonment by "illegally" hunting Dall sheep for his father's funeral potlatch, without which, he felt, it would have been impossible to carry out a proper ceremony.[40]

Relations between KFN and CAFN are friendly, and there is considerable day-to-day social interaction between Kluane and Champagne/Aishihik citizens, many of whom, including Joe, have very close relatives (e.g., spouses, parents, children, siblings, or cousins) in the other

40 I put "illegally" in quotes because he killed them in the Kluane Game Sanctuary; had he been caught, he would have been charged under Yukon law. The Yukon Court of Appeal, however, subsequently ruled in *R. v. Michel and Johnson* (1983) that status Indians did, in fact, have an aboriginal right to hunt in the sanctuary.

Figure 8 Joe Johnson at Fourth of July Creek hunting camp, August 2005 (photo by author)

First Nation.[41] Hence my surprise when I learned about his choice to obtain a Yukon hunting licence rather than go through the CAFN lands department. When I asked him why he had done so, he explained that the summer before, the last time he and I had hunted together up Fourth of July Creek, he had asked CAFN for permission to hunt. In response, they sent him a letter granting him permission to hunt there for one specific week only. After telling me this, he looked at me for a while, his eyes smouldering. Then he went on to say that if a CAFN citizen asks for permission to hunt in Kluane territory, "we give them as much time as they want." He said he had decided to get a Yukon licence so he could hunt wherever he wanted and not have to put up with such insulting treatment anymore.

41 Some of Joe's closest relatives were citizens of CAFN, including his paternal uncles, who helped raise him and taught him to hunt.

Two decades before, it would have been almost unthinkable for a Yukon Indian person to deny or limit another's right to hunt anywhere he or she wanted. In light of the continuing cultural and economic importance of First Nation hunting in the Yukon (see Nadasdy 2003: chap. 2) and the colonial legacy of wildlife management in the territory, it is hard even now to imagine one Yukon Indian person denying another's right to hunt. In the case of Joe's application to CAFN the previous year, wildlife officials were able to restrict his ability to hunt in the way they did only because of the prior creation of a bureaucratic apparatus for managing fish and wildlife, a development that was itself wholly dependent upon the creation of jurisdictional boundaries between the two First Nations. CAFN's agreements have been in place since 1995, so by 2006 they were much further along in the process of establishing their own government institutions than KFN, which had been self-governing only since 2004. CAFN had by then established a formal permitting process to deal with requests like Joe's. As a result, the limitation on Joe's ability to hunt was issued not by a specific person, but by the First Nation's bureaucratic apparatus. Thus, Joe's anger was directed not at a specific person acting in a culturally inappropriate manner, but at CAFN's impersonal management bureaucracy.

Joe's impression that KFN regularly and routinely granted citizens from other First Nations permission to hunt in their territory was rooted in his many years of experience in the KFN office where he served in various capacities, including several terms as chief, until his retirement in 1996. During those years, KFN dealt with requests for permission to hunt in an informal, ad hoc, and personalized manner. From my own observations in the KFN office between 1995 and 2003 I, too, got the impression that KFN always granted such requests from citizens of other First Nations; the issuance of letters of permission – mostly to CAFN hunters – had seemed to me little more than a formality. But things began to change after KFN's agreement came into effect on 2 February 2004. On 15 April of that year, the director of KFN's lands department told me that she was regularly fielding calls from CAFN citizens requesting permission to hunt in KFN territory. Since the newly self-governing KFN as yet had no policy in place for dealing with these requests, she said, she had no choice but to deny them permission. She admitted this was a difficult situation, because many of them got quite angry when she told them they could not hunt. She said she hoped KFN and CAFN would soon sign a sharing accord to deal with the problem. In fact, KFN and CAFN, along with the Ta'an Kwäch'än Council (the third member of the Southern Tutchone Tribal Council), had signed a sharing accord back in 1997; but KFN had never ratified it because of concerns about whether they had the legal authority to do so given their 100 per cent overlap with White River First Nation.[42] The legal implications of the overlap issue did not disappear when KFN became self-governing, with the result that there was still no sharing accord in place in 2006 when Joe Johnson wanted to hunt on Fourth of July Creek.

Overlap with WRFN was not the only obstacle to formalizing reciprocal hunting rights between CAFN and KFN citizens. By 2006 there was a growing concern, especially among some younger Kluane citizens, about possible overhunting of moose in KFN's territory owing to encroachment by CAFN citizens. Several of them independently expressed to me their concerns about the number of CAFN citizens who had recently been hunting in the Donjek River valley, deep in Kluane territory. One man – the same, incidentally, who orchestrated the raising of signs on the Alaska Highway to mark the boundaries of Kluane territory (see figure 5) – told me it was imperative that KFN get its government up and running as soon as possible so that Kluane people could control hunting by citizens of other First Nations and thereby protect their animal populations. The implication of his statement was clear: without an impersonal bureaucratic screen of laws and regulatory processes in place, it would remain very difficult for any KFN citizen to deny – or provide only limited approval to – requests by citizens of other First Nations to hunt in Kluane territory.

As of 2016, the Southern Tutchone First Nations have yet to ratify a sharing accord. In fact, much of what I describe above has since become institutionalized: as a matter of policy, CAFN issues permits that are valid for two weeks only and are also species-specific. CAFN is a bit unusual because of its proximity to Whitehorse; other First Nations generally respond to requests for permission to hunt by issuing permits that are good for the whole season. By contrast, KFN does not currently

42 Kluane and White River First Nations emerged as distinct political entities following the 1990 break-up of the Kluane Tribal Council (KTC itself had been the result of the 1961 amalgamation of the Kluane and White River bands). Because traditional territory boundaries had by then already been agreed upon by the parties to the UFA, Kluane and White River found themselves with 100% territorial overlap. See chapter 4 for an extended discussion of this overlap and the social and political complications to which it has given rise.

grant citizens of other First Nations permission to hunt in its territory at all. One Kluane citizen who worked for a time in KFN's lands department acknowledged that this causes anger among those whose requests are denied, but defended the policy as necessary for protecting Kluane animal populations.

The Instability of the Territorial System

It is becoming increasingly common to hear Yukon Indian people invoke the language of territoriality to assert their First Nation's exclusive rights to control the resources within its traditional territory. But territorial sentiments of this sort do not always take precedence over cross-cutting relations of kinship and reciprocity. Non-territorial principles governing social relations remain strong among Yukon Indian people and provide the basis for a trenchant moral critique of the new territorial regime. Vandergeest and Peluso (1995: 389–91) note that territorialized resource management regimes are often unstable due to factors ranging from the state's inability to enforce them in the face of local resistance to conflict among government agencies with competing territorial mandates. Because of "the lack of fit between lived space and abstract space," they argue, a government's territorial strategy for controlling resources is "often a utopian fiction unachievable in practice because of how it ignores and contradicts peoples' lived social relationships and the histories of their interactions with the land" (ibid. 389). The territorialized resource management system in the Yukon is unstable for some of the same reasons.

One source of the new territorial regime's instability is its own complexity. Even a cursory comparison of maps 1, 2, and 4–7 reveals inconsistencies across and among the internal territories created for wildlife management in the Yukon; they cross-cut, overlap, and otherwise fail to correspond to one another. The result is a territorial regime of such complexity that even officials in the Yukon Department of Environment can sometimes get confused. In 2007, for example, a member of the Dän Keyi Renewable Resources Council (DKRRC)[43] told me that Yukon government officials had recently contacted the

43 This is the Renewable Resources Council established pursuant to KFN's final agreement.

council to inform them that they were planning to conduct fisheries research in two lakes within the council's jurisdiction: Tincup and Wellesley Lakes. He told me that the council had thanked them for the heads-up but politely informed them that Wellesley Lake was actually well outside the council's jurisdiction. Shaking his head, he told me that the government biologists had seemed completely unaware of the terms of KFN's agreement and the jurisdictional implications it has for wildlife management in the region.[44] Similarly, in 2011 I learned that a CAFN citizen had recently shot a moose within the no-hunting corridor along the Alaska Highway near the Duke River on KFN settlement land. KFN officials wanted the Yukon government to charge him for hunting illegally,[45] but the regional conservation officer had refused, claiming he had no authority to do so because KFN and CAFN were both signatories of the Southern Tutchone sharing accord. The conservation officer had then been surprised to learn that KFN had never ratified the accord (back in 1997) and promised that in the future he would bear that in mind.[46]

If even Yukon government officials – whose job it is to know these things – can sometimes be unclear on the details of the new resource management regime, it should hardly come as a surprise that Yukon Indian hunters and the general public, too, sometimes have trouble keeping it all straight. This general ignorance of a complex regime contributes to its instability; yet, for many Yukon Indian hunters, something

44 The situation here is particularly complex because it involves special provisions in KFN's agreement designed to deal with the fact that Kluane and White River First Nations have 100% overlap. See chapter 4 for a detailed discussion of the situation and a map (9) from KFN's agreement that shows Wellesley Lake well outside the area over which the DKRRC has jurisdiction.

45 Unless and until KFN negotiates terms by which it will assume powers of law enforcement and justice (see Kluane First Nation 2003a: 17–19), it is Yukon – rather than KFN – officers who are charged with enforcing both KFN and Yukon laws.

46 There are different ways one might interpret these incidents of official ignorance. Andrew Mathews (2008) shows that the "ignorance" of state officials is sometimes the product of delicate negotiations with their political superiors, on one hand, and their "clients" and/or the local population, on the other. See also Nadasdy (2003: 56–9). I do not have sufficient information about these incidents to offer an analysis of this sort, but the possibility certainly exists that something other than simple ignorance was involved, especially in the second case.

more than mere ignorance is at work. Unlike Yukon government officials, who accept – even take for granted – the underlying territorial premise of the new management regime, the same cannot be said for many Yukon Indian hunters.

Yukon Indian people, like indigenous peoples elsewhere, long chafed under hunting and trapping regulations imposed upon them by state wildlife managers. It was not merely the specific regulations that they resented (although some of these were, in fact, quite onerous), but also the very idea of management itself. The idea of wildlife management, rooted as it is in the political and economic context of capitalist resource extraction (Bavington 2010; Nadasdy 2007a) and based on an agricultural metaphor (Nadasdy 2011), sits uneasily alongside Yukon Indian people's ideas about proper human–human and human–animal relations. For them, hunting entails participation in a complex web of reciprocal social relations among human and other-than-human persons (Nadasdy 2003: chap. 2; Nadasdy 2007b). To be sure, these relationships can at times be difficult and fraught with danger, so hunters must manage them with considerable care. But this kind of "management" is an intensely personal affair, involving introspection and self-control rather than the coercion of others. The idea that some outsider – who is by definition ignorant of the delicate and complex web of social relations in which the hunter is enmeshed – should dictate the terms of the hunt is anathema to the maintenance of proper interpersonal relations among persons. And the idea that regulations, along with the authority to make them, should vary according to arbitrarily defined geographical areas, rather than the particularities of those interpersonal relations, verges on the nonsensical. Finally, I would note that the very act of regulating the behaviour of others by telling them directly what they are permitted to do and where is itself deeply inconsistent with the norms of proper social interaction among Athapaskan peoples (Goulet 1998; Nadasdy 2003: 102–8).

Thus, although the new agreements do grant First Nation governments significant new powers to manage and co-manage renewable resources throughout their territories, the very exercise of those powers threatens to transform the ways in which Yukon Indian people relate to animals and, perhaps even more significantly, to one another with respect to animals. The fact that it is now First Nation – rather than Yukon – government officials who claim the authority to interfere with the interpersonal relations of the hunt by dictating to hunters what they may and may not do and where does not seem like much of an improvement to many Yukon Indian hunters.[47] As a result, some – even among those who may be otherwise supportive of the new agreements – find ways around the territorial regime of resource management or else refuse to comply with it altogether.

A case in point: one of the first acts of the newly self-governing Kluane First Nation in 2004 was to institute a permit system for the cutting of firewood on its settlement lands. Nearly five years earlier, a fire had raged through the area, nearly burning down the village and leaving a 12-kilometre-long swathe of easily accessible standing dead timber. The new permit system was primarily intended to control the harvest of firewood by commercial cutters from as far away as Haines Junction and even Whitehorse. Permits to cut firewood for personal use were issued free to Kluane citizens and other local residents, although they did specify where the permit holders were allowed to cut. For non-Indian people, including commercial cutters, the new system was but a minor change; it simply meant getting a permit from KFN rather than from the federal government, as they had previously been required to do. For KFN citizens, however, who up until then had had the aboriginal right to cut firewood anywhere they wanted without a permit, it meant submitting to the territorial authority of a government, in this case that of Kluane First Nation. Even though permits were free to KFN citizens, and the lands department granted its citizens permits to cut wherever they requested, there was a great deal of grumbling in the village about the new policy. Some KFN citizens refused outright to obtain permits on the grounds that no one had the right to tell them when, where, or how much firewood they could cut to heat their homes. Indeed, it seems that Yukon Indian people now increasingly view their own First Nation management bureaucracies – along with co-management bodies such as the Renewable Resources Councils – with considerable suspicion, simply because they have assumed the role of "managers." In 2007, the executive director of the Dän Keyi Renewable Resources Council and two of its members independently complained to me that local residents seemed to regard the RRC as "the enemy" – even though RRC members are all local residents as well.

---

47 For a similar dynamic at Lac du Flambeau in northern Wisconsin, see Nesper (2007).

Even when Yukon Indian people do abide by the new rules, they are sometimes able to subvert the impersonal bureaucratic control imposed by the new territorializing agreements. The agreements may even be giving rise to new kinds of social relationships that cross-cut traditional territory boundaries. For example: because Yukon Indian hunters can effectively avoid the need to obtain a hunting permit from another First Nation if they are accompanied on the hunt by a citizen of that First Nation (who can claim to have done the shooting), at least some hunters are cultivating a Yukon-wide network of "hunting buddies" upon whom they can prevail when they want to hunt outside their own First Nation's territory. One KFN hunter told me that he has hunting buddies all over the Yukon. The first thing he does if he wants to hunt in another First Nation's territory is to phone one of his buddies there. Only if none of them is available to hunt with him does he formally request permission to hunt from the First Nation government in question. By 2016, this practice had become so widespread that a member of the Dän Keyi Renewable Resources Council complained to me that so many citizens of other First Nations were now hunting with KFN citizens in KFN's traditional territory that the First Nation's refusal to grant them hunting permits had become almost irrelevant.

In light of all this, it would be inaccurate to claim that Yukon Indian people have internalized the new management regime and its territorial assumptions. Nor can one say that the new agreements have completely transformed Yukon Indian people's relationship to the land and resources. But there can be little doubt that the new territorializing maps and boundaries function as "models for" a powerful new system of legal and administrative relations. While this system has not replaced indigenous ways of relating to one another and the land, it does undermine them and poses a serious obstacle to those Yukon Indian people who would continue to relate to the land and animals – and to one another – as their grandparents did. Those who choose to do so often transgress not only Yukon but now also their own First Nation's laws, risking fines and possibly even imprisonment in the process. Even when Yukon Indian people find creative ways to subvert the new territorial system (through the cultivation of hunting buddies, for example), they must grapple with and adjust their practice to accommodate it. Thus, the new territorial system must be seen for what it is: a powerful engine for social-ecological change.

Conclusion

Although I maintain that land claim and self-government agreements in the Yukon are imposing a new territorial political order in the Yukon, I do not mean to imply that this imposition emanates – in some straightforward top-down fashion – from the Canadian government. Rather, it stems from the agreements themselves. These agreements resulted from decades of struggle against colonial policies; and they grant Yukon First Nations significant powers to govern their peoples and resources. Those powers, however, come in the currency of territorial sovereignty, and to wield them Yukon Indian people have had to alter their forms of social and political organization in dramatic and often unforeseen ways.

In this chapter, we have seen that the territorialization of resource control effected by the agreements has led to a process of bureaucratization that subjects Yukon Indian people to the authority of newly created First Nation states, transforming in the process how they can relate to the land and animals – and to one another with respect to the land and animals (though not always in the ways resource managers intend). The fact that the agreements are having such a transformative effect on human–animal–land relations is significant because the preservation of hunting practices – and the social relations they entail – was one of the principal goals motivating Yukon Indian people to enter into land claim negotiations in the first place. There is, then, a certain political ambiguity in the territorially ordered political system currently emerging in the Yukon. Rooted as it is in colonial administrative practices, the new configuration of territorially constituted First Nations must be viewed as a legacy of colonial rule, of federal efforts to incorporate Yukon Indian peoples more firmly into the Canadian state. At the same time, however, this territorial system is also the product of First Nation resistance to colonial incorporation, a result of more than forty years of struggle and compromise. The new territorially ordered system must therefore be viewed as both an assertion of territorial sovereignty by Yukon First Nations (and recognition of that sovereignty by Canada) and, simultaneously, as a process of internal territorialization that is creating new territorial units within the Canadian state.[48]

48 For an extended discussion of this ambiguous political space in the US context, see Bruyneel (2007).

The territorializing changes wrought by the agreements affect more than just people's access to and control over resources; they impinge on nearly every aspect of Yukon Indian people's lives. And, as we shall see, all the changes associated with the imposition of territoriality have the same ambiguous political character that we see in the territorialization of resource control. Among the most significant of these other changes is the emergence of multiple ethno-territorial identities – and corresponding nationalist sentiments – among Yukon Indian peoples. The rise of First Nation nationalism is a profoundly significant process that not only affects the lives of Yukon Indian people in myriad ways but also has important implications for processes of governance – in the Yukon certainly but also across much of the rest of Canada where similarly territorializing agreements have either already been signed or are currently under negotiation. In the next two chapters, I examine this phenomenon in some detail by looking at the everyday ways of thinking and acting that are engendered by Kluane First Nation's land claim and self-government agreements and analysing how these serve to enact Kluane First Nation as a culturally homogeneous sociopolitical unit, or nation, that is ethnically distinct from other similarly constituted First Nations in the Yukon.

In my analysis, I follow historian Eric Hobsbawm (1992), who distinguishes between two senses of the term *nation*: (1) a political sense in which "the 'nation' … [is] the body of citizens whose collective sovereignty constituted them a state which was their political expression" (ibid.: 18–19),[49] and (2) an ethnic or nationalist sense, in which the nation is comprised of all those who supposedly share a common language, history, or broader ethnic and/or cultural identity.[50] Katherine Verdery (1993a: 38) argues that much confusion in the study of nationalism stems from the conflation/confusion (by nationalists and scholars alike) of these two senses of nationalism. After all, as Hobsbawm (1992: 19) himself notes, there is "no logical connection between the body of citizens of a territorial state on one hand, and the identification of a 'nation' on ethnic, linguistic, or … other characteristics which allowed collective recognition of group interests" on the other. Hobsbawm also

49 He goes on: "For, whatever else a nation was, the element of citizenship and mass participation was never absent from it" (Hobsbawm 1992: 19).

50 Rogers Brubaker (1992: 123) makes a similar distinction between "state-national" and "ethno-national" views of the nation.

notes, however, that although these two senses of the term may be logically distinct, they are seldom so in practice. As we shall see over the course of the next two chapters, the very notion of a "sovereign people," in whose collective interests the state (or state-like First Nation) is supposed to act, implies the existence of a collective citizenry with a set of common interests that set them apart from the citizens of other states (or First Nations); and these common interests often come to be seen as rooted in a set of shared cultural characteristics (e.g., language, history, ethnicity). Indeed, the very act of constituting a collective citizenry through the creation of a state (or state-like political organization) can and often does lead to practices of cultural homogenization and the emergence of ethno-nationalist sentiments.[51] Thus, "nations [in the ethnic sense] are more often the consequence of setting up a state than they are its foundation" (Hobsbawm 1992: 78). The distinction between the two senses of the term *nation*, then, is in practice more often a matter of differing perspectives on a complex historical process than it is a difference between two kinds of nations: "For nationalists the creation of the political entities which would contain [the nation] derived from the prior existence of some community distinguishing itself from foreigners, while from the revolutionary-democratic point of view the central concept was the sovereign citizen-people = state which, in relation to the remainder of the human race, constituted a 'nation'" (ibid.: 22).

In the two chapters to follow, I examine the rise of Yukon First Nation nationalism, though in each chapter I foreground a different one of Hobsbawm's senses of *nation*. In chapter 3, I focus on the institutions and practices of Yukon First Nation citizenship. I show that the very process of constituting the "sovereign people" of whom Yukon First Nations are comprised is simultaneously transforming – in quite profound ways – social relations not only among Yukon Indian people,

51 Many scholars have remarked on the homogenizing tendencies of the state, see e.g., Foster (1991), Handler (1988), Verdery (1996: 89), Williams (1989). Hobsbawm (1992: 19–21) illustrates this tendency nicely in his discussion of the French language and its evolving role in constituting the French nation during the French revolution. Although the ability to speak French was not initially viewed as a criterion for membership in the new French nation (which was determined solely by one's citizenship), one's willingness to acquire French – along with a range of other rights, responsibilities, and characteristics – did quickly come to be viewed as evidence of one's commitment to – and proper belonging within – the French nation (a similar argument can be made regarding English in the United States today).

but also between them and the land and animals with whom they share their territory. Although one may begin to get some inkling in this chapter of how the practices and institutions of citizenship are contributing to the emergence of distinct First Nation ethnicities, it is not until chapter 4 that Hobsbawm's second sense of *nation* (nation-as-ethnicity) moves to the forefront of my analysis. In that chapter, I focus on the rise of ethno-territoriality and associated nationalist sentiments in the southwest Yukon. This development is closely related to processes discussed in chapter 3, but my explicit focus on ethno-territorial nationalism, as opposed to citizenship, provides a somewhat different perspective on the social and environmental changes ushered in by the Yukon land claim and self-government agreements. In both chapters, however, I examine the everyday interactions and practices that produce a sense of belonging to something called the Kluane First Nation[52] (and concomitant sense of separation from other similarly constituted First Nation states in the region). It is through these interactions and practices that Yukon Indian people not only enact Kluane First Nation as a state-like organization but also themselves, collectively, as a nation.

52 This is similar to what John Borneman (1992: 339) refers to as "nationness."

Chapter Three

Citizenship

I'm not a citizen; I'm an Indian.

Gerald Dickson

One afternoon in June 2011, I was drinking coffee with Gerald Dickson in his smoke-filled kitchen in Burwash Landing. Inevitably, the conversation turned to self-government. Although he had worked for many years on Kluane First Nation's land claim and self-government agreements as a researcher and negotiator, Gerald is one of the agreements' staunchest critics. On that day, he recounted a disagreement he had just had with his cousin, a young woman who had recently returned to Burwash to take up her position as KFN's newly elected chief. Because he had voted against the ratification of KFN's agreements, Gerald had told her, he did not see why he should have to abide by them. In response, she had insisted that he must do so because he is a citizen of Kluane First Nation. At this point in the story, he became a bit agitated and told me he had replied: "I'm not a *citizen*; I'm an *Indian*." His grandparents, he went on, had taught him that he was "*dän*, an Indian"; they had never mentioned anything to him about being a "citizen of KFN." What does it even mean, he asked, to be a citizen of KFN? No, he told me, he prefers to continue "living as an Indian," particularly if assuming the status of KFN citizen means being subject to an agreement he explicitly rejected at the ballot box.

Gerald's critique of Kluane First Nation citizenship raises some important and difficult questions about northern First Nation land claim and self-government agreements, and about tribal/First Nation citizenship more generally. To fully understand his critique, however, we need to consider in a bit more detail the meaning of the two terms he used – *Indian* and *dän*. Although he seems to use them interchangeably, they are not, in fact, perfect synonyms. *Dän*, the Southern Tutchone term of self-designation, means "people." It is often used to distinguish Southern Tutchone people from *guch'än* (whitemen), and it is in this sense that Gerald used it as a synonym for *Indian*; but the two words generally have quite different connotations. The meanings of *dän* and *Indian* are both complex and context-dependent but in different ways that do not correspond to one another. For instance, depending on the context of its use, *dän* can either be more or less encompassing than *Indian*. McDonnell (1984) points out that when used in its broadest sense the term *dene* (the cognate of *dän* used by Kaska speakers in the southeast Yukon) encompasses not only all humans (Indian and non-Indian) but other-than-human persons as well. This includes animals along with some objects and phenomena that Euro-Americans would generally not even classify as being alive (Hallowell 1960; Nadasdy 2007b). As we shall see below, this expansive meaning of *dän/dene* is relevant to the discussion of First Nation citizenship, because it encompasses a range of persons generally excluded from the category of citizenship – and so from the realm of politics.

At another level, McDonnell points out, *dän/dene* can be used to distinguish Indians from non-Indians. As noted, this is how Gerald uses it in the above example. Attempts to use the term in this manner are not always successful, however, because Athapaskan audiences are sometimes not receptive to this more restricted meaning (see Goulet 1998: 103). Finally, as McDonnell notes, *dän/dene* can sometimes also be used to indicate the degree of social difference *among* Indian people. In Burwash, for example, *dän* can be used to differentiate Yukon Indian people from other Indians. When used in this way, *dän* does not include Cree people, for instance, whom the northern Athapaskan Indians of the Yukon regard as culturally distinct.[1]

1 The fact that various Athapaskan languages each have their own distinct cognate of this word (in neighbouring Upper Tanana, for example, it is *Dineh*) suggests that they might be used to differentiate among Athapaskan peoples in the Yukon (e.g., *dän* from *dineh*), but I have never heard anyone do this. It is conceivable, however, that with the rise of ethno-territorial nationalism among First Nations discussed in chapter 4, people may begin to use these terms in this way.

A second important difference between the terms *dän* and *Indian* is a legal one; unlike the term *Indian*, *dän* does not invoke the Indian Act, a piece of colonial legislation that defines the legal category *Indian* in Canada and specifies how people who fall into this category are to be governed. Gerald has long been an outspoken critic of the Indian Act, so his preference to "remain an Indian" rather than embrace his KFN citizenship cannot be read as nostalgia for that act or the legal status it created. Indeed, by using *Indian* and *dän* as synonyms, he signalled that he was referring not to the legal definition of *Indian*, but to his self-identification as an indigenous person of the southwest Yukon – that is, to his understanding of what it means, culturally, to be a Yukon Indian person. By explicitly opposing his KFN citizenship to his status as *dän*, Gerald was asserting that KFN citizenship is somehow incompatible with the cultural practices of being *dän* and, thus, that the agreements themselves are somehow incompatible with indigenous ways of being in the Yukon. My goal in this chapter is to explore that incompatibility.

In light of previous chapters, it should come as no great surprise that Gerald's grandparents never impressed upon him the notion that he is a citizen of Kluane First Nation. *Citizenship* is not an indigenous concept in the Yukon. The very term *citizen* implies the existence of a state, or at least a state-like political organization. Although there is considerable debate among scholars about the nature of citizenship and the rights, obligations, and forms of belonging it indexes or should index (Aleinikoff 2002; Brubaker 1992; Hall and Held 1990; Marshall 1950), the category – in its modern use – only makes sense in the context of the territorial state (Brubaker 1992: 21–31).[2] Brubaker has noted that the "the modern state is not simply a territorial organization but a membership organization, an association of citizens" (21) and that these two central aspects of the state, territory and membership (citizenship), are inextricably intertwined: "The emergence of the modern state and state system cannot be understood apart from the emergence and institutionalization of citizenship … Political territory, as we know it today – bounded territory within a system of territorial states, to which access

2 The *American Heritage Dictionary* defines a *citizen* as "a person owing loyalty to and entitled by birth or naturalization to the protection of a state" (348). On the centrality of the state (and state-building projects) to conceptions of citizenship, see also Kipnis (2004: 264–6), Sassen (1999), Torpey (2000), Turner (1990: 193), Isin and Turner (2007: 14).

is controlled by the state – *presupposes* membership" (ibid: 72, emphasis added; see also 22–6, 62–3, and Turner 1990: 211). For political and administrative purposes, territorial states (and other state-like politico-territorial units) must distinguish between their members (citizens) and non-members (non-citizens), and the social boundaries that are established in the process are just as critical to the proper functioning of the territorial state system as are the geographical boundaries between state territories.[3]

Citizenship is also essential to ideas about the legitimacy of the state. In liberal democracies, such as the United States and Canada, it is the collective citizenry – in theory at least – that is the very source of sovereign state power. Brubaker (1992: 28) points out that, "almost all modern states ... subscribe to the legitimating doctrine of national or popular sovereignty. Almost all claim to derive state power from and exercise it for (and not simply over) a nation, a people" (see also Johnson 1973: 990–2; Tully 1995: 194). Thus, for ideological as well as practical reasons, territorial states and state-like polities *presuppose* – and therefore (in ways that we shall explore in this and the following chapter) help bring into being – sovereign peoples, "nations" in Hobsbawm's first sense of the term. The laws and institutions of citizenship are the mechanisms for determining who exactly constitute the sovereign people – and who are subject to the rights and duties associated with that status.[4] Citizenship is therefore essential to the process of state formation.

Given (1) the centrality of *citizenship* to our concept of the territorial state and (2) the decided lack until very recently of territorially ordered, state-like political entities in the Yukon (see chapter 2), it is little wonder

3 Brubaker notes that citizenship has become "virtually universal" insofar as "it is axiomatic that every person ought to have a citizenship, that everyone ought to belong to one state or another. And this principle is largely realized in practice. The vast majority of persons possess the citizenship of at least one state" (Brubaker 1992: 31). Indeed, citizenship has come to seem such a natural and universal category that the tiny minority of people in the world who are not citizens of any state (tellingly referred to as "stateless" peoples) "are not simply lacking a privilege, they are fundamentally anomalous, and are accommodated in our state-centred world only precariously and in an ad hoc fashion" (ibid.: 198 n. 31; see also Malkki 1992). From a global perspective, then, citizenship can be viewed as "an international filing system, a mechanism for allocating persons to states" (Brubaker 1992: 31).

4 The first formal codification of citizenship was during the French Revolution. For various discussions, see Brubaker (1992: chap. 2); Torpey (2000); Wallerstein (2003).

that Gerald and some other Yukon Indian people view their First Nation citizenship as a foreign – even colonial – imposition. In this chapter, I examine the institutions and practices of Kluane First Nation citizenship to show that First Nation citizenship is not simply the recognition in law of an already existing indigenous form of political subjectivity. Rather, citizenship is a new category of political belonging, a recent product of the Yukon land claim and self-government agreements and the statist assumptions upon which they are based. I show that the very process of constituting the "sovereign people" of Kluane First Nation is simultaneously transforming – in quite profound ways – social relations not only among Kluane people, but also between them and the land and animals. Then, in chapter 4, I will examine how the creation of political boundaries among sovereign peoples and their corresponding territories can also give rise to ethno-nationalist sentiments, notions that particular *kinds* of people, "nations" in Hobsbawm's second sense of the term, belong to particular territories.

First Nations, Sovereignty, and Citizenship

Gerald's impassioned disavowal of his Kluane First Nation citizenship on cultural grounds cuts against the grain of much contemporary critical scholarship on citizenship in Indian country. Although a number of American Indian and indigenous studies scholars have levelled powerful critiques against the category of *citizenship* in recent years (e.g., Blackburn 2009; Bruyneel 2007; Deloria 1974: 18–19; Henderson 2002; Porter 1999; Audra Simpson 2008: 203– 6; Witkin 1995), they have for the most part focused their critiques on settler state citizenship, arguing that the unilateral imposition of US/Canadian citizenship upon Indian peoples was part of the larger colonial agenda of forced assimilation and that it is therefore incompatible with First Nation sovereignty. These scholars, however, have largely exempted tribal or First Nation[5] citizenship from the same critical scrutiny they bring to bear upon settler state citizenship. More than that, they tend to valorize First Nation citizenship as an antidote to the political ills caused by the imposition

5 In the US context, scholars and activists refer to "tribal" citizenship, while in Canada – where the term "First Nation" is generally used in place of "tribe" – the accepted term is First Nation citizenship. For simplicity's sake and because of my focus on the Yukon, I will refer hereafter simply to First Nation citizenship.

of US/Canadian citizenship and as an integral aspect of First Nation sovereignty.[6] The argument runs something like this: indigenous polities were sovereign prior to the foundation of either Canada or the United States. Insofar as settler governments recognized and affirmed the sovereignty of indigenous polities by making treaties with them, they also implicitly recognized that those polities must be composed of citizens. First Nation citizenship, then, like First Nation sovereignty, precedes, stands outside of, and is incompatible with settler state citizenship (Porter 1999: 997–1000; Johnson 1973). Henderson (2002) refers to this form of indigenous citizenship (and its recognition through treaty) as "*sui generis* and treaty citizenship," suggesting that First Nation citizenship is an indigenous category that is fundamentally different from, and largely incompatible with, citizenship in a settler state such as the United States or Canada. Such reasoning leads Porter (1999), Henderson (2002), and others to urge Indian people to reject their US/Canadian citizenship as a legacy of colonial oppression and embrace instead their First Nation citizenship as the only way to enact true First Nation sovereignty. From this perspective, when First Nation self-government agreements explicitly define the legal category of First Nation citizenship, they merely recognize in law a political status that already exists in historical fact. In so doing, they enable Indian people to assume once again their rightful identities as citizens of long-standing sovereign collectivities.

This view of First Nation citizenship is a powerful one, but it is difficult to reconcile with the position taken by Gerald, who clearly regards his status as a citizen of Kluane First Nation as an unwelcome and foreign imposition. While I am sympathetic to the above critique of settler state citizenship and its imposition upon Indian people, Gerald's critique suggests that we should not perhaps be quite so quick to embrace First Nation citizenship as an unproblematic alternative. If, as I argued in the preceding chapters, Yukon First Nations – as territorially organized political entities representing culturally and ethnically distinct peoples – are themselves recent products of Yukon Indian peoples' struggle against settler colonialism, then it makes little sense to view

6 As we saw in chapter 1, however, a few indigenous studies scholars are more critical. Political theorist Taiaiake Alfred (1999: xiv), for example, rejects the concept of sovereignty altogether – along with related concepts such as *citizenship* – as colonial impositions that constrain the possibilities for indigenous politics.

citizenship in those First Nations as an indigenous or sui generis category. I agree with scholarly critics of settler state colonialism when they argue that First Nation citizenship is an integral aspect of First Nation sovereignty (as citizenship is of sovereignty everywhere); but if *sovereignty* itself is a Euro-American concept whose imposition upon/adoption by indigenous people has helped transform – rather than merely gain recognition for – indigenous forms of political organization, then perhaps a less celebratory view of the associated concept of First Nation citizenship is called for as well. Indeed, it is precisely because of the close connection between *state sovereignty* and *citizenship* that a critical examination of First Nation citizenship is essential to the analysis of contemporary First Nation state formation.

None of this is to say that indigenous people did not have their own forms of political subjectivity prior to contact. It is only to suggest that the term *citizenship* – like *sovereignty*, to which it is inextricably tied – is so loaded with conceptual baggage that its use in an indigenous context is fraught with both theoretical and practical dangers. To cast Indian peoples' ideas about how they should relate to wider social collectivities as a form of *citizenship* is to engage in a highly complex and imperfect process of cultural translation.[7] As we have already seen in this book, translations of this sort can have a host of unintended consequences, which may vary from one indigenous context to the next. As noted earlier, the language of sovereignty – which includes citizenship – is a better fit for some First Nations than others. Because the fit in the Yukon is particularly poor, the consequences of mistranslation are perhaps more obvious there than in some other parts of the continent.[8]

As part of the nearly hegemonic discourse on territorial state sovereignty, the category of *First Nation citizenship* – and the practices associated with it – are deeply implicated in the socio-political transformations discussed in this book. Its assumption by/imposition on Yukon Indian people is altering the nature of interpersonal relations, generating new political subjectivities, and subjecting Yukon Indian people to new forms of governance (and governmentality). First Nation citizenship, then, like other forms of citizenship, must be viewed as a

7 Henderson himself is well aware of this; he warns indigenous people not to "conform to Eurocentric concepts such as sovereignty or citizenship" (2002: 432).

8 To be fair, none of the proponents of First Nation citizenship cited above writes about the Yukon or any subarctic context.

mechanism for creating a certain kind of political subject. Insofar as it entitles people to a set of rights and privileges, First Nation citizenship can be empowering; but, as we have seen, empowerment is hardly a straightforward notion. To avail themselves of the rights and privileges attendant upon their First Nation citizenship, Yukon Indian people must submit to the authority of their First Nation and the territorially ordered political system within which it is embedded – and in doing so, they help enact them. In other words, the *empowerment* associated with First Nation citizenship entails *subjection to* the territorial state form.

All of this suggests that while Gerald's critique of KFN citizenship may sit uneasily alongside much of the literature on First Nation citizenship, it is very much in line with some of the recent theoretical critiques that have been levelled against the category of *citizenship* more broadly. Before engaging with these critiques, however, we must consider in a bit more detail the nature of First Nation citizenship. Central to this inquiry is the question of whether or not First Nation citizenship really is an indigenous or sui generis category that is distinct from – and incompatible with – non-indigenous notions of citizenship. After all, if First Nation citizenship is a fundamentally different thing than US or Canadian citizenship, then it makes little sense to subject it to the same kinds of critique. What is called for, then, is a consideration of First Nation citizenship in comparative perspective.

Is First Nation Citizenship Sui Generis?

Claims to the effect that First Nation citizenship is an indigenous and/or sui generis category – and therefore fundamentally different from the Euro-American concept of citizenship – emanate from both ends of the political spectrum. Advocates of First Nation sovereignty (e.g., Henderson 2002; Porter 1999) make assertions of this sort as part of an effort to indigenize *citizenship*, to reframe it in ways that are more in line with indigenous ideas about politics and governance. At times, however, their arguments bear an uncomfortable, if superficial, resemblance to those made by those who reject First Nation sovereignty altogether (or accept it only in very limited form). Anthropologist Carole Blackburn (2009: 71), for example, describes how a member of the federal team negotiating the Nisga'a final agreement in British Columbia suggested to her that the Nisga'a could have saved themselves a lot of trouble by agreeing to refer in their treaty to First Nation "members" rather than "citizens," because in the end, "[the term] citizen [in the treaty] doesn't mean more than if we had used the word member … It's used in a way that does not in any way imply sovereignty." In such a view, the term "citizen" has a radically different meaning in the Nisga'a agreement than it does in standard political discourse in Canada. For those who reject First Nation sovereignty as a starting premise, the term *First Nation citizenship* becomes nonsensical. It cannot refer to "real" citizenship, so clearly it must have some other meaning (e.g., be reducible to *membership*).[9]

Despite the differences in their arguments, both the champions of and detractors from First Nation sovereignty all tend to share the assumption that First Nation citizenship is *too different* from territorial state citizenship to be regarded as the same thing (though they differ significantly in how they understand the nature of that difference). For both camps, the conflation of First Nation and settler state citizenships is simply a confusion that arises from the fact that the same word is being used to denote different concepts. Yet, scholars of non-indigenous citizenship (e.g., Turner 1990: 195) note that the principles, laws, practices, and institutions that characterize territorial state citizenship vary widely from one territorial state to the next – sometimes in fundamental ways. The principles underlying German citizenship, for example, differ substantially from French and even more fundamentally from US or Canadian citizenship (Brubaker 1992). Those who would make the claim that First Nation citizenship is fundamentally different from territorial state citizenship, then, must demonstrate not only that First Nation citizenship is different from US or Canadian citizenship, but that it falls outside the already wide range of variation in citizenship codes found among states worldwide. That is, they must show that First Nation citizenship is somehow *more different* from all the various forms of state citizenship than those are from one another. This, it seems to me, is a tall order. For while there are marked differences between First Nation citizenship and US or Canadian citizenship, many of those differences fall away if territorial states other than the United States or Canada – Germany or Ireland, for example – are used instead as the comparators (Aleinikoff 2002: 144; Brubaker 1992: 14). Indeed, most

9 Such an argument, of course, plays right into the hands of anti-treaty activists, as well as many members of the general public who reject (or are confused by) the idea that First Nations are sovereign entities composed of citizens.

arguments for the sui generis status of First Nation citizenship seem to be based on an implicit contrast with US or Canadian citizenship in particular, rather than on an analysis of how First Nation citizenship compares to the whole range of citizenship forms among territorial states (Steinman 2011: 67–9). This is significant because the United States and Canada (along with most Latin American countries) – in part as a result of their settler colonial histories – are actually somewhat unusual in their approach to citizenship (Brubaker 1992: 33).

Perhaps the most common argument in favour of treating First Nation citizenship as fundamentally different from other types of citizenship is that it is based upon descent rather than territory (see, e.g., Steinman 2011: 67–8). Most, if not all, First Nation citizenship codes require would-be citizens to prove that they are related by descent to a set of apical ancestors,[10] regardless of where they happen to have been born.[11] Kluane First Nation's citizenship code is fairly typical in this regard. It stipulates that a person is eligible for KFN citizenship if:

(a) the person has 25 per cent or more Kluane First Nation blood and was ordinarily a resident of Kluane First Nation traditional territory prior to 1 January 1940;
(b) the person is a descendant of a person who is/was eligible;
(c) the person establishes that he or she is an adopted child of a person eligible to be enrolled under 2.1 (a) or (b); or
(d) the person is deemed by the Enrolment Committee to be eligible for enrolment (Kluane First Nation 1995: 23).

From this it is clear that a child born of non-Kluane First Nation parents cannot become a KFN citizen simply by virtue of being born within the boundaries of KFN territory, while a child of Kluane First Nation parents is generally eligible for citizenship regardless of where he or she

10 An apical ancestor is an ancestor from whom descent is traced.

11 It is impossible to make hard generalizations about this, since there is considerable variation among First Nation citizenship codes, and not all of them are available to the public. In her survey of 737 current and historical tribal constitutions and membership codes (representing 586 different tribes/First Nations) in the United States, Canada, Australia, and New Zealand, however, Kirsty Gover (2010: 77) found that "*all* the tribes in [her] study base their membership governance on a concept of descent" (emphasis added).

was born.[12] Most proponents of First Nation sovereignty defend descent-based citizenship as necessary for maintaining the cultural integrity of the First Nation, though some do express misgivings about it (e.g., Borrows 2002: 153). By contrast, many critics of First Nation sovereignty/citizenship decry descent-based citizenship as race-based, even racist, and therefore antithetical to the very concept of citizenship in a democratic society. Citizenship, they assert, should be universally available to all who reside within the territorial borders of the state, regardless of race. In her analysis of the debate over the Nisga'a agreement that took place on the floor of the Canadian Senate, for example, Carole Blackburn (2009: 72) notes that "critics argued that the treaty was a set of race-based rights and railed against the establishment of ethnic enclaves on Canadian soil. Some senators were uncomfortable with the ethical and political implications of having a government entity within Canada that did not practice universal citizenship. How, they asked, could the Senate sanction the formation of a government that would base its membership, and the ability to vote, on ancestry?" The model of descent-based citizenship practised by the Nisga'a, along with nearly all other First Nations on the continent, does indeed contrast sharply with the territory-based citizenship practices of the United States and Canada. But to assert on this basis that First Nation

12 The situation is actually a bit more complicated than described here. For many First Nations in the United States, descent is not merely a yes or no proposition. Rather, the notion of blood quantum is used to calculate one's degree of descent, allowing for someone to be classified as a descendant, but not enough of a descendant to qualify for citizenship. A great deal has been written on the politics surrounding the use of blood quantum as a criterion for First Nation citizenship/membership (Biolsi 1995; Jaimes 1992; Kauanui 2008; Sturm 2002). Unlike the United States, Canada never used blood quantum as a measure of Indian identity. As a result, very few First Nations in Canada use blood quantum, and those that do have only implemented the practice relatively recently (Gover 2010: 83). Instead, most use a broader notion of ancestry (see, e.g., Blackburn 2009: 72 on the Nisga'a citizenship code). Many First Nation citizenship codes also have provisions allowing for people who are not related by blood to qualify for some or all the benefits of citizenship, for example through adoption, marriage, and/or the granting of "honorary citizenship" (again, see Blackburn [2009] on the Nisga'a and Gover [2010: 36–9] for a survey of these types of provisions across North America). The essential point here is that First Nation citizenship codes – regardless of how they handle blood quantum, marriage, adoption, and the like – are all based primarily on descent rather than territory.

citizenship codes are inconsistent with the institution of citizenship in a democratic society (or, alternately, that it is an important and necessary solution to a problem that is unique to First Nations and unlike anything with which territorial states have to contend) is to ignore much of the rest of the world.

In fact, there are two distinct principles upon which territorial states have historically based their citizenship codes and practices: *jus soli* (right of the soil) and *jus sanguinis* (right of blood). Jus soli is the principle that a person's citizenship is determined by his or her place of birth; anyone born within the territory of a state that has a citizenship code based on jus soli is automatically deemed a citizen of that state. This stands in contrast to the principle of jus sanguinis, which holds that people derive their citizenship not from territory but from descent. In a state with a citizenship code based on jus sanguinis, people do not qualify for citizenship simply because they were born within its territorial borders; rather, they are deemed to be citizens of the same state as their parents. While these two principles may at first glance seem incompatible with one another, in practice they easily coexist within a single citizenship code. As it turns out, very few states have citizenship codes based exclusively on one or the other of these principles; most have adopted some hybrid system that incorporates elements of both.[13] Indeed, we might think of state citizenship codes as existing on a spectrum from those based primarily on jus sanguinis at one end to those tending towards jus soli at the other.

The United States and Canada are notable in that their citizenship codes are both located at the far end of this spectrum. They are built almost exclusively on the principle of jus soli, incorporating only a few elements of jus sanguinis.[14] By contrast, the citizenship codes of Europe are primarily built on the principle of jus sanguinis, though they vary considerably in the degree to which they temper their descent-based

---

13 This link between jus soli and jus sanguinis is not simply a matter of practicality. It arises out of the dual nature of the state, which we have seen is simultaneously a territorial and a membership organization.

14 Both countries, for example, confer citizenship on children born abroad whose parents are citizens, a clear application of the principle of jus sanguinis (although even here territory is a factor, since citizen-parents still have to meet certain minimal residence requirements for their children to qualify for citizenship).

codes with territorial considerations.[15] Thus, while the descent-based citizenship codes of First Nations across North America may appear anomalous in the US and Canadian context (but see Aleinikoff 2002: 142–4),[16] they fit right in among the liberal democracies of Europe (ibid.: 117).

It is worth noting in this regard that – contrary to the assertions of those who accuse First Nations of racism for having descent-based citizenship codes – neither abstract principle of citizenship can be viewed as inherently superior to the other from an ethical standpoint. Brubaker (1992: 177–8) points out that although jus sanguinis can, indeed, lead to intolerance and racism when taken to its extreme (as, for example, in Nazi Germany), more enlightened applications of the principle can result in what he termed the "benign differentialism"[17] of the Habsburg empire, for example, which granted "special rights [and] privileges to persons in their capacities as members of ethnocultural groups, as a means of guaranteeing the free practice of their religion, language,

15 Germany is often held up as an extreme example of a state with a citizenship code rooted in jus sanguinis. It is extremely difficult for a non-ethnic German to gain German citizenship – even for those who were born in the country and whose families have been residents for generations. On the other hand, it is relatively easy (and was especially so prior to 1990) for ethnic Germans from other countries to become German citizens, regardless of how long they have resided in the country (see Brubaker 1992: chap. 4). This contrasts with France, which is sometimes mistakenly described as having a citizenship code based primarily on jus soli. Although France's citizenship code is, in fact, based primarily upon jus sanguinis, it has extended a modified form of jus soli citizenship to second-generation immigrants (who do not automatically become citizens because of their birth in French territory, but who may choose French citizenship when they reach the age of maturity; see ibid.: chap. 5).

16 Erich Steinman (2011: 67) notes that it is the contrast between tribal citizenship and the "normative lens of US [and Canadian] citizenship" in particular that delegitimates tribal citizenship in the eyes of many non-Indians in North America. Aleinikoff (2002: 117) points out that tribes' descent-based citizenship codes appear even more anomalous when viewed in relation to sub-national political communities in the United States, such as states, congressional districts, and municipalities. Unlike US citizenship, citizenship in these political communities is based purely on residence. Although the requirements for establishing residency can vary, they have nothing to do with descent. Assuming you are a citizen of the United States, you are also a citizen of the state in which you reside, simply by virtue of your residence within its borders. The same is true of the Canadian provinces and territories.

17 Compare this to Iris Marion Young's notion of "differentiated citizenship," to be discussed below.

[and] culture" (ibid.: 177). And jus soli, too, has more than one possible ethical valence. When North American critics of descent-based First Nation citizenship (e.g., the Canadian senators cited above) extol the virtues of universal citizenship rooted in the principle of jus soli, they ignore the fact that territory-based citizenship codes can and often do lead to virulently assimilationist policies. Brubaker (1992: 112–13) notes, for example, that the extension of jus soli citizenship to second- and third-generation resident "foreigners" in France was in large part fuelled by a xenophobic urge to stamp out their foreignness and turn them into proper Frenchmen. For their part, indigenous people in the United States and Canada are only too familiar with the extension of jus soli citizenship as a tool for forcibly assimilating resident "others"; so they can perhaps be excused for not sharing the Canadian senators' high regard for territory-based "universal" citizenship.

The Territorial Dimensions of First Nation Citizenship

The fact that First Nation citizenship codes are primarily based on jus sanguinis does not mean that territory is unimportant to First Nation citizenship (no more so than it is unimportant to German citizenship). Most Indian people – like indigenous people everywhere – regard their connection to land as an integral part of their identity. Indeed, territory – along with descent – is central to the concept of indigeneity itself (see Ingold 2000: chap. 8). As Gover (2010: 16) points out, the central assertion of indigenous land claims is that the First Nation "is the legitimate successor to a historic community and so entitled to inherit its jurisdiction and property." Some link to indigenous territory, then, is an integral part of what it means to be a First Nation citizen. As one Nisga'a citizen told Carole Blackburn (2009: 70), "the self-description as citizens is really a declaration that we've always had this inherent connection to our land." For this reason, considerations of territory are always at least implicit in efforts to articulate and codify First Nation citizenship.

Like territorial states, First Nations are both territorial and membership organizations in which notions of territory and membership are closely linked (Brubaker 1992: 22–3; Dussias 1993). So although all First Nations rely principally on jus sanguinis to govern their membership, we should not be surprised to find that their citizenship codes – like the state citizenship codes on which they are modelled – are hybrid forms that incorporate (to varying degrees and in different ways, depending on the First Nation) elements based on territory as well as descent.[18] But because First Nation citizenship codes are based primarily on descent, the role of territory in the constitution of citizenship is often very complex, indirect, and inconsistent.

A closer look at Kluane First Nation's citizenship code will be instructive here. We saw above that it is built upon the principle of descent; all citizens must be able to trace their descent from a set of apical ancestors. Territory, however, figures centrally in constituting that set of ancestors, since to qualify as such a person must be or have been of "25% or more Kluane First Nation blood and ... ordinarily a resident of Kluane First Nation traditional territory prior to January 1, 1940" (Kluane First Nation 1995: 23). Before we can fully appreciate the importance of territory in this clause, we must first consider in a bit more detail the role played by "Kluane First Nation blood."[19] The appearance of this term in the clause gives one the impression that the ancestors of today's Kluane First Nation citizens were related to one another by blood and that by virtue of this shared substance they together constituted the socio-political collectivity now recognized as the Kluane First Nation (a kind of "proto-Kluane First Nation"). In fact, however, this set of citizen-ancestors shared neither common ancestry nor membership in a single political collectivity.

In 1940, the indigenous population of the southwest Yukon was characterized by a high degree of ethno-linguistic heterogeneity. Included among Kluane First Nation's citizen-ancestors are people who came to the Kluane region from all over the Yukon and Alaska and spoke a wide variety of different indigenous languages, including dialects of Southern Tutchone, Northern Tutchone, Tlingit, Tagish, and Upper Tanana (McClellan 1975: 25–32; Nadasdy 2003: 17). Although today Kluane First Nation is nominally a Southern Tutchone First Nation,[20] no

---

18 Indeed, Robert Lowie (1927: chap. 4) long ago argued that while consanguinity and territoriality might be logically distinct unifying principles, in practice they are both always present to some degree and complexly intertwined with one another.

19 It is worth pointing out that the term "Kluane First Nation blood" is never defined, either in KFN's constitution or in its land claim or self-government agreements. Combined with the intractable difficulties surrounding its use (as discussed in the main text), this renders the meaning of the term deeply ambiguous.

20 KFN is a member of the Southern Tutchone Tribal Council. See chapter 4 for a discussion of tribal councils in the Yukon.

citizen-ancestor falls below the 25 per cent threshold by virtue of their Tagish, Tlingit, or Upper Tanana ancestry. Rather than distinguishing members of one indigenous group from another, then, the reference to "Kluane First Nation blood" in KFN's citizenship code serves primarily to distinguish those of (at least 25%) indigenous ancestry from Euro-Canadians. Any indigenous people living in what is now KFN territory prior to 1940 could qualify for KFN citizenship and inclusion in the set of KFN's apical citizen-ancestors.[21] It is thus a particular relationship to land – one that derives from a combination of indigeneity and residence within a specific territory – that lies at the heart of KFN citizenship. This relationship is far from straightforward, however, since as it turns out many of those who could qualify for apical ancestor status under these criteria are not, in fact, viewed as having been KFN citizens at all (or else their status is ambiguous). These people and their descendants (or at least some of the latter) are citizens of other Yukon First Nations instead. The most obvious examples of this are the citizens and ancestors of the White River First Nation.

Because KFN and WRFN share a single traditional territory (a situation that will be discussed in considerable detail in chapter 4), nearly all citizens of WRFN could also qualify as citizens of KFN according to the residency requirement in KFN's code.[22] Indeed, in one case a man elected to enrol as a citizen of KFN while his brother and father chose WRFN citizenship. But WRFN and KFN were hardly unique in sharing a pool of potential citizens. Because of high rates of mobility and intermarriage among Yukon First Nation people, many citizens of other First Nations across the Yukon can trace their descent back to an ancestor who resided in what later became KFN territory (and vice versa). With the settlement of land claims and the resulting creation of First Nations, Yukon people had to choose the First Nation to which they wanted to belong (in the parlance of the Yukon land claim, they had to "enrol" in a First Nation), and many could choose from among

21 Despite appearances, then, the requirement that people have "Kluane First Nation blood" to be eligible for apical ancestor status is actually more pan-Indian than First Nation–specific in character. In this, KFN's citizenship code follows the standard pattern in Canada (see Gover 2010: 83–6). It is also consistent with the lack of indigenous tribal categories in the Yukon, as discussed in chapters 2 and 4.

22 The possible exception here is a subset of those WRFN citizens who reside – and/ or whose ancestors resided – in what is now Alaska.

multiple First Nations. This lends an element of circularity to efforts to determine who has/had "Kluane First Nation blood." On the one hand, someone can only qualify as a citizen of Kluane First Nation if he/she can trace descent from an ancestor who had Kluane First Nation blood. On the other hand, indigenous people who before 1940 were resident in what became Kluane First Nation territory are only deemed to possess (or have possessed) Kluane First Nation blood if they or their descendants now claim KFN citizenship.[23] Those citizen-ancestors whose descendants are now all citizens of White River First Nation, for example, are not generally considered to possess or have possessed Kluane First Nation blood.

This circularity can lead to ambiguity about just what kind of "blood" is/was circulating in the veins of these citizen-ancestors. In the example mentioned above, for example, the two brothers – one a citizen of KFN, the other of WRFN – both qualify for First Nation citizenship through their father (their mother is German), himself a man of mixed Upper Tanana and Norwegian ancestry who has lived the great majority of his life – since before 1940 – in the shared KFN/WRFN territory. The father was a member of the amalgamated Kluane Tribal Council (comprised of the previously separate and now once again distinct Kluane and White River First Nations – see chapter 4) and even served as its elected chief for a time; but he was a vocal advocate for de-amalgamation, and when White River and Kluane First Nations finally split again in 1991, he and one of his sons opted for White River citizenship. He is not, therefore, a Kluane First Nation citizen, nor does it make much sense in this context to claim that he possesses Kluane First Nation blood (a suggestion I suspect he would vehemently deny). Yet, his other son, who was born after 1940, qualifies for Kluane First Nation citizenship solely by virtue of his ability to trace descent from his father. Thus, for purposes of reckoning his son's citizenship, the father necessarily qualifies as one of KFN's apical ancestors, possessing by definition at least a quarter Kluane First Nation blood. The point here is not to reveal

23 There are, of course, some ancestral figures without any direct living descendants who, by virtue of kinship, would likely be regarded by all or most contemporary Kluane First Nation citizens (if pressed on the matter) as having possessed "Kluane First Nation blood." In the absence of anyone actually claiming KFN citizenship by virtue of descent from an ancestral figure, however, there is seldom – if ever – any reason to make assertions about the nature of that ancestor's blood.

inconsistency[24] but to highlight the importance of territory in constituting the set of apical ancestors from whom today's Kluane First Nation citizens descend. In fact, these citizen-ancestors did not constitute a kin group at all; rather, they might better be viewed as a voluntary[25] association of (some of the) indigenous people who had/have a strong personal connection to what is now Kluane First Nation territory.

What, then, are we to make of the claim, implicit in KFN's code, that the ancestors of today's Kluane First Nation citizens shared something called "Kluane First Nation blood" – as opposed to "White River" or "Champagne and Aishihik First Nation blood" – long before any of these political entities even existed? Although it may not hold up to logical scrutiny, the claim that, say, Jimmy Johnson (an iconic Kluane ancestor who died in 1946 and about whom songs are still sung across the southern Yukon and Alaska) had "Kluane First Nation blood" is really no different from similarly anachronistic claims to the effect that "Goethe was a great German" or that "Dante was an Italian poet." The post hoc attribution of national identity/citizenship to prominent and respected ancestors is part of the standard repertoire of nation building. It is a powerful means of evoking (and naturalizing) the nation, and nationalists everywhere have used this strategy to create a sense of their nation's great historical depth – even when "outsiders" have only recently recognized its existence (e.g., Anderson 1991: 11 n. 4).

Indeed, provisions 21 (a) and (b) of KFN's citizenship code, above, provide a blueprint for building the "imagined community" that is a (First) nation. The references to blood and descent in the two provisions together conjure an image of the nation as a group of people related by kinship marching together down through history. The reference

24 Some inconsistency of this sort seems an inevitable result of efforts to impose a territorially ordered political system upon one as fluid and non-territorial as that of Yukon Indian people prior to 1940.

25 There is an important caveat here. Although some citizen-ancestors were still alive when KFN came into being, and can be viewed as having voluntary consented to their KFN citizenship (see discussion on consent below), the same cannot be said of those citizen-ancestors who died prior to the creation of KFN – or even the *idea* of KFN – and who could not, therefore, have "volunteered" for anything of the sort. In the latter case, however, descendants can be viewed as having implicitly "volunteered" their deceased ancestors for *post hoc* citizen-ancestor status through the simple act of choosing KFN citizenship themselves (thereby asserting in effect that their ancestor must have had "Kluane blood").

to territory in provision 21(a) explicitly links that nation to a specific homeland. I will discuss this all in greater detail in the next chapter.

First Nation Citizenship, Indigeneity, and Territory

National citizenship implies that the members of a nation have a special connection to their national territory (and should therefore be loyal to the national state that governs it), but various citizenship codes can enact very different theories about the nature of that connection and how it gets perpetuated and reproduced. Those based on the principle of jus sanguinis, for example, take it for granted that children inherit a connection to their national territory from their parents (Brubaker 1992: 89). As a result, children of citizen-parents are deemed to have a special relationship to the national territory even if they themselves have never been there. It is this notion that underlies the "right of return" in its various manifestations around the world. By contrast, citizenship codes rooted in jus soli assume that one has a special connection to the territory where one is born,[26] while a heavily hybridized system such as France's, which allows second-generation immigrants to assume French citizenship upon reaching the age of majority, assumes that people have a special connection not so much with their place of birth, but with the territory in which they grew up (Brubaker 1992: 110). In the case of First Nations, ideas about the connection between nation and territory are further complicated by the concept of indigeneity.

We have seen that although KFN citizenship is based primarily on descent, territory nevertheless plays a crucial role in constituting the set of its apical citizen-ancestors. Despite the importance of territory in KFN's code, however, the principle of jus soli is completely lacking; place of birth is irrelevant to the citizenship status of both citizen-ancestors and their descendants alike. Nor is it enough for someone to have lived in KFN territory before 1940 for him or her to qualify as a citizen-ancestor. The code's insistence on the indigenous status of its citizen-ancestors (through reference to "Kluane First Nation blood") implies that not all ways of relating to the territory qualify one for citizenship. There were, for example, several Euro-Canadian men who,

26 As Brubaker (1992: 89) shows, however, there is often a strong territorial component underlying jus sanguinis citizenship as well.

before 1940, lived in what would later become KFN territory.[27] They lived most of their lives in the region, married indigenous women, and their descendants are now are citizens of various First Nations across the Yukon. Although their First Nation descendants certainly regard these men as their ancestors, they are not citizen-ancestors because one cannot qualify for KFN citizenship by tracing one's ancestry back to them alone. This implies that although they had a long-term connection to Kluane territory, it was not the right kind of connection to qualify them for citizenship.[28]

A similar distinction between indigenous and non-indigenous ways of relating to territory is evident – more explicitly – in the KFN citizenship code's eligibility criteria for *honorary citizenship*, a status open to non-indigenous people.[29] In addition to a residency requirement (i.e., that one be a "long-term community member"), candidates for honorary citizenship must also demonstrate (among other things) "knowledge of and respect for the land and the traditional way of life" (Kluane First Nation 1995: 25). Notably, however, there is no such requirement for the descendants of Kluane citizen-ancestors, who derive their citizenship solely through the application of jus sanguinis. Thus, to qualify as a citizen-ancestor or honorary citizen, a person (or someone acting on his/her behalf) must successfully lay claim to a very particular way of knowing and relating to Kluane territory;[30] yet, because of the application of jus sanguinis, the nature of a citizen-descendant's relationship to the land is irrelevant to his or her citizenship. And, as it turns out, there are some KFN citizens who have never set foot in KFN territory, or even the Yukon. As with jus sanguinis systems everywhere, the

27 These include Thomas Dickson, an RCMP officer from Ontario who settled in Burwash Landing, along with Gene and Louis Jacquot, brothers from Alsace-Lorraine who established the trading post there.

28 This resonates with Brubaker's (1992: 124) assertion that "from a state-national perspective, it is the *strength* of the attachment [to territory] that is decisive ... [whereas] from an ethnonational point of view, it is the *kind* of attachment that matters."

29 The rights and responsibilities of honorary citizens vary from First Nation to First Nation. Honorary citizens of Kluane First Nation are not permitted to vote in KFN elections, but they may participate and vote in general assemblies (where, among other things, KFN laws are passed).

30 For citizen-ancestors, it is taken for granted that this way of knowing/relating is an essential aspect of their Indian-ness; honorary citizens, by contrast, must demonstrate "knowledge of and respect for the land and the traditional way of life" to the satisfaction of KFN's enrolment committee.

implicit assumption is that these citizen-descendants have inherited a connection to Kluane territory from their parents, so if they should ever "return" there, they would, by virtue of their descent from an indigenous citizen-ancestor, relate to the land in a manner appropriate to their citizenship (i.e., as an indigenous Kluane person).[31]

As noted above, some indigenous scholars have expressed misgivings about the theoretical and political implications of descent-based First Nation citizenship, arguing instead for a more properly territorial approach. Anishinabe legal scholar John Borrows (2002: 153), for instance, notes that "nothing in blood or descent alone makes an Aboriginal person substantially different from any other person," and warns that "despite the best of intentions, exclusion from citizenship on the basis of blood or ancestry can lead to racism and more subtle forms of discrimination that destroy human dignity." His solution is to extend First Nation citizenship to "non-Aboriginal people provided that they meet certain standards that allow for the reproduction of [the aboriginal] communities' values." And chief among these values, he argues, is the "'special bond' between Aboriginal people and the lands they have traditionally occupied. These bonds should be reflected in the discourses of Aboriginal citizenship" (ibid.: 157). Borrows's suggestion for extending First Nation citizenship to non-indigenous people in some ways resembles the set of territory-based criteria for honorary citizenship contained in KFN's citizenship code, except that he advocates full – rather than honorary – citizenship for those non-indigenous people whose relationship with the land qualifies them for citizenship (as we shall see below, he also elaborates somewhat on the nature of the "special relationship" with the land that should be required for citizenship). Although Borrows maintains that descent should not be necessary for First Nation citizenship, he (like KFN's citizenship code) remains silent on the question of whether it is sufficient. If the "special bond between Aboriginal people and the lands they have traditionally occupied" is so important an aspect of First Nation citizenship, then why is it that

31 Nowhere is this assumption expressed explicitly; indeed, I suspect that many Kluane First Nation citizens would be uncomfortable with such an explicit formulation. Nevertheless, it follows logically from the way jus sanguinis and indigeneity are codified in KFN's citizenship code. See Ingold (2000: 132–51) for a cogent discussion of the tension between descent and attachment to territory that is inherent in standard notions of indigeneity.

descendants of citizen-ancestors retain their citizenship regardless of how they relate to the land – or whether they have ever even set foot upon it?

Although there is much to recommend in Borrows's approach (to which I will return later), it is important to point out that while his proposed (partial) substitution of territory- for descent-based eligibility requirements does indeed avoid the dangers of racism, it is – like all territory-based citizenship codes – fundamentally assimilationist. He makes it quite clear that non-indigenous people should be eligible for First Nation citizenship only if they adopt indigenous peoples' beliefs, values, and ways of relating to the land.[32] This is a classically assimilationist view and one that bears a close resemblance (but in reverse) to how the United States and Canada handled Indian citizenship before its blanket extension (in 1924 and 1956 respectively) to all Indian people within their borders. Prior to that time, individual Indians were eligible for US or Canadian citizenship only providing they could demonstrate that they were sufficiently assimilated to Euro-American culture (Biolsi 1995).[33] The point here is not to damn Borrows for being a

---

32 Interestingly, Borrows (2002: 146) is concerned that his argument will be misconstrued as assimilationist in the other direction (i.e., that Indian people will have to assimilate to Euro-American society). He justifies his reverse assimilationist approach by arguing that the special bond between Indian people and their lands is more conducive to human dignity and proper environmental stewardship; so, if non-indigenous people would adopt Indian beliefs and values, everyone (including the environment) would benefit. This may be true, but it does not make his position any less assimilationist. After all, advocates of assimilationist policies *always* believe that their own beliefs and values are superior to those of the people they would assimilate.

33 The history of Indian citizenship in Canada is considerably more complicated (and ambiguous) than in the United States, in part because of the particularities of Canadian history and in part because of the way citizenship and enfranchisement were decoupled from one another there. Canadian citizenship – as distinct from British citizenship – did not even exist until the Canadian Citizenship Act of 1947. In theory, Indian people in most parts of Canada had the right to vote in Canadian elections from Confederation (1867) on – but only if they formally renounced their legal status as Indians (a procedure referred to in the Indian Act as "enfranchisement"), a process few were willing to undergo. There were, however, some exceptions to this requirement, most notably for Indian men who served in the Canadian military. In addition, at various points in time the federal government enacted provisions for the compulsory enfranchisement of individual Indian people (accompanied by a compulsory loss of Indian status), and Indian women who were stripped of their Indian status under the Indian Act by virtue of their marriage to non-Indian

reverse assimilationist. On the contrary, citizenship codes of the sort he advocates are quite commonplace among nation states, and variants of the general type run the gamut from virulently assimilationist to relatively benign, depending upon the specifics of the code and the larger legal and political context in which it is embedded. Rather, the point is to show that, like all other forms of citizenship, First Nation citizenship must steer a course between the Scylla of racist exclusion and the Charybdis of virulent assimilation.

The assimilationist policies of Canada and the United States regarding Indian citizenship were particularly noxious because they not only barred non-citizen Indians from voting; they also routinely denied them access to many of the rights, resources, and legal protections afforded citizens under US/Canadian law. In this context, the offer of settler state citizenship in exchange for one's Indian status was a profoundly coercive one (Blackburn 2009: 75; Johnston 1993). It is easy enough to conceive of a less virulently assimilationist citizenship policy in which citizen and non-citizen residents share equal access to rights (excepting perhaps a few political rights, such as the right to vote), resources, and protections under the law. Such a context would dramatically reduce the degree of coercion involved in one's choice of citizenship, allowing people a freer choice between different systems of beliefs and values and the citizenship statuses associated with them. In fairness to Borrows, he seems to have in mind this latter form of benign assimilation; and, of course, existing power relationships make it extremely unlikely that First Nation citizenship will emerge as a tool for the coercive assimilation of non-Indian people anytime in the foreseeable

men also experienced involuntarily enfranchisement (or at least could choose to vote without fear of losing that which they had already lost). In 1956, the Canadian government amended the Citizenship Act to extend blanket Canadian citizenship to all Indians *retroactively* to 1947, but it was not until 1960 that Indian people received the right to vote in federal elections without forfeiting their Indian status. Even then, some could not vote in provincial/territorial elections. The extension of provincial/territorial voting rights varied by jurisdiction (Indian people gained the right to vote in Yukon elections in 1961; see Coates 1991: 225). But those who had been compulsorily enfranchised under the Indian Act (and their children) were unable to regain their Indian status until the Indian Act was amended in 1985. On the history of Indian citizenship and the vote in Canada, see Bartlett (1979); Henderson (2002); Johnston (1993); Kingsley (2007: 83–7). Bartlett and Johnston, in particular, highlight the assimilationist intentions underlying Indian citizenship/enfranchisement policy in Canada.

future. Nevertheless, whenever citizenship – First Nation or otherwise – is based (in whole or in part) on territory, there is always at least the potential for virulently assimilationist forms to emerge.

Even when citizenship status is not used to effect the routine exclusion of some residents from important rights, resources, and legal protections, however, the symbolic stakes of citizenship remain high. Because citizenship plays a key role in the process of state formation and at the same time functions to institutionalize the concept of nationhood (Brubaker 1992: 48–9; Torpey 2000: 6, 14–15), it is intimately bound up with the nation-state ideal, the notion that the boundaries of the state are coterminous with those of the nation. As Brubaker puts it, "citizenship ... is inevitably bound up with nationhood and national identity, membership of the state with membership of the nation ... Debates about citizenship ... are debates about what it means to belong to the nation-state" (Brubaker 1992: 182, see also p. 28). It is citizenship's role in helping to forge the symbolic link between nation (with its connotations of shared descent, ethnicity, language, history, and culture) and the state (a politico-territorial unit) that underlies the assimilationist drive inherent in territory-based approaches to citizenship.[34] If someone qualifies as a French or First Nation citizen by virtue of their personal relationship to French or First Nation territory, it is generally expected that they will then also *think* and *act* in ways considered appropriate to a French or First Nation national.

So far, I have tried to show that the institutions of First Nation citizenship are not so very different from those of territorial states. Insofar as First Nation citizenship indexes full membership in a state-like politico-territorial organization, this should not really be surprising. The codes and institutions of First Nation citizenship fall well within the (already quite wide) range of variation among states. Like states, First Nations make use – in varying degrees – of both descent-based and territorial principles in constructing their citizenship codes; and First Nation citizenship, like territorial state citizenship, plays an important role in the

34 Descent-based approaches to citizenship tend not to be assimilationist because they are based on the ethno-nationalist assumption that assimilation is extremely difficult if not impossible for those who are not already members of the "community of descent" that is the nation. In such a view, naturalization would require "a change in nature, a change in political and cultural identity, a social transubstantiation that immigrants [and citizens] have difficulty imagining, let alone desiring" (Brubaker 1992: 78; see also 176–8).

construction and enactment of the (First) nation, that imagined community bound together by an ideology of common descent and special attachment to a territorial homeland. The nature of that attachment in the case of First Nations bears further consideration. First, however, I consider some of the socio-political effects resulting from the recent creation of First Nation citizens and citizenship institutions in the Yukon.

Critiquing First Nation Citizenship

In recent years, social theorists have looked critically at the concept of citizenship and found it to be a profoundly ambivalent institution, shot through with internal tensions and contradictions. Citizenship, they note, is simultaneously a form of empowerment and of subjection, a mechanism for inclusion as well as exclusion, and it is rooted in both consensus and coercion. Although the vast majority of this literature focuses on territorial state citizenship, all of these contradictions can be found in First Nation citizenship as well.

Consensus and Coercion

One of the central principles of liberal political theory is that "political membership ought to be founded on individual consent" (Brubaker 1992: 32).[35] The collective citizenry, as the ultimate sovereign, is supposed to be composed of those persons who have consented to be governed under a state's constitution (Brubaker 1992: 28; Johnson 1973: 994; Porter 1999: 137; Tully 1995: 194).[36] Those who criticize the US and Canada's blanket extension of citizenship to Indian people on the grounds that it was done without their consent (e.g., Henderson 2002; Porter 1999; Witkin 1995) draw on the liberal theory of consensual citizenship to make their argument. Yet the role of consent in the construction of citizenship is not at all straightforward – even in liberal democracies. Schuck and Smith (1985: 9–41) note that despite the importance of consent in liberal political theory, citizenship in the United

35 In *Federalist* 22, Alexander Hamilton wrote: "The fabric of American Empire ought to rest on the solid basis of THE CONSENT OF THE PEOPLE. The streams of national power ought to flow immediately from that pure original fountain of all legitimate authority" (Hamilton et al. 2005: 123, emphasis original).

36 See Schuck and Smith (1985: 22–41) on the history of the principle of consent in liberal political theory.

States (their analysis is also relevant for Canada, see Carens 1987: 414) has, in fact, always been rooted in two distinct – and often opposed – principles of political membership: the principle of ascription and the principle of consent, each of which has its own merits and shortcomings. The problem is that each principle, in its pure form, leads to intractable theoretical and practical difficulties.[37] As a result, the United States (along with other states, including Canada) has combined ascriptive and consensual elements – often in a very ad hoc and theoretically inconsistent manner – when fashioning the laws and institutions that govern citizenship; and, as it turns out, consent is by far the less important of the two principles.

Brubaker (1992: 32) points out that, for the vast majority of people in the world – including those living in liberal democracies – citizenship is an ascribed status; it is imposed upon most of us – without our consent – at birth (via some combination of jus soli and jus sanguinis). This is no accident. The ascription of citizenship at birth is essential, Brubaker says, because the alternative, a system of voluntary or contractual citizenship that leaves people unassigned to any state until they make a choice, would be an administrative nightmare. Perhaps even more importantly, it would be politically unacceptable: "All states regard their citizens as bound to them by obligations of loyalty and service … These core obligations are too important to the state to permit individuals to opt into or out of them at will."[38] For these reasons, "the state is not and cannot be a voluntary association" (ibid.). I would add that the territorial nature of the state itself also contributes to the essentially ascriptive

37 What is more, neither principle has a particular moral valence. Although the tendency in liberal democracies such as the United States and Canada is to favour consensual processes and look askance at ascribed statuses of all kinds, it is worth bearing in mind that the 14th amendment of the US constitution, which formally ratified jus soli (a form of citizenship by ascription) as the principal means for constituting the citizenry of the United States, was passed with the express purpose of extending citizenship to freed slaves, whereas consensual theories of citizenship had long been used to deny them citizenship (Schuck and Smith 1985: 66–71).

38 Schuck and Smith (1985: 32) point out that the threat of expatriation was in fact one of the central concerns associated with the idea of consensual citizenship in the United States prior to the 14th amendment: "If individuals could relinquish their political subjectship whenever they wished, then the state was always in danger of losing its members through unilateral expatriation, probably at the very times it needed them most, such as during periods of war or economic emergency" (see also ibid.: 54–63).

nature of citizenship. Because the administration and enforcement of the rights and obligations of citizenship are necessarily ordered and constrained by state territoriality (it is difficult, for example, to compel someone living in another state's territory to provide military service), territorial considerations – such as place of birth and residence – are necessarily of central importance when it comes to state membership and active participation in political society (Schuck and Smith 1985: 39–40).[39]

Long aware of these issues, liberal political theorists have struggled to develop ways of understanding a system that is necessarily based primarily on birthright (ascriptive) citizenship as at least minimally consistent with the principle of consent. One important mechanism for this has been the notion of "tacit consent." Although all agree that children cannot possibly consent to citizenship status conferred on them at birth, many liberal theorists have argued that upon reaching the age of majority, birthright citizens tacitly consent to the social contract by continuing to reside in the country, owning property, voting, or otherwise demonstrating their membership in the political community of the state (Schuck and Smith 1985: 32–3, 44–7). But this assumes that they have a practical alternative; what looks like tacit consent from one theoretical vantage point may be, from another, simply a lack of realistic alternatives (ibid.: 34–5, 38, 88). For this reason, some theorists reject the notion of tacit consent altogether.

A pure form of consensual citizenship is only found in cases of naturalization (and naturalization's flip-side, expatriation). It is only when someone adopts a citizenship status not conferred on him or her by birth that would-be citizens are generally required to give their explicit consent to be governed. Most naturalization laws, however, are so restrictive as to limit severely the number of people who can pursue this route to citizenship, and the number of naturalized citizens in any state is nearly always insignificant compared to the total population of citizens. What is more, not all instances of naturalization require consent, particularly not those involving the naturalization of collectivities, in which individual consent would be difficult if not impossible to obtain.

39 Along these lines, Torpey (2000: 19) notes that the territorial state has a fundamental interest in being able to control the flow of particular categories of people across state boundaries precisely because such control is "decisively bound up with the rights and duties … associated with membership – citizenship – in the nation-state" (see also Brubaker 1992: 25; Aleinikoff 2002: 17).

In *Boyd v. Nebraska* (1891), the US Supreme Court explicitly considered cases of collective naturalization.[40] It ruled that in all these cases, "the sovereign to which the naturalized individual had formerly owed allegiance either disclaimed dominion by treaty or was incorporated as a state of the Union" (Johnson 1973: 995). The court invoked the notion of tacit consent by presuming that in such cases the newly naturalized citizens had tacitly consented to be governed by the United States either (1) through the actions of their elected representatives (in the case of new states admitted to the Union) or (2) in the absence of specified declarations to the contrary (Johnson 1973: 995–6; Porter 1999: 136–7).[41]

Because the US Supreme Court had previously ruled in *Elk v. Wilkins* (1884) that Indians were not birthright citizens, despite their having been born within the territory of the United States,[42] the blanket extension of citizenship to Indians must be considered an instance of collective naturalization.[43] As critics rightly point out, however, tribal sovereigns never disclaimed dominion, nor did the blanket imposition of settler state citizenship meet the standards of tacit consent laid out in *Boyd v. Nebraska*. Because of this lack of consent, they argue, the extension of settler state citizenship to Indians in both the United States and Canada was fundamentally flawed and illegal (Johnson 1973: 996–7; Porter 1999: 137). I find it hard to argue with this logic, but how does it apply to First Nation citizenship? If critics of settler state citizenship subscribe to a consensual theory of citizenship, then surely they must apply the same logic to First Nation citizenship as well. Did First Nation citizens ever give their consent to be governed by First Nation

---

40 These included the admission of new states into the Union as well as some situations in which subjects of another sovereign had automatically became US citizens as a result of treaty and/or land cession (e.g., following the Mexican War). Significantly for our purposes, also included in the court's deliberations were several instances in which specific Indian tribes had been collectively naturalized by treaty.

41 After the Mexican War, for example, all Mexican citizens in the ceded territory were given one year to declare their allegiance to Mexico; those who failed to do so were automatically deemed US citizens.

42 It also ruled that they could not become US citizens simply by unilaterally renouncing their tribal citizenship. As citizens of a foreign power, it asserted, Indians must undergo a formal process of naturalization to become US citizens.

43 Prior to this, Indian people in both the US and Canada had had the option of naturalizing (or, in Canada, of becoming "enfranchised") as individuals, a process that entailed an express declaration of consent.

governments? If so, when and how? Although this is a question to be answered empirically on a case-by-case basis, Gerald Dickson's attitude towards his own Kluane First Nation citizenship (discussed at the beginning of this chapter) suggests that, in the Yukon at least, they have not always done so.

We have seen that in the Yukon the category of *First Nation citizen* is a recent product of the land claim and self-government agreements. For children born in the years since those agreements were ratified, First Nation citizenship is an ascribed status; children are born into it in the manner described above (principally through the application of jus sanguinis). Those who were already alive at the time of ratification, however, cannot be considered birthright citizens, since the First Nations to which they now belong did not exist at the time of their birth. It stands to reason, then, that they must at some point have undergone a process of naturalization, either individually or collectively. Although many Yukon First Nation constitutions lay out a set of (generally very restrictive) procedures for individual naturalization, none of a Yukon First Nation's original citizenry (i.e., those who became citizens on the effective date of its land claim and self-government agreements) had to follow such procedures; they became citizens the instant those agreements came into effect. In fact, it is not at all clear exactly when – or even whether –these original citizens consented to be governed by their First Nation. It is true that Yukon Indian people did have to enrol under a First Nation Final Agreement (and, as noted above, because many of them were eligible to enrol under more than one agreement, they often had to "choose" the First Nation to which they wanted to belong). One might plausibly argue that those Yukon Indian people who have enrolled subsequent to the ratification of the agreements did in this way consent to be governed by the First Nation in which they chose to enrol (indeed, this is what is involved in the "naturalization procedures" to which I referred above). The vast majority of each Yukon First Nation's original citizens, however, had enrolled long before their First Nations' agreements had even been negotiated, much less ratified (indeed, it was they who cast ballots in the ratification vote). Thus, when they enrolled they could not have had any idea what powers their First Nation governments would eventually have, what their rights as First Nation citizens would be, nor what rights they would be giving up as a result. For these original citizens, then, it makes very little sense to view the act of enrolling under a First Nation's final agreement as a declaration of consent to be governed by that First Nation.

Casting a ballot in favour of ratification might more plausibly be viewed as a form of consent, but what of all those Yukon Indian people who, like Gerald, voted against ratification? The number of such people is considerable. Kluane First Nation's agreement, for example, was ratified by only 60 per cent of eligible voters.[44] This means that 40 per cent of them never consented to be governed by the Kluane First Nation, nor – and this is very significant – did they ever consent to a system of governance that would bind them all to the will of the majority in a ratification vote. Indeed, an electoral system based on majority rule was itself an imposition of the Indian Act in an indigenous context where political relations were organized along very different lines (see chapter 2).[45] And, as it turns out, even the figure of 60 per cent overestimates the number of people who knowingly gave their consent to be governed by KFN.

To assume that a citizen's vote in favour of ratifying KFN's agreements constitutes consent to be governed by KFN is to assume that the citizen understood what he or she was voting for. I am not suggesting that people must have perfect knowledge of how a government works before they are in a position to give their consent, but a basic understanding of the rights and obligations that accompany citizenship – and also of any rights and freedoms relinquished by accepting citizenship – would seem to be a minimal requirement for any definition of what it might mean to grant one's consent to the social contract. For many of the original citizens casting ballots in Kluane First Nation's ratification vote, this was manifestly not the case.

Shortly after the ratification of KFN's agreements, for example, I was discussing the ratification vote with a Kluane elder. During our

44 96 out of 161 eligible voters cast votes in favour of ratification.

45 Voting is, of course, the key decision-making mechanism in contemporary liberal democratic states, and it is central to notions of democracy and popular sovereignty. As anthropologist David Graeber (2004: 88–92) points out, however, voting is entirely dependent on the existence of a coercive apparatus that can compel those who "lost" the vote to abide by the decision of the majority: "If there is no way to compel those who find a majority decision distasteful to go along with it, then the last thing one would want to do is hold a vote: a public contest in which someone will be seen to lose. Voting would be the most likely means to guarantee humiliations, resentments, hatreds, in the end the destruction of communities" (89). As we saw in chapter 2, no such apparatus of coercion existed in the Yukon until recently. Instead, Yukon Indian people engaged in the kind of consensus-based decision making Graeber argues is so widespread among stateless peoples.

conversation, it became evident that she had no idea that a vote in favour of ratification had also been a vote to relinquish one's status under the Indian Act. In fact, she became quite upset when I explained this to her. Although she herself had voted against ratification, she assured me that many of the elders who had voted in favour of ratifying the agreements would never have done so if they had known this meant losing their Indian status, an assertion I later confirmed in discussions with some of those other elders.[46] The exchange of Indian status (and membership in an Indian Act band) for First Nation citizenship is not some esoteric part of the Yukon self-government agreements; rather, it is the central premise upon which those agreements were built. Indeed, the ratification process was carefully structured with this fact in mind.[47]

46 KFN elders' dismay at losing their Indian status should not be read as support for the colonial dictates of the Indian Act. In addition to subjecting one to the provisions of that infamous piece of legislation, Indian status also constitutes formal recognition by the state of one's identity as an Indian. Thus, for all the problems associated with it, Indian status is a potent symbol of Indian-ness in the Yukon – as it is elsewhere in Canada. Indeed, some of the elders in question had gone to great lengths in the late 1980s and early 1990s to (re)gain their Indian status after the passage of Bill C-31 amended the eligibility requirements for enrolment under the Indian Act. They were not at all pleased to discover they had lost their status again.

47 The ratification of KFN's land claim and self-government agreements consisted of an up-down vote on the following question: "Do you approve of the Kluane First Nation Final Agreement, the Collateral Agreements, the Kluane First Nation Self-Government Agreement, the dissolution of the Kluane First Nation Band, and the transfer of all of its liabilities and assets, including Burwash Landing Reserve No. 1, to Kluane First Nation?" (Kluane First Nation 2003a: 46).

Because the two agreements (land claim and self-government) had somewhat different constituencies, however, there was a complex procedure for tallying the votes. In advance of the ratification vote, KFN generated three separate voter lists: list 1 consisted of those who were members of the Kluane Indian band and were also enrolled under the Kluane First Nation final agreement; list 2 was made up of those who were not members of the Kluane Indian band but who were enrolled under KFN's final agreement; and list 3 consisted of those who were members of the Kluane Indian band but were not enrolled under KFN's agreements (Kluane First Nation 2003b: 28–9). In tallying the votes to see if the agreements had been ratified, there were two separate requirements for ratification. The first (often referred to as "the final agreement test") was that a majority of those enrolled under KFN's land claim agreement (lists 1 and 2) had to vote in favour of the agreements. The second (the self-government test) was that a majority of Kluane band members (lists 1 and 3) had to vote in favour of dissolving the Kluane Indian band and replacing it with the self-governing Kluane First Nation (which necessarily entailed replacing Indian

It would therefore be difficult to sustain an argument that someone who did not understand this most basic aspect of the self-government agreement could have knowingly consented to the terms of the social contract it represents.

In the case of KFN, there is another reason to question the assumption that a vote in favour of ratification amounted to consent. There were external issues – having nothing to do with the provisions of the final or self-government agreements themselves – that had a powerful influence on how people voted. Principal among these was a letter circulated in mid-July 2003 by a group of Kluane band members calling themselves CARES (Coalition Against Ratification – Endorsing Sovereignty) that outlined a series of objections to the agreements and urging a no vote. While some of their objections had merit, the letter enraged many in the community because it claimed that Kluane people who were of Tlingit and Tagish descent were "visitors" who had migrated to KFN's traditional territory "less than a hundred years ago," and that therefore they represented "3rd party interests" and should not be allowed to cast ballots in the ratification vote. Many interpreted this (I think rightly) as an attack on the large and influential Dickson family. Although I heard Kluane people from all families and linguistic backgrounds denounce the letter, many members of the Dickson family took it as a personal affront. Two prominent members of the family told me that as soon as they had read the letter they had immediately gone to the telephone and began urging their relatives to vote in favour of the agreements – just to spite the authors of the letter. As a result, I know of at least five people who claim to have changed their ratification votes from "no" to "yes" in response to the CARES letter (and I suspect there were considerably more than that). Since all of these were members of the Kluane Indian band, it seems quite likely that the letter changed the outcome of the self-government test – which passed by

status with First Nation citizenship). Both tests had to pass for the agreements to be ratified (Kluane First Nation 2003a: 46–7). It is worth pointing out that the ratification of KFN's agreements nearly foundered on the second test. Only 55% of Kluane band members voted in favour of ratification. This may seem like a comfortable margin, but because of the small number of voters involved (there were only 93 voters on lists 1 and 3 combined), the second test in fact passed by only five votes – a number that includes those citizens who told me they would have voted against the agreements if they had understood that it meant losing their Indian status.

only five votes – and led directly to the ratification of KFN's agreements (see note 47 for a discussion of the Byzantine structure of the ratification vote). Several Kluane people, including Bob Dickson, chief of KFN at the time, and Robin Bradasch, KFN's chief negotiator, themselves both staunch advocates of the agreements, told me point blank that they were quite sure that the CARES letter had changed the outcome of the ratification vote.[48]

It seems, then, that only a minority of Kluane band members voted in favour of the agreements because they "approved of the Kluane First Nation Self-Government Agreement, the dissolution of the Kluane First Nation Band, and the transfer of all of its liabilities and assets ... to Kluane First Nation" (see note 47). For this reason, I feel confident in asserting that only a minority of Kluane band members ever really consented to relinquish their Indian status and become Kluane First Nation citizens. In light of all this, it is easy to sympathize with Gerald's question that opened this chapter – why should he be bound by an agreement he rejected in the voting booth? Why should he be bound by a social contract to which he never consented? He does at times seem to enact both his Canadian and Kluane First Nation citizenship by living in Canada and in KFN territory; by voting in national, territorial, and First Nation elections; by observing the property regimes sanctioned by different levels of government, and so on; but I do not think we can infer from all this that he has somehow tacitly consented to be governed by Canada and/or the newly constituted Kluane First Nation. After all, what choice does he really have? If he wants to continue living with his family in the place where he was born and to have some say in how he and the land are treated, he has to participate in existing political processes – regardless of the fact that he has never consented to either Canadian or Kluane First Nation citizenship. Similarly, if he wants to keep driving his truck on Yukon roads and hunting in the places he hunted with his grandparents, he has to abide by existing jurisdictional

48 Despite her personal support for the agreements, Robin told me she had gotten into an argument with a member of the Dickson family who told her she was going to vote "yes" as a result of the CARES letter. Robin had urged the woman to cast her vote based on the agreements, not on her personal dislike of the CARES letter writers: "If you don't like the agreement, vote 'no.' The agreement didn't change just because [name of letter writer] wrote that letter."

and property regimes – even though he may object to them in principle. Regardless of consent, citizenship in a First Nation subjects one to the authority of the First Nation government and the terms of its land claim and self-government agreements.[49]

The Universality of Differentiated Citizenship

In addition to objecting to the way Kluane First Nation citizenship subjects him to an agreement he despises, Gerald had another criticism that morning in 2011. He objected to the way the agreements erase important differences among Kluane people. By way of illustration, he complained, "These days everyone is hunting moose down Young Duke." This rich moose hunting area about five miles northwest of Burwash Landing had been part of his grandfather Sam's hunting area. When Sam was alive, Gerald said, no one would ever have dreamed of hunting there without first obtaining his grandfather's permission to do so.[50] Today, though, other Kluane families hunt there without even bothering to ask for permission. They can do this because the whole area is now within KFN's traditional territory, and all KFN citizens are legally entitled to hunt wherever they please within that territory. But this is not right, Gerald said; if people from other families want to hunt down Young Duke, they should ask him for permission – or, better yet, they should ask his uncle Kirk, Sam's eldest living son. How can you possibly refer to the current situation as "self-government," Gerald wanted to know, when the new system ignores – even undermines – the social mechanisms Kluane people long used to regulate social relations and land use among themselves? Some Kluane people would no doubt disagree with the way Gerald characterized the hunting situation down

49 Although he approaches the question very differently than I do, Burke Hendrix (2008: 68–72), too, argues that consent is as unworkable a principle for justifying the authority of tribes/First Nations as it is for states.

50 Sam's authority over his hunting area was a form neither of individual ownership nor of political jurisdiction. As discussed in chapter 2, although local headmen regulated access to certain areas that were "owned" by their moiety, in practice "it was always possible … for a man to manipulate his kin ties so that in effect he could exploit almost any area which attracted him" – so long as he asked the headman's permission first (McClellan 1975: 483).

Young Duke,[51] but the point he raised is nevertheless an important one that resonates with a long-standing debate in citizenship theory: the debate over universal versus differentiated citizenship.

Universal citizenship is simply the idea that all citizens are equal before the law, that they all have the same rights, duties, and protections vis-à-vis the state to which they belong. This ideal of universality is a long-standing and, to many, essential aspect of citizenship.[52] Recall that the Canadian senators' objections to Nisga'a citizenship, cited above, were based on the assumption that anything other than universal (Canadian) citizenship is inimical to democracy. Many people, including many liberal political theorists, would agree with the senators that universal citizenship is an essential component of substantive democracy and that the granting of "special rights" to any particular subgroup of citizens is fundamentally undemocratic. It is, of course, widely recognized that universal citizenship has seldom if ever been realized in practice; various categories of people within democratic societies have historically been excluded from citizenship and subjected to discriminatory treatment. As an ideal, however, universal citizenship is appealing to many because of its promise of equality; and this ideal has often

51 Gerald assumes that authority over the area would have been passed down from father to son; and, indeed, Sam seems to have inherited authority over the area in question from his own father, Jimmy Johnson. In other cases in the region, however, such authority seems to have been passed down to sister's son or daughter's husband – and thus to members of the same moiety (e.g., see Easton et al. 2013: 56). McClellan (1975: 481–8) suggests that headmanship had more to do with competence and strength of personality than either matrilineal or patrilineal succession. It is also possible that the ambiguity described by McClellan is evidence of a partial shift from matrilineal to patrilineal practices (evident also in some other aspects of contemporary Kluane life), a shift that no doubt owes much to the legacy of the Indian Act and its imposition of patrilineal mechanisms for the inheritance of Indian status (see Jamieson 1978; Lawrence 2004).

52 Brubaker (1992: 54) argues that the amalgamation of different social statuses into the universal status of citizenship was an essential part of the effort to replace a complex feudal system of "special law communities, valid only for their members, with a single general legal order, valid for the entire territory." As such, it was integral to the production of state territoriality, a "product of rulers' drive toward unitary internal sovereignty" (ibid.: 52). And, indeed, Biolsi (2005: 240) points out that the ideal of universal citizenship entails what he refers to as "panoptical sovereignty," which "implies the more or less equal treatment of citizens, who become, from the imputed standpoint of the state, interchangeable as objects of the state's gaze."

proved useful to marginalized people attempting to improve their social position within the state context (as, for example, in the struggle for women's suffrage and US civil rights movement).

While the emancipatory potential of universal citizenship should not be discounted, its effects are not always emancipatory – nor have all marginalized peoples embraced universal citizenship as an ideal for which to strive. To begin with, critics point out that the successful extension of citizenship to marginalized groups has hardly brought about an end to their discrimination. In part, this is a result of unequal/selective application of the law. Drawing on Aiwha Ong's (1999: 215–17) notion of graduated sovereignty, Biolsi (2005: 240–1) notes that *all* states – even the most powerful and democratic of them – sometimes refuse or are unable to "exercise full, flat and even jurisdiction over space, at least as far as some of its 'citizens' [are] concerned." He argues that every state "graduates or zones its sovereignty so as to benefit some citizens systematically and, just as systematically, to disempower or otherwise harm other citizens" (see also Holston 2008; Young 1989: 251). Yet the problems with universal citizenship run deeper even than this.

Legal and political theorists of various stripes have criticized the very idea of universal citizenship as inherently flawed and unable to accommodate the needs of underprivileged minorities (Deloria 1988: 179; Hall and Held 1990; Kymlicka 1995; Young 1989; Young 1990).[53] Iris Marion Young, among the most influential of these critics, notes that the ideal of universal citizenship is based upon an assumption that there exists "a point of view and interests that all citizens have in common which transcends their differences" (Young 1989: 252). Thus, "in exercising their citizenship, all citizens should assume the same impartial, general point of view in transcending all particular interests, perspectives, and experiences" (ibid.: 257). The problem with this, she asserts, is that no such "impartial general perspective" exists. Rather, everyone's political views and perceptions of society are necessarily shaped by their own particular experiences. It is the perspectives of the

53 Concerns about minority rights in a popular democracy are hardly new. In the Federalist Papers, James Madison warned of "the violence of the majority faction" (Federalist 10) and Tocqueville (1945) famously wrote on the dangers of a "tyranny of the majority."

powerful that often get mistaken for the mythical "general will," and when this happens the ideal of universal citizenship actually serves to reinforce privilege and silence the already marginalized (ibid.: 257).[54] Thus, "where differences in capacities, culture, value, and behavioral styles exist among groups, but some of these groups are privileged, strict adherence to a principle of equal treatment tends to perpetuate oppression or disadvantage" (ibid.: 251).[55]

What is more, Young argues, the myth of a common good, a general will, a shared public life has "in practice excluded groups judged not capable of adopting [the] general view, so that its imposition exerts a homogenizing force on the citizenry" (Young 1989: 251–3). Indeed, she notes that "European and American republicans found little contradiction in promoting a universality of citizenship that excluded some groups, because the idea that citizenship is the same for all translated in practice to the requirement that all citizens be the same" (ibid.: 252). It is this logic that accounts, at least in part, for the assimilationist tendency in efforts to expand state citizenship, as already discussed in relation to Indian people.[56] But if citizenship is homogenizing, exactly what kind of homogeneous persons does it produce (or take for granted)? Various scholars (Hall and Held 1990: 177; Ong 2003: 8–9; Macpherson 1962; Marx 1972: 41–6) have observed that the modern liberal category of the *citizen* is built upon (and reinforces) a distinctly

54 Hall and Held (1990: 183) agree: "'The people' is, after all, also a discursive figure, a rhetorical device, a mode of address … It represents as a 'unity' what are in fact a diversity of different positions and interests … 'The people' has … functioned so as to silence or marginalize the conflicts of interest which it claims to represent." Similarly, Turner (1990: 194, 197) notes that citizenship requires the creation of a universal political subject in opposition to local particularities of ethnicity, etc., which must be subordinated or erased.

55 See Aleinikoff (2002) for a discussion of how the rhetoric of universal citizenship in the United States has changed from a tool for inclusion and assimilation during the civil rights era to a mechanism for exclusion and denial of collective rights in the current era.

56 Indeed, the expansion of citizenship to include new groups has often been accompanied by overt efforts to assimilate them (Turner 1990: 194, 197). As discussed above, this certainly is true of efforts to expand settler state citizenship to include Indian people in both the United States and Canada, which were always closely and explicitly linked to the project of assimilation (e.g., Biolsi 1995: 30; Henderson 2002: 422–3; Porter 1999:115, 118, 120).

capitalist vision of society as composed of autonomous possessive *individuals*.[57] Thus, the *citizen* – like the territorial state itself – can be viewed as an ideological construct arising from – and in the service of – capitalism. For this reason, some suggest that citizenship should be viewed as a form of governmentality, a type of subjection in the Foucaultian sense (Brubaker and Cooper 2000: 15; Ong 1996); insofar as states successfully identify people – and get them to identify themselves – as *citizens*, they produce certain kinds of political subjects (i.e., possessive individuals that have a particular set of rights and responsibilities with respect to one another and the state). This process of subjection shapes and constrains the ways people can act – and even think – in relation to the state and capitalism.[58]

Concerns about universal citizenship lead Hall and Held (1990: 176–7) to question the utility of the citizenship concept altogether; they ask "whether there is now an irreconcilable tension between the thrust to equality and universality entailed in the very idea of the 'citizen,' and the variety of particular and specific needs, of diverse sites and practices which constitute the modern political subject?"[59] Rather than rejecting the concept of citizenship, however, Young suggests we simply abandon the ideal of universal citizenship, with its mythical assumptions of

57 Hall and Held (1990: 177) in particular highlight the connection between the ideal of universal citizenship and its individualizing nature when they point out that "though citizenship is a social status, its rights are entitlements to individuals" and that individual citizens enjoy these rights solely "on the basis of a fundamental equality of condition – their membership of the community." That citizenship is necessarily productive of "individuals" is consistent with Corrigan and Sayer's (1985) view of state formation as an inherently individualizing process. See also Foster (1991: 246–7).

58 Biolsi (1995) provides some powerful examples of this kind of subjection in his analysis of governmentality on the Rosebud reservation in the late nineteenth and early twentieth centuries. He notes, for example, that even though most Lakota were opposed to the allotment of their reservation lands, once they became "empropertied as individuals, each man, woman, and child had a material stake in the protection of private property relations … and in a social apparatus – the state – that could claim to 'stand above' and, in doing so, represent their 'common interest' and guarantee protection" (34). They even began to sue one another in federal courts for property-related infractions, thus helping enact the colonial state. Similarly, Larry Nesper (2007) shows that tribal citizens enact the "tribal state" and themselves as individuals through their use of tribal courts.

59 In fact, Hall and Held end up calling for a reconceptualization of citizenship along the lines laid out by Iris Marion Young (1989), as discussed below.

the general will, and embrace instead what she calls "differentiated citizenship," in which some groups within a state should be entitled to different rights and responsibilities *in addition* to those that are common to all citizens.[60] As Will Kymlicka (1995: esp. chap. 4) notes, liberal democracies have in fact long used a variety of mechanisms to grant group-specific rights to minority populations within their borders – from Indian treaties to affirmative action programs. Indeed, it is precisely in these group-differentiated terms that a number of theorists (e.g., Blackburn 2009; Cairns 2000; Kymlicka 1995) defend the idea of First Nation citizenship and self-government in Canada against critics' charges that this amounts to the granting of "special rights" to some citizens.

Anthropologist Carole Blackburn (2009), for example, has argued explicitly that Nisga'a citizenship must be viewed as a form of differentiated citizenship within Canada. Like Yukon First Nation citizens, Nisga'a citizens are also citizens of Canada, with all the rights, responsibilities, and protections that accompany that status (at least in theory). In addition, however, they *also* have the rights, responsibilities, and protections that are afforded by Nisga'a citizenship as spelled out in the Nisga'a Final Agreement signed in 1999. Blackburn sees the category of Nisga'a citizenship as an explicit challenge to received notions of citizenship, nationhood, and sovereignty. By providing a set of rights, responsibilities, and protections over and above those of Canadian citizenship, Nisga'a citizenship disrupts the notion

60 "Different social groups," Young asserts, "have different needs, cultures, histories, experiences, and perceptions of social relations which influence their interpretation of the meaning and consequences of policy proposals and influence the form of their political reasoning" (ibid.: 257). These differences must be recognized and respected as "irreducible" and "a democratic public ... should provide mechanisms for the effective representation and recognition of the distinct voices and perspectives of those of its constituent groups that are oppressed or disadvantaged within it" (ibid.: 261). For a somewhat different approach to solving the problems posed by universal citizenship – which he sees as a key element of what he calls "modern constitutionalism," see Tully (1995, esp. chap. 6). In that earlier work, Tully, like Young, Kymlicka, and other theorists of differentiated citizenship, takes sovereignty for granted as the precondition for politics (see Shaw 2008: chap. 5). Recently, however, he has become more critical of sovereignty, leading him to suggest what appears, at least at times, to be a non-sovereign approach to citizenship (Tully 2014). See the conclusion to this book for some discussion of this later work of Tully's.

that Canadian citizenship confers a uniform set of rights, responsibilities, and protections. This differentiated citizenship and the treaty rights with which it is associated, she argues, creates a "novel political space" (ibid.: 76) that enables Nisga'a citizens to resist the assimilationist tendencies of universal Canadian citizenship.

There is certainly something to be said for this argument; but, as it happens, the idea of differentiated citizenship does not really solve the problems of universal citizenship identified by Young and others – it only displaces them. Even as proponents of differentiated citizenship reject the idea that a state's entire citizenry can and should be treated as a homogeneous group with a unitary will, they take for granted the idea that that same citizenry can be subdivided into a set of homogeneous bounded minority "groups" that, when viewed internally, have these same impossible characteristics (see, e.g., Young 1989: 258–60 for discussion of social groups along these lines). Indeed, Brubaker and Cooper (2000: 32) argue that Young's notion of differentiated citizenship is flawed insofar as "social and cultural heterogeneity is construed [in Young's work] as a juxtaposition of internally homogeneous, externally bounded blocks. The 'principles of unity' that Young repudiates at the level of the polity as a whole – because they 'hide difference' – are reintroduced, and continue to hide difference, at the level of the constituent 'groups.'"[61] As it turns out, this is precisely what we see in the case of Kluane First Nation citizenship.

Although KFN citizens, like the Nisga'a citizens discussed by Blackburn, now have group differentiated rights (as laid out in their final and self-government agreements) vis-à-vis other (non-KFN) citizens of Canada, KFN citizenship is itself universal and individualizing. That is, the agreements construct Kluane First Nation citizens as individuals who stand as equals before Kluane, Yukon, and federal law. In fact, Kluane citizens as a whole are no more homogeneous than Canadians, yet there are no provisions for differentiated citizenship rights *among* Kluane citizens. Kluane First Nation citizenship hides differences among Kluane citizens in exactly the same way that universal expressions of Canadian citizenship hide differences between Kluane people and other Canadians. And this is precisely what Gerald was objecting to when he complained about what he saw as indiscriminate hunting

61 For a general critique of what Brubaker refers to as "groupism," see Brubaker (2002).

activity in his grandfather's hunting area.[62] To the extent that it is used as a justification for hunting there, the category of "Kluane First Nation citizen" steamrolls the complex particularities of local social relations and land use practices, and erects in their place a simplified and universal set of relations among Kluane citizens and between them and the environment.[63] Those Kluane hunters who would defend themselves against Gerald's charge that they have been hunting inappropriately have a choice. They can either attempt to establish their bona fides in accordance with locally accepted indigenous practice (either by proposing their own interpretation of traditional rules of access or by drawing upon their own kinship relations to establish the legitimacy of their actions), or they can invoke their individual rights, as KFN citizens, to hunt anywhere within KFN's traditional territory. To the extent they do the latter, they help enact Kluane First Nation as an external entity with legitimate authority to adjudicate disputes among individual Kluane people, and they enact themselves as citizen-subjects of the Kluane First Nation state.

Citizenship as Exclusion

Many scholars have remarked on the inherently exclusionary nature of citizenship (Gordillo 2006; Hall and Held 1990; Kipnis 2004; Munasinghe 2002; Wallerstein 2003; Glenn 2011); for, although the institutions and practices of citizenship can forge bonds among fellow citizens,[64] they

62 Indeed, Gerald's objections to this aspect of KFN citizenship were strikingly similar to those he and others registered in response to universalistic expressions of Canadian and Yukon citizenship during land claim and self-government negotiations when, for example, they insisted that their long-term relationship to the land should give their interests in the region precedence over those of more recently arrived non–First Nation citizens of Canada.

63 Indeed, one might productively view the imposition of universal citizenship as another form of state simplification to add to those critiqued by Scott (1998).

64 Indeed, some argue that citizenship should promote social cohesion and stability (Kymlicka and Norman 2000: 1). But see Holston (2008: 5) for an account of how citizenship can be "used as a measure of differences and a means of distancing [fellow citizens] from one another." He shows that in Brazil, for example, institutions of citizenship have long been used to "exclude and discriminate on the basis of selected differences among citizens. Through laws, institutions, and social performances, this differentiating citizenship produces and maintains inequality" (ibid.: 22).

also erect boundaries of various kinds: between insiders and outsiders, passive and active citizens, citizens and non-citizens.[65] Because states are territorial organizations, they have a fundamental interest in territorial closure; that is, in being able to control or restrict the flow of people into their territory – whether or not they choose to actually exercise that control (Brubaker 1992: 25; Torpey 2000). Because states are also membership organizations, they have an interest in membership closure as well; that is, in having the power to differentially distribute rights, duties, privileges, and services to members (citizens) and non-members who are within their territories (visiting or resident non-citizens).

As Brubaker points out, both territorial and membership closure can serve material interests (e.g., by limiting or denying non-citizens access to domestic resources and costly programs and services) and ideological ones (e.g., limiting full participation in the state to those who are deemed ethnically, racially, or culturally appropriate). Ideological rationales for closure, however, are arguably the more prominent in the world today, since citizenship status is less often the basis of routine exclusion than it once was (in many countries, legal long-term non-citizen residents are eligible for most of the same benefits and services as citizens).[66] This leads Brubaker (1992: 182) to claim that "the politics of citizenship today is ... a *politics of identity*, not a *politics of interests* (at least not in the restricted, material sense) ... The central question is not 'who *gets* what?' but 'who *is* what?'" Answers to this question nearly always invoke the "nation." Because citizenship denotes membership in a state, and states are inextricably entwined with nations and nationalism, the politics of citizenship is "first and foremost a politics of nationhood" (ibid.). As we shall see in chapter 4, territorial states and the administrative forms associated with them tend to give rise to nationalist sentiments. The politics of citizenship/nationhood can (and often has) taken on racist overtones when certain "types" of people

65 As Brubaker (1992: 29) puts it, "The non-citizen is a residually defined outsider."

66 This, of course, ignores non-resident non-citizens and "illegal" aliens. Kipnis points out that because the institutions of citizenship allocate rights and privileges to some people (citizens) and not others (non-citizens), they necessarily produce social inequality. From this perspective it becomes clear that even those policies that are meant to mitigate the effects of social inequality *within* a state (e.g., health, education, and welfare benefits) can appear – from the vantage point of excluded non-citizens – "to be little more than policies acting to reproduce the inequalities that result from differential access to citizenship" (Kipnis 2004: 268).

are deemed unworthy – or less worthy – of national membership (see Aleinikoff 2002: chap. 2; Ong 1996), but even in the absence of virulent forms of nationalism, the politics of citizenship/nationhood is characterized by what Brubaker, following Dunn, refers to as "the routine, ordinary, taken-for-granted nationalism that is the 'natural political sentiment for modern states'" (Brubaker 1992: 28).[67] The exclusion of non-citizens (even those who are long-term residents) from the franchise indicates just how deep-seated is this everyday nationalism:

> Domestic closure against non-citizens rests on [the] understanding … of modern states as bounded nation-states – states whose telos it is to express the will and further the interests of distinctive and bounded nations, and whose legitimacy depends on their doing so, or at least seeming to do so. The routine exclusion of non-citizens from modern systems of "universal" suffrage is exemplary in this respect … That the exclusion of non-citizens from the franchise in national elections has nowhere been seriously challenged, even in the many European states with sizable populations of long-term resident non-citizens, testifies to the force – indeed the axiomatic status – of nationalism in modern states … The closure of suffrage (and other institutions) to non-citizens, based on the axiom that a state may, in fact must, discriminate between members and non-members, is one expression of this "normal," "legitimate," "rational," nationalism. (Brubaker 1992: 28)[68]

Because they create differences of this sort between "us" (members of the state) and "them" (non-members), the laws and institutions of citizenship serve to define – and give substance to – the imagined community that is the nation.

---

67 This is similar to what Anthony Smith calls "methodological nationalism" (see chap. 4).

68 Aleinikoff (2002: 5), however, notes that, in fact, "although the citizenry may be the location of sovereignty, citizenship neither defines the category of the governed nor that of the governors … The category of those who either exercise state power or elect those who do has never been coterminous with citizenship. Throughout the nineteenth century, white male immigrants were entitled to vote in a number of [the United] states, even as women and African American citizens were not. Today, residents of Puerto Rico and of the District of Columbia are not represented by voting members of Congress, and millions of citizens who have been convicted of felonies are disenfranchised."

Because Yukon First Nations are state-like, First Nation citizenship is necessarily exclusionary in many of the same ways just discussed. Although Yukon First Nations do not possess significant powers to exclude non-citizens from their traditional territories,[69] they do wield the power to exclude non-citizens from a wide array of rights, programs, and services. Indeed, the vast majority of programs and services provided by Yukon First Nations are accessible by citizens only, and we saw in chapter 2 that First Nations can and do routinely limit or deny non-citizens', including citizens of other Yukon First Nations, access to resources (e.g., the right to hunt) within their traditional territories.[70]

Although exclusions of this sort are often ostensibly about regulating access to resources (e.g., limiting the hunting rights of non-citizens in the interests of conservation), they also play a critical ideological role insofar as they incline Yukon Indian people to make new distinctions between "us" (citizens) and "them" (non-citizens) among themselves, distinctions that we shall see (in chapter 4) now sometimes override cross-cutting bonds of kinship and reciprocity. As in territorial states, then, the politics of First Nation citizenship must be seen as "first and foremost a politics of nationhood." Indeed, the brand of ethno-territorial nationalism currently emerging among Yukon First Nations closely resembles Brubaker's "routine, ordinary, taken-for-granted nationalism that is the 'natural political sentiment for modern states.'" This should not be surprising because Yukon First Nations, like the liberal democratic states that form the basis of Brubaker's analysis, are built on the principle of popular sovereignty. Yukon First Nation governments are conceived as being of and for the people of the First Nation.[71] The everyday nationalism entailed in this notion of sovereignty is evident in the routine exclusion of non-citizens – including Yukon

69 Yukon First Nations do have some powers to exclude non-citizens from their settlement lands (see chap. 2 for the distinction between traditional territory and settlement land), but these more closely resemble private property owners' ability to exclude others from their property than a sovereign state's power to exclude foreigners from its territory (Kluane First Nation 2003b: 81–8).

70 We also saw, however, that non-citizens can often access those resources through the Yukon territorial government (e.g., by obtaining a Yukon hunting licence), though in such cases they are bound by Yukon laws and regulations. It is only on settlement lands that First Nations have the full authority to exclude non-citizens from access to resources.

71 The preamble of Kluane First Nation's constitution, reproduced in chap. 4, asserts this clearly (see page 207).

Indian people who may count KFN citizens among their close relatives and/or who are long-term residents of the traditional territory – from a wide array of rights and benefits. As we saw in the chapter 2, not all of these exclusions go uncontested; relations of kinship and reciprocity remain strong among Yukon Indian people, and they provide a basis for a trenchant moral critique of exclusionary practices based on First Nation citizenship. That some routine exclusions, such as the exclusion of non-citizens (even kin and long-term residents) from voting in First Nation elections, do go largely unquestioned,[72] however, shows that Yukon Indian people have begun to internalize and take for granted the everyday nationalism of their First Nation states.

In chapter 4, I will further examine some of the exclusionary practices that are inclining Yukon Indian people to draw distinctions between "us" and "them" and explore some of the consequences of these everyday forms of nationalism. Before doing so, however, I turn to a different facet of exclusionary citizenship, one that has received considerably less attention in the literature on citizenship. The institution of citizenship not only separates "us" (citizens) from "them" (non-citizens); it also implicitly divides the human realm (where citizenship is possible) from the non-human (where it is not).

First Nation Citizenship and Other-Than-Human Persons

Non-humans are not eligible to become Kluane First Nation citizens. Only humans – not moose, caribou, or spruces trees – can be citizens of Kluane First Nation. This is not really surprising; the same can be said of citizenship everywhere. Indeed, most scholars of citizenship would regard such a statement as a truism; the restriction to humans is so basic an aspect of citizenship that no citizenship code in the world (including those of the Yukon First Nations) bothers to state it explicitly.[73] Yet, the

72 To my knowledge, no one in the Yukon has seriously questioned the idea that non–First Nation citizens should be denied the franchise in First Nation governments. Some of the effects of this exclusion may be mitigated by provisions in First Nation constitutions for the granting of honorary citizenship status to long-term residents of the traditional territory, but the provisions governing the rights and privileges of honorary citizens vary by First Nation.

73 Interestingly, however, KFN's citizenship code does not explicitly preclude non-humans from becoming citizens either. It refers only to "persons" (see eligibility criteria above), leaving open the possibility of a more expansive interpretation that could include all *dän*, including the non-human variety (Nadasdy 2007b).

exclusion of non-humans from citizenship reflects a fundamental – if implicit – assumption of Euro-American political theory: only human persons can be political subjects. Animals, plants, and other non-human entities may be the objects of politics, but they cannot be its subjects. This no doubt accounts for the fact that – for all their detailed analysis of the exclusionary nature of citizenship – very few scholars theorizing citizenship (with a couple of significant recent exceptions to be discussed below) have so much as remarked on the fact that citizenship excludes non-humans from membership in the sovereign political community.

Although the exclusion of non-humans from the political realm is generally taken for granted among Euro-American political theorists and constitution-makers, it represents a radical departure from Yukon Indian ways of being in the world. We saw in chapter 2 that indigenous society in the Yukon was not territorially ordered. Rather, social relations there were – and in many cases still are – ordered by principles of kinship and reciprocity that cross-cut the territorial boundaries of today's First Nations. These social relationships are not restricted to human persons. On the contrary, other-than-human persons (who, we have seen, are included in the category *dän*) engage with humans in the same web of kinship and reciprocity that characterizes social relations among humans. For this reason, many Yukon Indian people view them as powerful agents who play a vital and ongoing role in indigenous Yukon society (Nadasdy 2003: chap. 2; 2007b). Indeed, Yukon Indian people generally regard themselves as among the *least* powerful of all the various kinds of persons inhabiting the landscape. After all, human people depend for their very survival on the goodwill of their animal benefactors; and if animals are offended they may refuse to give themselves to hunters in the future. For this reason, most Yukon Indian people explicitly recognize their indebtedness to the powerful other-than-human persons upon whom they depend, and they cultivate a sense of humility in their dealings with these powerful beings.[74]

74 This attitude is widespread among northern indigenous hunting peoples. Indeed, many say that animals are moved by pity to help humans. As anthropologist Jean-Guy Goulet (1998: 66) puts it: "Dene Elders always emphasized how pitiful they were when they encountered their animal helpers. The poverty and pitifulness in question is not so much a material one as an existential one. The recognition of one's existential poverty compared to other beings is the necessary condition to become

Animals and other non-human persons are not merely powerful actors in Yukon indigenous society, however; they also play an overtly political role. They can understand human speech (whether spoken or merely thought), and it is they – not humans – who authored many of the laws that still govern not only human–animal interactions, but also social relations among humans. The sharing of meat, for example, is a central aspect of social relations among indigenous hunting people across the north who have made it clear that they share meat not only out of a sense of duty to family and friends, but also – and perhaps even more importantly – because the animals demand it.[75] Animals communicated their laws, including the requirement to share their bodies with kin and neighbours, directly to particular humans in the distant past; and these laws have been passed down from one human generation to the next as a body of stories that teach people how to behave properly towards one another and towards the various animal and other non-human people inhabiting their world.[76] Despite the ancient origins of these laws, animals and other non-human persons continue to enforce them – sometimes quite harshly.[77] They also continue to communicate with humans by speaking to them in their dreams, visions, and the occasional waking encounter (Nadasdy 2007b: 33–4). Perhaps most importantly, animals play an ongoing role in the political education of Yukon Indian people by cultivating in them the attitudes and interpersonal skills they will need if they are to assume their roles as fully competent adult members of human-animal society.[78] Despite the

the recipient of gifts and powers from these other beings." Similarly, Mary Black-Rogers (1986: 367) points out that among the Anishinabe, to "be pitied" by and to "receive a gift" from a more powerful being are one and the same thing (for a discussion of similar beliefs among the Rock Cree, see Brightman 1993: 81).

75 For a list of sources providing examples of this belief among a wide range of Northern Athapaskan and Algonquian peoples, see Smith (2002: 61). On this belief among the Inuit, see Omura (2013) and Wenzel (1991).

76 That traditional stories must be considered a body of indigenous law on par with Canadian common law is a point made powerfully by Borrows (2002, esp. chaps. 1 and 2). In the Yukon, the Northern Tutchone First Nations in particular have taken the lead in seeking to reframe what is commonly referred to as the "traditional knowledge" contained in long-time-ago stories as *Dooli*, or "traditional law" (Natcher, Davis, and Hickey 2005: 245).

77 On enforcement, see Nadasdy (2003: 94), Nelson (1983: esp. 21–7).

78 For a discussion of how animals teach humans patience and respect, and of the importance of these attitudes for the proper conduct of interpersonal relations, see Nadasdy (2003: 100–8).

dramatic changes that have taken place in Yukon Indian society over the past hundred years, many Yukon Indian people (like other hunting peoples across the circumpolar world) continue to act in accordance with the laws received from animals in the distant past as they try to maintain proper relations with one another and with the other-than-human persons upon whom they depend (Nadasdy 2003; Nadasdy 2007b; Nadasdy 2011).[79]

Because it draws a firm boundary between human and other-than-human persons, KFN citizenship is fundamentally incompatible with this view of society. Indeed, KFN citizenship is an integral part of a system of governance that explicitly precludes non-humans from participation in the political realm. As a politico-territorial organization modelled on the liberal democratic state, Kluane First Nation is conceived by all as of and for the *human* people of Kluane First Nation. The non-human residents of KFN's traditional territory are excluded from this notion of popular sovereignty; the government of KFN is neither *of* nor *for* them, nor do KFN's land claim and self-government agreements envision any role at all for these non-human persons in the running of KFN government or society. Instead, the agreements treat them as a set of resources, and they divide up ownership of and jurisdiction over these resources among the three signatory governments. In chapter 2, for example, we saw that under its final agreement KFN "retains" ownership and jurisdiction over its settlement lands. This includes the power to enact laws regarding the "use, management, administration and protection of natural resources under the ownership, control or jurisdiction of Kluane First Nation" (Kluane First Nation 2003b: 14). While advocates of First Nation rights might applaud such a formulation, the attitude towards the non-human world that underlies it is utterly foreign to indigenous thought and practice in the Yukon.

The notion that the Kluane First Nation government – on behalf of its (human) citizens – has "jurisdiction and control over" the non-human residents of Kluane territory, and that it is therefore KFN's job to manage and administer them in the best interests of those (human) citizens, stands in stark contrast to ongoing practices, knowledge, and values that are predicated on the assumption that these other-than-human

79 For a discussion of these issues in other parts of the North American subarctic see Brightman (1993), Nelson (1983), Tanner (1979).

persons are powerful sentient actors in their own right. Although these beings are enmeshed in a complex web of social relations with human persons, they are neither subject to human law nor do they respect human assertions of territoriality – jurisdictional or otherwise.[80] In fact, assertions to the effect that the Kluane First Nation government has the responsibility to unilaterally manage and control the lives and affairs of the non-human persons within its territorial borders, even when it is ostensibly for their own good (e.g., in the interest of conservation), smacks of paternalistic colonialism – or would if applied to human persons. Indeed, these aspects of the agreements bear an uncomfortable resemblance to the Indian Act, which asserted the Canadian state's responsibility to manage and control the lives and affairs of Indian people (who, until relatively recently, were also non-citizens) – also ostensibly for their own good.

Anishinabe legal scholar John Borrows (2002) is one of the very few theorists who addresses the exclusion of non-humans inherent in Euro-American conceptions of citizenship.[81] First Nation citizenship as it is currently formulated, he says, "is not consistent with holistic notions of citizenship that must include the land, and all beings upon it" (141). To accurately reflect Anishinabe views of political community, he argues, citizenship would have to be radically reconceptualized to include other-than-human persons:

> Our births, lives, and deaths on this site have brought us into citizenship with the land. We participate in its renewal, have responsibility for its continuation, and grieve for its losses. As citizens of this land, we also feel the presence of our ancestors and strive with them to have the relations of our polity respected. Our loyalties, allegiance, and affection are related to the land. The water, wind, sun, and stars are part of this federation. The fish, birds, plants, and animals also share this union. Our teachings and stories form the constitution of this relationship and direct and nourish the obligations it requires. (Borrows 2002: 138)

---

80 This last point is readily conceded by wildlife biologists, especially those involved in complex inter-jurisdictional efforts to manage migratory species, such as geese or caribou, whose migrations routinely cross political boundaries.

81 Others include Will Kymlicka and Sue Donaldson in their book *Zoopolis* (2011) and James Tully with his notion of "Gaia citizenship" (2014: 65–6; 2016). I will refer to both of these efforts below.

Despite significant cultural differences across the north, Borrows's notion of "landed citizenship" would, I think, strike a chord with many northern Indian people, including those in the Yukon, who continue to think of themselves as "part of the land, part of the water" (McClellan et al. 1987: 1).

If we read Borrows as simply advocating the extension of liberal citizenship to include animals and other non-human entities, his vision of landed citizenship raises a host of theoretical and practical questions. First Nation citizenship is, after all, defined in First Nation self-government agreements and constitutions, and it is enacted daily by citizens who participate in political debate, vote in First Nation elections, avail themselves of First Nation administered programs and services, serve as First Nation appointees on co-management boards, and so on. It is one thing to assert that the abstract concept of Kluane First Nation citizenship-as-political-community should be expanded to include moose, caribou, and black spruce trees; it is quite another to suggest that these same beings should be eligible to vote, sit on co-management boards, and participate in processes of First Nation governance. But this is an important part of what First Nation citizenship entails. As we have seen, the notion of citizenship connotes more than a sense of shared community and interdependence; it also signals membership in a state (or state-like political organization), and it implies a particular relationship – entailing both obligations and benefits – between individual citizens and the state to which they belong. Fulfilling these obligations and receiving these benefits is an integral part of what it means to be a citizen. How exactly are moose, spruce trees, and other non-human persons supposed to assume their proper roles as individual citizens vis-à-vis the First Nation state? The fact that Borrows does not attempt to answer this question[82] suggests that he views his notion of landed citizenship less as a mechanism for expanding the concept of liberal citizenship than as a provocation to

82 To my knowledge, the only scholars who do attempt to answer such questions are Donaldson and Kymlicka (2011), whose explicit goal is to expand the liberal concept of citizenship to include (some) animals. For reasons I discuss elsewhere (Nadasdy 2016), however, their model of animal citizenship is incompatible with indigenous Yukon ideas about animal personhood and political agency.

get readers to think critically about the inadequacy of liberal notions of citizenship for Anishinabe politics.[83]

The problem lies in the statist implications of the citizenship concept. Other-than-human persons were indeed full political subjects in indigenous Yukon (and Anishinabe) society, but they no more derived that status from their membership in some territorially ordered indigenous polity than did Yukon Indian people themselves. Rather, their political role emerged through their participation in ongoing relations of kinship and reciprocity with all the various kinds of persons with whom they came in contact. Flexible though it is, the concept of citizenship is simply unable to accommodate this view of the world. This suggests that Taiaiake Alfred may be right to view the liberal concept of *citizenship* as fundamentally incompatible with a genuinely decolonized indigenous politics. By contrast, the relevant political community referenced by Borrows's concept of "landed citizenship" is not the state (or state-like First Nation), but all of creation. Far from representing a straightforward expansion of liberal citizenship, Borrows's concept of landed citizenship implies a radical rethinking of law and politics from the ground up.[84] In such a politics, viewing the land and animals as full

83 It is actually a bit difficult to pin Borrows down with respect to citizenship. In parts of his essay on landed citizenship (e.g., 2002: 157) as well as in some of his subsequent writings on the topic of citizenship (Borrows 2010a: 156–9), he does appear to advocate for the extension of liberal-style First Nation citizenship (i.e., full membership in the First Nation body politic, including voting rights and everything else that would entail) to those non-indigenous (human) people who live in First Nation territory and agree to participate in processes of First Nation governance.

84 Taken as a whole, Borrows's work can be read as an attempt to develop just such a decolonized political and legal framework (Borrows 2002; Borrows 2010b; Borrows 2010a). In formulating his notion of "Gaia citizenship," Tully draws explicitly on the writings of indigenous scholars, including Borrows, as well as iconic environmentalists, such as Aldo Leopold, who famously urged us to regard ourselves as "plain members and citizens" of the biotic community (cited in Tully 2016: 5). In Tully's account, Gaia citizens (who are human) recognize that they are bound up in relationships of reciprocal interdependence with non-humans and thus have a responsibility to care for them and the biotic systems within which we all live. Although he recognizes non-humans as kin (13), however, he does not seem to consider them as political subjects/actors (citizens) in their own right or to consider what non-human citizenship would look like. The effect, as in Borrows's work, is to make one wonder whether "citizenship" is really an appropriate term at all for what he is trying to describe.

political actors would be common sense; it would not require elaborate justification but would seem as natural as the denial of citizenship to non-humans seems to those whose politics are rooted in the ontological assumptions of the state.

If the citizenship concept is not flexible enough to accommodate Yukon Indian people's ideas about the proper relationship between humans, animals, and other beings in the world, then what are the consequences of its imposition through the land claim and self-government agreements? In their capacity *as citizens*, Kluane people are privileged residents of their territory, because collectively they exercise exclusive jurisdiction and control over the management of animals, plants, and other non-human persons on their settlement lands. None of the non-human residents of the region have such rights and responsibilities under the new agreements. Thus, Kluane citizens stand apart from – and above – the non-human inhabitants of their territory. As *citizens*, Kluane people can be good and responsible stewards of their land, but they cannot be "part of the land, part of the water"; and it is this (among other things) that makes people like Gerald Dickson profoundly uncomfortable with his status as a Kluane First Nation citizen. It is perhaps too early to say exactly how this change in perspective will affect human–animal relations (to say nothing of human–human relations), but there cannot be much doubt that people who see their role as one of "managing animal populations in their jurisdiction" are bound to relate to animals differently than those who view them as politically powerful and intelligent persons with whom they have to learn to live.

Conclusion

Citizenship is not an indigenous concept in northern Canada. Modern citizenship is the mechanism used by states – and some state-like political organizations, such as the self-governing First Nations that have recently come into being across northern Canada – to formally define their membership, that is, the body of people in whose name they govern. In the absence of a system of territorially ordered states – or, in the case of northern Canada, a system of state-like First Nations – citizenship would be meaningless. And indeed, the idea that the indigenous people of northern Canada were citizens of specific bounded First Nations each with jurisdiction over its own distinct territory would have made little sense to them until just a few generations ago. Before that, there were no First Nations citizens, because there were no First

Nations for them to be citizens *of*. Yet, citizenship and the power to regulate citizenship are essential aspects of state sovereignty; so to the extent indigenous people frame their arguments against the state in the language of sovereignty, First Nation citizenship becomes an obligatory category.

Proponents of First Nation sovereignty by and large agree with the assertion that citizenship and sovereignty are linked, and they champion First Nation citizenship – and First Nation governments' power to regulate it – as key expressions of that sovereignty. In this they are undoubtedly correct; First Nation citizenship *is* essential to First Nation sovereignty. But if sovereignty is itself a cultural import that is transforming – rather than merely recognizing – indigenous political forms, as it surely is for the indigenous people of the western subarctic, then First Nation citizenship must be viewed as a key mechanism of that transformation. First Nation citizenship, like all varieties of state citizenship, is imposed through a complex mixture of coercion and consent. Like other varieties of citizenship, First Nation citizenship is a universalizing concept that takes for granted – and so helps enact – a particular kind of person, the rights-bearing possessive individual, and a particular political form, the state. To the extent that Yukon First Nation people adopt the attitudes and practices of First Nation citizenship, they enact First Nations as (semi-) sovereign state-like organizations, one another as individual members of those organizations, and animals as resources owned and managed by whatever state-like polity has jurisdiction over where they happen to be found. And finally, like other forms of citizenship, First Nation citizenship is exclusionary, drawing distinctions between "us" (citizens) and "them" (non-citizens) as well as between human citizens (the subjects of politics) and non-human resources (the objects of politics).

In the coming chapter, I relax my focus on the official/legal aspects of First Nation membership (i.e., citizenship) and look more squarely at the ways land claims and self-government have increasingly caused Kluane First Nation citizens to view themselves as particular "kinds" of people who differ significantly from the citizens of other First Nations – despite the fact that these "foreign" citizens are often their close relatives. I foreground the everyday practices that create the (First) nation in Hobsbawm's second sense: a community bound together by common language, history, culture, and/or ethnicity and distinct from members of other such communities.

Chapter Four

Nation

We have made Italy, now we have to make Italians.

Massimo d'Azeglio, cited in Hobsbawm (1992: 44)

Thus far, I have focused on the Yukon land claim and self-government agreements primarily as boundary-making mechanisms. They create new geographical boundaries by demarcating First Nation traditional territories and settlement lands, and they establish new social boundaries through the institution of First Nation citizenship. These geographical and social boundary–making projects are inextricably intertwined with one another. By drawing lines on the map and then using them as the basis for differentially distributing rights, duties, privileges, and services among citizens and non-citizens, the agreements create a series of everyday legal, administrative, and practical distinctions between "us" (citizens) and "them" (non-citizens). Indeed, many – though by no means all – of the distinctions between First Nation citizens and non-citizens are framed in explicitly territorial terms (i.e., as rights and privileges vis-à-vis a First Nation's territory).

In chapter 2, I argued that although many people assume that First Nation traditional territories reflect "traditional" patterns of land-use and occupancy, they are in fact something quite new in the Yukon. Because indigenous Yukon society was not composed of distinct political entities each with jurisdiction over its own territory, the new agreements cannot be viewed as simply formalizing jurisdictional boundaries among pre-existing First Nation polities. Instead, I argued, they are mechanisms for creating the legal and administrative systems that bring those polities into being. Much as they tend to view First

Nation traditional territories as traditional, many people also assume that the cultural stuff contained by those territories, too, is somehow traditional – that is, that First Nation traditional territory boundaries separate peoples who are – and have long been – linguistically and culturally distinct from one another. In such a view, the creation of a traditional territory boundary between, say, Kluane and White River First Nations merely reflects and formalizes already existing differences in language and culture between two distinct ethnic groups or "peoples." In fact, however, prior to the land claim process, the indigenous people of the Yukon were no more divisible into discrete linguistic/cultural groups than they were into discrete territorially ordered polities. While First Nation land claim and self-government agreements are certainly not productive of all linguistic and cultural differences among Yukon Indian people, they *are* largely responsible for the fact that today those differences are increasingly being framed in ethno-nationalist terms.

In chapter 2, I also suggested (following Hobsbawm) that the distinction between civic and ethnic nationalism is an analytical rather than historical one, and that, in practice, legal and administrative differences between (in this case, First Nation) citizens and non-citizens often come to be framed in ethno-nationalist terms. Having now examined some of the ways the Yukon agreements create political, legal, and administrative differences among the citizens of different First Nations, I now ask how and why it is that Yukon Indian people have increasingly begun to frame these differences in ethno-nationalist terms. In other words, how and why have Yukon First Nation citizens begun to regard themselves collectively as different *kinds* of people than the citizens of other First Nations?

Anthropologist Katherine Verdery (1993a: 38) writes that "nation," a term denoting the relationship between states and their subjects, has become one of the most potent symbols of our times. Like all symbols, its meaning is ambiguous; such that it can mean different things to different people, and its meaning can vary according to context (as I have already noted, for example, in pointing out its civic and ethnic variants). Second, like all symbols, its use can evoke powerful emotions – powerful enough, Benedict Anderson (1991) notes, to incite a willingness to sacrifice one's own life in its defence. In large part, the emotional power of *nation* derives from the way its use tends to naturalize certain social relations. Derived from *natio*, meaning birth, the word *nation* has always – despite significant changes in meaning over the centuries – referred to social groups supposedly rooted in nature;

one is *born into* a nation.[1] In its modern incarnation, these supposedly natural groupings are viewed metaphorically as "collective individuals": single, coherent, and bounded entities, each of which possesses its own character, attributes, desires, and agency (Handler 1988: 39–43).[2]

Indeed, the very notion of "self-government," so central to both the concept of the nation state and to the process of decolonization, is an instantiation of this metaphor, since it implies the existence of a collective national "self" as the rightful subject of autonomous governance. National selves are viewed as deserving of autonomy precisely because, like individuals, they supposedly possess distinct characters, attributes, desires, and destinies that set them apart from other ethno-national selves. The idea that a nation should govern itself, then, depends, first, upon the construction of a unitary ethno-national self and, second, upon the clear differentiation of that self from other ethnonational selves (which are themselves deserving of self-government). As Katherine Verdery (1996: 78) succinctly puts it: "'Nation' as an idea generally posits simultaneous sameness (we are all one) and difference (we are unlike the others)." This implies that two closely interrelated processes lie at the heart of nationalism: external differentiation and internal homogenization.[3] Before people can begin to view themselves as members of an ethno-national self worthy of autonomy, they must first

1 At first glance, this may seem to apply to *nation* only in its ethnic guise; after all civic nationalism (citizenship) is viewed explicitly as a legal/political category rather than a biological one. As we saw in chapter 3, however, the vast majority of people on earth are, in fact, assigned citizenship on the basis of birth, and the principle of jus sanguinis formally acknowledges the role of descent in the construction of the civic nation. It is no accident that the process of assuming citizenship not conferred by birth is referred to as "naturalization." On the etymology of "nation," see Hobsbawm (1992: chap. 1).

2 Drawing on Macpherson (1962), Verdery (1993a) argues that the nation must be viewed not merely as a collective individual, but as a collective *possessive* individual. The nation-as-collective-individual metaphor has many entailments. One of these, a central trope of nationalist thought, is that members of a nation share bodily substances, such as blood or genetic material (Malkki 1992: 38 n. 7). Along these lines, anthropologists (Borneman 1992; Schneider 1977; Verdery 1994a; Verdery 1999: 41; see also Anderson 1991: 5) have long noted the structural similarity between idioms of kinship and nationalism.

3 Many scholars (e.g., Cohen 1986; Sahlins 1989: 270–3; Cooper and Stoler 1989: 615) have observed that nationalism is inherently oppositional insofar as it requires those who view themselves as members of one national self to draw a collective distinction between themselves and foreign "others." Peter Sahlins (1989: 271), for example,

differentiate themselves – culturally, linguistically, historically – from the members of other nations, while simultaneously erasing – or at least downplaying – any such differences among themselves.

To say that nationalism requires the creation of ethno-national differences is not to say that the differences that eventually come to be viewed as diagnostic of national identity are imaginary or somehow invented by nationalists; linguistic and cultural variation, after all, are real enough and long predate nationalism. It does mean, however, that myriad social differences must somehow be "yoked" together and framed as *national* in character. In his process-oriented account of social entities, Andrew Abbott (1995: 871) defines "yoking" as the "connection of two or more proto-boundaries such that one side of each becomes defined as 'inside' the same entity." Thus, for a nation to emerge as a social entity, a particular language or dialect might be yoked to a particular religion and both in turn to a set of dietary preferences, and so on. Prior to the rise of the nation (or First Nation) as a social entity, these are all just social differences: one person speaks Southern Tutchone, another Upper Tanana; one is Christian, the other is not; one eats Dall sheep and gophers, the other prefers muskrat. But if differences get yoked to one another such that one side of each difference comes to be seen as emblematic of a particular ethno-national self, then those on that side of the yoked linguistic, dietary, and religious boundary (e.g., Southern Tutchone-speaking, Christian, sheep-eaters) come to be viewed as "inside" the nation, while those on the other are outsiders, properly part of some other ethno-national self.

This account is, of course, much too neat. The criteria for national membership are historically contingent and always open to negotiation. They can be contested and weighted differently by different actors in different contexts. Thus, the yoking together of Abbott's proto-boundaries is never final, nor is there anything natural about the resulting social entity. Rather, it is a product of ongoing negotiation and struggle, requiring constant justification if it is to retain a semblance of reality.

---

notes that "national identity ... is contingent and relational: it is defined by the social or territorial boundaries drawn to distinguish the collective self and its implicit negation, the other." Meanwhile, other scholars (Foster 1991; Verdery 1993a; Williams 1989) have also emphasized the flip side of this process of external differentiation: the tendency towards internal homogenization.

> The emergence of an entity [such as a nation] is the assemblage of various sites of difference ... into a set of boundaries ... that define an inside and an outside. But the work of creating an entity must also be seen as the work of rationalizing these various connections so that the resulting entity has the ability to endure, as a persistent thing, in the various ecologies in which it is located. (Abbott 1995: 872)

Thus, there will always be people who question the various criteria for national inclusion and the links among them. To return to our only partially hypothetical example: is it really necessary for someone to eat Dall sheep to belong to the (First) nation? Or is it enough that they (or their parents) speak Southern Tutchone? Or perhaps other criteria – ancestry, race, or personal history within the national territory, for example – may be invoked in certain contexts as even more relevant to the question of First Nation membership. The point is that discussions/negotiations over national identity are almost never made in the abstract. Instead, they occur in particular social contexts where the question of identity has real social stakes. And when it comes to questions of national identity, one's relationship to the state is always a critical part of the context. Accordingly, I begin with a general discussion of how and why the imposition of state territorial boundaries so often leads to the rise of ethno-nationalist sentiments.

Sovereign Territoriality and the Construction of First Nation Homelands

Among the many consequences of territoriality identified by Sack (1986: 33) is that "territoriality acts as a *container* or *mold* for the spatial properties of events." This aptly characterizes the territorial state, which Giddens (1987: 172) has famously described as "a power-container whose administrative purview corresponds exactly to its territorial delimitation."[4] As many scholars (e.g., Anderson 1991; Giddens 1987; Mitchell 2002) have noted, the administrative power of the state

4 For extended discussions of the state-as-container metaphor and its entailments, see Agnew (1994), Taylor (1994), and Walker (1993). For an account of how this metaphor of "vertical encompassment" is naturalized though everyday bureaucratic practice, see Ferguson and Gupta (2002).

depends in large part on its ability to gather and manipulate statistical and geographical information about the populations, lands, and resources within its borders (censuses, maps, economic indicators, etc.). Indeed, the rise of the territorial state was accompanied by the emergence of a vast machinery for the production of these official data, and it was the state itself, as container, that provided the spatial unit for their collection and analysis (Murphy 1996: 102–3; Agnew 1994: 68–71). Because the emerging social sciences relied heavily upon official data generated by the state (and, indeed, were intimately involved in their production) and because the assumptions underlying those data (territorial and otherwise) informed the operational categories of the new social science disciplines, these disciplines have tended to regard the boundaries of "society" as congruent with those of the state (Agnew 1994: 69–70; Smith 1979: 191; Wolf 1982: 7–19).

These official data, then, are not just "about" the state as a preexisting social entity, they are in part *constitutive* of it and of the particular notion of society it engenders and contains (Giddens 1987: 180). As historian Thongchai Winichakul (1994) points out, maps played a key role in this process. By defining the "geo-body" of the Thai Nation, he shows, national maps were instrumental in bringing about the rise of the Thai nation, the collective individual whose "geo-body" was inscribed on those maps.[5] And if the state is a container for society, then the borders of the state must separate members of distinct societies; that is, they serve to divide an "us" from a "them." It is this tendency to assume that the borders of the state separate distinct peoples – along with all the data-gathering activities entailed in such an assumption – that Anthony Smith (1979: 191) has referred to as "methodological nationalism" (see also Anderson 1991: 52–3). The territorially bounded institutions, knowledge, and practices associated with the state generally play an important role in creating the imagined political-economic-cultural community that is a nation. "England," as Corrigan and Sayer (1985: 192) put it, "was ... 'hammered into a nation,' primarily through the machinery of state." Indeed, numerous scholars have argued that the emergence of the territorial state system preceded and contributed

5 On the importance of maps in constructing historical narratives of the nation, see also Anderson (1991: 174–5).

to the rise of nationalism – and not the other way around (Hobsbawm 1992: 78; Murphy 1996: 95).[6]

The link between territorial state and nation is so intimate that there is a widespread tendency (oft lamented by scholars of nationalism) to conflate the two concepts.[7] The very term *nation state* assumes that the state and the nation are conterminous, an ideal that has rarely if ever been achieved. Yet the tendency to conflate state and nation in this way is not simply the result of sloppy word choice. Rather, it reflects the nationalist ideal, an ideal that animates the nation-building visions of state politicians as much as it does the state-building dreams of ethno-nationalist separatists (Gellner 1983: 1).[8] Nationalism, then, is fundamentally a territorial ideology, one that is intimately and dialectically bound up with the territoriality of the state system. Geographer Edward Soja (1971: 16) puts it succinctly: "The nation-state is probably the most territorial of human political organizations. Its basic ideological force – nationalism – is, in essence, the drive by a particular group for a state – a territory – of its own."[9]

This provides a new perspective for thinking about Yukon First Nation traditional territories, discussed at length in chapter 2. Clearly, traditional territory boundaries do more than simply indicate the jurisdictional boundaries of a few management boards. If that were really

---

6 This is not to say that nationalist movements have never led to the creation of new states. It is simply to point out that nationalism owes its existence as a coherent and compelling ideology to the existence of an international system of territorial states (Rée 1992). As Gellner (1983: 3) puts it, "The problem of nationalism does not arise in stateless societies … Nationalism emerges only in milieux in which the existence of the state is already very much taken for granted."

7 Hobsbawm (1992: 177), for example, complains of the "semantic illusion which today turns all states officially into 'nations' (and members of the United Nations), even when they are patently not."

8 It is for this reason that "all movements seeking territorial autonomy tend to think of themselves as establishing 'nations' … and all movements for regional, local or even sectional interests against central power and state bureaucracy will, if they possibly can, put on the national costume, preferably in its ethnic-linguistic styles" (Hobsbawm 1992: 177–8).

9 There is widespread agreement among scholars of nationalism and political/historical geographers about the essentially territorial nature of nationalism. For discussions of the central importance of territory and territoriality for the ideology of nationalism, in particular the drive for a national "homeland," see Anderson (1986; 1988), Gellner (1983), Kaiser (2002), Knight (1982), Murphy (1996), Paasi (1996), Penrose (2002), Smith (1981), Williams and Smith (1983).

all they did, then it would not be so difficult in practice to resolve territorial overlap, nor would efforts to do so incite the deep emotions that they do.[10] Instead, as I noted in chapter 2, Yukon Indian people often have very strong feelings towards their First Nation traditional territories, which have become symbolic of what they see as their special connection to the land and their long history upon it *as a people*. In our very first meeting, for example, Joe Johnson, then chief of Kluane First Nation, told me that when driving north on the Alaska Highway, he feels that he has "come home" when Kluane Lake comes into view, and that he gets that same feeling driving south once he crosses the White River. I did not know it at the time, but his characterization of "home" corresponded exactly to the traditional territory boundaries he and other KFN delegates were then advocating at overlap negotiations with the White River First Nation (which I will describe in detail below).

What is interesting about Joe's statement is not simply that it shows a strong emotional attachment to place, but rather its implicitly nationalist framing.[11] As we saw in chapter 2, traditional territory boundaries were drawn up in a rather ad hoc way, and they do not always correspond very well to the personal experiences of individual First Nation citizens. This was certainly the case for Joe, who, as we also saw in that chapter, spent a significant part of his youth living and hunting in places like Kloo Lake, McKinley Creek, and Fourth of July Creek – all of which are south and east of KFN's traditional territory boundary. Significantly, however, his characterization of "home" at our first meeting left many of those places out. If he had been referring to his own personal experiences on the land, I would expect him to have told me that he felt at home once he reached Kloo Lake (which northbound drivers on the Alaska Highway encounter well before they catch their first glimpse of Kluane Lake). This suggests that he was referring not to his own personal home territory, but instead to the "home" of Kluane

10 See the general discussion of traditional territory overlap and sharing accords in chapter 2 and the specific account of Kluane/White River overlap below.

11 It is clearly possible for people to develop powerful attachments to place without framing them in either territorial or ethno-national terms. For a brilliant and evocative analysis of an extremely rich yet non-ethno-territorially ordered sense of place among southern Athapaskans, see Basso (1996).

First Nation.[12] This is not, of course, to suggest that he did not have very real and deep emotional attachments to Kluane First Nation's homeland. He was born at Redtail Lake in Kluane territory and grew up in Burwash Landing. He had an intimate knowledge of Kluane First Nation's territory from a lifetime of hunting, trapping, and guiding. But he also had intimate knowledge of areas well *outside* KFN's traditional territory. The fact that he chose to frame his concept of "home" in national – rather than personal – terms is, I think, significant. Indeed, Peter Sahlins (1989: 8) suggests that "national identity means replacing a sense of local territory by love of national territory." While I would not want to claim that Joe – or any other citizen of Kluane First Nation – ever "replaced" their personal attachment to place with a love for their national territory, I do believe he developed strong emotional bonds with Kluane First Nation's traditional territory and that these territorial sentiments were intimately bound up with a growing sense of himself as a member of the Kluane First Nation *people*. Both the territory and the people – as unitary and connected entities – emerged directly out of the land claim process.

I shall explore in some detail the processes contributing to the emergence of a Kluane ethno-nation, but first I consider more generally why it is that purely political/administrative boundaries such as those demarcating First Nation traditional territories so commonly come to be viewed as separating people of different cultural or ethnic groups.

Internal Territoriality and the Rise of Ethno-Nationalism

As we saw in chapter 2, states are internally as well as externally territorial; and internal boundaries, even when created for purely administrative purposes, can be constitutive of new – and sometimes oppositional

12 Again, Joe said this to me at our very first meeting. He did not know me at all then, other than that I was there to do research; so, he may well have been speaking quite strategically, perhaps even in the hope that this southern researcher would repeat his definition of KFN's homeland in writing and so strengthen KFN's position in their negotiations with WRFN. It is worth pointing out, however, that in subsequent years other Kluane citizens described their conceptions of "home" to me in very nearly the same words as Joe (the first sighting of Kluane Lake from Boutellier summit nearly always figures in such descriptions).

– political identities (Anderson 1997: 107).[13] Geographer Anssi Paasi (1996: 32–8) refers to this as the "institutionalization of regions," a process that can lead to the rise of local/regional identities which, like national identities (which they can become), distinguish an "us" from a "them" along territorial lines. One need only glance at a map of the post-colonial world to see that what were once internal administrative boundaries of empire ended up shaping in fundamental ways the nationalist movements that arose in opposition to imperial rule and the geographical configuration of post-colonial states that resulted from those nationalist struggles. Indeed, Benedict Anderson (1991: xiv) notes that "the nineteenth century colonial state (and policies that its mindset encouraged) dialectically engendered the grammar of the nationalisms that eventually arose to combat it" (see also Chatterjee 1993). Among the key components of this grammar are the institutionalization of regions associated with state processes of internal territoriality and the related emergence of ethno-territorial identities.[14]

As we saw in chapter 2, the process of internal territorialization is not always a top-down one. Even when initially imposed by powerful outside forces, political and administrative boundaries derive their local significance and meaning from the way people interact with them in their everyday lives. Peter Sahlins (1989), for instance, shows that French and Spanish identities emerged in the frontier zone of the southern Pyrenees not so much as a result of assimilationist policies emanating from distant Madrid or Paris, but rather from how local people responded to the imposition of the border in their midst. He argues that the territorial boundary between France and Spain in the Cerdan

13 Murphy (1989: 441) notes that "to create an area with legal or administrative significance is to bring into being a functional spatial unit that can profoundly alter ideas about social groupings"; Bourdieu (1991: 222) asserts that "the frontier, that product of a legal act of delimitation, produces cultural difference as much as it is produced by it"; Biolsi (2005: 253) notes that "spatializations are constitutive of subjectivities"; and Peter Sahlins (1989: 270) asserts that "political constraints [accompanying the imposition of political borders] became meaningful boundaries of territorial and social identities."

14 Anderson (1991: 53–65) himself actually offers a somewhat different explanation for "how administrative units could, over time, come to be conceived as fatherlands" (53). Although his explanation accounts nicely for the rise of nationalist (and anti-imperial) sentiments among settler colonial populations (whom he refers to as "creoles"), it is much less relevant to the rise of such sentiments among indigenous populations within settler states.

had relatively little sociological relevance locally until Catalan peasants began to use it for their own purposes in (often long-standing) struggles with their neighbours over lands and resources. Although cultural differences between these local protagonists – all of whom regarded themselves as Catalan – likely played little or no role in these local disputes, at least initially, the legal and political realities of the Spanish/French border made it increasingly useful for disputants to strategically invoke their own and their opponents' identities as Spaniards or Frenchmen. As citizens of different states, they sought to gain advantage in their struggles with one another by invoking their differential rights to particular lands and resources.[15] And once Catalan peasants began invoking their status as members of different nations, they increasingly justified doing so by framing those differences as cultural – even where it is unlikely that any significant cultural differences existed between French and Spanish Catalans *in general* (Sahlins 1989: 265). By thus framing their local interests in national terms, Sahlins argues, Catalan peasants literally created the Spanish and French nations in the local context.[16]

There are some striking similarities between the emergence of national consciousness in the southern Pyrenees of the eighteenth and nineteenth centuries and the rise of Yukon First Nation identities in the early twenty-first century. In both places, the imposition of territorial borders initiated a process of ethno-national differentiation among people who until then shared very similar histories and cultural practices. This is not to say the populations in either place were culturally homogeneous prior to the drawing of the boundaries, but

15 Sahlins clearly draws on situational models of ethnicity here, but he is quick to point out that Catalans were not free to adopt whichever national identity suited their interests at the moment. On the contrary, he shows that local people – more so even than the central governments – were extremely intolerant of "political amphibians," those who adopted national identities instrumentally, switching between French and Spanish to maximize their advantage in any situation (Sahlins 1989: 225–7). It seems that initially people living on the border had considerable freedom to choose between French and Spanish national identities; but once they had done so, it became increasingly difficult for them to switch.

16 Of the French Catalans, he says: "Before 1870, the French Cerdans had defined their national identities less by participating in the life of the nation than by using the state for their own ends. In the process, they drew their local boundaries of territory and identity in opposition to Spaniards on the other side of the political boundary, despite sharing with them a common Catalan ethnicity" (Sahlins 1989: 267).

only that social differences were not framed as national differences. In both cases, it was the imposition of political boundaries – rather than pre-existing cultural differences – that provided the impetus for ethno-national differentiation. Recall, for example, the story from chapter 2 , where I recounted Joe Johnson's anger towards Champagne and Aishihik First Nations for limiting his hunting rights in CAFN territory. The language of "us" and "them" that Joe used at the time is, I think, significant. Some of Joe's closest relatives, including his paternal uncles who helped raise him and taught him to hunt, were citizens of CAFN. Yet, because of the territorial boundary and the regulatory regime it engenders, it had become possible for him to draw a distinction between "us" – Kluane people – and "them" – Champagne/Aishihik people[17] – in a manner that would have been unthinkable just two decades earlier. Such expressions are becoming increasingly common in the Yukon. This is not to say that ethno-territorial sentiments of this sort always take precedence over cross-cutting relations of kinship and reciprocity. In fact, as we have already seen, such social relations remain strong and provide the basis for a trenchant moral critique of the growing ethno-territoriality and nationalist sentiments. Yet, the new boundaries – and accompanying maps – function as "models for" a powerful new system of legal and administrative relations, a system that is transforming how Yukon Indian people think of and relate to one another vis-à-vis land.

Sahlins (1989: 271) points out that national identities "do not depend on the existence of any objective linguistic or cultural differentiation but on the subjective experience of difference. In this sense, national identity, like ethnic or communal identity, is contingent and relational: it is defined by the social or territorial boundaries drawn to distinguish the collective self and its implicit negation, the other." Everyday encounters such as Joe's run-in with CAFN's management bureaucracy not only enact First Nations as "state-like" political organizations (as I argued in chapter 2), they also cause Yukon Indian people to draw qualitative distinctions between themselves on the one hand and the

17 In light of the effects of band amalgamation to be discussed later in this chapter, it is worth noting that the Champagne and Aishihik First Nations, as the plural form of its official name suggests, is itself a product of the 1970 amalgamation of the previously distinct Champagne and Aishihik Bands. These, in turn, had been composed of people not only from settlements at Champagne and Aishihik, but from Nesketaheen, Klukshu, Hutchi, Kusawa, and Kloo Lake as well.

citizens of other First Nations on the other. To invoke Brubaker again, this is "the routine, ordinary, taken-for-granted nationalism that is the 'natural political sentiment for modern states'" (1992: 28).

The indigenous people of the Yukon are presently responding to the imposition of First Nation traditional territory boundaries in much the same way as Sahlins's Catalan peasants responded to the imposition of the Spanish/French border in their midst: by using them – and the political, legal, and administrative differences they engender – for their own purposes. And, again like those Catalan peasants, they are increasingly likely to frame such differences in ethno-nationalist terms, as though the political and legal differences between citizens of First Nations derive from pre-existing differences in culture, language, and history, rather than the other way around. In the process, they rationalize the political, legal, and administrative differences produced by First Nation territorial boundaries by yoking them to cultural, linguistic, and historical differences in ways productive of First Nations as distinct ethno-territorial entities.[18]

Ethno-territoriality and Ethnogenesis in the Yukon

Geographer Adam Moore (2016: 4) usefully defines ethno-territoriality as "a social and political project the goal of which is to establish an explicitly spatial basis for claims involving ethnic identity, cultural rights, and political authority by identifying and constructing certain places or territories as belonging to or appropriate for certain ethno-national categories of people and practice." He notes that ethnic/national categories are themselves often created (or given new significance) by ethno-territorial strategies, which allow "others to be imagined as members of the same cultural and political community based upon a shared relationship with a given territory" (ibid.: 12). This suggests that the process of internal territorialization currently taking place in the Yukon is dialectically linked to the emergence of new "imagined

18 Building on the work of Fried and Williams, Katherine Verdery (1994b: 47) argues explicitly that it is national differentiation associated with state-making that causes ethnic differentiation, and not the other way around: "Ethnicity (and race with it) is the product of state-making, not its precursor (cf. Fried 1968; Williams 1989). It is not from ethnic identities that national identities develop; rather, the latter create the frame that generates the former – the frame within which ethnicity *qua* difference, in its broadest sense, acquires social significance."

communities" corresponding to the new First Nation territories created by land claim and self-government agreements. Indeed, arguably one of the most important changes associated with the agreements' territorial ordering of First Nation political space is precisely the emergence of these new ethno-territorial identities – and corresponding nationalist sentiments – among Yukon Indian peoples.

Studies of ethnogenesis in many parts of indigenous North and South America have viewed the emergence of relatively distinct ethnicities/nations/tribes associated with fixed territories as largely the product of colonial interactions. Indeed, it has been over fifty years since Morton Fried (1966; 1975) argued that "tribes" in this sense, far from being a primordial political form, are nearly always "secondary phenomena" because they emerged almost everywhere as a result of – and in complex relationship with – states.[19] In her account of ethnogenetic processes among the Assiniboin, Cree, and Ojibwe of the northern plains, for example, Patricia Albers (1996: 91) argues that

> ethnicity in the generic and highly abstract sense of a "tribal" name did not always function as a marker of geopolitical boundaries. Given a pluralistic pattern of land use and alliance making, most of their ethnic categories did not have a high level of salience or any a priori power to organize and distribute people across geographic space ... It was only after the imposition of US and Canadian sovereignty that their ethnic names took on any real importance, and then it was only because these were invested with the legal power of treaties written by nation-states.[20]

Tribal categories did not exist in the Yukon either prior to European contact. The aggregate "tribal" terms used in the Yukon today, such as *Southern Tutchone, Northern Tutchone,* and *Upper Tanana,* are essentially linguistic categories. They refer to languages or major (and, as we shall see, now contested) dialectical divisions drawn by early ethnographers rather than to any pre-contact cultural or political units

19 See also the resulting discussion in Helm (1968) and Southall (1970). For a more recent analysis along these lines of the emergence of "tribalism" in southern Africa and Madagascar, respectively, see Vail (1991), Graeber (2004: 54–60); for Indonesia, see Li (2000: 158–9). Recently, James Scott (2009) has further elaborated on Fried's argument.

20 See Innes (2013) for a recent critical assessment of Albers's work that actually takes her critique of "tribe" in this context considerably further than she did herself.

(Easton, Kennedy, and Bouchard 2013: 135).[21] As I will discuss below, the contemporary practice of using these terms to refer to bounded ethno-cultural units is quite recent, having become common only with the establishment of tribal councils in the mid-1990s. Indeed, early ethnographers agreed that Yukon Indian people did not regard themselves as divided into distinct territorially organized "tribes" or "peoples." Cornelius Osgood, the author of the Athapaskan tribal distribution map that formed the basis for most subsequent linguistic and ethnographic maps of the western subarctic, was quick to point out that "Athapaskans do not consider themselves as composing neat political or cultural units," and noted that in the 1930s when he had constructed his map, they "generally align their village with the nearest surrounding villages and exclude those beyond a certain range, thus forming

---

21 McClellan and Denniston note that Yukon Indian people did recognize "a commonality of linked dialects, shared customs, and contiguous territory, but it was the Whites who gave them their overall 'tribal' names" (McClellan and Denniston 1981: 384). Regarding these "tribal" names, Legros notes that as late as the 1970s, "the indigenous people who were called Tutchone in ethnological literature were then totally unaware of this name … They were also unaware of the terms Han, Kaska, Mountain Indians, etc. – names that ethnographers had been using to classify the indigenous people of the Yukon Territory into different cultural and linguistic units … Consequently, I quickly discovered that there was no point in asking the members of each of the Southern and Northern Tutchone regional groups about the meaning of the names Tutchone, Han, etc. Even when pronounced in different ways, these terms remained foreign to their respective vocabularies. In their culture, there is [*sic*] no categories equivalent to those which ethnologists use to distinguish for instance the Han linguistic group from the Tutchone linguistic group. When asked about the name of their group, the Tutchone replied that they call themselves *dan* (human beings). With a little more prodding, they classified the people around them into *huč'an* (people) of such and such a place. In the past, the term *huč'an*, accompanied by its geographic qualifier, designated a regional group that would meet at least once a year at a predetermined trading place. The four to six local groups of a regional group had no proper name. They were referred to as a 'bunch' descended from 'so-and-so,' generally a grandmother. A local group consisted of two to a maximum of around 10 to 12 nuclear families whose female members were matrilineally related and formed one moiety. To designate their own local group, a woman or man would use the word *'eh yaa' dlant'* which English-speaking Tutchone translate as 'my friends'" (Legros 2007: 100–1).

This situation is hardly unique to the Yukon; the ethnographic literature is replete with cases in which the "larger ethno-linguistic units recognized by the ethnologist are useful for descriptive and administrative purposes but have little basis in native society" (Eggan 1960, cited in Southall 1970: 36).

units which overlap if depicted graphically" (Osgood 1936: 3). For his part, anthropologist Robert McKennan (1981: 563) remarked, "The Athapaskans on the Tanana and Yukon Rivers, from the Tutchone to the Ingalik, do not easily fall into a number of discrete cultural or linguistic blocks; rather, they constitute a continuum of local bands whose respective microcultures and dialects differ only slightly from those of their immediate neighbors." Similarly, in his impressively comprehensive ethno-historical account of the Tutchone of the central Yukon, Dominque Legros (2007: 103 n. 147) argues that

> there is in fact no rigid ethnic clustering of the northern Athapaskans. The overall ethnic situation in the Yukon Territory and adjacent regions of Alaska can be visualized by imagining the distribution of the Athapaskan peoples as a piece of fabric woven over millennia. Some parts woven under special circumstances have a particular texture and look of their own. Others, worn over the centuries were mended and the portions of the fabric they form also appear as very distinct from the others. Taking a look at eleven regional groups [who form the basis of his study] is a little like cutting out a swatch in order to examine the special texture which characterizes it. The operation is valid as this part of the fabric is different from the rest. However, by cutting out only a swatch, we also cut the weft of the fabric which holds the swatch together. At its edges, the swatch immediately frays and we realize just how the periphery, which seemed to be one with the centre, depended on the threads to attach it to the rest of the fabric.

None of this is to suggest that Athapaskans did not have ways of classifying one another. They just did not classify themselves as members of discrete ethno-cultural entities. McClellan sketched the outline of a very complex indigenous system for classifying people that, she maintained, "is highly relative, depending on the particular vantage points in time and space of both the classifier and the classified. Also, various modes of classification crosscut each other. Finally, the Yukon Indians prefer to think in terms of selected individuals rather than of total geographically bounded groups" (ibid.: 14). Among the more important indigenous criteria for classifying people were "the kinds of technology, the specific food staples or the natural environment most closely associated with the group, the group's distance and direction from the speaker, the name of the particular place where families are congregated at a given point in time, or the histories and kin ties of important persons within a group" (ibid.). For the most part, indigenous classifications were relative rather than categorical. Legros, too, describes a system of classification among the Tutchone that was entirely devoid of ethnic/tribal labels, but was, instead, "based entirely on notions indicating relative geographic position defined in relation to the place where the speaker lives" (2007 102).[22]

Notably absent from McClellan's (and Legros's) list of relevant criteria for indigenous classification is language. Although McClellan notes that Yukon Indian people "easily distinguish dialectical variations and are quick to comment that an individual speaks either 'the same as' they do, or 'a little bit different,' or that they 'can't hear [understand] him at all,'" these linguistic differences were cross-cut by other, often more salient kinds of difference, so that in practice, "Yukon Indians rarely single out language as a primary guide in circumscribing or naming a geographical group" (ibid.: 13–14; but see her entire discussion, on pp. 13–16). The low social salience of linguistic difference among nineteenth-century Athapaskans may be attributable in part to the fact that many Yukon Indian people spoke multiple indigenous languages/dialects (McClellan 1975: 14; see also Easton 2005: 54–5; Easton, Kennedy, and Bouchard 2013: 37–8).[23] In any case, as we shall see, language has become a much more salient marker of social difference in the years since McClellan conducted her research.

Yukon Indian peoples' ways of classifying one another have changed significantly in recent decades. As on the northern plains, it was their interactions with the expanding Canadian state that first led to the rise

---

22 On the relative nature of social classification among other northern Athapaskan peoples, see Goulet (1998: 103). There is nothing unique about the Yukon or Athapaskan society here. Citing numerous examples of relative classificatory schemes from Africa and southeast Asia, Southall (1970) argues that this is likely the norm among stateless peoples. His characterization of the situation in southern Africa is equally apropos of indigenous Yukon society: "It was not that these peoples were an undifferentiated mass, but that they were differentiated in many subtle and complex ways for different purposes" (ibid.: 35). Interestingly, traces of this relational way of thinking have survived the transition to English. When describing the location of a place or event, for example, Yukon Indian people today will nearly always do so in relative terms, as in the phrase: "x happened just the other side of Swede Johnson Creek," where "this" or "the other" side is always relative to the speaker's current location. This can sometimes lead to confusion among Euro-Canadian listeners.

23 Kluane elders, too, confirmed for me the multilingual abilities of their grandparents' generation.

of "tribal" or ethnic identities distinguishing them clearly from their neighbours. Of central importance in the early stages of this process was the Canadian government's organization of the indigenous population into administrative bands. As we saw in chapter 2, the composition of these bands did not correspond to any cultural or linguistic differences on the ground, but had more to do with the relocation of Indian populations to highway settlements and with federal officials' financial and administrative considerations. Although each band elected its own chief and council (these offices were not indigenous, but were created by the Indian Act), these officials had very little power; instead, they helped administer federal policy and served as intermediaries between the federal government and band members. As elsewhere throughout the colonial world (e.g., see Vail 1991), the imposition of indirect rule in the Yukon helped create and institutionalize ethnic differences – often cast as tribal. Despite the arbitrary imposition of the band structure, band membership gradually became a significant aspect of social relations for indigenous people throughout the Yukon. Different administrative bands began to have different collective interests vis-à-vis the state (and one another); band members accessed federal programs and services through their respective bands; and, despite their relative lack of power, band officials often came to see themselves as working on behalf of their fellow band members who, in turn, collectively voted them into and out of office.

The social relevance of band membership increased dramatically with the advent of land claims. As we saw, it was individual bands that entered into land claim negotiations with the federal and territorial governments and – with the signing of their agreements – evolved into today's self-governing First Nations. Membership (citizenship) in those bands-cum-First Nations is today a profoundly salient aspect of social relations in the Yukon. It was largely through their participation in the oppositional land claims process that Yukon Indian people first began to perceive themselves as members of distinct political and cultural units,[24] but the land claim process itself built upon lines of difference previously created by Canadian colonial policy – in particular the creation and management of administrative bands. As a result, Yukon Indian people began to differentiate not only between their own

24 Jenson and Papillon (2000) make a similar claim regarding the James Bay Cree.

and Euro-Canadian governments, but increasingly also among First Nations. Because the process of differentiation was so closely tied to particular historical circumstances, it is worth examining a specific case in more detail. It will then be possible to take a close ethnographic look at some of the mechanisms contributing to the genesis of specific ethnonational identities.

The Birth of Kluane First Nation

The preamble to Kluane First Nation's constitution, modelled on that of the United States, explicitly invokes the collective citizenry of Kluane First Nation as a distinct "people" with its own collective language, culture, right to self-government, genealogy, and ancestors:

> We, the people of Kluane First Nation, have developed and maintained a system of sustainable living that has allowed for the nourishment of our land and our people since time immemorial. Our government structure ensures the survival of our culture, language, spirituality and physical well-being through laws that show great respect for the land and the water. We have inherited our right of self-governance from our elders, our medicine people, our spirits, and from our mothers and fathers. Now, with the guidance and the wisdom of our ancestors, we assert our right to determine and control our lives as Kluane First Nation people and hereby adopt this *Constitution* as our supreme law. (Kluane First Nation 1995: 3)

The impression one gets from this preamble is that of a distinct and homogeneous people marching together down through history, a people that has finally regained "its" natural right to govern itself.[25] Yet the Kluane First Nation itself, as a membership organization with claim to a particular territory, is only of very recent vintage.

Generally, Yukon First Nations have their origins in the administrative bands created by the Canadian government, but the historical relationship between band and self-governing First Nation is not always quite so straightforward as this suggests. Given its brevity, the history of the Kluane First Nation is surprisingly complex, and it is intimately

25 Segal and Handler (1992: 10–12) point out that the "We the people" of the US constitution had a similar homogenizing effect, historically refiguring the diverse settlers of the United States as one unified "people."

bound up with that of its neighbour to the northwest, the White River First Nation. In fact, these two First Nations emerged in their current form as distinct political and administrative entities only in 1990, well into the land claim process. In 1956, the federal government created the original White River Band, composed primarily of Upper Tanana and Northern Tutchone speakers and based in the present-day village of Beaver Creek, by amalgamating the previously distinct Snag and Stewart River Bands (see map 8). Meanwhile, further to the south, the government had created the Burwash Band, based in the village of Burwash Landing. Then, in 1961, in the interests of economy and efficiency of administration, the government amalgamated the Burwash and White River bands.[26] In their place, it created the Kluane Band (which was subsequently renamed the Kluane Tribal Brotherhood and then the Kluane Tribal Council). This amalgamation led to the forced relocation of former members of the White River band from Beaver Creek to Burwash Landing, causing severe hardship and anguish. In 1990, the Kluane Tribal Council – amidst a great deal of acrimony – separated again into the distinct Kluane and White River First Nations (and WRFN filed a wrongful amalgamation suit against the federal government). This final split did not occur, however, until *after* the amalgamated Kluane Tribal Council had already established its traditional territory under the Yukon Umbrella Final Agreement.[27] Although the amalgamation of the White River and Kluane bands predated the land claim process, and the reasons for the KTC's subsequent break-up are multiple and complex, the eventual emergence of both Kluane and White River First Nations – as state-like entities towards which people are beginning to feel a sense of nationalist attachment – can only be understood as part of this longer colonial history of the region.

In a relatively last-minute scramble to adjust the Umbrella Final Agreement to reflect the new configuration of bands in the southwest Yukon, negotiators divided the land quantum and compensation money that had been earmarked for the amalgamated Kluane Tribal Council and reallocated it on a per capita basis to the now distinct White River and Kluane First Nations. Negotiators also included a provision (UFA

26 See Memorandum Regarding Amalgamation of Indian Bands written by F.E. Anfield, Indian commissioner for British Columbia, on 8 February 1961 and sent to all Indian superintendents in British Columbia and the Yukon.

27 The final traditional territory map was submitted in 1988.

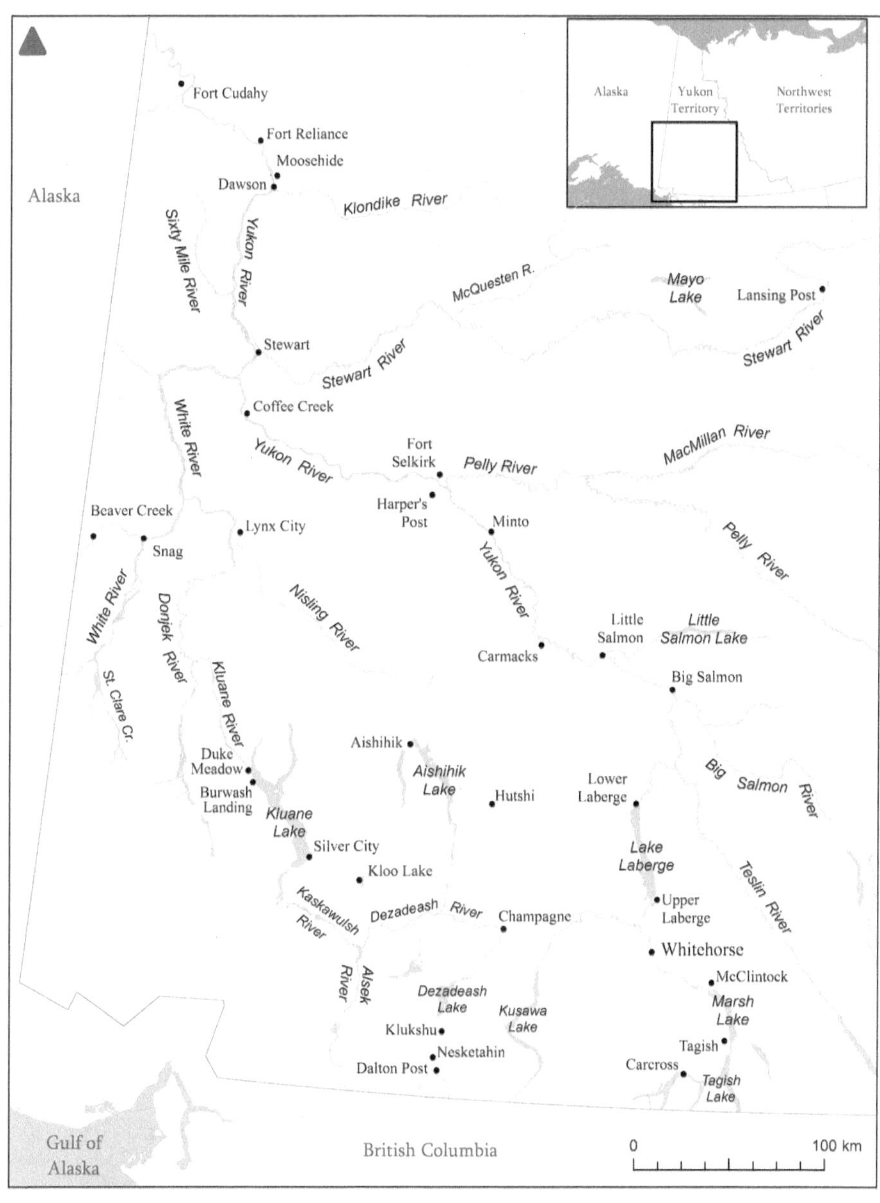

Map 8 Some early Yukon trading posts and camps by Tracy Sallaway (Maps, Data and Government Information Centre, Trent University).

2.9.1) requiring that the KFN and WRFN submit amended traditional territory maps prior to its ratification.[28] For reasons that will become clear, this never occurred. As a result, KFN and WRFN are currently in the unique position of having identical traditional territories – or, in the parlance of Yukon land claims: 100 per cent overlap.[29] This situation has caused considerable tension and has profound implications for KFN's final and self-government agreements, since, as we saw in chapter 2, significant parts of those agreements – especially those related to the management of fish and wildlife – do not apply in overlap areas (recall that WRFN rejected its agreements, so it is still an Indian Act band). Because of these potential implications, the First Nations worked hard to resolve their overlap prior to the ratification of KFN's agreement. Despite years of effort, however, they failed to do so.

At one meeting in 1995, elders from both First Nations met to discuss the overlap issue. After two days of talks, they unanimously agreed to share the traditional territory, in effect refusing to draw a line resolving the overlap (see the discussion of overlap resolution boundaries in chapter 2). Central to their discussions was the belief that a boundary was incompatible with their cultural values; they had always shared the land and intended to continue doing so. As Bessie John, a respected White River elder, put it:

> We are one nation to this country where we was born! That's what they should tell the government, I say. Where is our mother? There was one that came from the ground to this earth here. And government people they think they're our bosses. We should be boss of our country. One trail from all the way to Alaska. All the way down from Alaska to that river there. I talk about that river, that Yukon River, belong to Indian for Earth. God, who made that river for Indian food. That's our food, that river.

---

28 Provision 2.9.2 of the UFA reads: "Prior to the ratification of the Umbrella Final Agreement by the Yukon First Nations, the Kluane First Nation and the White River First Nation shall provide maps, at a scale no smaller than 1:500,000, of their Traditional Territories, which Traditional Territories shall be delineated within the Traditional Territory map provided by the Kluane First Nation pursuant to 2.9.1" (Kluane First Nation 2003b: 21).

29 Two other Yukon First Nations, Ta'an Kwäch'än Council and Kwanlin Dun First Nation, also split late in the land claim process and are in substantially the same situation. Although TKC and KDFN do have distinct traditional territories, these are very nearly – though not quite – identical to one another (see map 1).

> No-one made for us, only Earth and God can make for us our food. Government should know that ... Every day I stay home I was thinking. We should share the land with each other. We are one First Nation. We are Indian on our land. We should share our land now, together.[30]

At the same meeting, White River elder Bill Blair Jr expressed a similar sentiment: "I don't know about borders. We never had borders. Now we have to make borders. I think that's very unfortunate. Very, very unfortunate ... I think we should share. I don't see nothing wrong with that" (cited in Easton 2001: 113). Yet another Kluane elder who attended those talks told me she had had ambivalent feelings about them, so she had consulted her own mother (who had been too old at the time to attend). She had asked her mother which areas had historically been used by White River people and which by Kluane people. She told me that for a long time her mother had not even understood what she was trying to ask – and that when she finally had understood, she had gotten angry, saying only that people had always shared the land with one another. Many elders at the meeting quite explicitly attributed the purported need for a boundary to a divide-and-conquer strategy on the part of government, and numerous elders talked about the need to reject any talk about a contiguous line for this reason.[31] In fact, a common theme in all the overlap talks I examined (taped talks from 1990, 1995, 2002) was that the government had imposed the need for a line, and that if it were left up to the people, they would just continue to share the land.

When I discussed this with a federal negotiator, he disagreed with that characterization of the government position. He acknowledged that neither he nor other government officials were qualified to make judgments on traditional use, so they had intentionally left the process of overlap resolution to the First Nations; government played only a facilitating role (e.g., they had paid for a moderator in the 2002 talks between Kluane and White River First Nations). In fact, he stressed to me that in the final overlap talks that took place in the spring and summer

30 Taped overlap discussions, Burwash Landing, YT, 5 June 1995. Yukon Archives, Kluane First Nation Collection, accession number SR234-50(A).

31 Brian Thom (2009: 189) encountered this same suspicion among Coast Salish people grappling with similar issues.

of 2002, Canada and the Yukon had been open to *any* solution at all that would have permitted Kluane and White River to finalize their agreements. At the time, he recalled, a number of the First Nations representatives at the table had suggested that there be no boundary line at all, that Kluane and White River should just share the entire traditional territory. He said that both Canada and the Yukon had been open to this approach, but that in the end it had been the First Nations representatives themselves who had rejected it.

When I later discussed the federal negotiator's comments with KFN's chief negotiator, she acknowledged that what he had told me was technically true; Canada and the Yukon had been willing to go with whatever the First Nations decided, even if that meant refusing to draw a line at all. She pointed out, however, that such a solution would have required one of two things: (1) the renegotiation of both First Nation final agreements to deal with the intractable jurisdictional issues that would arise from 100 per cent overlap – essentially a completely different kind of agreement, or else (2) the re-amalgamation of Kluane and White River First Nations. Practically speaking, the first option was out of the question. The federal negotiating mandate was set to expire, memoranda of understanding had already been signed committing the parties to take the existing deals to ratification, and federal funding for negotiations had just about come to an end. This left re-amalgamation as the only viable option. Legally speaking, it seems the more straightforward of the two (although in practice, this option, too, would have required a renegotiation, since it would have meant combining two different agreements into one). Re-amalgamation also seems consistent with the First Nation preference for sharing the land. Politically, however, it was completely out of the question. Their wrongful amalgamation and forced relocation in 1961 has become for the people of both WRFN and KFN one of the most salient symbols of the history of their oppression at the hands of the federal government. They spent years fighting to be allowed to separate, so that White River people could return to their homes in Beaver Creek; and the split, when it finally came, was messy. In talking to me about the split with White River, several KFN citizens likened it to a divorce; there was fighting over who would get the property (i.e., band assets), which led to bitter feelings that still have not completely healed. To imagine that re-amalgamation was a viable solution is to completely ignore the colonial history of the region. In fact, this same KFN negotiator added that even those elders who had advocated sharing the entire territory at the 2002 meeting had ultimately baulked when she had pointed out to them that it would effectively have meant re-amalgamation.

In this light, it is worth noting that at the 1995 elders meeting mentioned earlier (at which the elders unanimously agreed to share the land) there was no discussion whatsoever of what an overlap resolution boundary actually is or its relation to the final agreements. Instead, the discussion was about who had historically used what land and when; so, it is not surprising that the elders ultimately decided to share the land (i.e., citizens of both First Nations could continue to hunt anywhere within the traditional territory). Recall, however, that they came to this decision *in spite of* the lingering bitterness over the 1990 split. This illustrates something, I think, about the power and ongoing importance of the belief among Yukon Indian people that the land and animals should be shared, a legacy from the time before the existence of territorially ordered First Nation polities. It is important to note, however, that the elders at this meeting never discussed the implications of their decision for their land claims agreements. This is probably because the negotiators, those familiar with the legal context of the discussions and who might have pointed out these implications, were not present at those talks.

Thus, the government negotiator's assertion that it was essentially up to the First Nations whether they wanted a contiguous line or not is only accurate if one ignores the legal and historical contexts in which the overlap discussions took place. This is not to say that the need for a contiguous line is part of a conscious government plot to divide and conquer, as some Yukon Indian people believed. Rather, it arises from the territorial structure and associated jurisdictional and administrative arrangements of the land claims agreements themselves.

The issue of overlap came to a head in 2002–3, as KFN's negotiations neared completion. Without an overlap resolution boundary, 100 per cent overlap meant that important provisions of KFN's agreement would not come into effect at all (e.g., the Dän Keyi Renewable Resources Council established under its agreement would not have jurisdiction *anywhere*). When it became clear that the First Nations were not going to reach a mutually agreeable solution, KFN, along with the federal and Yukon territorial governments, came up with a solution that would allow those provisions of their agreement to come into effect in at least part of their traditional territory. They divided the overlapped territory into three sections: a WRFN Core Area, a KFN Core Area, and a shared Secondary Area between them (see map 9). Each First Nation

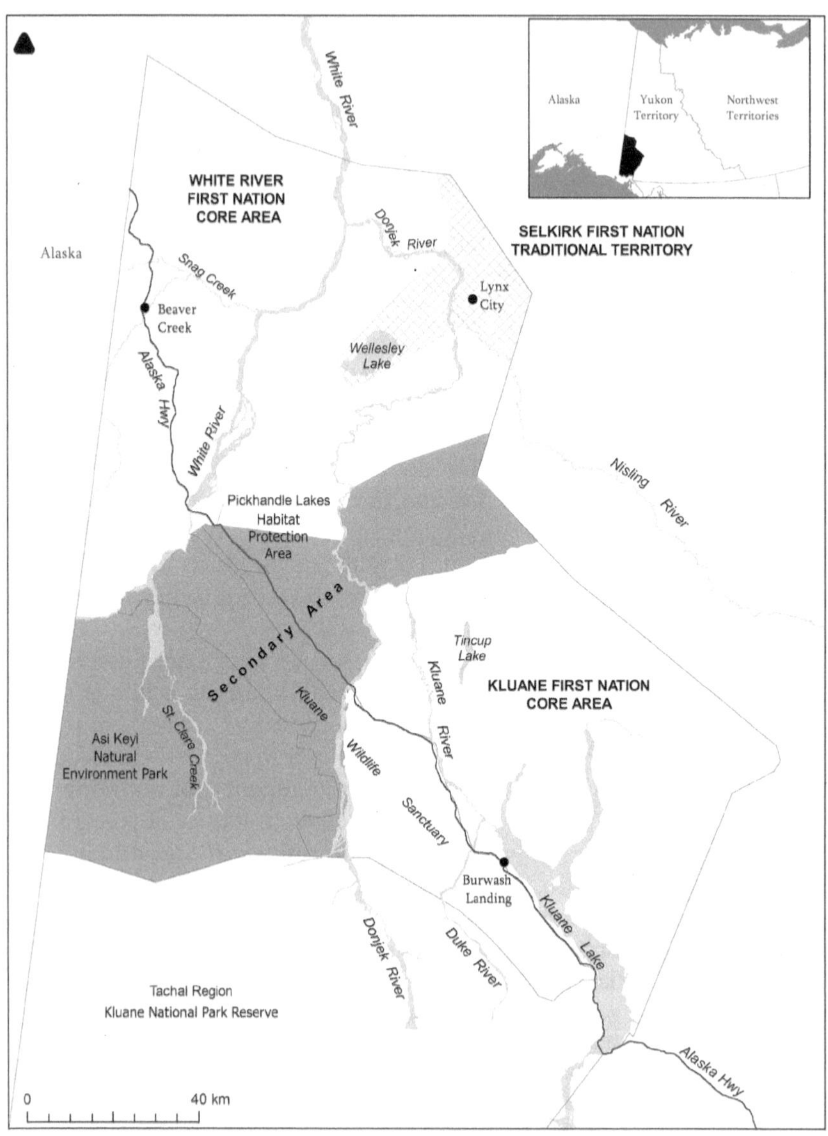

Map 9 White River and Kluane First Nation core and secondary territories by Tracy Sallaway (Maps, Data and Government Information Centre, Trent University) based on map 22 (Core Concept Area) of the Kluane First Nation Final Agreement, Appendix B – Maps.

would enjoy exclusive jurisdiction in its core area and only limited shared jurisdiction in the secondary area. This solution allows KFN to exercise jurisdiction in at least part of its traditional territory, but the solution is only provisional (and possibly illegal, since WRFN was not party to this agreement even though it clearly affects them and their traditional territory). It is subject to change depending on the terms of any future WRFN Final Agreement, any overlap resolution boundary the two First Nations might negotiate in the future, and/or a successful court challenge (and WRFN threatened at one point to mount one). Creative though it may be, this solution still takes for granted the territorial assumption of the state system, based as it is on a clear demarcation of the two First Nations' (core area) jurisdictional boundaries.[32]

The Kluane and White River First Nations emerged as distinct political entities amid a contentious struggle over band assets, a struggle whose origins lie in the federal government's policy of amalgamating Indian bands and forcibly relocating Indian people for its own administrative and fiscal convenience. Although some of the causes of conflict between Kluane and White River First Nations predate the land claim process, the conflict derives its shape from the territorializing nature of the Yukon agreements, the negotiation of which had profound effects on Yukon Indian society long before they were ever signed and ratified (Nadasdy 2003: chap. 6). Although enmity and conflict among Yukon Indian people is certainly nothing new,[33] what *is* new is people's tendency to frame such conflict in ethno-territorial terms. Whereas in the past Yukon Indian people drew on relations of kinship, reciprocity,

32 At first glance, this solution – with its provisions for shared jurisdiction in the secondary area – may appear inconsistent with the territorial state model; but, in fact, international law allows for the existence of condominia, territories over which two or more sovereign states agree to share dominium, or sovereignty. Although relatively rare, condominia have long been a feature of the political landscape within the international system of territorial states. In North America, for example, the United States and Britain formally shared jurisdiction over the Oregon Territory (which the British referred to as the Columbia District) from 1818–1846. Perhaps more directly relevant, Thomas Biolsi (2005: 245–7) argues that the power to co-manage resources, now widely exercised by indigenous peoples across North America, is rooted in the idea that indigenous people retain certain sovereign powers over their ceded lands; thus, co-management represents a form of shared sovereignty.

33 On conflict in the region prior to contact, see McClellan (1975: 510, 518–26).

and co-residence to enlist allies in their conflicts with one another (with the consequence that one could often find both allies and enemies in any camp), today Yukon Indian people are increasingly likely to view conflict as taking place between territorially ordered ethno-national entities, such as the Kluane and White River First Nations. And indeed, as a result of amalgamation and the legacy of territorial conflict it engendered, many Indian people of the region now distinguish clearly – at least in some contexts – not only between Kluane and White River *territories*, but also between Kluane and White River *people*, a distinction that would have made little sense to their grandparents (which is, after all, why Kluane and White River elders insisted on sharing the land). None of this is to suggest that citizens of one First Nation do not have close friends and relatives in the other; it is simply to note that Kluane and White River First Nations have increasingly become the repositories of ethno-territorial sentiments and loyalties that cross-cut – and in some instances now override – relations of kinship and reciprocity. It is no exaggeration to say that these two First Nations, along with people's increasing nationalistic attachment to them, are in large part products of the conflict created by Canada's colonial policies in the region and given territorial form by the land claim and self-government agreements.[34]

People are most apt to invoke cultural or historical distinctions between Kluane and White River people in the context of specific disagreements over resources or other land claim–related matters. They are, however, increasingly inclined to view Kluane and White River people as culturally, linguistically, and historically – in a word, ethnically – distinct in a more general sense as well. As we have seen, this requires that a whole array of social differences be yoked together to form a boundary between the putatively homogeneous Kluane and White River First Nations. I turn now to a consideration of some of the mechanisms by which this is accomplished.

34 Eric Cheyfitz (2000) describes a similar process in the American Southwest. He argues that the ongoing Navajo-Hopi land dispute is the product of US colonialism rather than of pre-existing enmity between a unified "Hopi Nation" and a "Navajo Nation." Indeed, he argues persuasively that those nations – as distinct ethno-territorial entities – are themselves the relatively recent products of that same colonial process (and, indeed, of the land dispute itself).

Cultural Differentiation among Yukon First Nations

In practice, the construction of ethno-nationalism's collective individuals consists of everyday social interactions in which people frame cultural differences as existing between one "kind" of person and another. These run the gamut from informal to more formal – even institutionalized – interactions. As an example of the former, a Kluane First Nation citizen once told me almost in passing that "White River people" do not eat Dall sheep. "You can't give sheep meat away up there [in Beaver Creek]," he said. Considering the central importance of meat and hunting to Yukon Indian people's ideas about their cultural identity (Nadasdy 2003: 75–9), and of sheep meat/hunting in particular for Kluane identity (ibid.: 151–2), this seemingly offhand comment served as a powerful way of constructing "White River people" as culturally distinct from "Kluane people." While the man's statement is not true in an absolute sense (there are, in fact, White River First Nation citizens who eat sheep meat just as there are some Kluane First Nation citizens who do not), it works well enough as an informal rule of thumb; and, by generalizing about the differences between Kluane and White River people, it becomes an assertion of significant cultural difference between distinct and internally homogeneous Kluane and White River "peoples," thus helping to enact them as separate cultural collectivities. For this reason, it must be viewed as an example of ethno-nationalist discourse.

Although there is always a political dimension to statements about what foods different "kinds" of people eat, this statement about White River people's gustatory preferences was especially charged when it was uttered in 1996, because both KFN and WRFN were at the time locked in negotiations with the federal and Yukon governments over hunting rights. Rights to hunt sheep were particularly contentious in those negotiations (see Nadasdy 2003: 153), and tensions over the KFN/WRFN split were still very high in both communities. When I relayed (without attribution) this man's comment to a group of White River First Nation citizens in Beaver Creek a short time later, they rejected it quite vehemently at first, though they did so only in very general terms: "Of course we eat sheep; it is a traditional food. We have eaten it for centuries." Although Upper Tanana speakers did historically eat sheep (McKennan 1959: 34), no one that night claimed sheep-eating status for White River people on personal grounds (e.g., "Of course we eat it; I just had some last week"). Upon further discussion, several people in the room did admit that, "well, there aren't any sheep around here anymore," so that, in fact, it turns out they do not eat sheep very often; but they stressed that for purposes of historical accuracy and contemporary land claim negotiations, the people of White River First Nation should be regarded, culturally, as a sheep-eating people.[35]

I did not bring up the Kluane citizen's comment about White River people's sheep-eating habits that evening to stir up tensions between nascent ethnic groups. Rather, I mentioned it in the context of good-natured joking among my White River companions about "Southern Tutchone" (read: Kluane) people's penchant for eating "gophers" (arctic ground squirrels) – in marked contrast to their own tastes as White River people (although, in fact, Upper Tanana people historically ate these animals too; see McKennan 1959: 35). As a statement of "fact," of course, this is no truer than the Kluane citizen's blanket claims about people's sheep-eating preferences in the region; there are, in fact, White River citizens who eat gophers, just as there are Kluane citizens who do not. The important thing to note here is that the citizens of both First Nations engage at times in this type of culturally homogenizing ethno-nationalist discourse. People can and do disagree (sometimes vehemently) with particular generalizations of this sort, but in the process they often end up reinforcing rather than undermining their ethno-nationalist framing. For example, rather than questioning the central premise underlying the Kluane citizen's generalization about people's sheep-eating habits (i.e., that Kluane people and White River people constitute separate collectives that have distinct cultures and dietary preferences) my White River companions merely asserted that he had gotten the dietary preference of the White River collectivity wrong: White River people, too, like Kluane people, eat sheep. Thus, everyone took for granted the existence of White River and Kluane as two culturally distinct peoples.

Everyday interactions of this sort are extremely important ways of enacting cultural/ethnic difference between the two First Nations, but there are also more formal and institutionalized means for producing and reifying cultural differences of this sort. Take, for example, Kluane First Nation's membership in – and White River's exclusion from – the

35 Indeed, I was told outright that under no circumstances was I to tell the Yukon government negotiators that White River people do not eat sheep, not that I had any intention of doing so.

Southern Tutchone Tribal Council (STTC). Established in the mid-1990s, the STTC is a regional organization comprised of the three putatively Southern Tutchone First Nations (Kluane, Champagne-Aishihik, and Ta'an Kwäch'än). Although envisioned from the beginning as having a political role (albeit a changing one),[36] the STTC's principal focus has always been on cultural preservation. Its current mandate is to "preserve, protect, and promote our way of life by working together on heritage, language, and culture" (Kushniruk 2012: 14). Over the years, the STTC has sponsored an array of cultural activities, including an annual hand game tournament, dance groups, language revitalization efforts, drum-making workshops, a bison hunt, and an annual cultural gathering. A key if implicit assumption underlying the creation of the STTC and all its activities is the correspondence of language and culture; so that the members of Southern Tutchone First Nations, by virtue of the fact that they (or their ancestors) speak southern Tutchone, also share (a homogeneous) Southern Tutchone culture, which is distinct from that of their neighbours. Not only does this move distinguish Southern Tutchone people/culture from the Upper Tanana people of White River First Nation but also from those of the three Northern Tutchone First Nations, who are members of their own separate Northern Tutchone Tribal Council.

The assumption of cultural homogeneity across the constituent members of the STTC (and other tribal councils in the Yukon) obscures the considerable linguistic and cultural variation that exists among its constituent First Nations – not to mention *within* each of them. Take language as an example. We have already seen that the ancestors of Kluane First Nation citizens were not, in fact, all Southern Tutchone speakers. Many spoke other languages, including Northern Tutchone, Upper Tanana, Tagish, Tlingit, and English; and many of those who did speak Southern Tutchone were multilingual – often speaking it as a second or third language. Much the same can be said of the other two First Nations that comprise the STTC. To classify them as "Southern Tutchone" First Nations, then, is to simplify what is in fact a much more complex social and linguistic situation. Yet, there is more to the simplification process even than this.

36 The STTC was recently given a new mandate and reorganized with the goal of enhancing the implementation of land claim agreements through regional cooperation.

"Southern Tutchone" itself is something of an abstraction. Linguists and anthropologists have long viewed northern Athapaskan languages as a "dialect complex, or complex of dialect complexes" rather than as a collection of discrete languages (Krauss 1964; see also Krauss 1973; McClellan 1964: 2). Indeed, although it was Catharine McClellan who first drew the distinction between the Northern and Southern Tutchone languages, by her own admission she did so on the basis of very little evidence, and she was quick to stress that "the classification stands open to revision. Further ethnographic and linguistic study may well suggest more apt designations" (1975: 21). There are at least four distinct dialects of Southern Tutchone, and the northern among them arguably have more in common with neighbouring dialects of Northern Tutchone than they do with Tlingitized Southern Tutchone dialects to the south.[37] What is more, Legros (2007: 101) suggests that there was so much linguistic variability that any attempt to draw sharp distinctions between languages and dialects is probably futile:

> As each regional group that occupied a part of a valley or the vicinity of a lake had its own distinct way of speaking or sub-dialect (vocabulary, sounds of vowels and consonants, cadence of speech, type of elision, intonation, etc.), a person's place of origin could always be identified through a particular way of speaking which was often particular only to some 40 individuals, or fewer; in fact, in some regions language would fragment into family dialects. (Legros 2007: 101)

37 Well aware of the problems with linguistic/ethnic/cultural classification in the region, Dominque Legros (2007: 100–14) refuses to distinguish between Northern and Southern Tutchone people on either linguistic or cultural grounds. Instead, in his ethnohistorical study of the "Tutchone" people, he focuses on eleven regional groups that were culturally similar and "interconnected through marital ties and trade between 1890 and 1920" (ibid.: 103). These include not only (some of the) immediate ancestors of people who are now citizens of various contemporary Northern and Southern Tutchone First Nations (Legros 2007: 106–7), but also those of ostensibly Upper Tanana (today's White River) and possibly Han (Tr'ondëk Hwëch'in) First Nations as well (Legros 2007: 107–9). Like McClellan before him, Legros (see, e.g., 2007: 107, 390–2) points out that culturally – and perhaps linguistically as well – the more northerly groups of Southern Tutchone people (including those living at Aishihik, Hutshi, and Kluane Lake) had at least as much in common with their putatively Northern Tutchone neighbours as they did with the Tlingitized Southern Tutchone groups to their south.

Even contemporary kinship practices belie the assumption that language and culture correspond. There have always been extensive relations of kinship and intermarriage among the supposedly distinct linguistic/cultural "tribal" groups. And, as we saw in chapter 3, siblings and other close relatives frequently ended up enrolling in different Yukon First Nations – and often enough, this resulted in close relatives becoming members of different tribal councils. Recall, for example, the case discussed in chapter 3 of the Kluane citizen whose brother and father (who raised them both) enrolled in WRFN. In what meaningful sense can one possibly claim that the brother who is a Kluane citizen belongs to a different cultural group than his brother and father in WRFN? And their case is not at all uncommon.[38]

What, then, are we to make of the contemporary practice of asserting rigid linguistic and cultural boundaries between the Southern Tutchone First Nations of the STTC and their Northern Tutchone, Upper Tanana, and Han neighbours? It is significant, I think, that efforts to institutionalize the linguistic and cultural differences among First Nations began in earnest in the mid-1990s – around the same time the Yukon Umbrella Final Agreement and first four First Nation final and self-government agreements were ratified. This suggests that they are part of the nation-building process associated with the creation of state-like First Nations. Thus, they can be viewed as part of an ethnic framing that helps rationalize/justify the distribution of differential rights and privileges among First Nation citizens by making the situation appear as though it derives from pre-existing differences in language and culture.

The notion that language and culture are coterminous is a standard element of ethno-nationalist discourse. Scholars of nationalism, however, have long viewed this as a myth, arguing that to the extent that it does approximate reality, it is almost always the result of state-sponsored programs of cultural and linguistic homogenization/standardization (Anderson 1991: chap. 5; Bourdieu 1991: 220–8; Handler 1988: chap. 7; Hobsbawm 1992: 51–63, 93–100; Sahlins 1989: 265). Indeed, James Scott (1998: 72–3) argues that state officials regularly pursue such programs, which often entail considerable violence, because the simplification that results is crucial for the expansion of state power. The very act of

38 To cite only one more example: the Kluane citizen who made the comment about White River people not eating sheep has a daughter and grandchild who are citizens of White River First Nation.

designating a First Nation as, say, "Southern Tutchone" – in both language and culture – is an ideological act of homogenization that radically simplifies the complexity of social relations that existed among the ancestors of today's putatively Southern Tutchone First Nations and their neighbours. Such a designation would have been both meaningless and pointless prior to the creation of First Nations as state-like political organizations.

The process of cultural differentiation initiated by the Yukon agreements, however, does not stop at the tribal council level. Despite the tendency to conflate language and culture (which arguably created a need for some sort of political organization at the tribal council level), the Yukon agreements actually treat individual First Nations, rather than tribal councils, as the principal bearers of culture and history. Indeed, the provisions in the agreements that deal with Yukon First Nation culture and heritage take First Nation territoriality entirely for granted. To wit: the agreements grant ownership and management rights over those heritage resources[39] that are "directly related to the culture and history of Yukon Indian people" to that Yukon First Nation "in whose Traditional Territory [they are] found" (ibid.: 190–2). Thus, the agreements take it for granted that "the culture and history of Yukon Indian people" is divisible along ethno-territorial lines.[40] This is especially evident in the language of those provisions that are specific to each First Nation's final agreement, provisions that deal specifically with heritage sites/resources found in that First Nation's territory. The specific provisions in Kluane First Nation's agreement, for example, refer to those heritage sites and resources as "directly related to the culture and

39 The agreements define "heritage" as a collection of documentary and non-documentary resources and sites that "are of scientific or cultural value for their archaeological, palaeontological, ethnological, prehistoric, historic, or aesthetic value" (for relevant definitions in KFN's agreement, see Kluane First Nation 2003b: 2, 4, 6).

40 Brown (2007: 184) suggests this logic is inherent in all claims to sovereignty. The Yukon agreements do recognize that First Nations attempting to divvy up heritage resources in this way might run into some practical difficulties – especially given the extensive territorial overlap among them, so they lay out a process for resolving disputes over heritage resources in the event that First Nations are unable to agree among themselves who is the rightful owner (e.g., Kluane First Nation 2003b: 191–2). This, however, takes it for granted that such a division is not only possible but also desirable.

heritage of Kluane People," thus implying that Kluane people's culture and history can be distinguished from those of their neighbours.

Subsequent to the ratification of their agreements, all self-governing Yukon First Nations acted upon this ethno-territorial framing of history/culture by creating government heritage departments. These bureaucratic entities correspond to those in the federal and provincial/territorial governments (with which they regularly interact). Just as the Department of Canadian Heritage and the Yukon Heritage Branch are charged with the tasks of managing "Canadian" and "Yukon" heritage, respectively, each First Nation heritage department is responsible for protecting and managing its own "First Nation's" heritage.[41] As Richard Handler (1988) has shown for the Quebec case, government agencies of this sort often play a very active role in the "nationalization" of culture and history and the cultivation of corresponding nationalist sentiments. Even when such agencies do not engage in explicitly nationalistic activity, however, their very existence – as governmental institutions with jurisdiction over culture and history within a defined territory – necessarily help "institutionalize" (in Paasi's terms, see page 198) the culture and history of that region. Every time First Nation heritage officers approve a research permit to study "Kluane First Nation culture" in KFN's traditional territory, say, or produce interpretive materials on "Champagne-Aishihik First Nation's history" within the southern region of Kluane National Park, they enact their respective First Nations as distinct social entities each possessing its own culture and history.

Despite the agreements' bureaucratic compartmentalization of "heritage," the production of individual First Nation histories/cultures is not yet far advanced (especially *within* tribal councils). Yukon Indian people – including First Nation heritage officers, who are presumably the most constrained by bureaucratic conceptions of heritage – are still very much aware of the historical and cultural relations that bind

41 The Tr'ondëk Hwëch'in First Nation heritage department (one of the largest and most effective First Nation heritage departments in the Yukon), for instance, describes its mandate as follows: "The Heritage Department is responsible for managing, protecting and presenting TH [Tr'ondëk Hwëch'in] heritage resources. This includes land-based research, traditional-knowledge protection, seasonal archeology projects, documentation of oral histories, storage of heritage material, development of significant heritage sites, Hän language documentation and programming and operation of the Dänojà Zho Cultural Centre" (see http://www.trondek.ca/heritage.php).

them to their neighbours. Yet, the administrative structure created by the agreements makes it difficult to avoid framing heritage in ethno-territorial terms. Such framing can manifest itself in subtle ways – even when First Nation heritage officers engage in discourse and practices that that at first glance seem to subvert such an ethno-territorial framing. CAFN's heritage department website, for example, states that, "in *kwädąy* times (olden days), there were no firm boundary lines between Champagne and Aishihik *dän* [people] and our neighbours. We had strong connections, through marriage and trade, with people living in adjoining areas, including Burwash Landing and Northway areas to the northwest, Carmacks and Fort Selkirk to the north, Whitehorse, Carcross and Tagish to the east, and Klukwan, Haines, Dry Bay and Yakutat to the south and southwest."[42] Yet, despite the author's explicit affirmation of First Nation connectedness in "olden days," he or she takes the ethno-national category, *Champagne and Aishihik people*, entirely for granted as the basic sociological unit even back then. Though the statement allows that "'we' [CAFN people] had strong connections, through marriage and trade with people living in adjoining areas," neighbouring groups' exclusion from the category of "we" suggests that "they" were in fact other "peoples," that is, members of other similarly constituted ethno-national entities. Rather than subverting ethno-territoriality, then, the statement enacts it by projecting the cultural collective of "Champagne-Aishihik people" into the immemorial past of *kwädąy* times.

The same subtleties of framing can be seen in First Nation heritage practices as well, even – or perhaps especially – in those collaborative practices that explicitly seek to transcend First Nation territorial boundaries. First Nation heritage officers from different First Nations, for example, regularly collaborate with one another (as well as with the Yukon government's Heritage Branch) on specific heritage projects, especially those that span First Nations' territorial territory boundaries, such as in recent high-profile research on ice patches across the southwest Yukon (Farnell et al. 2004; Hare et al. 2004). Such practices clearly indicate First Nation heritage officers' recognition of shared culture and history. Such recognition is even more apparent in the case of the Yukon First Nation Heritage Group, a political body composed of representatives from all Yukon First Nation heritage departments. In explicit

42 See http://cafn.ca/government/departments/language-culture-heritage/history-and-genealogy/.

recognition of their shared history and culture – and of their common political interests, particularly vis-à-vis the Yukon government, First Nation heritage officers created the group in the early 2000s to pursue common goals in the realm of heritage management, to facilitate collaboration, and to present a united front in high-stakes political processes such as environmental assessments. Despite the collaborative nature of such practices, however, they generally take it for granted that it is *First Nations* that do the collaborating, and their involvement in any particular project is generally based on its relationship to their territorial territories.[43] Although First Nations may choose to collaborate with one another (much as states often choose to collaborate under the auspices of the UN), such efforts actually reinforce the assumption that it is First Nations, as the rightful bearers of culture and history, who are the main players in the heritage game.

The emergence of First Nations as distinct ethno-national entities, however, entails more than just the divvying up of First Nation culture and history along ethno-territorial lines. Indeed, before culture and history can be divided up in this way, they must first be conceived of as the kinds of things that are amenable to such division. As we shall see, this entails the imposition of a radically new conceptualization of the past. Before taking up that topic, however, I turn from my examination of cultural differentiation *among* First Nations to consider (related) processes of cultural homogenization *within* them. As has been the case with nation states more generally, the creation of First Nation states has provided an impetus for the homogenization of Yukon Indian languages and cultural practices in a manner conforming to the new ethno-territorial political configuration in the Yukon. And these processes of internal homogenization are closely tied to the project of extending state power through the simplification/standardization of local cultural practices (Scott 1998).

---

43 Members of the First Nation Heritage Group gain their seats on it by virtue of their roles as First Nation government heritage officials. Similarly, although not everyone involved in the ice patch research was a government heritage official, the research was framed as a collaboration among government "partners" (Yukon and various First Nations), each of which had an interest in the research because of the ice patches found in their respective territories. First Nations without ice patches in their territories did not collaborate on the project. See, for example, the acknowledgments in Farnell et al. (2004: 257).

The Homogenization of First Nation Language and Culture

As noted in the introduction to this chapter, those sharing a First Nation identity must not only differentiate themselves – linguistically, culturally, historically – from the nationals of other First Nations, they must also begin to view themselves as all somehow sharing the same language, culture, and history. Indeed, this notion of *sameness* is implicit in the very idea of a national *identity* (Brubaker and Cooper 2000), and some scholars (Foster 1991; Verdery 1993a; Verdery 1996; Williams 1989) have argued that all nationalist movements share a tendency towards cultural homogenization,[44] noting that beliefs about a collective self require the erasure of difference within the nation – along with a corresponding devaluation of those who do not conform to the dominant criteria of national inclusion. In fact, of course, there is considerable heterogeneity within any First Nation; not all First Nation citizens will possess all the characteristics or engage in all the practices that come to define the interior of the First Nation-as-entity. In the discourse on civic nationalism, the drive for internal homogeneity manifests itself as an ideology of universal citizenship, which, as we saw in chapter 3, is hostile to the recognition of group difference within states and seeks instead to impose visions of the "general will" and the "common good," which, in point of fact, are neither "general" nor "common," but instead serve particular interests within the state. By erasing differences in this way, the ideology of universal citizenship normalizes the beliefs and practices of some citizens while marginalizing those of others.

In its ethno-nationalist guise, the drive for homogeneity can and often does lead to policies that selectively promote a subset of cultural and linguistic practices from among the variety of those practised within the national territory (Handler 1988; Williams 1989; Verdery 1993a; Verdery 1996). Those policies assume – and so help produce – a universal, homogeneous, "national" culture. Those whose beliefs and practices do not conform to the emerging standard of the national culture are rendered increasingly marginal, both culturally and politically, and

44 Katherine Verdery (1996: 89), for example, notes that "modern states are based on control of territory, with a tendency to strive for homogeneity of the population contained within."

their very belonging to the nation can become suspect.[45] It is precisely in the context of the nation state's drive for internal homogenization that many differences among citizens become socio-politically salient.[46] This is certainly the case for language, which we saw had little socio-political salience in the Yukon prior to the land claim era.

Perhaps not surprisingly, the standardization of national languages often goes hand in hand with the rise of literacy, the spread of print capitalism, and the need for an administrative lingua franca (Anderson 1991; Scott 1998: 72–3). Despite the symbolic importance of indigenous languages to nation-building efforts in the Yukon, every First Nation in the territory currently uses English as its official language of administration. There are two principal reasons for this. First, there simply are not enough fluent speakers for any Yukon indigenous language to serve as the medium for official business.[47] Second, closely linked as they are to a hunting way of life, none of these languages currently possesses the specialized administrative and legal vocabulary that would be required for use in First Nation offices. Before Southern Tutchone – or any other indigenous language of the Yukon – could become a language of bureaucratic administration, it would have to undergo the same kind of conscious language reform that swept Europe in the nineteenth century, the central goal of which was to transform largely spoken vernacular languages into languages of state (Anderson 1991: chap. 5; Seton-Watson 1977).

---

45 It is because of this potential mismatch between civic and ethnic conceptions of the nation, Verdery (1993b: 180) notes, that the two views can sometimes be at odds with one another.

46 "By instituting homogeneity or commonality as normative, state-building renders difference socio-politically significant ... The most comprehensive possible agenda for the study of nationalism is ... the study of historical processes that have produced a particular political form – nation-states – differently in different contexts, and of the internal homogenizations that these nations have sought to realize in their different contexts" (Verdery 1993a: 43).

47 Although all the indigenous languages of the Yukon are considered endangered, this problem is especially acute for the smaller First Nations in the Yukon, such as Kluane First Nation. Not only do many Kluane citizens themselves not speak Southern Tutchone fluently, but the overall lack of Kluane citizens qualified to serve as government bureaucrats means the KFN government must hire considerable numbers of non-citizen staff (including both citizens of other First Nations and Euro-Canadians). It is hard enough to hire and retain qualified Euro-Canadians to work in remote Yukon villages even without requiring them to speak or learn Southern Tutchone.

There have been some efforts along these lines. Over the past several decades, linguists at the Yukon Native Language Centre (YNLC) have been working with native speakers to develop written forms for the indigenous languages of the Yukon (for a critical analysis of their efforts, see Meek 2010). Although language preservation has perhaps been the principal motivating factor in their efforts, there has been less emphasis on recording the languages for posterity than on facilitating their continued use in a society now heavily dependent on the written word. Rather than focusing on the production of dictionaries and grammars, for example, they have concentrated instead on training native speakers to teach these languages in their home communities, and most of the written and online materials produced by the YNLC are intended for classroom use. One (sometimes implicit) goal animating much of this literacy work – as it was in nineteenth-century European language reform – has been to lay the groundwork necessary for transforming these languages into official administrative languages of the First Nation state; indeed, given the central importance of First Nation offices (and the services they provide) in village life, it is hard to see how any of these languages could be restored to everyday use unless it was adopted for use in the administration of First Nation affairs.[48] And there are some who would clearly like to see this happen.

Several Kluane citizens – particularly those most involved in language revitalization efforts – told me explicitly that they would like to see Southern Tutchone someday become the official language of KFN government. One proponent of this view, who was at the time working in KFN's administration, began posting signs in KFN's office each day with the Southern Tutchone "word of the day," and he organized several language lessons for KFN staff (who reacted to his initiative with varying degrees of enthusiasm). He envisioned a day in which KFN's daily business would be carried out in Southern Tutchone, and

48 The other important objective of nineteenth-century European language revivals was to transform oral vernaculars into literary languages that could then serve as the basis for national literatures. This has been less of an explicit focus in the Yukon, though it is worth pointing out that many of the literacy materials developed by the Yukon Native Language Centre have been written versions of traditional northern Athapaskan stories (see YNLC website), and there have been other efforts to adapt Yukon native languages to modern literary/cultural contexts (e.g., the Juneau Award–winning music of Jerry Alfred, who sings in a dialect of Northern Tutchone).

new employees (both native and non-native) would have a few years to achieve fluency or lose their jobs. Part of the motivation behind such aspirations was a belief that this would help revive the language by forcing people to use it in everyday settings. Another rationale, however, was explicitly nationalistic; several people told me point blank that since Kluane First Nation is composed of Southern Tutchone people, official First Nation business should be conducted in Southern Tutchone, rather than in the language of the colonizer. Given the constructed nature of Southern Tutchone (as both language and ethnicity), this sentiment must be regarded as ethno-nationalistic, rather than as simply anti-colonial.[49]

The process of language standardization is not yet far advanced in the Yukon, largely because Yukon First Nation languages are still almost exclusively oral; despite the heroic efforts of the YNLC, there is still relatively little written material available in any of them. Even so, YNLC's efforts have provoked some misgivings. Although YNLC linguists have made significant efforts to avoid privileging any particular dialects in their production of language materials,[50] some fluent speakers are still wary of their efforts precisely because of their potential for standardization. This was evident, for example, at a week-long STTC-sponsored Southern Tutchone Literacy Workshop I attended in 1998, one of a series of such workshops the YNLC has organized over the past several decades. There are at least four mutually intelligible dialects of Southern Tutchone (although, as noted above, this categorization itself depends on a somewhat arbitrary distinction between the dialects of Northern and Southern Tutchone – and possibly of Upper

49 Although no First Nations in the Yukon have come close to achieving this goal, the Kaska Nation, which is composed of several First Nations lying astride the Yukon, BC, and NWT borders (which it does not recognize), made a powerful symbolic statement along these lines by adopting a constitution with a title and preamble written in Kaska. Although I do not read Kaska, the English translation of the preamble, which follows immediately after the original Kaska, explicitly constructs the Kaska Nation as a culturally and linguistically homogeneous ethno-nation ("we share a common history, language, culture, and traditional laws") whose existence as such long preceded the arrival of Euro-Canadians: "Our Kaska Dena Nation has existed from time immemorial as has our inherent right to govern ourselves" (Kaska Dena Constitution Working Group 2008: 5).

50 They have, for instance, often produced variants of their teaching materials in each of the different dialects, and they have taken pains to record dialectical variations of different words in many of the materials they have produced.

Tanana as well). Fluent speakers of all the Southern Tutchone dialects were brought to Burwash Landing for the week to advise in the preparation of written texts. Over the course of the week, it became clear to me that some of the fluent speakers were resistant to the process. One elder expressed to me her frustration quite explicitly. She worried that in his effort to develop a generic written form of "Southern Tutchone," the linguist leading the workshop was conflating the different dialects; as a result, she feared, he was going to end up with a mishmash that does not correspond to the way anyone actually speaks and that this would hasten the language's disappearance. Although the linguist leading the workshop, himself a fluent speaker of Southern Tutchone, is well aware of this dialectical variation and has taken pains to record the dialectical variants of different words, even the division of the language into distinct "dialects" has a homogenizing effect because it flattens out the linguistic diversity *within* each putative dialect.[51] The point here is not to condemn his work, which many (and I include myself here) view as critically important, but merely to point out that standardization and homogenization are inevitable in any attempt to transform a purely oral language into a written one, a necessary prerequisite for its adoption as a national language.

The creation of a standardized official state language not only serves the administrative needs of the territorial state, it also puts pressure on citizens to conform linguistically or risk political marginalization or loss of access to state programs and services. Barbra Meek (2014) illustrates this nicely in her analysis of a sociolinguistic interaction among speakers of Kaska (an Athapaskan language spoken in the southeast Yukon, northeast British Columbia, and southwest NWT). In her case, speakers of two dominant Kaska dialects marginalize another Kaska speaker and the dialect she speaks. Such interactions contribute to the standardization of the Kaska language, simultaneously rendering the

51 Although cited earlier, it is worth recalling here Legros's (2007: 101) characterization of linguistic variation in the region: "As each regional group that occupied a part of a valley or the vicinity of a lake had its own distinct way of speaking or sub-dialect (vocabulary, sounds of vowels and consonants, cadence of speech, type of elision, intonation, etc.), a person's place of origin could always be identified through a particular way of speaking which was often particular only to some 40 individuals, or fewer; in fact, in some regions language would fragment into family dialects."

speakers of non-standard dialects as "non-speakers" (or at least "non-fluent" speakers) whose cultural authority is therefore much easier to dismiss.

These processes of standardization and marginalization are not restricted to the realm of language. Given the conflation of language and culture discussed above, any failure – in either ancestry or practice – to live up to the standardized ethno-national ideal can serve as a justification for marginalization. If one views the possession of "Southern Tutchone" language and culture as essential to one's identity as a Kluane person (and therefore to one's status as a "proper" citizen of Kluane First Nation), for example, then anyone who does not eat Dall sheep, say, or who has Tlingit or Tagish ancestry, can be cast as an "outsider," their loyalties automatically rendered suspect by virtue of their supposed cultural inauthenticity.[52] This is, in fact, exactly what happened in the case of the CARES letter, described in chapter 3. Recall that in that letter, a group of Kluane citizens opposed the ratification of KFN's land claim and self-government agreements in explicitly ethno-nationalist language. The letter writers sought to disenfranchise those Kluane citizens of Tlingit and Tagish ancestry, whom they described as "visitors" and "3rd party interests," despite the fact that those citizens' ancestors moved to Kluane territory over one hundred years ago and formed an integral part of the original Kluane band.[53]

Interlude: Animals and the Ethnic Nation

Thus far, we have considered the twin processes of external differentiation and internal homogenization only insofar as they involve humans. It went without saying that the ethno-territorial processes we

---

52 As Duara (1995: 15) notes, "The nation, even where it is manifestly not a recent invention, is hardly the realization of an original essence, but a historical configuration designed to include certain groups and exclude or marginalize others – often violently."

53 In fact, as we have seen, intermarriage among different "tribal" groups was a common feature of pre-contact Yukon society and continues today. Indeed, if Tlingit ancestry really disqualified one from "authentic" Southern Tutchone-ness, then there have been precious few authentic Southern Tutchone people anywhere in the Yukon since the mid-nineteenth century. The letter writers were also notably silent on the matter of Northern Tutchone and Upper Tanana ancestry, which, if included along with Tlingit and Tagish as grounds for disenfranchisement, would have disenfranchised nearly everyone in Kluane First Nation, the letter writers included.

examined serve to differentiate various groups of *humans* from one another, because animals – almost by definition – cannot be members of the nation. And what need is there for homogenizing processes like those described above to exclude and/or marginalize animals from the ethnic nation when the fundamental assumptions of ethnic nationalism *presuppose* their exclusion from the nation?

We saw in chapter 3 that the Yukon land claim and self-government agreements deny First Nation citizenship to the animals and other non-human persons who inhabit the boreal forest. Because Euro-American political theorists almost uniformly assume that such beings cannot possibly be the subjects of politics, self-government negotiators never even contemplated granting them citizenship in the new First Nation polities; there is simply no space for such beings in the civic nation. If anything, this is even more true of the ethnic nation. Indeed, the exclusion of animals from the ethnic nation is so utterly taken for granted that, while animals are (to my knowledge) completely absent from the vast literature on nationalism, no nationalist or scholar of nationalism that I am aware of has ever bothered to make a case for their exclusion.[54] Just as Euro-American political theorists of all stripes generally view animals as lacking political subjectivity, so, too, do nationalist thinkers and the scholars who study them regard animals as entirely lacking in history, culture, language, and all of the other characteristics that might mark them (if they were human) as fellow members of an ethnic nation. And, to the extent that ethno-nationalism is viewed as a form of kinship relation writ large, animals' inclusion in the ethno-nation is rendered even more unlikely. After all, what nationalist would seriously argue that animals should be considered fellow nationals by virtue of their shared "blood" or common descent from the founding fathers of the nation?

Yet, the idea that humans and animals are linked to one another by bonds of kinship is not at all bizarre to Yukon Indian people. Indeed, in the Long Time Ago stories, human- and animals-people regularly

54 Contrast this to chapter 3, where we saw that there are at least a few scholars (e.g., Borrows 2002; Donaldson and Kymlicka 2011) who have considered – though in very different ways – extending membership in the civic nation to animals.

intermarried and had children together.[55] Still today, people sometimes use kinship terms to address animals, and they recognize relations of kinship not only between themselves and animals but also among different animal species.[56] Nor would most Yukon Indian people concur with any suggestion to the effect that animal-people are lacking in history, language, or culture. As I have taken pains to describe elsewhere (Nadasdy 2007b), they believe that animals are able to understand – and sometimes even speak – human languages and that they are enmeshed in the very same complex web of social relations as human-people. Indeed, many Yukon Indian people continue to believe animal-people, despite their superficial differences (fur, etc.), to be fundamentally similar kinds of beings as themselves. If the human-people of the Yukon have sufficient culture and history to qualify as members of the newly emerging ethno-nations across the territory, then why not animal-people?[57]

My point here is not to argue that animal-people *should* be considered members of these ethno-nations (as either co-ethnics or perhaps minority ethnic groups within First Nations). The concept of *ethnicity* is no more flexible than *citizenship* in that regard. Indeed, it is probably less so, since *ethnicity* – in both its primordial and situational guises – is

55 Probably the most famous story of this sort in the Yukon is "The Girl Who Married the Bear." For multiple versions of this story, along with many other such stories, see McClellan (2007). Significantly, animals are not the only other-than-human persons who can enter into kinship relations with humans, as evident from stories such as "The Sun's Daughter" and "Star Husband," versions of which can also be found in McClellan (2007).

56 For an overview of human-people's relationships – including often those of kinship – with various animal-peoples, see McClellan (1975: chap. 4). See also Nelson (1983) for a similar, but more extensive, overview for the Koyukon people of interior Alaska. The kin relationship between various animals (e.g., the fact that wolf and wolverine are brothers-in-law) is revealed in many Long Time Ago stories (for the Southern Yukon see especially the volumes of McClellan 2007).

57 Interestingly, Leanne Simpson (2008) writes that the Nishnaabeg did, in fact, conceive of animals as constituting their own nations (i.e., that there is a moose nation, a deer nation, a caribou nation, and so on) that were capable of entering into treaty relations with human nations. There are superficial parallels here with Donaldson and Kymlicka's (2011) assertion that "wild animals" should be considered citizens of their own sovereign polities that stand outside of those composed of humans and their domestic animal partners (though they write exclusively about citizenship and not ethnic nationalism). As far as I am aware, however, no one has suggested that humans and animals should be considered members of *the same* ethnic nation.

fundamentally about subdividing the *human* species; it is by definition a social – or in some views, biological – distinction among humans. *Species* is similarly a differentiating/homogenizing concept but at a different scale. Thus, it would be a category mistake to claim that members of a different species can be members of an ethnicity that includes some, but not all, humans. My point, rather, is to illustrate just how incompatible ethno-nationalism is with indigenous Yukon peoples' ideas about proper relationships between human- and animal-people. To the extent Yukon Indian people view themselves as members of ethno-nationalist collectivities, they adopt a view of society that necessarily excludes animals. There is simply no way to include animals – or other non-human persons – within the ethno-national self that does not transform the concept beyond recognition. After all, if Upper Tanana people can be excluded from (or marginalized within) a Southern Tutchone First Nation on cultural grounds, what chance do moose or spruce trees have of being included? To do so would render the very idea of the ethnic nation nonsensical.

We have now seen that the rise of First Nation states has entailed the homogenization of indigenous languages and cultures and to sociocultural differentiation among the (human) people of different First Nations. But the putatively homogeneous First Nation cultures that result from these processes are not free floating. Rather, they are anchored to – even inscribed upon – the landscape in a manner that serves to naturalize the nation's claim to its homeland and produce a sense of its deep history there.

Inscribing the Nation in the Landscape

All nation states have their founding myths and historical narratives that serve to justify their existence and ongoing practices of rule. Not only are these nationalist histories necessarily rooted in place (all events must, after all, take place somewhere), they are also framed in explicitly ethno-territorial terms. They justify the state's peculiarly territorial form of rule by forging a deep historical link between the collective individual of the nation and the geo-body of the national territory/homeland. The nationalist histories of northern Canadian First Nations have yet to be written, but the raw materials from which such histories get built are already at hand, in the lives and deaths of peoples' ancestors on the land.

Ancestral Bodies and the Production of National Homelands

One of the most powerful ways of anchoring the nation to its homeland is via the actual physical bodies of its collective ancestors. Katherine Verdery (1999: 105) notes that "the connection among kinship, burial, nationalism, and soil is a very potent and widespread one." To get at this nexus of ideas, she suggests that we might usefully conceive of nationalism as a form of ancestor worship (ibid.: 104; see also Renan 1990: 19), noting that "burying or reburying ancestors and kin sacralizes and nationalizes spaces as 'ours,' binding people to their national territories in an orderly universe" (ibid.: 110). Of course, it is not only those living in nation states who revere their dead. Verdery argues that it is precisely because of the very old and widespread tendency among humans to "link ... people with the geographical emplacement of their dead," that ancestral bodies and graves can so often become culturally and politically powerful in a nationalist context (ibid.). Nationalism, then, does not create the sacred links between people, their ancestors, and the land in which they are buried; it merely reframes those links in national – rather than family or lineage – terms. As it happens, this is precisely how the Yukon First Nation final and self-government agreements frame the relationship between Yukon Indian people, their ancestors, and the land.

We already saw in chapter 3 that Yukon First Nation citizenship codes subtly recast ancestors as "citizen-ancestors." As the wellsprings of "Kluane First Nation blood" and the apical ancestors from whom all contemporary and future Kluane First Nation citizens must trace descent, these ancestors are transformed into the founding fathers and mothers of the new First Nation. In this light, we saw, a prominent historical figure such as Jimmy Johnson, who played an important role in the early history of Burwash Landing and was well known throughout the Yukon and interior Alaska, suddenly – and quite naturally – appears as one of the founding heroes of the Kluane First Nation. This despite the fact that Jimmy Johnson himself died in 1946, well before the formation of the original Kluane band – much less the creation of Kluane First Nation – and that his descendants are now counted as citizens and/or residents of perhaps a dozen First Nations and Alaska native villages. I emphasize that there is nothing unusual about this; the post hoc attribution of national identity/citizenship to prominent and respected ancestors is part of the standard repertoire of nation building.

Once the ancestors of Kluane citizens have been reframed as founding ancestors in this way, however, it is but a small step to viewing their bodies as sacralizing the national homeland. Ancestral bodies, which have *literally* become a part of Kluane First Nation territory, transform that territory into a sacred space that is of – and belongs to – their descendants, the Kluane people/nation.

In chapter 3, we not only saw that Kluane First Nation's citizenship code casts Kluane citizens' ancestors as citizens-ancestors, it also explicitly ties them to "Kluane First Nation territory." The link between the ancestors and the national territory is such a central trope of nationalist thought (Verdery 1999)[58] that no one at KFN's negotiating table – neither First Nation nor government negotiators – ever questioned it. Everyone simply took it for granted that the existence of indigenous graves at any particular site rendered KFN's bid for control over that site not merely legitimate but ironclad. Although government negotiators could and regularly did contest Kluane First Nation's specific land selections (see Nadasdy 2008 for a description of the land selection process), they never once contested KFN's selection of a grave site. Indeed, Yukon First Nation final agreements not only give First Nations complete authority over gravesites on First Nation settlement land, they also grant them an unusually strong say over what happens to indigenous graves found on non-settlement land within their traditional territories.[59] Of particular interest here is the fact that all the provisions regarding Indian burial sites in the Yukon final agreements

58 Indeed, Katherine Verdery points out that the adoption or rejection of national ancestors often has territorial implications, and vice versa, sometimes with violent consequences (e.g., Verdery 1999: 109).

59 Regarding land use management off settlement lands within a First Nation's traditional territory, the Yukon agreements typically require the Yukon and or federal government to "consult with" the relevant First Nation. In the case of managing burial sites, however, the wording of the agreements is much stronger. They "require the joint approval of Government and the Yukon First Nation in whose Traditional Territory the Yukon First Nation Burial Site is located" (Kluane First Nation 2003b: 199). In the case of any future discoveries of indigenous grave sites, the agreements do allow for an arbitration process in the event that the relevant First Nation refuses to allow excavation, exhumation, or reburial to proceed (thus presumably holding up some development project); even then, however, "any exhumation, examination, and reburial of human remains from a Yukon First Nation Burial Site ordered by an arbitrator under 13.9.3 shall be done by, or under the supervision of, that Yukon First Nation."

take for granted contemporary First Nation territoriality. For example, gravesites in a First Nation's traditional territory are assumed to contain that First Nation's ancestors simply by virtue of the fact that they are located within that territory. It is the First Nation within whose traditional territory a gravesite is found that has authority over it (e.g., Kluane First Nation 2003b: 199–200).[60] In this way, the agreements apportion the bodies of the ancestors out on the land among the newly emerging politico-territorial units created by the agreements; and those bodies, in turn, help legitimate each First Nation's claim to its territory.

But it is not only specific gravesites that are at issue here. In recent decades, most Yukon Indian people have been buried in centrally located village graveyards, but this is a relatively recent practice dating back less than a century.[61] Prior to their permanent settlement in villages, Yukon Indian people were buried out on the land. Thus, there are gravesites

60 The situation is considerably more complicated in KFN's case due to its territorial overlap with White River First Nation. The graves of known ancestors are claimed either by WRFN or KFN primarily based on kinship relations with the deceased. The First Nation affiliation of unknown burial sites, however, depends largely on where in the territory the grave is located. Even when people know who is buried in a grave, however, post hoc determinations of First Nation affiliation can be difficult and contested. Bodies are not viewed as either White River or Kluane ancestors purely on the basis of *whom* they are related to (as we have seen, First Nation citizenship even of living people is underdetermined by kinship); *where* they are buried is also always an important consideration. So, for example, when in the summer of 2002 human remains were discovered near the old trading post of Sourdough just north of Beaver Creek (well inside White River First Nation's Core Area), it was assumed by everyone to be a White River First Nation burial site, and WRFN assumed authority over it.

61 Because Burwash Landing trading post was built in 1903, the Burwash graveyard contains some graves dating back to the early twentieth century. Even then, however, when someone died out in the bush, it was sometimes impractical to transport the body back to the village, so they were buried close to where they died. It is also worth noting that prior to the arrival of missionaries, Indian people of the southern Yukon practiced cremation, though McClellan (1975: 249) notes that "the Southern Tutchone, at least, sometimes just covered the corpse with heavy logs," and that shamans' bodies were never burned but rather were "laid out in an isolated grave house." After cremation, the remains were much more easily transported, and McClellan does suggest that ashes were sometimes transported to their final resting places (at which point, by the late nineteenth century, they were usually placed within a grave house). Several residents of Burwash Landing reported that prior to the creation of the village graveyard, cremations were carried out on a small island "down below" (near the point where the Kluane River flows out of Kluane Lake).

scattered all over the Yukon landscape. People still recall who is buried in the more recent gravesites, but the names of the deceased inhabiting many of the older graves have long since been forgotten – as indeed, have most of the gravesites themselves. Kluane First Nation, like other Yukon First Nations, made a point of mapping – and selecting as settlement land – all known burial sites within their traditional territory (with the exception of those "White River" gravesites selected by WRFN, see note 60) – whether they knew who was buried there or not. If anything, the unknown dead are even more potent national symbols than the known dead. Indeed, their very namelessness enhances their symbolic power because, lacking personal identities, they can so easily be portrayed simply as, say, dead "Canadians" or "Frenchmen."[62] The fact that "ancestors of the First Nation" were buried across the land so long ago that no one even remembers their names stands as a powerful testament to First Nations' claims to have been occupying their territories since time immemorial, and these nameless graves are more easily "nationalized" than the graves of grandparents and other known ancestors whose personalities and (complicated) kinship ties are well remembered. Thus, there are Kluane First Nation ancestors – known and unknown – buried throughout Kluane First Nation's territory; and this wide distribution of gravesites throughout First Nation traditional territories is powerfully symbolic of First Nations' connection to those territories as a whole. There is a palpable sense in which the earth itself is thought to be composed of the very blood, flesh, and bones of generation after generation of forgotten ancestors, who could be buried anywhere.[63]

62 On the symbolic importance of the unknown dead in the national imagination, see Anderson (1991: 9–10). Verdery (1999: 20–1), too, points out that the "anonymous dead" can become particularly potent symbols of the nation when, for instance, they can be framed as victims of nationalist or ethnic persecution (such as the bodies found in mass graves in the former Yugoslavia).

63 See Deloria (1992: 146), who notes that such a belief, widespread among the indigenous people of North America, "speaks to an identity so strong as to be virtually indistinguishable from the earth itself." Deloria errs, however, when he claims that "nowhere else on the planet do we find this attitude" (ibid.). On the contrary, it is quite a common belief worldwide, and one that has often been reframed and harnessed for use in nation-building projects. Indeed, the use of graves as land claim-making devices is extremely common in nationalist rhetoric. Verdery (1999: 98) reports a striking claim to this effect made by Serbian nationalist Vuk Drašković: "Serbia is wherever there are Serbian graves."

KFN negotiators and elders at KFN's negotiating table regularly legitimated their claim to the land – and simultaneously questioned the government's authority on that same land – by explicitly drawing attention to the graves of their ancestors, as elder Lena Johnson did in 1997:

> Where is the right of government taking over, all over the country? All over Yukon and Canada? Those native people lived here ... My dad and my mum were married here. My grandparents, they lived here, and they died here, and they're buried here. My parents died here. I remember when my first cousin died, my uncle's first baby. I was three years old. Down by Redtail [Lake]. I can remember they carried that baby's body up the hill. It's buried there. And that's where, you know, people are buried all over the place too. And I don't know *how*, what kind of God, who *created* this *land* for government to take over.[64]

As Lena's statement suggests, it is not only the dead bodies of the ancestors that sacralize First Nation territories and bind First Nations to them. It is also their lives – their histories – on the land that come to be viewed as the source of the deep and lasting bond between First Nation and territory.

Place Names and the Production of National Homelands

Despite the lack of written histories, accounts of ancestors' lives upon the land – and their close relationships with its other-than-human inhabitants – are preserved in songs and stories (from the mythical to the mundane) passed down from generation to generation. Always rooted in place, these songs and stories – along with the rich and frequently evocative names of the places to which they refer – now increasingly constitute "evidence" of the ancient link between First Nation and territory. I do not mean to suggest here that either those place names or the stories they invoke have been "invented" by First Nation nationalists. Once again, it is a matter of framing. To the extent people now frame these place names and stories as evidence of a *First Nation's* history on

64 Lena Johnson, 31 January 1997. Taped land table negotiations. Yukon Archives, Kluane First Nation Collection, accession number SR234-61(B), 18:30–20:01.

the land – as if that First Nation has always existed – they enact not only the unitary First Nation but also its link to a bounded homeland. Scholars have written extensively about Athapaskan place names and how they situate people within the rich particularities of place, thus entangling them in the social and moral life of their communities (Basso 1996; Cruikshank 1981; Cruikshank 1990a). As Julie Cruikshank (1990b; 1998) so eloquently shows us, however, stories are always polysemous, their meaning(s) in any instance deriving from the context in which they are told. First Nation nationalism is simply a new social context within which to deploy and understand stories and the places to which they are tied. Cruikshank (1990a: 64) points out that interest in indigenous place names in the Canadian north increased considerably with the advent of land claims. This suggests that it may be worth reflecting a bit more on the nationalist context within which place names – and their stories – are increasingly being invoked.

It almost goes without saying that one of the most powerful ways of creating a link between a nation and its homeland is through the use of place names. Scholars have noted that the act of naming geographical features is a powerful way of claiming possession over territory (Boelhower 1988: 220–1; Seed 1995: 163–4, 174–6, 189–90). Indeed, it was standard colonial practice around the world to replace indigenous names with those assigned by Europeans.[65] Besides satisfying the self-aggrandizing desires of European explorers,[66] this practice served to assert symbolic control over territory. It is no surprise, then, that decolonization has nearly always been accompanied by the widespread replacement of colonial era place names with their pre-colonial (or supposedly pre-colonial) counterparts. Historian Ray Craib (2004: 44–52), for example, describes the near obsession among nineteenth-century Mexican nationalist scholars with pre-colonial place names, which they sought to "resurrect" and "actively perpetuate" precisely because they deemed these names essential for any attempt to narrate the "true"

65 Seed (1995), however, points out that European colonial powers had very different views on how the assignation of place names related to territorial control.

66 Carter (1988), however, warns us that even in apparently clear-cut cases of topographical self-aggrandizement, we need to be attentive to the other logics and motivations that animated explorers' naming practices. And Cruikshank (1981: 79) points out that some explorers, at least, such as Edward Glave in the Yukon, actually advocated – though to little avail – the preservation of indigenous place names.

history of the Mexican nation (ibid.: 45). Even when faithfully and accurately "resurrected," however, these "old" names are infused with new meaning, having become emblematic of the brand new nations emerging from the ashes of empire.

In northern Canada, as elsewhere, emerging First Nation governments have seized upon place names, newly invented as well as resurrected, as a means to symbolically assert their new-found control over land. Jenson and Papillon (2000: 249, 255, 257), for instance, note that a key move in the land claims struggle in James Bay was Cree leaders' act of naming Cree national territory *Eeyou Astchee* [Cree/the People's land], and insisting upon its use in English/French political discourse. Because this territorial moniker explicitly ties a particular human collectivity, *the Cree*, to "its" territory, it was instrumental, they argue, in constructing "an image of a single people [as opposed to a collection of different regional bands], with a common history and relation to the land" (ibid.: 251).

Traditional territory names in the Yukon are perhaps not as institutionalized as *Eeyou Astchee*, but insofar as they are used, they function in largely the same way. Signs at the borders of KFN's traditional territory on the Alaska Highway,[67] for instance, welcome drivers to *Łù'àn Män Keyi* [Kluane Country] (see figure 5),[68] and KFN's final agreement created the *Dän Keyi* [our people's land] Renewable Resources Council.[69]

67 Interestingly, the sign at the northern border was erected near Long's Creek, which is well south of the White River bridge. It is also a bit south of the KFN/WRFN Secondary Area boundary; so its placement corresponds with neither Joe Johnson's idea of the Kluane national homeland (discussed at the beginning of this chapter), nor with any of the territorial boundaries ultimately created by KFN's final agreement. The reason for this is that the signs were erected well before the finalization and signing of KFN's agreement. At the time, overlap talks between KFN and WRFN were ongoing, and Kluane negotiators had proposed Long's Creek, which is approximately midway between Burwash Landing and Beaver Creek, as a possible overlap resolution boundary. The notion of core and secondary areas was then still years in the future.

68 The literal translation is "Kluane Lake Country," but the placement of the signs, along with the English translation of the term that appears on the signs themselves (which leaves out "Lake"), suggests that *Lù'àn Män* refers not to the lake itself but to *Lù'àn Män Ku Dän*, the people of Kluane Lake.

69 In chapter 3, I discussed the multiple possible meanings of the word *dän*. KFN's final agreement, however, explicitly translates the term *Dän Keyi* as "our people's land" (see Kluane First Nation 2003b: 241), and in that context "our people" clearly refers to the citizens of Kluane First Nation.

Most of the time, however, people refer to Kluane territory using the English-language name officially assigned to it in KFN's agreement: *Kluane First Nation traditional territory.*[70] Regardless of the variant used, all these names assume the existence of a single unified *people*, the Kluane people, who have a special political and historical relationship to a clearly defined and bounded territory.[71] Like *Eeyou Astchee*, all of these names are new. There was neither an *Eeyou Astchee* nor a *Dän Keyi* prior to the land claim era, because neither the bounded territories nor the socio-political collectives to which they refer existed as such. These new territorial names help bring those national collectivities into being while at the same time affirming their long-standing historical ties to the territory.

It is not just the overall name of the national territory that can do this kind of ethno-territorial work; more localized place names, too, can help create unitary peoples and bind them to particular territories by invoking "their" history upon the land. As Cruikshank (1990a: 64) notes, Yukon First Nation negotiators initially deployed place names research as evidence of a First Nation people's land use and occupancy. Increasingly, however, now that most First Nations have ratified their agreements, First Nation officials have set about the task of "restoring" indigenous place names on the official government maps of the Yukon. Indeed, all the parties to the Yukon land claim negotiations

70 "Kluane" is an English version of the Southern Tutchone word *Łuane*. "Ł" is the symbol used to indicate an un-aspirated "l" sound (not found in English) in the orthography developed for Southern Tutchone by linguists at the Yukon Native Language Centre. Interestingly, during KFN's land claim negotiations, Kluane negotiators made some effort to get the name of Kluane National Park changed on the grounds that "Kluane" is not a Southern Tutchone word and that it is a misspelling. The federal government adamantly refused to consider a name change, however, on the grounds that "Kluane" Park was already internationally known. KFN then attempted to have Kluane Park divided into two separate parks. The southern park (the part in CAFN's traditional territory) could retain the name "Kluane," while the northern park (in KFN's territory), they proposed, should be given the name *Tachäl*, after *Tachäl Dhäl*, the S. Tutchone name for Sheep Mountain, the most popular tourist site in the northern part of Kluane Park. The federal government refused this as well, but it did consent to dividing Kluane Park into distinct administrative areas. The northern of these is now officially referred to as the Tachäl region of Kluane Park.

71 We also saw in chapter 3 that the invocation of "Kluane First Nation traditional territory" in KFN's citizenship code makes the relationship between Kluane "territory" and Kluane "people" explicit.

Figure 9 Gerald Dickson hunting Dall sheep above Tásàn Zhät Nji Chù' (Copper Joe Creek), August 2003 (photo by author)

anticipated the restoration of indigenous place names. The Yukon Umbrella Final Agreement includes provisions for the establishment of a Yukon Geographical Place Names Board and gives individual First Nations a formal role in the "naming or renaming" of geographical features within their traditional territories (see, e.g., Kluane First Nation 2003b: 201),[72] and First Nations wasted little time in submitting proposed name changes to the Board. Kluane First Nation, for example, submitted a list of ten such names in 1997, long before it had finalized

72 First Nations have sole authority to "name or rename places or geographical features" on their settlement lands (see provision 13.11.3). When considering the naming or renaming of geographical features elsewhere in a First Nation's traditional territory, the Geographical Place Names Board must consult with the First Nation(s) in question (provision 13.11.2), and First Nations are permitted to submit proposed name changes directly to the board.

Figure 10 Joe Johnson hunting moose in the Burwash Uplands above Shär Ndü Chù (Duke River), February 1997 (photo by author)

its own agreement.[73] Significantly, all of the proposed name changes were of creeks/rivers along the Alaska Highway or prominent features within Kluane National Park.[74] Thus, the new names were chosen for maximum visibility; they would appear on highway signs or in Parks Canada's interpretive materials. Indeed, one of the Kluane citizens who helped compile this list of names described to me his vision of tourists and non–First Nation residents alike having to use (and learn to pronounce) these Southern Tutchone names. It is hard to imagine a

73 As a Yukon-wide board created by the Yukon Umbrella Final Agreement (UFA) rather than any particular First Nation's final agreement, the Yukon Geographical Place Name Board was constituted in 1995 upon the ratification of the UFA.

74 The ten names submitted were: Tachäl Dhäl (Sheep Mountain), A'ay Chù' (Slims River), Shézät Chù' (Swede Johnson Creek), Shär Ndü Chù' (Duke River), Tl'äw K'à Chù' (Burwash Creek), Dänzhür Chù' (Donjek River), Łù'àn Män (Kluane Lake), Khär Shän Nji (Congdon Creek), Tl'el Nji Chù' (Quill Creek), and Tásàn Zhät Nji Chù' (Copper Joe Creek).

Figure 11 Agnes Johnson setting fishnet for grayling at Shézät Chù (Swede Johnson Creek), April 2004 (photo by author)

more direct way of inscribing Kluane language and culture upon the land. Yet official renaming efforts barely scratch the surface of this inscription process.[75]

Interest in indigenous place names has only increased with the finalization of Yukon First Nation agreements. Much of this work has resulted in maps and GIS databases housed in First Nation offices or made

75 Despite the fact that the Yukon Geographical Place Names Board approved all ten names as early as 10 November 1997, the renaming process dragged on for nearly two decades. Finally, on 30 May 2013, six of the names were formally approved. Tachäl Dhäl was approved as a new name ("Sheep Mountain" had never been officially recorded, since it refers to a spur of Mount Wallace), and A'ay Chù' officially replaced "Slims River." The other names (Tl'äw K'à Chù', Shär Ndü Chù', Dänzhür Chù', and Khär Shän Nji) were accepted as official dual/alternate names. What exactly this means is still unclear, but it does mean they can now appear on official signs and other documentation (either by themselves or alongside the English names).

available to the public in interactive form.[76] Relatively few of the place names contained in these databases will ever be candidates for formal submission to the Geographic Place Names Board, for the simple fact that there are so many of them.[77] Nearly every feature of the land has an indigenous name – or, more typically, several (in the various languages and dialects of the region). As Cruikshank (1990a) has noted, many of these names refer, often in richly descriptive language, to the activities of Yukon Indian people's ancestors, historical and mythical, thus evoking their long histories on the land. Many of the geographical features in these databases have no English names at all, so their public dissemination – either through public release or through the use of First Nation GIS databases in land management processes – has largely the same effect as official name changes; it inscribes the collective history of the First Nation's people upon the land.

While neither these place names nor the stories to which they refer are themselves new, their nationalist framing is. Significantly, when KFN submitted its list of ten place names to the Yukon Geographical Place Names Board, they selected the Southern Tutchone names for these places – rather than their Tlingit, Upper Tanana, or Northern Tutchone variants. Even more specifically, those names were in the Kluane dialect of Southern Tutchone. There is nothing surprising about this, but it means that the "restoration" of these place names is only partial. The application of the English name, "Kluane Lake," for example, did not replace a single agreed-upon indigenous name, but rather several names in various languages and dialects. Thus, officially re-designating the lake *Łuan Män* (Southern Tutchone) – rather than, say, *Luug Cho Mann'* (Upper Tanana) – is, like the act of officially naming it "Kluane

76 The most prominent example of this for Southern Tutchone place names is the *Dákeyi (Our Country)* project. Produced by the Yukon Native Language Centre, this set of ten interactive maps, first released on CD in 1996 and then made available on the web in 2007 (see http://www.ynlc.ca/culture/dakeyi/index.html), includes over 60 significant place names. Clicking on the names gives one access to detailed descriptions (in Southern Tutchone and English), photographs, and audio files. The maps were intended for use "by high school students and others studying Southern Tutchone language and culture." Notice the conflation of language and culture here.

77 As an illustration of the density of place names, Norman Easton, working with the White River First Nation, has documented over 700 Upper Tanana place names in a narrow band (visible from the Alaska Highway) between the White River in the Yukon and Northway, Alaska.

Lake," a simplification, albeit one now in service of Kluane First Nation as well as Canada. In addition to according well with the simplifying/homogenizing tendencies of the state (Scott 1998), this renaming also serves to legitimize the claims of the Kluane First Nation (as the First Nation state associated with the Kluane dialect of Southern Tutchone) to the lake in question and to the territory in which the lake is located. This not only strengthens the link between Kluane First Nation and its territorial homeland; it also contributes to the homogenization of Kluane First Nation by rendering invisible the fact that some ancestors of today's Kluane First Nation citizens would themselves have called the lake by a different name.

First Nations in History

Once appropriately reframed in national terms, ancestral bodies and place names – along with the lives, stories, and songs they index – link the collective individual of the First Nation to the geo-body of its national territory/homeland. Significantly, however, they also produce a sense of the First Nation collective's long history upon the land. This history is essential for any conception of the First Nation as a social entity that exists in and across time, and it produces a powerful image of the First Nation – if not the First Nation state associated with it – as an ancient, even primordial, social entity. And, indeed, it is increasingly common to hear Yukon Indian people speak in ways that take for granted the antiquity of their First Nations. In 1997, for example, a Kluane elder, frustrated with what he saw as KFN negotiators' tendency to accede to government demands just so they could get an agreement more quickly, urged restraint with the following words: "We [citizens of Kluane First Nation] have been waiting 300 years for this treaty; what's the rush all of a sudden?"[78]

Benedict Anderson (1991: 11–12) notes that such a historical sensibility is endemic to nationalism: "If nation states are widely considered to be 'new' and 'historical,' the nations to which they give political

78 His statement is reminiscent of Anderson's (1991: 11 n. 4) comment that "the late President Sukarno always spoke with complete sincerity of the 350 years of colonialism that his 'Indonesia' had endured, although the very concept of 'Indonesia' is a twentieth-century invention, and most of today's Indonesia was only conquered by the Dutch between 1850 and 1910."

expression always loom out of an immemorial past, and, still more important, glide into a limitless future."[79] He argues that the very idea of the nation as "a sociological organism moving ... steadily down (or up) history" is predicated on a conception of "homogeneous empty time" as the neutral medium through which nations trace their stately (and linear) historical progress (ibid.: 26). Historian Prasenjit Duara (1995) agrees but goes even further, arguing that the very notion of linear narrative *history* is inseparable from the concept of the *nation*: "Nations emerge as the subjects of History just as History emerges as the ground, the mode of being, of the nation" (27). Indeed, for Duara, contemporary history – as practised by both professional and popular historians – is in large part a metaphysical project in service of the nation state:

> History and the modern nation are inseparable. The nation – hence nationalist leaders and the nation-state who act in the name of the nation – attains its privilege and sovereignty as the subject of History; modern History is meaningless without a subject – that which remains even as it changes. Our own practice of history shows us that what endures ... is the silent space of reference: the nation. We take for granted that the histories we study are the histories of China, India, Japan, France. It is in this way that the nation insinuates itself as the master subject of History into the very assumptions of both professional and popular history. This nation-space is never innocently silent. It comes with claims to territories, peoples, and cultures for all of "its" history, and the historian is often already implicated with the project of an evolving subject simply by participating in the received strategies of periodization. That even the best social and local historians do not find themselves challenging this assumption or theorizing an alternative to the already-always nation-space is testimony to the complicity of History and the nation-state. (Duara 1995: 27–8)[80]

79 At least since Renan (1990), scholars of nationalism have made much of the essential role of history – and of historical "error" – in the production of the nation (see Foster 1991: 240–4 for a discussion of some of this literature).

80 He notes, too, that "the birth of professional History in the universities of the West was deeply tied to national concerns, and the profession derived its authority from its role as the true spokesman of the nation" (1995: 21). For more on what Duara means when he claims that history is a form of metaphysics, see Duara (1995: 28–33).

This suggests that treating ancestors, place names, and the stories they index as evidence of a First Nation's long history in "its" homeland is, as I suggested above, not simply a matter of reframing "history" in term of the nation rather than principles of kinship and reciprocity. To describe the process in this way is to take the nationalist category of *history* itself entirely for granted. The emergence of First Nation nationalism, then, requires not the replacement of a kin-focused sense of history with a nation-focused one, but the imposition of a notion of linear progressive history as *the* principal means for relating to the past (and, thus, to the present and future as well). Once this has been accomplished, then "pre-national" modes of relating to the past can be appropriated, transformed, and subsumed into national history. Duara (1995: 27) describes the process thus: "History was the principal mode whereby non-nations were converted into nations ... Modern nationalism seeks to appropriate these pre-existing representations [of the past] into the mode of being of the modern nation – that is, the nation as existing in the time of History and embodied in the nation-state."[81]

The vast majority of the histories written since the rise of the nation state have been nationalist histories, not simply because they explicitly "narrate the nation" (Bhabha 1990), but because the nation itself becomes a lens, "a hallowed means of imposing a temporal order – a chronology – upon the contingencies and multiplicity of what has come before to tell a coherent, delimited, encoded story" (Craib 2004: 49). Thus, linear, narrative, progressive history is hardly the "transparent means of understanding" that it so often appears to be; rather it is "a discourse enabling historical players (including historians) to deploy its resources to occlude, repress, appropriate and, sometimes, negotiate with other modes of depicting the past and, thus, the present and future" (Duara 1995: 5).

But what do such thoroughly non-national ways of relating to the past – and to time – even look like? Duara himself is acutely aware of how hard it is – for those of us embedded in the nationalist conception of history – to think outside of it, even when we are consciously

81 For a discussion of the production of American Indian histories by nineteenth-century Indian nationalists and the centrality of these histories to their nationalist projects, see Lyons (2010: 129–31).

attempting to do so.[82] As I shall discuss in chapter 5, those who take linear progressive history to be "a transparent means for understanding" have trouble conceiving of the past – and of time – in other ways precisely because from such a vantage point those other temporal modes cannot but appear to them as so much mystical and irrational nonsense (Chakrabarty 2000 makes a similar point). Yet, if we hope to understand how the emergence of ethno-territorial nationalism is affecting Yukon Indian society, we must not ignore or deny the existence of these alternative modes of apprehending the past. Rather, we need to confront them head-on, paying particular attention to how the new First Nation national histories – and historical framings – "occlude, repress, appropriate and, sometimes, negotiate" them.

The ethnographic literature, as it turns out, is replete with descriptions of alternative ways of conceiving of time and depicting the past. I will discuss these at greater length in chapter 5, but for now a single example – drawn from Keith Basso's (1996) analysis of Western Apache place names (on which I have already drawn) – provides an ethnographic counterpoint to the production of First Nation histories. In the process of explicating how Western Apache people use place names, Basso also describes a way of relating to the past that differs fundamentally from the linear progressive First Nation histories currently under production. Western Apache people, Basso maintains, are deeply interested in events that took place in the past, and they have their own experts on the topic; but, in marked contrast to historians, they relate to it primarily in spatial terms: "What matters most to Apaches is *where* events occurred, not when, and what they serve to reveal about the development and character of Apache social life" (ibid.: 31). His work with Charles Henry, a skilled Apache "place-maker" (the term he uses to refer to Apache experts on the past) taught him that most Apache people are not particularly interested in generating supposedly definitive chronologies of past events, because there is an important sense in which they view those events as not having taken place in *the past* at all:

82 "Although my goal is to critique the nation as the subject of History, I am acutely aware that it is – as yet – impossible to radically displace the nation as the locus of history, if for no other reason than that our values, whether as historians or individuals, have been intimately shaped by the nation-state" (Duara 1995: 6).

> Weakly empirical, thinly chronological, and rarely written down, Western Apache history as practiced by Apaches advances no theories, tests no hypotheses, and offers no general models. What it does instead, and likely has done for centuries, is fashion possible worlds, give them expressive shape, and present them for contemplation as images of the past that can deepen and enlarge awareness of the present. In the country of the past, as Apaches like to explore it, the place-maker is an indispensable guide ... For the place-maker's main objective is to speak the past into being, to summon it with words and give it dramatic form, to produce experience by forging ancestral worlds in which others can participate and readily lose themselves ... The place-maker often speaks as a witness on the scene, describing ancestral events "as they are occurring" and creating in the process a vivid sense that what happened long ago – right here, on this very spot – could be happening now ... Thus performed and dramatized, Western Apache place-making becomes a form of narrative art, a type of historical theatre in which the "pastness" of the past is summarily stripped away and long-elapsed events are made to unfold as if before one's eyes. It is history given largely in the active present tense. (Basso 1996: 32–3)

By contrast, Basso notes, most Apache people find Euro-American history, with its focus on chronologically ordered narratives, largely irrelevant and (ironically, despite its typical ethno-territorial framing) strangely placeless. Clearly, any attempt by historians (Apache or otherwise) to mobilize Apache place names and their stories as "evidence" in constructing the Western Apache people's history in their homeland would entail more than a simple "reframing" of "Apache history." It would require, instead, a thoroughgoing transformation of those places – along with the conceptions of time and appropriate ways of relating to the past with which they are entwined.

Although Basso himself sticks scrupulously to his Western Apache case, the spatiotemporal order he describes is by no means unique to the Apache. As we shall see in chapter 5, a spatial orientation towards past events that are never truly past but continue to unfold in the present is widely reported not only among other indigenous peoples of North America, but also among peoples around the world – including Europeans and Euro-Americans in certain times, places, and social contexts. What Basso does not do, except in passing, however, is to acknowledge the existence of other ways of engaging with the past among the Western Apache. What happens, for instance, when the ethnonationalist tendencies of the Apache tribal state confront the spatialized view of the past he describes so beautifully? As we have seen, any claim by a tribe or First Nation to sovereign status necessarily entails, among other things, a notion of itself as an ethno-territorial entity marching inexorably forward through (linear) historical time. Just as claims to sovereignty take for granted the existence of state-like polities that contain distinct peoples or "nations" whose membership is defined and regulated by the institutions of citizenship, then, they also imply a particular spatio-temporal framework.

In chapter 5, I will argue against the idea that any "culture" is characterized by a single totalizing view of time, but I will also show that a spatialized sense of time like that described by Basso does indeed – at certain times and in certain contexts – inform how Yukon Indian people relate to one another, to animals, and to the land. The Yukon agreements, however, cannot accommodate such a view of the past. Rather, as we shall see, they take the homogeneous empty time of the nation state entirely for granted. Insofar as Yukon Indian people and others implementing the Yukon agreements mobilize ancestral bodies and place names – along with the lives, stories, and songs they index – in the service of the "First Nation," then they, too, must, in Duara's words, "occlude, repress, appropriate and, sometimes, negotiate with other modes of depicting the past." In the coming chapter, I examine these spatio-temporal politics by looking closely at the spatial and temporal dimensions of two different views of human–animal relations in the Yukon: indigenous hunting, on one hand, and state-bureaucratic wildlife management (as established under the Yukon agreements), on the other. I then pay particular attention to the imposition of national bureaucratic space-time upon human–animal relations in the Yukon and its political, social, and environmental consequences.

Chapter Five

Time

To a large extent, Western rational disbelief in the presence of ancestors and the efficacy of magic rest [*sic*] on the rejection of ideas of temporal coexistence implied in these ideas and practices.

Johannes Fabian (1983: 34)

Time, Colonialism, and Anthropology

An apparent contradiction lies at the heart of anthropological analyses of time and colonialism. On one hand, as Johannes Fabian (1983) argued so convincingly, colonial practice (including anthropology) was – and often still is – shot through with evolutionary assumptions and other "time-distancing" devices that locate colonized "others" in some other time – usually the static past. It is as though "they" somehow got stuck in the past, while "the West" continued its steady progress through history. From this temporal vantage point, which Bruyneel (2007: 2) refers to as "colonial time," it is the sacred duty of the colonizers, those magnanimous inhabitants of the present, to drag the "primitive" and "backwards" peoples they colonized – kicking and screaming if need be – into the temporal framework of the modern world. These days, recognition of the ways this "denial of coevalness" (Fabian 1983: 31) helped motivate, facilitate, and justify the colonial project is widespread enough among anthropologists that any suggestion to the effect that indigenous people might be governed by a different sense of time – especially anything smacking of "timelessness" – is often met with suspicion. We must, after all, take great care to represent colonized peoples as marching together with us down through historical time lest we be accused of treating them as people "without history."

On the other hand, as we saw at the end of the previous chapter, the modern concept of *history* – with its presumption that time is a neutral and homogeneous medium through which we all progress (in one direction) together – is itself hardly neutral. Indeed, Duara (1995: esp. chap. 1) convincingly argues that the same evolutionary assumptions identified by Fabian undergird our concept of history too. From this perspective, the denial of coevalness appears in a rather different light. The claim that Yukon Indian people, for example, were (and in some contexts, perhaps, still are) "people without history" is not necessarily the colonialist slur so many contemporary scholars suppose it to be. Nor does such a claim necessarily imply that Yukon Indian people were uninterested in – or somehow unable to conceive of – the past until Euro-Canadians came along to teach them how to *do* history. It is, rather, at least potentially a way of rejecting the supposed universality of linear progressive history and of drawing attention to the fact that indigenous peoples have ways of engaging with the past that do not take the *nation* as their subject and thus do not serve, in Duara's words, as "the ground, the mode of being, of the nation" (1995: 27).

As we saw in chapter 4, scholars critical of the link between *history* and *nation* assume that prior to the emergence of nationalism people must have had very different ways of relating to the past – and to time more generally. And, indeed, the ethnographic literature is replete with descriptions of temporal frameworks that do not seem to conform to dominant Euro-American ideas about time as a uniform and linear (or even cyclical) progression, and anthropologists have long argued that conceptions of time vary considerably across cultures (e.g., Bourdieu 1977; Durkheim 1915; Evans-Pritchard 1940a: 100–4; Geertz 1973; Hallowell 1937; Leach 1961: 114–36; Whorf 1956). In light of all this apparent evidence that indigenous peoples do, in fact, live in another kind of time, what does it actually mean to treat them as coeval? Does it really do them a service to insist that they be inserted alongside Euro-Americans in their supposedly inexorable march through (a culturally specific notion of) historical time?

Confronted with this apparent contradiction, anthropologists have largely responded in one of two – admittedly related – ways.[1] The

---

1 Some, however, like Keith Basso, whose (1996) work we examined along these lines in the previous chapter, do not engage with the question of colonialism at all and instead continue to produce ethnographic accounts of alternative senses of time and ways of engaging with the past.

first has been to dismiss all those ethnographic accounts of alternative forms of time as mistakes; indeed, some scholars (e.g., Malotki 1983) have expended considerable effort debunking the classic anthropologies of time. In one of the most widely cited refutations of this sort, Maurice Bloch (1977: 283) asserts that, "if other people really had different concepts of Time, we could not do what we patently do, that is to communicate with them." In such a view, anthropologists' "discovery" of different kinds of time is a mistake that requires explanation, and some scholars (Gell 1992; Krech 2006) have gone to considerable lengths to "explain away" nonlinear, non-uniform, non-progressive forms of time. Among the best known of these, Alfred Gell (1992: 315) flatly asserts that

> there is no fairyland where people experience time in a way that is markedly unlike the way in which we do ourselves, where there is no past, present, and future, where time stands still, or chases its own tail, or swings back and forth like a pendulum ... There are only other clocks, other schedules to keep abreast of ... There is nothing out there to affect our estimation of the logical possibilities inherent in the world with which we are already familiar.

I shall have more to say about Gell shortly. For now, it is enough to point out that we could just as easily invert his argument: it may not be that he rejects alternative forms of time because they are based on mystical beliefs and practices (which is presumably what he means when he consigns them to "fairyland"); but rather that he has no choice but to regard those beliefs and practices as mystical nonsense because he has *already* rejected the temporal frameworks on which they are based. And, I would add, he *must* reject them because he has already committed himself to a concept of time (to say nothing of space) as a neutral, abstract, and content-less medium that serves as the backdrop for all human activity (see especially Gell 1992: 315–16).

The second, related, strategy for dealing with the apparent contradiction described above has been to dismiss alternative forms of time as examples of Fabian's pernicious "time distancing" devices. Although Fabian himself at times seems unsure of what to make of the ethnographic literature on alternative forms of time (1983: 153–4), he does argue forcefully that the relativist notion that each culture has its own "culturally constructed" sense of time is problematic because it implicitly privileges the anthropologist's own temporal assumptions as the "reality" against which to compare these constructions (1983: 29, 41–2).[2] Citing Carol Greenhouse, Justin Richland (2008: 23) characterizes the argument thus: "Insofar as anthropological investigations of social time have always 'proceeded from the double assumption that linear time – "our" time – really *is* our time and really is *real*' (Greenhouse 1996: 3), any act of finding relativities of time 'out there' among the West's 'Others' only leads to the reassertion of anthropology's authority to diagnose what time 'really is.'"[3] To the extent that anthropologists assert that indigenous societies were/are embedded in a different temporal order than "the West," then, we become guilty of denying their coevalness and thereby helping to perpetuate the colonial order.

Both of these strategies for dealing with the contradiction, however, run into problems. Scholars studying the temporal politics of colonialism (see, for example, Anderson 2011; Burman 1981; Pickering 2004; Schieffelin 2002) have shown that attempts to assimilate (or "civilize") colonized peoples nearly always have an important temporal dimension; that is, attempts to transform colonized peoples into workers, students, Christians, or consumers can be viewed in large part as efforts to instil in them a particular notion of time.[4] As colonial practice, of course, such efforts fit right in with the view from colonial time, that colonized peoples must be dragged kicking and screaming into the modern world (and, indeed, such colonial policies were often explicitly justified in just this way). But this leaves us with a series of troubling questions. If the alternative forms of time that supposedly characterize the practices of the colonized are really only figments of

2 He notes: "In most ethnographic studies of other time conceptions the difference between standardized clock time and other methods of measuring provides the puzzle to be resolved" (Fabian 1983: 29). Subsequently, Tim Ingold (1996) made an analogous argument regarding the standard anthropological idea that there exist different "cultural constructions" of nature.

3 I would add that much of the ideological work alluded to by Greenhouse and Richland is done by the modifier "social" in the phrase "social time" – as if it were possible for an anthropologist to speak authoritatively about the social construction of different "beliefs" about time from the privileged vantage point of "non-social" time.

4 These arguments parallel – and often explicitly draw upon – E.P. Thompson's (1967) argument that the rise of industrial capitalism was closely accompanied and facilitated by efforts to instil a new sense of time among members of the emergent working classes.

anthropologists' (colonial) imagination – then why is it that colonial officials had to expend so much effort trying to impose their own sense of time upon their colonial subjects? And what to make of the fact that colonized peoples themselves so often and strenuously *resist* efforts to impose capitalist/colonial time frames upon them – sometimes explicitly celebrating their own alternative view of time in the process?[5] And if anthropologists deny a priori that indigenous people could possibly be embedded in a different temporal order and insist instead that they are – and have always been – embedded in "real" time (which also just happens to be the time of the capitalist nation state), then how exactly are we different from those colonial officials who refused to respect indigenous senses of time – and the "superstitious beliefs" associated with them? Does such a denial make us complicit in efforts to force compliance with the temporal rhythms of colonial capitalism and national history? These are questions that troubled Fabian as well, leading him near the end of his book to ask, "Is the theory of coevalness which is implied … in these [his own] arguments a program for ultimate temporal absorption of the Other …?" and to wonder whether "there are … criteria by which to distinguish denial of coevalness as a condition of domination from refusal of coevalness as an act of liberation?" (Fabian 1983: 154). Following either of the two strategies outlined above, then, appears to lead us right back into the apparent contradiction they were supposed to resolve.

The contradiction is only apparent, however, because it depends upon an untenable assumption: that cultures are characterized by a single totalizing notion of time; that "we," for example, live in historical, linear, homogeneous, abstract, clock time (to use a few of the terms regularly invoked to characterize "the" dominant Western sense of time), while "they" either live alongside us in "our" time, *or else* they live in ahistorical, circular, task-oriented, and/or messianic time (to invoke a range of popular alternatives). This assumption is surprisingly widespread in the literature on time and colonialism. Even Fabian, though he focuses almost entirely on anthropological/Western notions of time (which he *does* see as multiple, see especially 1983: 21–5), nearly always refers to "the Time of the Other" in the singular, as when he asserts that

5 A now classic celebration of the "Indian" approach to time is Deloria (1992: esp. chap. 4).

"the substance of a theory of coevalness, and certainly coevalness as praxis, will have to be the result of actual confrontation with the Time of the Other" (153). Indeed, his pronouncement that "it takes imagination and courage to picture what would happen to the West (and to anthropology) if its temporal fortress were suddenly invaded by the Time of its Other" (35) takes it for granted that the "Time of the Other" is not only singular but also different from the "Time of the West." While Fabian was hardly the first to frame the problem in this way (e.g., see Hallowell 1937), his agenda-setting critique did lend impetus to the view that colonialism consists of the wholesale (and often violent) replacement of one kind of time (indigenous) by another (colonial, capitalist). This has become a central trope in the literature on time and colonialism, but the assumption of temporal uniformity upon which it is based is completely unwarranted.

While it is true that anthropologists have long viewed time as a cultural construction, we have *also* long recognized that cultures are not characterized by a single unified notion of time.[6] It is only relatively recently, however, that anthropologists and others (Anderson 2011; Bender and Wellbery 1991; Gurvitch 1964; Miyazaki 2003; Traweek 1988) have really begun to focus their analytic gaze on temporal heterogeneity *within* societies and the social and political implications of this heterogeneity. In recent years, some have even described "task-oriented" or "messianic" time at work in the heart of the modern industrial nation state. Ingold (2000: 336–8), for example, finds non-homogeneous task-oriented time deeply embedded in industrial labour patterns, while Turnbull (2004) and Richland (2008: 21) both argue that, because of the law's reliance on the use of "precedent," which both scholars liken to indigenous notions of "tradition," the "sovereign time" (Richland's term) of state legal systems is in an important sense "timeless."[7] As Turnbull (2004: 171) puts it: "This makes law very like the Australian Aboriginal notion of the Dreaming; law is not in the ancient past – it is continually present." The

6 Durkheim (1915), for example, distinguished between "sacred" and "profane" time in all societies; while Evans-Pritchard (1940a) differentiated "oecological" from "structural" time among the Nuer.

7 Although not writing specifically about time, legal scholar John Borrows (2002: esp. chaps. 1–2), too, argues convincingly that Anishinabe "traditional" stories must be viewed as analogous to precedent-setting legal cases.

recognition of temporal heterogeneity *within* societies inevitably raises questions of power.[8]

Indeed, among the first to attempt a systematic exploration of the multiple forms of social time, Georges Gurvitch was also one of the first to conceptualize time in explicitly political terms: "Each society, each social class, each particular group, each micro-social element – indeed every social activity … has a tendency to operate in a time proper to itself … No society, no social class, no structured group … can live without trying to control these times" (Gurvitch 1963, cited in Rutz 1992: 15). In this view, the temporal order of any society is not a cultural given but rather the product of struggles among social actors to exert control over which of the multiple possible forms of time should constitute the basis for any particular social interaction or process. It is for this reason that "the social construction of time must be seen as a political process" (Verdery 1992: 37). In his introduction to *The Politics of Time*, anthropologist Henry Rutz (1992: 7) notes that "a *politics* of time is concerned with the *appropriation* of the time of others, the *institutionalization* of a dominant time, and the *legitimation* of power by means of the control over time" (emphasis original). A fine-grained analysis of these temporal politics – in all their particularity – provides a means

8 Early models of temporal heterogeneity were fairly simplistic, usually admitting to only two kinds of time and leaving little or no room for developing an analysis of temporal politics. Maurice Bloch (1977), for example, loosely follows Durkheim in distinguishing between the linear time that governs everyday activities and other forms of time that govern ritual activities. Everyday "mundane" activities, he suggests, are rooted in a system of "normal communication based on universal notions of time and cognition, and in which people are visualized in ways which seem to differ little from culture to culture," while alternative non-linear conceptions of time are confined to "that *other system* of cognition which is characteristic of ritual communication, another world which unlike that manifested in the cognitive system of everyday communication does not directly link up with empirical experiences" (1977: 287). Thus, for him, linear time, which is "real" and universal (insofar as it corresponds to empirical reality and is necessary for the practical business of living), can coexist with ritual time, which is a cultural construction that varies by culture. Because they supposedly govern completely separate and non-overlapping systems of cognition and practice, however, linear and ritual time need never come into contact with one another. Because he rigidly separates different kinds of time and the practices associated with them, he leaves no space for temporal politics. Even Hallowell (1937), who explicitly examined the temporal heterogeneity resulting from the colonial encounter, did little more than hint at the possibility of analysing temporal politics.

for escaping the apparent contradiction I described above. No longer constrained to view colonialism as a process that replaces one totalizing indigenous sense of time (or timelessness) with an equally totalizing enlightenment/capitalist one, we are free instead to examine a multitude of struggles over which sense of time – among many – should govern any particular interaction, activity, or process. To be sure, the anthropologist engaging in such analysis must still guard against implicitly privileging one sense of time as more "real" than others, but this kind of temporal agnosticism becomes a bit easier to maintain if we recognize that the choice is not – and has never been – between "our time" and "their time" writ large but rather from among the multiple temporal framings that might govern any particular social process or interaction.

It would be easy enough to get caught up in the contradiction described above when analysing the temporal politics of colonialism in northern Canada. Canadian policy towards northern indigenous people has long been framed from the perspective of colonial time. As elsewhere, evolutionary assumptions about subarctic Indian peoples' primitive backwardness pervaded colonial rhetoric about the need to "civilize" – and later "assimilate" – them. Although even "assimilation" has now officially gone out of vogue as a policy objective in both the United States and Canada, and government officials scrupulously avoid the use of words like "backward" and "primitive," the basic assumption that Indian people live in the past and must be "modernized" if they are to play a productive role in contemporary society still informs a great deal of Indian policy in both countries. Glen Coulthard (2014), for example, draws on Patrick Wolfe's (2006) analysis of settler colonialism to lay bare the temporal dimensions of Canada's contemporary "politics of reconciliation," which casts colonialism as an event that took place in the past – a sad chapter in Canadian history that has fortunately come to a close – rather than as a structure of oppression that is still very much in place today. From such a perspective, Canadian Indian peoples' "bitter indignation and persistent anger at being treated unjustly by a colonial state both historically and in the present" gets cast instead as a "seemingly pathological inability to get over harms inflicted in the past" (Coulthard 2014: 126; see also Irlbacher-Fox 2009: esp. 3, 31–4, 107–13). Portrayals of Indian people as stuck in the past are hardly accidental, nor can they be written off as the unfortunate perspective of particular government officials or political parties. Indeed, as Michael Asch (1999) has so convincingly argued, the Canadian government *has to* portray Indians as stuck in the past, because Canada's claim to sovereign jurisdiction over its own territory is rooted firmly in the doctrine of *terra nullius* – with its underlying assumption that contact-era indigenous peoples were too primitive to have sovereign governments of their own (see chapter 1). Thus, the very legitimacy of the Canadian state is premised upon an assumption of Indian backwardness.

Since northern First Nation land claim and self-government agreements take Canadian sovereignty entirely for granted, we really should not be surprised if they, too, are premised on a denial of coevalness. This was evident even in the negotiations themselves. Yukon First Nation negotiators were forced again and again to counter veiled – and sometimes not so veiled – suggestions that they were "not yet ready" for self-government (i.e., that they were too "primitive" to govern themselves). Since the only permissible evidence of a capacity for self-government was the ability to establish and run a territorially ordered government based on the Euro-Canadian model, they had no choice but to counter such suggestions with assurances that they would, indeed, develop Euro-Canadian style laws and political institutions, which they then proceeded to do (Nadasdy 2003: 250–1). That such attitudes survive into the self-government era is illustrated by the now ubiquitous and largely taken-for-granted calls in the Canadian self-government discourse for First Nations to "build capacity," a euphemism for Euro-Canadian-style training that will enable them to serve as the bureaucratic functionaries increasingly required by land claim and self-government agreements – as if they had lacked the "capacity" to govern themselves before the arrival of Euro-Canadians (Irlbacher-Fox 2009).[9]

The assumption of Indian backwardness was evident not only in the day-to-day practice of land claim negotiations; it is also built right into the structure of the agreements themselves. As we saw in previous

9 Similarly, in his analysis of the Nunavut government's efforts to "build capacity" while simultaneously attempting to govern according to Inuit cultural principles, political scientist Graham White (2009: 76) argues that "many of the defining characteristics of the modern Weberian bureaucracy, as it has come to dominate government throughout Canada, are either inconsistent with or completely antithetical to key elements of Inuit culture." Ultimately, however, he takes a much more sanguine view of the relationship between "capacity" and "culture" than either Irlbacher-Fox or I do.

chapters, indigenous society in the Yukon was/is composed not only of human but also a host of non-human persons. These powerful non-human persons play a key role in governance and the management of social relations. Indeed, it is they who instituted and continue to enforce many of the "timeless" laws (laid out in an extensive body of "Long Time Ago" stories) that continue to govern social relations among all the different kinds of persons who inhabit the boreal forest. Yet, as we have seen, the Yukon self-government agreements do not recognize the political subjectivity of non-human persons at all. Nor did Yukon First Nation negotiators ever argue that they should, doubtless knowing full well how Euro-Canadian negotiators would perceive and react to such a suggestion. Many aspects of the relationship between human and non-human persons (e.g., human–animal reciprocity, animals understanding human speech, the existence of spiritual beings, reincarnation) seem like "magic" from a mainstream Euro-Canadian perspective. Because most Euro-Canadians would view such beliefs as "primitive" superstitions rather than as the basis for a "modern" system of government, any attempt by First Nation negotiators to advocate for a system of self-government based upon them would certainly have been a non-starter at the negotiating table. As it turns out, there is an important spatiotemporal component to all this.

Fabian (1983: 34) writes that, "to a large extent, Western rational disbelief in the presence of ancestors and the efficacy of magic rest [*sic*] on the rejection of ideas of temporal coexistence implied in these ideas and practices" (see also Chakrabarty 2000: chap. 3). Similarly, indigenous forms of "self-government" seem irrational and primitive to anyone who does not already accept the alternative temporal framework upon which they are based. In this chapter I will examine some of the temporal assumptions underlying many Yukon Indian beliefs and practices – particularly in relation to hunting – and show that they are incompatible with standard Euro-Canadian notions of time as linear or even cyclical. This is not to say that Yukon Indian people live – or have ever lived – out their lives solely in the timeless realm of the Long Time Ago stories; like all societies, theirs has always been characterized by a multiplicity of temporal frameworks. In certain very important contexts, however, (e.g., hunting and wildlife management) the temporal framework of those stories continues to inform how many of them interact with one another, with animals, and with the land. Anyone who insists on viewing the temporal framework of the Long Time Ago stories as "just" a cultural construction (however ethnographically interesting and socially useful) – while confidently assuming that time "really is" uniform and linear – cannot help but view the beliefs and practices that flow from that temporal framework as superstitious nonsense.

First Nation land claim and self-government agreements have imposed a new temporal order in the Yukon. This is not to suggest that a unitary "agreement time" has replaced "indigenous time" in a straightforward manner. Rather, the agreements have introduced a whole range of new temporal frameworks for the management and governance of both people and resources. Just as they are rooted in a set of spatial/territorial assumptions (see chapter 2), the Yukon agreements are also built upon a set of temporal assumptions. They take it for granted that the various processes of management and governance unfold in particular kinds of time (though not always the same one!); and that these processes stand in particular temporal relationship to one another and to the First Nation state as a whole. To the extent, then, that Yukon Indian people engage in and/or abide by the practices of management and governance as spelled out in the agreements (which, of course, they do not always do), they must adopt – or at least adapt to – those new temporal frameworks. This is not simply a matter of altering the *timing* of their activities (as when a hunter, say, is constrained by a state-imposed hunting season); it also often involves substantive change in the nature of the activities themselves. As we shall see, activities such as *hunting* and *wildlife management* as envisioned and "temporalized" (Fabian 1983: 74) in the Yukon agreements are qualitatively different kinds of activities than they are in the eyes of many Yukon Indian people (and would have been in the eyes of nearly all of their indigenous ancestors). A focus on the temporal politics of these agreements, then, can provide new insights into the nature of the social and environmental changes they bring.

Many of the temporal assumptions that undergird the Yukon agreements, like the spatial/territorial assumptions we examined in previous chapters, flow from the idea that First Nations are sovereign entities, that is, that they are (geographically and socially) bounded collectivities marching down through historical time. Indeed, the spatial and temporal assumptions of sovereignty are so closely linked to one another that I find it necessary throughout the remainder of this chapter to refer to the *spatio-temporal*, rather than simply the *temporal*, assumptions of the Yukon agreements; and, to some degree, this chapter can be viewed as focusing on the temporal aspects of phenomena I have already analysed in predominantly spatial terms elsewhere in the book.

A full examination of the spatio-temporal politics (à la Rutz) of the Yukon agreements is beyond the scope of this book; so in this chapter I focus primarily on the imposition of what Benedict Anderson has referred to as "homogeneous empty time," a temporal framework that he argues is an essential prerequisite for the rise of nationalism. We saw in the previous chapter that without such a temporal framework one cannot even begin to conceive of "nations" as social collectives that "loom out of an immemorial past, and, still more important, glide into a limitless future" (Anderson 1991: 11–12). While I agree with Anderson about the importance of homogeneous empty time (or, more accurately, "space-time") for the rise of nationalism, I will not focus as he does on the role of print capitalism in its development but instead on *bureaucratization*, which has played a much more central role in the emergence of First Nations as territorially bounded ethno-nationalist entities. In fact, it seems likely, for reasons I will discuss, that homogeneous empty space-time is as essential to bureaucracies as it is to nations.

Yet, if homogeneous empty space-time is necessary for bureaucracy, it is not sufficient. As we shall see, bureaucratic practice entails – and in large part consists of – imparting a complex and endlessly negotiated structure to ostensibly "homogeneous" and "empty" space-time through the production and use of schedules, work plans, budgets, and the like. Structured "bureaucratic space-time" of this sort organizes – and is presumed by – the processes of governance and management laid out in the Yukon land claim agreements, which are themselves profoundly bureaucratizing (Nadasdy 2003). I devote the bulk of this chapter, then, to analysing the spatio-temporal dimensions of two different views of human–animal relations in the Yukon: indigenous hunting, on one hand, and bureaucratic wildlife management (as established under the Yukon agreements), on the other. I then examine the temporal politics resulting from the way the agreements impose bureaucratic space-time upon human–animal relations in the Yukon.

The Spatio-temporal Dimensions of Hunting and Wildlife Management

A useful way to get at the spatio-temporal differences between indigenous hunting and the wildlife management regime established under the agreements is to analyse competing ways of understanding the notion of *renewable resources*. The Yukon agreements classify fish and wildlife (along with trees and other wild flora) as *renewable resources*

– in contrast to *non-renewable resources*, such as oil, gas, and gold. The very notion of resources as renewable implies a particular sense of time, one that is distinct from that implied by the notion of non-renewable resources (see Ferry 2008; Limbert 2008). The phrase *renewable resource* conjures up an image of temporal cycles, of periods of renewal and regrowth punctuated by episodes of exploitation. And, indeed, this image of cyclical growth and renewal resonates with Euro-American wildlife managers and Yukon Indian people alike; both are apt to think about animals in relation to temporal cycles,[10] although, as we shall see, there are important differences in how they understand these cycles.

Anthropologists have described notions of cyclical time among various peoples the world over. They have long argued that a sense of time as cyclical arises naturally from the cycling of days, tides, and seasons and how these natural cycles structure human activities.[11] Agriculture is among the most important domains of human activity to be shaped by these natural cycles, and the agricultural cycle features prominently in anthropological analyses of how people conceive of time. At first blush, it seems that these anthropological insights should be directly applicable to a study of renewable resource management, a set of practices clearly rooted in an agricultural world view. Indeed, managers of some renewable resources, such as trees, quite explicitly see themselves as engaged in a kind of long-term farming; the planting, care, and cultivation of trees are as important (at least in theory) as harvesting in the "silvicultural" cycle.

Wildlife management, too, is clearly rooted in an agricultural world view. As I have discussed elsewhere (Nadasdy 2011), Aldo Leopold, the founder of scientific wildlife management, drew on his experience as a forester to conceive of wildlife management explicitly as a *form of*

10 Some scholars (e.g., Notzke 1994: 1–2) argue that the resource concept is firmly rooted in Euro-American notions about human superiority over nature and so is incompatible with indigenous world views. The concept certainly implies a view of the world that foregrounds utility to humans, but, for reasons I elucidate elsewhere (Nadasdy 2005a), I am convinced neither that all such perspectives *necessarily* imply human superiority over nature, nor that they are necessarily incompatible with indigenous views of the world. Be that as it may, Yukon Indian people do regularly talk about fish and wildlife as renewable resources.

11 The classic work in this regard is by Evans-Pritchard (1940a), from whom E.P. Thompson (1967) drew heavily in his own celebrated article.

agriculture (and not as merely analogous to it). Despite a supposed paradigm shift in the field (but see Nadasdy 2010), agricultural metaphors still pervade the discipline,[12] and wildlife managers still largely view what they do as akin to the agricultural production of crops. They see fish and wildlife populations as renewable in much the same way as, say, a wheat crop. Like domestic species, fish and wildlife have natural life cycles; they are born, grow, reproduce, and die. Each cycle is similar to those that have gone before, though the individual organisms themselves are continually replaced. Humans can exert a degree of control over those cycles by "harvesting" animals, killing predators, rearing fish in hatcheries, and so on, but they must be very careful about these interventions. Like farmers, they need to limit the overall harvest in any year to allow for the survival of sufficient "seed" for the propagation of future generations. Through their intervention and control, wildlife managers are expected to *ensure* the continued renewal of wildlife populations. From this perspective, humans do not merely adapt to the "natural" cycles of animal populations; rather, they are critical to their maintenance. Indeed, the notion of human *control* over other species is as central to wildlife management as it is to agriculture (see Nadasdy 2011).

The situation is quite different, however, for Yukon Indian people, who are not – nor have their ancestors ever been – farmers. Indeed, Yukon Indian people, like hunting peoples elsewhere, are often quite explicit in their rejection of the agricultural metaphors of wildlife management. At a wildlife management meeting I attended in 1995, for example, Mary Jane Johnson, a citizen of Kluane First Nation, objected to the use of the term *harvest*. Kluane people, she maintained, are hunters, not farmers: "We don't 'harvest' animals; we kill them." She objected to the term *harvest* in particular, because its use implies ownership and

---

12 Wildlife biologists and government hunting regulations, for example, regularly substitute the verb *harvest* for the less metaphorical *shoot* or *kill* when talking about what hunters do to animals, and they refer to the overall number of animals within a species killed by hunters in a given territory each year as the *annual harvest*. Similarly, Yukon biologists studying Dall sheep populations, for example, are keenly interested in obtaining an estimate of the annual *lamb crop*, or the number of lambs born into a population in any given year. See Nadasdy (2011) for a detailed analysis of agricultural metaphors in wildlife management and the political consequences of their ongoing use.

control; people harvest crops that they themselves plant and so are entitled to harvest them all. Because farmers replant annually, they expect to harvest their entire crop every year. She argued that this is a very dangerous mindset when it comes to wildlife management and urged all meeting participants to use words like *hunt* and *kill*, rather than *harvest*[13] (see also Stevenson 2006: 170).

Although Yukon Indian people generally reject the agricultural metaphors of wildlife management, there is nonetheless something compelling to them about the cyclical temporality implied by the idea of a *renewable resource*. They are, of course, very knowledgeable about animal life cycles and seasonal patterns of animal behaviour; and scholars have written extensively about northern hunters' annual subsistence round, their strategy for adapting to those seasonal patterns (e.g., McClellan 1975: 95–105). However, they understand the temporality of at least some of aspect of their relationship with animals in very different terms than do biologists. I suggest that this difference has to do with what Alfred Gell (1992: 30–6) referred to as the "topology" of time.

Gell noted that two very different senses of time – each with its own distinct topology – have been confused with one another because they are both "cyclical." He argued that we must distinguish between *cyclical* time, characterized by the periodic recurrence of events of the same type (as one summer follows another), and *circular* time in which the *same event* recurs over and over again. Gell himself introduced this distinction to discredit the idea that there are alternative cultural conceptions of time, arguing that what he calls cyclical time is essentially linear-progressive, while circular time cannot and does not exist:

> Were the topology of time to assume this form [circular], it would never be possible to distinguish the occurrence of an event, *e*, from the recurrence of the same event *e* the next time around the cycle. We would not have

13 For the rest of the day, everyone at the meeting attempted to follow Mary Jane's advice, but it proved to be quite difficult to do so, because of the frequency with which the term is used in such contexts. Over and over again throughout the day biologists – and First Nation representatives as well – caught and corrected themselves. The effort did not seem to make a lasting impression on meeting participants, however, because at subsequent meetings (and I attended many with the same people over the next three years) they all lapsed back into old habits. I never again heard anyone explicitly object to the term in a meeting.

> "another summer" coming round again ... but simply "summer" full stop. There would be only one summer, because the event "summer" would occur only once in the whole of time. (Gell 1992: 34)

He argues that anthropologists have mistaken people's assertions about the (usually ritual) "recurrence" of events for evidence that they have a circular conception of time when, in fact, the very notion of recurrence "assumes a linear time-axis, because it is only with respect to such a linear time-axis that such an event could ever be said to have 'repeated' itself" (ibid.: 35). Thus,

> The collective representations of "time" [described by anthropologists] are not representations of the topology of the time dimension, but are representations of what characteristically goes on in the temporal world, i.e., the periodic realization of expectable sequences of events. The only "form" of time which will accommodate these collective representations, these standardized expectations, is linear-progressive time, no different, in its logical layout, from the temporal forms that underlie our own collective representations appertaining to time. The relevant distinction does not lie between different "concepts of time,"' but different conceptions of the world and its workings. (ibid.: 36)[14]

While I agree with Gell that "different conceptions of the world and its workings" are at play here, his dismissal of circular time as a logical impossibility is based on an overly narrow characterization of the problem. His error, it seems to me, was to focus exclusively on time, without taking into account its relationship to space. As a result, he cannot help but conclude that anyone conceiving of time as circular would be locked in a closed temporal loop, reliving the same events over and over again as if for the first time. Like Gell, I have a hard time imagining anyone conceiving of time in this way (except, perhaps, in extremely long-term cycles far exceeding the human lifetime). As we shall see, however, the notion of circularity becomes far less restrictive when applied to space-time than when applied to time by itself. In that case,

14 Gell seeks to preserve a single unitary and abstract notion of time precisely because it provides a means for comparison, interdisciplinary as well as cross-cultural (315–16).

circularity implies not so much a closed temporal loop as it does the disarticulation of space and time – along with a corresponding change in the notion of *simultaneity*. In such a view, people can distinguish between different iterations of the same event, but each iteration entails the simultaneous presence of beings from "different" times in the same place. As I shall discuss below, such a view of the world is common enough in the ethnographic and historical literature, but it is utterly nonsensical if one assumes that time "really is" the neutral and linear substrate Gell assumes it to be. To see what I mean, let us consider the spatio-temporal dimensions of Yukon hunting in more detail.

Like other northern hunting peoples, many Yukon Indian people conceive of hunting as a reciprocal relationship between humans and animals. In their view, fish and animals are other-than-human persons who give themselves to hunters in exchange for the hunters' performance of certain ritual practices. These practices vary across the North – as well as by animal – but they commonly include the observance of food taboos, ritual feasts, and prescribed methods for disposing of animal remains, as well as injunctions against overhunting, and talking badly about, or playing with animals. Hunting in such societies should not be viewed as a violent process whereby hunters take the lives of animals by force, but, rather, as a long-term social relationship between animal-people and the humans who hunt them.[15]

Central to any understanding of the spatio-temporal dimensions of such a relationship is northern hunters' belief in the reincarnation of both human- and animal-people. As long as a hunter follows the prescribed ritual procedures, the animals he or she kills do not really die but will instead be reborn to give themselves to the hunter again in the future (see Brightman 1993). Thus, many Yukon Indian people view hunting as part of an ongoing social relationship between human- and animal-people that transcends the lifetime of any individual hunter or prey animal. McClellan (1975: 72) suggests that the idea of reincarnation, "bring[s] together the past and the future, which probably helps to

15 For the classic description of animals as other-than-human persons and hunting as a part of the reciprocal relationship between human- and animal-people, see Hallowell (1960); see also Brightman (1993). For more on the specifics of the Yukon case, see Nadasdy (2003: chap. 2), and for reflections on the theoretical and political significance of such accounts, see Nadasdy (2007b).

produce an amorphous sense of time quite different from our own. In fact, the fundamental aspect of time is probably its quality rather than its quantity or diachronic nature."

As we have already seen, the complex nature of human–animal relations is expressed in a large body of "Long Time Ago" stories. These stories concern events that ostensibly occurred in the mythical past, and they explain events such as the origin of the world and how animals and people came to assume their current forms and roles. Although most non-Indian people regard these "myths" as "just stories," many Yukon Indian people maintain that they are not "just stories," but that they are true. What is more, although the events they recount occurred "a long time ago," there is another sense in which they are quite contemporary. Indeed, Kluane people's use of the English phrase "long time ago" suggests this apparent temporal ambiguity. Although people commonly use it to introduce events that took place back in mythic times before humans and animals assumed their current forms, they also regularly use it when referring to historical events (e.g., "long time ago, before the [Alaska] highway was built ...") and even sometimes to events that took place just a few years earlier. I remember being taken aback when I first heard a young man, perhaps fourteen years old, use the phrase to refer to his own childhood. McClellan noticed the same broad use of the phrase among Yukon Indian people across the southern Yukon back in the 1940s,[16] noting that, "while myth time is thought of as generally preceding the more recent period when a man's immediate ancestors were alive, the two periods seem to merge imperceptibly" (McClellan 1975: 71). Indeed, the ritual practices in which Yukon Indian hunters engage and which continue to structure reciprocal relations among humans and animals *presuppose* the contemporary and real-life existence of animal-people as they appear in Long Time Ago stories (Tanner 1979; see also Nelson 1983).

There is, then, an important sense in which all the people – animal and human alike – from Long Time Ago are still alive today. When Yukon Indian hunters kill a moose, say, they do not merely participate in an event that is *similar* to those in which they have participated in

16 She writes that the phrase "'a long time ago' ... may refer either to early myth time, or to an event as recent as five or six years before the present" (McClellan 1975: 70).

the past. Rather, they take part in yet another iteration of *the same event*, an event that they have participated in over and over again since the relationship between human- and moose-people was first forged in the distant past of the Long Time Ago stories. The hunt is the instantiation of an ongoing social relationship between *the same* human- and animal-people across multiple lifetimes. This means that the temporality of Yukon Indian hunting is not *cyclical*, as it is for farmers who harvest the same crop (but different individual plants) every year; rather, it is *circular*. This distinction has important implications for how Yukon Indian people understand the role of human agency in relation to animal populations.

Like bureaucratic wildlife managers, Yukon Indian people see themselves as intimately involved in animal cycles and as able to affect those cycles in important ways. Through the observation of certain ritual practices and the maintenance of proper social relations, Yukon Indian hunters play an important role in the renewal of animal populations (e.g., proper disposal of animal remains is critical if the animals are to be reborn). Although Yukon Indian hunters may resort to trickery and even a degree of coercion in their conduct of social relations with animals (Nadasdy 2007b), they do not generally subscribe to the view that humans *control* animals, who may abandon hunters at any time if they decide that their human partners are not living up to their social obligations. This is in sharp contrast to Euro-American wildlife managers, who attempt to control animal cycles in much the same way that a farmer seeks to control the agricultural cycle. Indeed, many Yukon Indian people find the assumption of control inherent in wildlife management at best ludicrous, possibly even offensive. As one Kluane First Nation hunter regularly noted at wildlife management meetings, the term *wildlife management* itself is a misnomer. Humans cannot "manage" wildlife populations, he said. Animals are quite capable of taking care of themselves; they make their own decisions about when to reproduce and where to go, decisions that are quite independent of any desires on the part of humans. Wildlife management, he said, is not about managing animals; it is about managing people (see also Natcher, Davis, and Hickey 2005).

Thus, Euro-American wildlife managers and Yukon Indian hunters can agree that wildlife is a renewable resource and that humans play an important role in the maintenance of the temporal cycles in which they, along with animals, are enmeshed. But the term *renewable resource* here is essentially contested.[17] Those employing such terms often assume that they "reflect a shared universe of meaning," when, in fact, they "actually represent non-congruent realities" (Morrow and Hensel 1992: 42). In such cases, participants in the discussion are seldom aware of the semantic discrepancy, and talk takes place *as if* they all shared an understanding of the term's meaning. This can lead to serious misunderstandings – often without the parties to the conversation even being aware of it; and these misunderstandings can have significant political consequences, especially in contexts of social inequality, since it tends to be the meanings ascribed to essentially contested terms by parties with access to power that get acted upon in broader socio-political contexts. In the next two sections, I examine in somewhat more detail the different spatio-temporal topologies underlying each conception of renewability: the circular and the cyclical. After dealing with each in turn, I examine the temporal politics that emerge from the Yukon agreements' imposition of cyclical time on human–animal relations.

The Circular Space-Time of Indigenous Hunting

As suggested above, hunting enmeshes Yukon Indian people in a spatio-temporal order that resembles what Walter Benjamin (1968) called *messianic time*. Following Benjamin, Benedict Anderson (1991: 24) notes that messianic time is characterized by "a simultaneity of past and future in an instantaneous present. In such a view of things, the word 'meanwhile' cannot be of real significance." Similarly, Gurvitch (1964: 31) describes a sense of time that he refers to as *enduring time*, in which "the past is relatively remote, yet it is dominant and projected into the present and future." Such a conception of time was prominent in

17 The classic discussion of essentially contested concepts is Gallie (1956), but see Weitz's (1977: 40–3) critique and revision of the idea. Without necessarily drawing directly on these philosophical works, a number of anthropologists have made productive use of the notion of essential contestability. See, for example, Lawrence Rosen (1984: 185–6) on "essentially negotiable concepts" and Fujimura's (1992) notion of "the standardized package," now widespread in the STS literature. For examples showing the analytic value of attending to essentially contested terms in the cross-cultural context of northern wildlife management, see Asch (1989), Morrow and Hensel (1992), Nadasdy (2011), and Usher (1986).

– among other places – medieval Europe (but see Le Goff [1980] for a description of temporal heterogeneity even then). As already noted, such a view is not purely about time; it implies a disjunction between time and space. In his analysis of the medieval world view, for example, Lewis Mumford (1962: 19) notes that time and space were relatively independent systems:

> The medieval artist introduced other times within his own spatial world, as when he projected the events of Christ's life within a contemporary Italian city, without the slightest feeling that the passage of time has made a difference … When a medieval chronicler mentions the King … it is often a little difficult to find out whether he is talking about Caesar or Alexander the Great or his own monarch: each is equally near to him. Indeed, the word anachronism is meaningless in medieval art: it is only when one related events to a coordinated frame of time and space that being out of time or being untrue to time became disconcerting … The connecting link between events was the cosmic and religious order. The true order of space was Heaven, even as the true order of time was Eternity.

Although there are many significant differences between medieval Christianity and the beliefs and values surrounding Yukon Indian hunting, they seem to share a similar spatio-temporal orientation. Henry Sharp (2001: 63) describes Dene notions of space-time – particularly in relation to animals – in terms similar to Mumford's:

> Dene culture is not dominated by the idea of a now, and time is not seen as a flow between a no-longer-existing past and a not-yet-existing future. There is a sense, and there are circumstances, in which the Dene conceive of reality as being "simultaneous," that is, time is treated as a dimension that is independent of any flow or directional change within that dimension. The past and the future are as real as the present. Communication and connection between the past, now, and the future are all possible … All places in time become equally accessible … The effect of this is to make it seem as if the Dene sometimes use time the way Western culture uses place.

Because of beliefs about reincarnation and human–animal reciprocity, there is a very important sense in which the animals encountered by twenty-first century Yukon Indian hunters are *the same animals* (just as the hunters are *the same hunters*) as those who appear in the Long Time Ago stories that teach Yukon Indian people how to relate properly to animal-people. This is only possible if time and space are disarticulated in the manner described by Mumford and Sharp.

For those who subscribe to such a view, animals are very different sorts of "resources" than they are for most Euro-Americans hunters and biologists. In his analysis of Rock Cree hunting in northern Manitoba, for example, Robert Brightman (1987; 1993) concludes that hunters historically did not believe that humans could affect animal populations through overhunting. Because animals do not die forever when hunters kill them (so long as the hunters observe all the necessary rituals), overhunting of the sort warned against by wildlife biologists is not possible. As a result, Brightman argues, there was no indigenous conservation ethic among the Cree. Still today, he notes, Euro-American notions about wildlife conservation coexist uneasily alongside aboriginal ideas about reincarnation and proper human–animal relations. Similarly, Ann Fienup-Riordan (1990) reports that many Yup'ik Eskimos of western Alaska continue to doubt that over-hunting is possible, which leads at times to serious tensions between Yup'ik villagers and state wildlife managers.

Yukon Indian people subscribe to many of the same beliefs and practices described by Brightman and others. Although the historical record is unclear on whether they ever regularly engaged in practices of overhunting and meat wastage like those described by Brightman and Fienup-Riordan, most contemporary Yukon Indian people do now believe that human hunting can affect the size of animal populations and have incorporated prohibitions against overhunting and waste into the set of obligations hunters incur towards animals through the act of hunting. This does not mean, however, that they have abandoned beliefs about animal reincarnation and human–animal relations. Indeed, one of the main objections by Yukon Indian people to the controversial (in the Yukon) practice of catch-and-release fishing is that it is a repudiation of the reciprocal act at the very heart of the relationship between human- and animal-people: "The fish comes to you as a gift. It's offering its life to you. And if you don't accept it, that's an insult. Sooner or later, the fish will stop coming to you" (Mark Wedge, quoted in Yukon Department of Renewable Resources 1997: 21).

So, although Yukon Indian people and biologists agree that overhunting can reduce the number of animals, they differ fundamentally in their understanding of *why* it can do so. At least some Yukon Indian people continue to believe that overhunting and waste affect the animals not because they reduce the number of animals in the total population, as biologists would have it, but because such practices offend the animals, making it less likely that hunters will be able to kill them in the future. For them, animals are still a potentially unlimited resource, their availability dependent on the maintenance of social relations between animal and human persons in accordance with the principles laid out in Long Time Ago stories. Indeed, it is through the reciprocal relations of hunting that humans and animals each contribute to the others' renewal.

Again, none of this is to say that Yukon Indian people live out their entire lives in the enduring space-time of the Long Time Ago stories. Indeed, it is hard to imagine a society that lacks some sense of time as linear and unidirectional, given the centrality of such a spatio-temporal framework to relations of physical cause and effect (you have to load the gun before you can shoot a moose; and, once shot, you cannot unshoot it). And, of course, Yukon Indian people have always been very knowledgeable about animal life cycles and seasonal patterns of animal behaviour, which in many contexts they do indeed view as cyclical rather than circular. They are as aware as anyone that there is a difference between last summer and this summer; and, as we shall see, contemporary Yukon Indian people have become quite adept at interacting with human- and animal-people in new social contexts that are structured by very different senses of space and time. Yet, Long Time Ago stories and the spatio-temporal framework associated with them continue to inform many Yukon Indian peoples' understanding of their interactions with animals, other humans, and the land.

The Cyclical Space-Time of Wildlife Management

Euro-Canadian wildlife managers conceive of the renewability of fish and wildlife very differently than many Yukon Indian people. For them, space and time are linked such that a given hunter can kill a given animal only once. Following Benedict Anderson (1991), I refer to this second spatio-temporal framework, within which the scientific management of animal cycles takes place, as "homogeneous empty space-time." Homogeneous empty space-time is characteristic of (and, indeed, essential to) the administration of the large and complex bureaucracies that govern corporations as well as nation states under contemporary capitalism.[18] According to Anderson, the development of a conception of homogeneous empty time was a necessary prerequisite for emergence of the "imagined community" that is a nation:

> The idea of a sociological organism moving calendrically through homogeneous, empty time is a precise analogue of the idea of the nation, which is also conceived of as a solid community moving steadily down (or up) history. An American will never meet or even know the names of more than a handful of his 240,000,000-odd fellow-Americans. He has no idea what they are up to at any one time. But he has complete confidence in their steady, anonymous, *simultaneous* activity. (Anderson 1991: 26, emphasis added)

Drawing an explicit contrast to messianic time, Anderson notes that in homogeneous empty time, "simultaneity is, as it were, transverse, cross-time, marked not by prefiguring and fulfillment, but by temporal coincidence, and measured by clock and calendar" (ibid.: 24). It is only in relation to such a notion of simultaneity, he notes, that the concept "meanwhile" can have any meaning, and it is only by means of measurements made with devices such as clock and calendar, he notes, that the concept of simultaneity-as-temporal-coincidence makes any sense.[19]

Although there is not necessarily a single spatio-temporal framework associated with clocks and calendars, they are both generally associated with notions of cyclical – as opposed to circular – time. Tributary states and capitalists alike have long used them as tools for controlling agricultural production, collecting taxes, regulating the length of the

---

18 This is not to say that homogeneous empty space-time is exclusive to capitalism; indeed, some conception of time as empty and homogeneous is probably essential to the administration of any large state or enterprise. Nor would I assert that homogeneous empty space-time is the only conception of time/space associated with large late-capitalist bureaucracies. Indeed, Michael Herzfeld (1992) identifies another important form of temporality (or, perhaps more accurately, "a-temporality") produced and reinforced by modern state bureaucracies. Although it would be interesting (and fully in keeping with the development of a politics of time) to explore alternative spatio-temporal orders and struggles over their use *within* bureaucracies, such an inquiry unfortunately lies outside the scope of the present study.

19 Peter Galison (2004) shows that our contemporary notion of temporal simultaneity had to be constructed, and that doing so took a massive amount of money and painstaking effort.

working day, and managing a host of other similarly cyclical processes, including those related to wildlife. As administrative tools, calendars and clocks help produce a sense of time as homogeneous and empty. Of the calendar, Bourdieu (1977: 105) notes: "Just as a map replaces the discontinuous, patchy space of practical paths by the homogeneous, continuous space of geometry, so a calendar substitutes a linear, homogeneous, continuous time for practical time, which is made up of incommensurable islands of duration, each with its own rhythm, the time that flies by or drags, depending on what one is doing."

Although of more recent vintage than the calendar, the mechanical clock has been in existence at least since the fourteenth century, and its invention facilitated dramatic changes in people's perception of time. "The clock," according to Lewis Mumford (1962: 15), "is a piece of power-machinery whose 'product' is seconds and minutes: by its essential nature it disassociated time from human events and helped create the beliefs of an independent world of mathematically measurable sequences." He noted that while there is little foundation in everyday human experience for a belief in such an abstraction,[20] once such a conceptual leap has been made, it has profound consequences: "When one thinks of time, not as a sequence of experiences, but as a collection of hours, minutes, and seconds, the habits of adding time and saving time come into existence. Time took on the character of an enclosed space: it could be divided, it could be filled up, it could even be expanded" (17).

It is no accident that Mumford – like Anderson – uses spatial terms to describe this notion of abstract time (i.e., as an empty space that people "move through"). Homogeneous empty time and the concept of simultaneity-as-temporal-coincidence with which it is associated *necessarily* imply a spatial dimension (e.g., *meanwhile* "x" is happening *somewhere* else). Indeed, Mumford notes that the emergence of abstract time coincided with similar developments in the conceptualization of space. At the same time the mechanical clock was spreading across Europe, artists were discovering the rules of perspective, and map-makers were developing modern cartographic methods. Just as the mechanical clock coincided with dramatic changes in the way people could think about

20 He does, however, suggest that it may have been the rhythms of labour (spiritual as well as physical) in the monasteries of medieval Europe that led to the invention of the mechanical clock in the first place (Mumford 1962: 12–14). See Zerubavel (1981: esp. chap. 2) for an elaboration of Mumford's ideas.

time, so the rules of perspective and proportional mapping both reflected and helped to bring about a fundamental shift in the way people conceptualized space: "Space as a hierarchy of values was replaced by space as a system of magnitudes" (Mumford 1962: 20; see also Harvey 1990: 240–59). Indeed, Renaissance paintings and maps implied and facilitated movement through space (imagined or real) in a way older medieval paintings and maps had never done, and it was movement that linked the concept of abstract empty space inextricably to that of abstract empty time: "Within this new ideal network of space and time all events now took place; and the most satisfactory event within this system was uniform motion in a straight line, for such motion led itself to accurate representation within the system of spatial and temporal coordinates" (Mumford 1962: 20–1). Thus, "the categories of time and space, once practically disassociated, had become united: and the abstractions of measured time and measured space undermined the earlier conceptions of infinity and eternity" (22).[21]

The concept of abstract, homogeneous, and empty space-time forms the basis for modern scientific inquiry; indeed, it was a necessary precondition for the development of Newtonian mechanics. It also underlies the development of capitalism. David Harvey (1990: 252) observed that a concept of "homogeneous universal time" is implicit in "conceptions of the rate of profit ..., the rate of interest, the hourly wage, and other magnitudes fundamental to capitalist decision-making" (see also Landes 2000, on time and value). Marx himself made it clear in his discussions of surplus value and the length of the working day, that capitalism depended in large part upon the institutionalization of a new way of thinking about time. It is by now well accepted that the rise of the capitalist labour process – along with the concept of value to which it was linked – led to new ways of thinking about time.[22] Considerably

---

21 Henri Bergson (1910) argued that "abstract time," the homogeneous medium of physics, is entirely reducible to space. He contrasted this to "duration," the experience of which he viewed as purely qualitative and immeasurable. Although I disagree with the implication that abstract space is a more fundamental category than abstract time, I agree that the two are wholly implicated in one another.

22 Culturally minded Marxist scholars (Le Goff 1980; Thompson 1967) built upon Marx's insights by examining how European conceptions of time (as well as technologies for keeping it) changed in association with the rise of the capitalist labour process. E.P. Thompson (1967), for example, citing Evans-Pritchard, characterized this change as a shift away from the irregular work rhythms of a "task-oriented" society – in which there is very little demarcation between "work" and "life" and people

less has been written, however, about the spatio-temporal imperatives of bureaucratic administration.

Under capitalism – especially industrial capitalism – production, distribution, and consumption become ever more complex processes linking far-flung peoples and places to one another. The activities of all these people must be coordinated if the whole system is to work at all (parts and raw materials must arrive at the factory on time, finished products must be transported to markets, payments must be sent, received, and processed on time, etc.). As the whole process speeds up (due to improvements in transportation and communication), coordination becomes all the more crucial. The calendar, no doubt invented at least in part to coordinate activities in the tributary state (Rotenberg 1992), becomes more crowded with events that require coordination. The clock, which can subdivide the calendar day into smaller and ever more precise units, becomes a critical tool for the fine-grained scheduling and coordination necessary for administration as well as production.

There are few if any social forms as well suited as bureaucracy to the task of coordinating events in a complex capitalist society. Max Weber (1946b: 215) noted that although bureaucracy pre-dates the rise of capitalism, it was the particular demands of the capitalist economy that led to the perfection of the bureaucratic form: "Today, it is primarily the capitalist market economy which demands that the official business of the administration be discharged precisely, unambiguously, continuously, and with as much speed as possible. Normally, the very large, modern capitalist enterprises are themselves unequalled models of strict bureaucratic organization." Although Weber was well aware of the many deficiencies of the bureaucratic form, he nevertheless argued that bureaucracy is by far the most effective means for administering large and complex social systems, such as corporations and modern industrialized states: "The decisive reason for the advance of bureaucratic organization has always been its purely technical superiority over any other form of organization. The fully developed bureaucratic

---

conform to the natural rhythms (seasons, tides, etc.) that govern their subsistence – to a labour process that is strictly governed by the clock, where for the first time it becomes meaningful to speak of "spending" and "wasting" time. Significantly, however, he does not argue that the capitalist conception of time replaced a pre-existing task-oriented conception. Rather, he points out that both continue to exist and that struggles over these alternate conceptions were intense and continue into the present (see also Ingold 2000: 336–8).

mechanism compares with other organizations exactly as does the machine with the non-mechanical modes of production" (1946b: 214, see also pp. 228–9).

Bureaucracies are "machine-like" in that they are complex hierarchical organizations characterized by an elaborate internal division of labour. Their various components are highly integrated with one another and replaceable (in theory at least), so that although each attends to only a small part of the overall problem of administration, their combined efforts enable the bureaucratic apparatus as a whole to administer the extraordinarily complex affairs of an industrialized state or corporation. Such activity is necessarily based on a notion of homogeneous empty space-time. To see why, consider what bureaucrats actually do.

Government bureaucrats in industrial states, for example, are faced with the daunting task of administering very large and complex systems of people, institutions, land, and resources. To accomplish this, they must, among many other things, keep track of and collect a multitude of different forms of revenue. They must schedule and execute the distribution of funds both internally and externally. They must plan and administer social programs throughout the state's territory. They must implement and enforce all laws and regulations – including those governing resource-use – throughout their territorial jurisdiction. They must plan, oversee the construction of, and maintain public infrastructure. They must negotiate and oversee political, economic, and social relations with their counterparts in the bureaucracies of other states, as well as those of corporations and other levels of government. To invoke Anderson in a new context, it is clear that all these administrative functions demand – indeed are premised upon – the conception of a "social organism [composed not only of the bureaucracy itself, but of the entire society] moving calendrically through homogeneous empty time." While one bureaucrat is making sure that sufficient funds are transferred to a government-sponsored health care program, for example, he or she has confidence that another bureaucrat somewhere else – whom he or she has probably never met – is tending to the collection of oil and gas revenues.

It is not enough, however, simply to assert that the administrative functions of bureaucracy are premised upon a conception of homogeneous empty space-time. Although homogeneous empty space-time may be a conceptual prerequisite for the administration of large and complex social systems, in practice the spatio-temporal framework of bureaucratic administration remains neither "empty" nor "homogeneous" for long. Indeed, imparting order and structure to the imagined abstraction of homogeneous empty space-time is a critical part of bureaucratic practice; it is a large part of what bureaucrats actually do on a day-to-day basis. Consider again the task of bureaucratic administration. Bureaucrats must accomplish all the diverse goals described above with a finite limit to the resources (time, money, personnel) at their disposal. For bureaucrats administering a complex social system, there is always more to do than can be accomplished in any given period of time. As a result, they must prioritize. They do so by engaging in elaborate processes of planning and evaluation which include, among other things, the preparation and approval of work plans and budgets (both of which they are continually revising), the negotiation of (inter- as well as intra-governmental) funding agreements, and the preparation, evaluation, and auditing of interim and annual reports (on the importance of scheduling, particularly in a bureaucratic context, see Zerubavel 1981). Work plans, budgets, reports, audits and similar administrative tools bring structure to the homogeneity and emptiness of abstract space-time. So, while bureaucrats plan and carry out the construction of a new road somewhere, they know that there are other roads and bridges elsewhere which, because of budgetary constraints, are not scheduled for construction until next year or the year after. And there are other bureaucrats who prepare, review, and approve (or reject) year-end reports and audits to make sure the government employees or contractors building the road adhere to proper timetables and budgets, so that there will be sufficient resources to construct those other roads and bridges in the future. It is precisely through the use of plans, budgets, reports, accounting techniques, and the other "soft technologies" of administration that bureaucrats seek to impose a particular spatio-temporal structure upon the abstract field of homogeneous empty space-time. This applies to wildlife management as much as to any other realm of bureaucratic management.

The Bureaucratization of Wildlife Management and the Spatio-temporal Politics of Human–Animal Relations in the Yukon

Environmental historians, anthropologists, and others agree that the development of bureaucratic wildlife management at the beginning of the twentieth century was inextricably bound up with the expansion of state power, as amply demonstrated by a voluminous literature on the relationship between colonialism, the exploitation of wild animals, and the rise of state-sponsored wildlife management (Beinart and Hughes 2007; Jacoby 2001; MacKenzie 1988; Marks 1984; Neumann 1998). Indeed, across the Canadian north it was the imposition of state wildlife management and conservation programs that first brought not only land and wildlife under the effective control of central governments, but local and aboriginal peoples as well (Feit 1998; Kulchyski and Tester 2007; McCandless 1985; Nadasdy 2003; Sandlos 2007). This was certainly the case in the Yukon, where the twentieth century witnessed the gradual development of an elaborate administrative apparatus for the management of fish and wildlife. Although wildlife management in the territory was rudimentary at the start of the century, the development of transportation and communication infrastructures in mid-century enabled bureaucratic managers to enforce an ever more complex set of management policies and regulations across hitherto largely inaccessible parts of the territory (see Nadasdy 2003: 38–41), and the hiring of staff biologists (beginning in 1970s) ushered in an era of scientific management with the aim of controlling the natural population cycles of fish and wildlife for the maximum benefit of humans.[23] The growing management bureaucracy increasingly made use of the administrative technologies discussed above, thus enmeshing the people and animals of the territory within a spatio-temporal framework structured by bureaucrats wielding budgets, work plans, accounts, and reports.

The Yukon First Nation land claim and self-government agreements have ushered in a new era of wildlife management in the Yukon, though their implications for Yukon Indian people are as ambivalent from a spatio-temporal perspective as they are from other perspectives explored in this book. On one hand, because they grant First Nations a genuine role in the management process, one might suppose that Yukon Indian people now possess the political means to challenge the spatio-temporal assumptions underlying scientific wildlife management and to advocate management strategies based their own very different perspectives. On the other hand, however, one can view the agreements as the culmination of the bureaucratizing process insofar as they incorporate Yukon Indian people into the wildlife management

23 As of 2017, the Fish and Wildlife Branch of the Yukon Department of Environment had 46 employees (down two from 2008), and Conservation Officer Services employed another 28 people (down four from 2008) Yukon-wide.

bureaucracy, thus actually making it *more* difficult for them to challenge the spatio-temporal assumption upon which it is built. To explore this ambivalence further, I need to provide some more details about how wildlife management works under the agreements.

Bureaucratic Wildlife Management under the Yukon Agreements

Chapter 16 of the Yukon Umbrella Final Agreement establishes a new regime for the co-management of fish and wildlife in the Yukon. One of the primary objectives of that chapter is "to enhance and promote the full participation of Yukon Indian People in Renewable Resource management" (Council for Yukon Indians 1993: 153). To this end, it provides for the establishment of the Yukon Fish and Wildlife Management Board (FWMB), a territory-wide body, and fourteen Renewable Resources Councils (RRCs), one for each of the fourteen Yukon First Nations. The UFA establishes the FWMB as the "primary instrument" for fish and wildlife management throughout the Yukon (Council for Yukon Indians 1993: 166) and each RRC as the "primary instrument" for renewable resources management within each First Nation's Traditional Territory (Kluane First Nation 2003b: 241). The FWMB and RRCs are considered co-management bodies, because the Yukon government and the Council for Yukon First Nations (or relevant First Nation government in the case of RRCs) each nominate half their members. These bodies are charged with the responsibility of carrying out public consultations on management issues (on either a Yukon-wide or Traditional Territorial basis) and making recommendations to the relevant government in any particular case.[24] Board and council appointees are neither government officials nor are they expected to act as representatives for the governments that appointed them; rather, they are "ordinary citizens" chosen on the basis of their interests in and knowledge about wildlife.[25] In other words, the board and councils are supposed to be external to the

---

24 As we saw in chapter 2, the question of jurisdiction can be fairly complex. In general, the Yukon government retains jurisdiction over fish and wildlife throughout the territory. First Nations, however, have jurisdiction over fish and wildlife on "settlement lands" retained under the agreements, and the federal Department of Fisheries and Oceans retains jurisdiction over the management of anadromous fish, such as salmon, throughout the Yukon.

25 Most of the First Nation final agreements have a provision requiring that RRC appointees be permanent residents of the Traditional Territory.

bureaucratic structures of government; as such, their role is to consult with the wider public and provide government bureaucrats (both territorial and First Nation) with recommendations based on those consultations. And, in fact, board and council members do come from all walks of life; very few of them are government officials or have any experience working in a bureaucratic setting.

Despite the conventional rhetoric about co-management bodies of this sort standing at "arm's length" from government and the fact that, for the most part, appointees to these bodies are not themselves professional bureaucrats, co-management of this sort does not represent as radical a break from centralized state management as is often supposed. Because the federal and territorial governments are themselves large bureaucracies, the formal mechanisms for intergovernmental relations created by the new agreements are necessarily bureaucratic in form (Nadasdy 2003). Thus, it is primarily at the bureaucratic level that the new agreements are implemented. I have argued elsewhere (Nadasdy 2005b) that far from representing an *alternative* to bureaucratic state management, co-management bodies like those created by chapter 16 of the Yukon final agreements are firmly *embedded within* that bureaucracy. Their creation was accompanied by a set of administrative rules and procedures regulating not only how they function internally, but also how they relate to external bureaucratic institutions in the territorial and First Nation governments (as we shall see below, however, those rules and procedures have been subject to fairly intense struggle). Such rules enable co-management boards to interface with existing offices and institutions of state management, and this is absolutely essential if they are to play their appointed roles. In this important sense, co-management boards are inherently bureaucratic. Rather than liberating Yukon Indian people from government bureaucracy, then, the creation of such boards has simply given them their own "slot" in the bureaucratic system.

As argued above, the spatio-temporal politics of wildlife management in the Yukon is not simply a matter of different actors invoking the spatio-temporal framework of "their culture." Rather, the space-time of human–animal relations is context dependent; certain social contexts are predicated upon particular spatio-temporal frameworks (which structure them). Under the new agreements, federal, territorial, and First Nation bureaucrats must work closely together, and their relations with one another are mediated (and in large part instantiated) by the administrative practices and technologies discussed above: budgets, work plans, financial reports, and audits. To assume their role within this bureaucracy, Yukon Indian people have no choice but to wield the administrative technologies discussed above, technologies that presuppose a bureaucratic notion of space-time as homogeneous and empty. This effectively institutionalizes the spatio-temporal assumptions of bureaucratic management, making it very difficult for Yukon Indian people who participate in (or abide by) these bureaucratic processes to challenge these assumptions and the power relations they support. One can reject that framework as inappropriate, as some Yukon Indian people do, but only by rejecting the whole bureaucratic context of wildlife management. There is however, plenty of room for complex spatio-temporal politics even *within* bureaucratic wildlife management.

Renewable Resources Councils and Struggles in Bureaucratic Space-Time

As we saw above, the administration of a large and complex state like Canada is necessarily premised on the conception of a "social organism moving calendrically through homogeneous empty time." The bureaucratic administrators of such a social system must have faith in the "steady, anonymous, simultaneous, activity" not only of other officials, but of all those people and processes they administer. Co-management bodies, such as the RRCs, being bureaucratic entities themselves, are necessarily part of all this steady, anonymous, simultaneous activity. As noted above, however, it is not enough simply to note that RRC members function in the homogeneous empty space-time of bureaucratic practice. Rather, they are necessarily caught up in the endless struggles – waged among bureaucrats wielding administrative technologies – to structure the abstract expanse of homogeneous empty space-time.

Stephen Lukes (1977) argues that structure implies power. If this is so, then the use of any administrative techniques to impose a particular structure upon the spatio-temporal order necessarily has a political dimension. And indeed, as historian John Sweetman (1984: 3) notes, "administration is the means by which power is exercised," an observation borne out by recent work on the political dimensions of accounting, audits, and other modern administrative practices (Neu 2000; Power 1997; Strathern 2000). This suggests that some understanding of these administrative technologies – and their histories – is crucial to any study of contemporary spatio-temporal politics in the Yukon.

Chapter 16 of each First Nation final agreement describes in broad strokes the roles, powers, and responsibilities of the Renewable

Resources Councils (see, e.g., Kluane First Nation 2003b: 241–6). First Nation final agreement implementation plans, which are legally binding parts of each agreement, provide a bit more information, including statements of each RRC's total annual operating budget for the year it is established and a multi-year financial forecast (see, e.g., Kluane First Nation 2003c: 432–6). Aside from these broad guidelines, however, the agreements provide very little detail about day-to-day operations of the RRCs, nor about the administrative context in which they are to operate. Thus, RRC members themselves, along with the First Nation and territorial officials responsible for dealing with them, have had to work out many of these practical details in the course of their day-to-day interactions. The result is an ongoing negotiation/struggle both within individual RRCs and between RRCs and territorial and First Nation bureaucrats, and one of the most important dimensions of this struggle in the ten years following the ratification of the original agreements was precisely over how to structure the homogeneous empty space-time within which the RRCs function. Much of this struggle took place in the realms of planning, budgeting, reporting, and other forms of administrative practice.

The final agreements state that "each Council shall prepare an annual budget, subject to review and approval by Government. The budget shall be in accordance with Government guidelines" (e.g., Kluane First Nation 2003b: 243). The agreements further specify that these budgets may include (1) "remuneration and travel expenses" for RRC members to attend meetings, (2) "the cost of public hearings and meetings," (3) "research review, public information and other activities," and (4) "other items as the Council and Government agree on" (ibid.). The implementation plans lay out each RRC's annual operating budget and also provide a recommended budget for their first year of operation, with spending broken down into only three major categories: "administration," "meetings," and "support." They further stipulate that "annual budgets prepared by the [RRC] in subsequent years will provide greater detail than that provided in the Year 1 Budget to better reflect the operational requirements of the [RRC]" (e.g., Kluane First Nation 2003c: 436). The Yukon government's role in approving RRCs' budgets and line items gives its officials an important role in defining and regulating the activities in which RRC members can engage.

The federal government ultimately bears the costs associated with the operation of the RRCs, but because it is the Yukon government that has jurisdiction over fish and wildlife in the territory, the federal government simply transfers the appropriate funds to the Yukon government on an annual basis; and it is largely Yukon officials who are charged with approving RRC budgets, negotiating contribution agreements with RRCs, distributing payments, and otherwise administering these funds. As we shall see, their control over the budgeting process enables them to exert direct influence over RRC activities.

As noted in the introduction, I served in 2003–4 as Kluane First Nation's representative to the Yukon Implementation Review Group (IRG), an intergovernmental body charged with conducting a formal nine-year review of the Yukon Umbrella Final Agreement and those First Nation final agreements that had been in effect for at least five years. The object of the review was to assess how well the parties had implemented the agreements and to identify problems or obstacles to their implementation – with an eye to possibly renegotiating any problematic sections. As part of the review process, the IRG invited written statements from each of the RRCs and invited them to appear before the IRG in person to present their concerns and answer questions. Territorial officials were also invited to appear before the IRG to do the same.

Disputes over reporting requirements and other aspects of administration have been a source of tension between RRCs and the Yukon government since the first RRCs were established in 1995. For the first few years, the projected annual budgets prepared by most RRCs were not much more detailed than those spelled out in the implementation plans. This should not be too surprising; as we saw, few RRC members were themselves bureaucrats or had any experience in preparing budgets, work plans, or other administrative documents of this sort. What is more, each RRC prepared its own budget, so there was considerable variation in the detail and quality of the budgets they submitted. Each RRC also used its own spending categories and budget format. The lack of standardized budgets made it difficult for Yukon officials to deal with the RRCs in a coordinated fashion and forced them to spend a great deal of time on the phone with RRCs clarifying what was going on. Yukon officials claimed that during the first few years, they even had trouble getting year-end audited financial statements from some of the RRCs.[26] So Yukon officials gradually introduced a series of new

26 In at least one case, Yukon government officials actually cut off the flow of funds to force an RRC to produce an audited statement.

reporting requirements. Some of these, such as requiring RRCs to use a standard budget form, were calculated to reduce the variation among individual RRCs and rationalize the overall process, and were viewed by RRC members as generally helpful. Other changes, however, were resisted by RRCs, who viewed them as onerous or as attempts by territorial officials to exert inappropriate influence over RRC activities.

Nearly all the RRCs – either in their written submissions to the IRG or in their oral testimony – expressed concerns over reporting requirements imposed by territorial officials. Several complained that reporting requirements changed every year and that territorial officials were constantly returning documents to the RRC to be revised to meet the current guidelines. What is more, RRCs complained that these requirements were becoming more and more onerous, using up excessive amounts of the RRCs' scarce time and resources on what they viewed as pointless paperwork. Yukon government officials, for their part, saw regular changes in the reporting requirements as a part of an effort to "fine-tune" the administrative process. They maintained that changes in the reporting process were not arbitrary, as they seemed to RRCs, but were leading to an increasingly rational and streamlined process. They did, however, admit that administrative changes could at times indeed be arbitrary – even counterproductive – but such changes, they noted, were nearly always "political" (i.e., extra-bureaucratic) and dictated from above.[27] Yukon officials also denied that the RRCs' reporting requirements were particularly onerous. On the contrary, they asserted that appropriate reporting was necessary to ensure that RRCs remain accountable to Canadian taxpayers whose money they were spending, and they described several incidents of inappropriate spending by RRCs to back up their position.

One particularly contested issue had to do with the production of annual work plans. Several years before my tenure on the IRG, that body (as part of a formal five-year review of the agreements) had agreed that the RRCs were underfunded and had recommended that the federal

27 They noted, for example, that certain new reporting requirements had recently been imposed at the request of federal bureaucrats by order of the federal minister whose government was under pressure from the right-wing Reform Party to increase the "accountability" of First Nations.

government provide an additional $20,000 per year to each council. The federal government agreed to increase RRC funding, but in return insisted that RRCs produce detailed annual work plans laying out how they would spend the extra money. Since it would have made little sense for RRCs to plan only how they would spend the *extra* $20,000 (and not do the same for the rest of their budgets), territorial officials were soon requiring that RRCs submit work plans detailing how they intended to spend their entire projected budgets. While some RRC members conceded that putting together an annual work plan was a potentially useful exercise (because it helped them set priorities for the coming year), most found the process at best irrelevant and many feared that it was actually undermining the RRCs' autonomy.

Because of their small budgets, RRCs are severely limited in the number of staff they can hire and the other resources at their disposal. At the same time, they are widely viewed as key institutions of the land claim agreements; Yukon and First Nation governments must (and do) consult with them on all manner of issues related to renewable resources: from the granting of water licences and land use permits, to proposed changes in hunting regulations, to plans for development anywhere in the traditional territories over which they have jurisdiction. In addition, new federal and territorial legislation is constantly increasing the role and responsibilities of Yukon co-management boards, usually without corresponding increases in their funding levels.[28] Many RRC members complained that, as a result of all this, it was impossible for them to be proactive; rather, all they could hope to do was to respond to the many demands placed on them by governments. Thus, although in theory the RRCs had the power to structure their time as they saw fit, in practice their priorities were often set for them externally, and any planning they may have done at the start of the year was largely irrelevant.

Worse yet, the RRCs felt that to the extent they *did* have the time and resources to pursue their own agendas, their ability to do so was being undermined by officials in the territorial government. Nearly all the

28 At the IRG review, for example, members of the Fish and Wildlife Management Board complained that the then-new federal Species at Risk Legislation created a number of new roles and responsibilities for the board, yet the federal government steadfastly refused to consider a corresponding increase in their funding.

RRCs complained that territorial officials were using the required work plans to interfere with council activities. Although RRC mandates are spelled out in the final agreements, there is considerable room for disagreement over how these mandates should be interpreted. RRC members felt that territorial officials were inappropriately using their power to approve/reject work plans to enforce their own particular (and, they felt, excessively restricted) interpretation of RRC mandates. Yukon government officials, for their part, denied that they were interfering inappropriately; they did, however, feel that it was their role to make sure RRCs stuck to their mandates. One of the most contentious areas of dispute in this regard was over whether RRCs should be allowed to fund wildlife research. Yukon government officials felt that funding and carrying out wildlife research was the sole responsibility of the Yukon government. They maintained that if RRC members decided that some particular wildlife study was necessary, they should make a recommendation to the Yukon government that it be carried out. Several of the RRCs vehemently disagreed, arguing that the Yukon government had its own research agenda that often did not correspond well with the interests of First Nations and RRCs. As a result, they argued, identifying significant gaps in existing knowledge about wildlife and devising ways to fill those gaps was a critical part of their mandate, and that might well include funding their own wildlife studies. In fact, the official RRC mandates – as spelled out in the agreements – are unclear on the issue of research; but because Yukon officials controlled the RRC's budgets and steadfastly refused to approve budgets and work plans that funded wildlife research, they were effectively able to enforce their own interpretation of the mandate. In this way, they were able to exert considerable influence over the ordering/structuring of events within the homogeneous empty space-time of wildlife management.

Yukon officials' control, however, was far from complete. The RRCs did not submit passively to Yukon officials' efforts to dictate to them the terms of their own mandates. In some cases, they simply funded research that was outside their approved budget and work plan, knowing full well that at year-end they would face the ire of territorial officials. Having been presented with a fait accompli, however, these officials could do little more than scold RRC members retroactively for having exceeded their authority. Another important means used by RRCs in their efforts to regain control over their mandates was to raise their own funds from non-governmental organizations, such as the Gordon Foundation. They could then use these funds to carry out research and other activities that they knew territorial officials would not approve.[29] "Resistance" of this sort, however, has its own temporal implications. Proposal writing is extremely time-consuming, and there is no guarantee that proposals will be successful. Given the time pressures faced by board members and staff, the choice to pursue non-governmental funding is a risky one; even when boards are successful at it, those that choose this route necessarily put off – or forsake entirely – engaging in other important activities.

We have now seen that government officials, RRC members, and others caught up in the wildlife management bureaucracy wield administrative technologies in their struggles with one another to impose a particular structure upon the empty homogeneous expanse of bureaucratic space-time. To the extent that they do so, however, they necessarily take for granted the spatio-temporal framework upon which those administrative tools are based. They take for granted the "steady, anonymous, simultaneous, activity" not only of humans, but also of the animals they would manage. This effectively enmeshes Yukon Indian people in a set of practices that are rooted in a spatio-temporal order that is in many ways incompatible with their notions of what constitute proper human–animal relations. The fact that these practices have become entrenched within the new institutions of governance and management created by land claim and self-government agreements,

29 It should be noted that fundraising of this sort was more than just a response to perceived "meddling" by territorial officials. In fact, the Fish and Wildlife Management Board and RRCs began seeking non-governmental funds almost immediately after they were established in an effort to augment what they saw as insufficient government funding. Nevertheless, they maintained that government officials had no right to tell them how to spend money obtained from outside grants – which in any case had to be spent according to the terms under which the grant was awarded. During IRG meetings, federal and territorial representatives challenged this practice, questioning whether it was appropriate for public co-management bodies to seek outside funding – because then they would be beholden to private foundations who have their own agendas. First Nations representatives, however, asserted that unless and until the federal government committed to providing these boards with sufficient funds to achieve their mandates, First Nations would not support any recommendation restricting their ability to look elsewhere for the funds they need to operate. In the end, the IRG recommended that "the Parties establish a base for the funding of each Board that eliminates the need for Boards to engage in fundraising activities to meet the financial requirements of their mandate" (Implementation Review Group 2007).

however, makes it very difficult for Yukon Indian people to question them. As we shall see, the only option for those who would challenge the dominant spatio-temporal framework is to reject the land claim agreements themselves along with the assumptions of bureaucratic management upon which they have been built.

The Spatio-temporal Politics of Catch-and-Release Fishing

As noted earlier, many Yukon Indian people do not regard human–animal interactions as occurring within homogeneous empty space-time; the simultaneity that connects a contemporary Yukon Indian hunter with the animal-people of Long Time Ago stories is of a very different kind than the simultaneity that informs practices of bureaucratic wildlife management. Similarly, although Yukon Indian hunters and Euro-American wildlife managers can agree that wildlife is a "renewable resource," they have very different ideas about the role humans play in the maintenance of animal cycles. As a result, many Yukon Indian people regard the basic assumptions and practices of bureaucratic wildlife management with suspicion. It is well known, for example, that many Yukon Indian people object to standard management practices such as the radio-collaring of animals by wildlife biologists because they see such treatment as insulting to animal-people. But the insult does not lie merely in the fact that such practices subject animals to the indignities of being drugged, handled, and forced to wear radio-collars. Equally problematic is the fact that through such practices, wildlife biologists impose upon animals their own time schedules, budgets, and research agendas. Rather than trying to understand animals on their own terms, biologists force them into the context of bureaucratic space-time in an attempt to wrest knowledge from them by force. This is completely at odds with Yukon Indian people's notions about what constitutes respectful behaviour towards all persons, whether human or non-human (Nadasdy 2003: 108–11).

Thus, many standard wildlife management practices are insulting to animal-people not merely because they subject them to physical indignities, but also because they impose on human–animal relations a new spatio-temporal framework, one that is geared specifically towards asserting what many Yukon Indian people see as an inappropriate degree of control over animals. No amount of wrangling over budgets and work plans can address the concerns of Yukon Indian people who object to bureaucratic management practices on these grounds. For them, the only option is to reject the spatio-temporal assumptions of bureaucratic wildlife management itself, an option that is becoming increasingly difficult because of the entrenchment of such assumptions in the provisions of Yukon land claim agreements. The struggle over catch-and-release fishing is a case in point.

In the late 1990s, the Fish and Wildlife Management Board, aware of Yukon Indian people's concerns about catch-and-release fishing, commissioned several studies to investigate whether voluntary catch-and-release was an appropriate technique for the management of fish stocks. As Easton (2008) reports, just the knowledge that the board was investigating the practice of catch-and-release generated a contentious public debate. Yukon government fisheries managers and most Euro-American sports fishermen and tourism operators supported catch-and-release because it enables fishermen to be selective about the fish they kill, allowing them to release the large spawners that are critical for the reproduction of fish populations. Clearly underlying this perspective on the practice are assumptions about the cyclical temporality of fish as a resource and the notion that humans can and should control their natural population cycles through the regulation of "harvest" levels (among other things).

In contrast, the vast majority of Yukon Indian people oppose the practice of catch-and-release fishing (Muckenheim 1998). They do so both because it subjects fish-people to the indignities of insulting treatment at human hands and because releasing the fish is a repudiation of the act of reciprocal exchange that lies at the heart of the relationship between human- and fish-people (see Easton 2008; Nadasdy 2003: 81–3; Natcher, Davis, and Hickey 2005: 246). Long Time Ago stories such as *The Boy Who Stayed with Fish*, a well-known tale about a boy who spoke disrespectfully about a piece of fish, make clear the dangers of such behaviour. As a result of his disrespectful behaviour, the boy was transformed into a fish, and he lived among the fish people for several years. Eventually, he regained his human form and taught people the proper way to treat fish.[30] In one of the reports prepared by the board, a Yukon Indian person objected to catch-and-release fishing because it "goes against the fundamental beliefs of the First Nations people ... They consider [it] to be 'playing with the fish' which is very disrespectful

30 For complete versions of this story, see Cruikshank (1990b: 75–8, 208–13). See also McClellan (1975: 185).

... [that] you only fish for food ... and that you never, never play with the animals. You must respect them or they won't come back" (cited in Muckenheim 1998; see also Easton 2008: 31). This phrasing suggests that if one treats a fish properly (i.e., one kills and eats it, rather than releasing it), it *will* "come back" to be caught again. Because both humans and fish are reborn, there is an important sense in which everyone in the story of the *Boy Who Stayed with Fish* – human and fish alike – is still alive today, and they continue to enact their age-old relationship of reciprocal exchange in the manner prescribed by the fish-people themselves and relayed to humans via the boy who lived with them.[31] In contrast to the perspective of biologists and sport fishers, then, the Yukon Indian perspective on catch-and-release fishing is based on the assumption that fish populations are *circularly* rather than *cyclically* renewable and that therefore fish management should be about maintaining social relationships, rather than controlling biological cycles.

Despite a great deal of talk about the need to find "common ground" on the issue, the Fish and Wildlife Management Board in 2000 recommended that voluntary catch-and-release continue to be used and promoted in the Yukon, although they did recommend that only barbless fishhooks be used in an effort to reduce the mortality of released fish. What is more, they created the Fish Think Tank, a working group charged with educating the public about catch-and-release fishing and promoting it as a management practice (Yukon Fish and Wildlife Management Board 2000: 20; see also Easton 2008: 33). Easton (2008: 33–5) is highly critical of the way the board disregarded Yukon Indian people's interests and values. He attributes this to a discursive strategy on the part of catch-and-release proponents to frame Yukon Indian concerns as "ethical" in nature (and thus not an appropriate basis for policymaking) in contrast to their own concerns, which were ostensibly rooted in biological and economic realities (the proper bases for the regulation of fisheries). Easton views as disingenuous proponents' self-proclaimed desire to "keep ethical decisions out of the fishing regulations," noting that "the law and its regulations are precisely the

31 For another example of a Yukon Indian person evaluating catch-and-release fishing in precisely this light, see Julie Cruikshank's (1998: 57–8) account of an interaction between a biologist and a Yukon Indian elder. The biologist explained the usefulness of catch-and-release as a management tool; in response, the elder told him the story of the boy who stayed with fish.

codification of ethics within a statutory frame by which they can be legitimately enforced by the State" (ibid.: 20).

I would add that the reason it is possible – indeed *necessary* – to dismiss Yukon Indian people's concerns as "merely ethical" is that their conceptions of animals and the *circular* spatio-temporality of human–animal relations are fundamentally incompatible with assumptions of scientific fisheries management. Because of this, there is *no way* to make fisheries policy that is consistent with *both* First Nation and biological ideas about management. To truly accept Yukon Indian people's concerns as the basis for making management decisions, one would first have to *reject* the cyclical spatio-temporality that underlies biological conceptions of fish and fishing. Indeed, at least one wildlife biologist recognized this explicitly. He told me that it is his impression that most non-Indian members of the various management boards try to take Yukon Indian people's beliefs and values seriously in their deliberations. Difficulties arise, however, when board members try to "operationalize" these beliefs in the realm of management, and the problem is especially evident when Yukon Indian people's beliefs and values contradict those of biologists. A good example of this, he noted, was the debate over catch-and-release fishing, because it was impossible to act on the beliefs and values of Yukon Indian people in relation to this issue without *denying* the insights of biologists (see Povinelli [1995] for a similar dilemma in the Australian context).

So why did First Nation members of the Fish and Wildlife Management Board go along with recommendations to continue and even promote catch-and-release fishing? One First Nation board member told me he had done so reluctantly and for pragmatic political reasons. He noted that Indian people make up less than a third of the Yukon population, and that "we all have to live together." He told me that while he would never practise catch-and-release fishing himself, he did not feel right dictating to non-Indian people how they should behave. Like all members of the board, he was also acutely aware of the fact that any recommendation to prohibit catch-and-release fishing would have ignited a political firestorm.[32] While such a position is certainly

32 Indeed, as Easton points out, the controversy over catch-and-release was so intense that the board felt compelled to announce – more than a year before it had completed its own study of the issue – that it did not intend to prohibit the practice (Easton 2008: 31).

understandable from a pragmatic standpoint, it is worth considering its full social and political implications. In the first place, when Yukon Indian people acquiesce to Euro-Canadian desires to practise catch-and-release, they are making a huge sacrifice. Because improper behaviour by Euro-Canadians can destroy the delicate social relationship between fish and *all* humans, Yukon Indian people consciously risk their own and their children's futures for the sake of social harmony with Euro-Canadians.[33]

Second, and perhaps more importantly, in acquiescing to catch-and-release, Yukon Indian people implicitly accept the biological assumptions about fish that underlie the practice. In so doing, they tacitly agree to use the framework of bureaucratic space-time as the only legitimate basis upon which to make – and contest – fisheries management decisions. So, while they are still free to engage in struggles over how to structure homogeneous empty bureaucratic space-time (in the ways described above), it becomes increasingly difficult for them to question the spatio-temporal bases of bureaucratic wildlife management.

Conclusion

I began this chapter by describing an apparent contradiction at the heart of anthropological inquiries into the relationship between time and colonialism, and I suggested that this apparent contradiction disappears when we stop thinking in terms of different cultures characterized by single totalizing senses of time. I argued that we should focus instead on the complex spatio-temporal heterogeneity *within* all societies and the politics associated with that heterogeneity. In this view, the secret to developing an anthropology that treats indigenous people as coeval is not to deny the existence of nonlinear senses of space-time, as Gell and others have done. It is, rather, to stop treating these alternate spatio-temporal frameworks – whether they inform indigenous hunting or the

33 That improper behaviour by Euro-Canadians can have a negative impact not only on their own relationship with fish, but on Yukon Indian people's as well is evident in the following. In the summer of 2006 some Yukon Indian people attributed low salmon numbers at Klukshu, a historically important fishing spot in the Southern Yukon, not to overfishing but to the fact that Euro-Canadians had insulted the fish by bathing in the creek. As a result of this behaviour, it was not only Euro-Canadian but also Yukon Indian people who were unable to catch fish.

use of legal precedent – as "historical relics of some long-lost past" and acknowledge them instead as "guiding norms that continue to operate in the present" (Richland 2008: 24). A sense of space-time as circular continues to inform many Yukon Indian people's interactions with the land, animals, and one another. By imposing a wildlife management regime rooted in bureaucratic space-time, the Yukon agreements did not *replace* the circular space-time of indigenous hunting. Rather, they superimposed a new spatio-temporal framework over the old – thus initiating a series of ongoing struggles over which of these spatio-temporal frameworks should govern various human–animal–land interactions.

In many ways, these two spatio-temporal frameworks are incommensurable, not only – or even primarily – because they are "out of synch" with one another, but, rather, because each is integral to a different view of reality. In the circular space-time of indigenous hunting, humans, animals, and other denizens of the boreal forest are fundamentally different kinds of beings – with very different relationships to space and time – than they are in the world of bureaucratic wildlife management. Ways of interacting with the beings that inhabit the hunters' world are often not appropriate for those populating the world of bureaucratic management and vice versa. Many Yukon Indian people, for example, continue to view animals as a potentially unlimited resource, their availability dependent only on the maintenance of social relations between animal- and human-persons, while non-Indian hunters and biologists tend to view animals as a finite resource vulnerable to over-exploitation. This in turn leads them to subscribe to different notions about the proper role of human agency vis-à-vis animals and about what constitutes appropriate management.

Despite this incommensurability, however, Yukon Indian people can and do operate in both spatio-temporal frameworks. Indeed, as we have seen, there is room for spatio-temporal politics not only *between* these two spatio-temporal frameworks, but *within* them as well (as when First Nation and Yukon government officials wrangle over budgets and work plans); and Yukon Indian people have become adept at the latter types of struggle. Yet, while they can and do assert some degree of control over space and time within the new bureaucratic context of wildlife management, that very context takes for granted the cyclical topology of bureaucratic space-time and so is incompatible with many of their views about proper human–animal–land relations. This is not to say that Yukon Indian people (even those working in First Nation wildlife management offices) have completely internalized the new management regime and its spatio-temporal assumptions – any more than they have internalized the social and territorial assumptions examined in earlier chapters. Nor can one say that the new agreements have completely transformed Yukon Indian people's spatio-temporal relationship to one another, the land, and animals. Indeed, many today reject the new spatio-temporal framework – and the beliefs and practices that flow from them – at least in some contexts. To the extent that they do engage in and/or abide by the practices of wildlife management spelled out in the agreements, however, they must adopt – or at least adapt to – the new spatio-temporal framework on which they are built. For this reason it is extremely difficult for Yukon Indian people to implement and/or abide by the agreements while at the same time interacting with the land and animals in a manner consistent with the Long Time Ago stories. To some extent, then, their participation in the bureaucratic wildlife management processes (and acquiescence to the spatio-temporal assumptions underlying them) makes it increasingly difficult for them to challenge dominant Euro-Canadian views of wildlife management and poses a serious obstacle to those Yukon Indian people who would prefer to relate to the land and animals – and to one another – as their grandparents did.

Conclusion

Anti-sovereignty

Comprehensive land claim and self-government agreements in the Yukon emerged from decades of struggle against colonial policies, and they grant Yukon First Nations significant powers of governance over their peoples, lands, and resources. As we have seen, however, those powers come in the currency of territorial sovereignty; and to wield them Yukon Indian people have had to draw new geographic, social, temporal, and epistemological boundaries, altering in the process how they relate to one another, animals, and the land in dramatic and often unforeseen ways. In this book, I have examined some of the everyday ways of thinking and acting to which the Yukon agreements give rise. These everyday practices take for granted – and thus help enact – Yukon First Nations as (semi-)sovereign state-like political entities. There is a widespread tendency to assume that Yukon First Nations are the modern heirs to fully sovereign indigenous polities whose existence long pre-dated the arrival of Euro-Canadians. In this view, Canada's assertion of sovereignty in the Yukon is unjust precisely because it ignores First Nations' prior sovereignty. If this were so, then the Yukon agreements could appropriately be viewed as part of a belated but necessary effort to recognize the indigenous polities of the Yukon, incorporate them more fully and fairly into the Canadian federation, and restore to them some of their territory and powers of self-government. In fact, however, there were no state-like social entities in the Yukon prior to Canada's assertion of colonial rule; the existence of geographically and socially bounded First Nations is a brand new phenomenon in the region. So rather than merely recognizing already-existing First Nations and restoring some of their powers, the agreements must be doing something else.

As we saw in chapter 2, social organization prior to the colonial era was flexible; social and political identities were relative and context-dependent rather than categorical and territorially constituted. Humans were bound up with one another, animals, and other features of the land in a web of kinship and reciprocal social relations that transcended linear notions of space and time and governed how human and other-than-human persons should interact with one another. In contrast, Yukon Indian people today are increasingly likely to regard themselves (at least at times and in certain contexts) as members of one or another culturally distinct "nation," each of which asserts partial control over the non-human "resources" within its clearly defined territorial boundaries and whose "people" (a category that not only excludes non-humans but also, at least ideally, implies cultural and linguistic homogeneity) travel a linear path together from time immemorial and into the distant future. These far-reaching changes in world view are essential aspects of a process of First Nation state formation that was born of Canadian colonial policies (and Yukon Indian peoples' struggles against them) and came of age with the signing of the Yukon land claim and self-government agreements.

It is hard to imagine how things could have been otherwise. Sovereignty, along with its ethno-territorial and temporal entailments, is so fundamental a premise of contemporary political thought that indigenous Yukon practices are hardly even recognizable to state officials as a form of politics at all, much less a viable "modern" alternative to colonial rule. There was simply no chance that the Canadian government would have signed off on a self-government agreement enabling Yukon Indian people to organize themselves as they had prior to the advent of colonialism – nor is it at all clear that such organization, if allowed, would serve to safeguard the interests of Yukon Indian people in the context of the contemporary settler state. First Nation self-government had to be state-like or it would not have qualified as "government" at all. In fact, a central challenge for Yukon Indian people when they were negotiating their agreements was to convince the federal officials that they were capable of self-government (i.e., that they were "no longer" too "primitive" to govern themselves), and the only permissible evidence of this capacity was the ability to establish and run a state-like government (Nadasdy 2003: 250–1). Yukon First Nation negotiators thus found themselves in a grimly ironic position: the only way they could convince federal negotiators that they were politically mature enough to handle "self-government" was to agree to the establishment of a political system that was not their own. So, although the emergence of state-like First Nations has indeed provided Yukon Indian people with powerful new tools for regaining some control over their lives and safeguarding their lands, those tools come at a price; to use them requires a radical transformation in how they relate to one another, animals, and the land.

This is not to say that the new statist ways of thinking about and relating to one another, the land, and animals have entirely replaced older ways. On the contrary, as I have argued throughout this book and elsewhere (see also Nadasdy 2007b; Nadasdy 2011), relationships based on kinship and reciprocity (among humans as well as between human and non-human persons) are alive and well in the Yukon. Not only are they surviving, but they continue to evolve as Yukon Indian people adapt to changing circumstances. For, while there are some Yukon Indian people, like Gerald Dickson whom we met in chapter 3, who reject outright their First Nation citizenship and all it stands for, there are others who subvert the changes brought about by the agreements in ways that are perhaps less confrontational but no less effective, such as the young hunter we met in chapter 2 who cultivates "hunting buddies" all around the Yukon to circumvent the territorializing provisions of the new wildlife management regime. Relationships of kinship and reciprocity remain strong and cut across ethno-territorial boundaries, in many cases mediating its effects (as we saw in Kluane and White River elders' refusal to draw a contiguous line between their respective territories; and, in other parts of the Yukon, through the negotiation of sharing accords). Many Yukon Indian people remain profoundly uncomfortable with the assumption of human control implicit in the idea that a First Nation has jurisdiction over the "resources" within its territory, so they often reject practices based on such assumptions and/or act in ways that are more compatible with their own ideas of human–animal relations (see chapter 2 and Nadasdy 2011). Yet, like it or not, ethno-territoriality has become an increasingly important principle in the lives of all Yukon Indian people.

First Nation citizenship now *matters* to Yukon Indian people in a way that Indian Act band membership previously did not (though, to be sure, band membership mattered too). One's First Nation citizenship has implications for where one lives and hunts and for what kind of government programs and services one is eligible. There are times and contexts in which it is no longer sufficient to draw on ties of kinship or reciprocity to make one's way in the world. Yukon Indian people who are not citizens of Champagne-Aishihik First Nation, for example, can no longer draw solely on their kinship ties if they want to hunt along Fourth of July Creek; instead, they must now obtain and abide by the terms of either a formal permit from CAFN or a hunting licence from the Yukon government. The new legal and political differences between "the people" of one First Nation and another are very real; and Yukon Indian people cannot help but be aware of them and take them into account in the everyday decisions they make about how to live their lives. As these legal and political differences become institutionalized – in, for example, the agreements' provisions for managing wildlife and heritage resources that we examined in chapters 2 and 4, respectively – there is a growing tendency to view them as rooted in and justified by differences in culture and history – rather than vice versa. Although still in its early stages, the emergence of ethno-nationalism, which is implicit in the notion of sovereignty, is clearly under way in the Yukon. So it should come as no surprise that citizens of Yukon First Nations are increasingly availing themselves of many of the classic techniques used by nationalists everywhere[1] to enact and narrate the nation as a socio-political entity with deep historical roots in its territorial homeland.

What are the implications of all this for thinking about "indigenous sovereignty"? Is such a thing possible? Or is *sovereignty* utterly incompatible with indigenous North American thought and practice, as Taiaiake Alfred (1999: xiv) has suggested? Given the cultural heterogeneity of indigenous North America, I would not presume to offer a general answer for the entire continent, but I hope to have made the case in this book that sovereignty *does* entail ways of being, knowing, and interacting with other people, animals, and the land that are incompatible with indigenous Yukon ways of living in and engaging with the world. These are not superficial incompatibilities that can be eliminated with some creative tinkering around the edges of what we mean by *sovereignty*, *citizenship*, and *nationhood*. They are more fundamental than that. Indigenous practices in the Yukon are rooted in a radically different way of being in the world and of organizing relations among humans, animals, and the land. The world such practices bring into being is fundamentally incompatible with the colonial state – and also with the First Nation states created in its image. In that world, terms like

1 This includes American Indian nationalists in other parts of the continent (see Lyons 2010: chaps. 3, 4).

sovereignty, jurisdiction, citizenship, nation, history, and even *indigeneity* are meaningless. Such ways of knowing and being in the world constitute a fundamental challenge to the state form itself and to the exercise of state(-like) power, whether by First Nation or settler state officials. It is precisely because they threaten the state order that indigenous Yukon knowledge and practices *must* be marginalized, dismissed as so much primitive and superstitious nonsense.

This suggests that "indigenous sovereignty" is something of a contradiction in terms (in the Yukon, at least). This is not to say that Yukon Indian people cannot or should not strive for political, economic, and cultural autonomy. It is merely to suggest that sovereignty – with or without "indigenous" as a modifier – is an inappropriate tool if the goal is to protect and maintain indigenous Yukon ways of knowing and being in the world. Rather than Yukon Indian people embracing their "indigenous sovereignty," it seems to me, such a goal requires the practice of a kind of radical "anti-sovereignty"; that is, a total rejection of the state form and all the cultural baggage that goes with it. It is worth thinking through the notion of anti-sovereignty a bit further.

One potential synonym of "anti-sovereignty," of course, is "anarchy." I hesitate a bit to apply this term to indigenous forms of social organization because of the ideological baggage that inevitably accompanies it.[2] As Holly High (2012a: 93) points out, the term typically invokes either "terrifying images of rudderless chaos [in] a world of brute force and pointless destruction" or romantic visions of a thoroughly egalitarian society characterized by "harmony between free agents, and human needs met through a multiplicity of voluntary associations" (Macdonald 2009: 5–6 refers to these as the "regressive" and "utopian" manifestations of anarchy). Over the years, each of these images of anarchy has played an important (and unfortunate) role in shaping both scholarly and popular understandings of indigenous peoples. We encountered the regressive image of anarchy-as-chaos in chapter 1, where we saw it serving as the essential "outside" of Hobbesian sovereignty, a realm of lawlessness and savagery so terrifying it compels all right-thinking

2 An alternative term, arguably with less – or at least different – ideological baggage, is "anarchism," but I prefer "anarchy" here, because it suggests a set of practices rather than a strand of (largely Euro-American) political philosophy (but see Craib 2015 on some of anarchism's non-Euro-American roots). Barclay (1982: 13–16) makes a similar distinction between anarchy and anarchism. Anarchism as political theory, however, is useful for thinking about the range of anarchical practices.

humans to band together in sovereign communities where they can enter into ordered political relations with one another. Recall that Hobbes himself used the indigenous peoples of North America as the prototypical example of the savage and superstitious denizens of that apolitical space. It is in this pejorative sense (anarchy-as-chaos) that the term has long been used to characterize stateless peoples as primitive savages utterly lacking in social and political organization – thus justifying all manner of harmful colonial interventions to "civilize" them (i.e., bring them into the protective embrace of sovereignty, where they will not only be safe from chaos and violence, but where they can also join the world of progress, science, and history).

One problem with this view of anarchy (apart from the racism that so often underlies it) is that it equates the absence of the state with the lack of any social and political order at all (an equation that follows logically from the Hobbesian assumption that sovereignty is the precondition for politics). Anthropologists are particularly well placed to correct this misconception, since we have studied non-state societies the world over, identifying in the process a wide range of strategies (particularly among hunting and horticultural peoples) for structuring social relations that rely on neither state institutions nor hierarchical decision-making processes.[3] From early on, anthropologists were careful to stress that "anarchy" is not the same thing as "chaos," as in Evans-Pritchard's famous characterization of the stateless Nuer: "The Nuer constitution is highly individualistic and libertarian. It is an acephalous state, lacking legislative, judicial, and executive organs. Nevertheless, it is far from chaotic. It has a consistent and coherent form which might be called 'ordered anarchy'" (1940b: 296).

Most anthropologists studying stateless societies have followed Evans-Pritchard in stressing the systematic, ordered, and logical ways people in non-state societies structure their social and political relations. Indeed, many – no doubt at least in part out of a desire to avoid the Hobbesian connotations of "anarchy" – have eschewed use of the

3 Indeed, anarchist thinkers have often turned to the ethnographic literature on indigenous/non-state people for inspiration and examples of "actually existing" anarchy (Kropotkin 1902; Maxwell and Craib 2015; Robinson and Tormey 2012; Scott 2009). And David Graeber (2004: 16–20) suggests that anarchist politics in fact animated the theoretical interests of some of the central figures in the discipline's early history, including A.R. Radcliffe-Brown and Marcel Mauss.

term entirely, preferring instead to write about "non-state," "egalitarian," or – again, following Evans-Pritchard – "acephalous" societies. This has changed in recent decades as anthropologists have begun to think explicitly about "anarchy" as a political form.[4] Harold Barclay, one of the first anthropologists to attempt a theorization of anarchic political systems, was explicit in his rejection of the Hobbesian equation of government and politics: "Not only do all societies have politics, but they have political organization or political systems – that is, standardized ways of dealing with power problems. Political organization is not a synonym for government. Government is *one* form of political organization. Politics may be handled in a variety of ways; government is just one of those ways" (Barclay 1982: 21).

If, following Barclay and others, we define anarchy not as "chaos" but simply as the condition of society in which there is no government or state apparatus,[5] then indigenous society in the Yukon was clearly anarchic prior to the arrival of Euro-Canadians. Its fluidity, decentralization, non-territoriality, and (from state officials' perspective)

4 Among the first to write explicitly about anarchy were Clastres (1987, originally published in French in 1974) and Barclay (1982). Since then, anthropologists have become increasingly interested in the topic; see, for example, recent works by Graeber (2004), Macdonald (2009), Scott (2009), High (2012b), and Bettinger (2015). Significantly, most anthropologists continue to stress the point that anarchy does not necessarily imply chaos/disorder and seek to describe and analyse the order underlying such systems. In what at first appears to be an exception to this rule, Judith Scheele has recently argued that some anarchic systems (in her case, the Tubu of northern Chad) are in fact characterized by disorder. But this is not the disorder invoked by Hobbes: "[The Tubu do not] live in some kind of a pre-social or spontaneous state of nature; 'disorder' is carefully codified, and part of public spectacle. Much effort goes into being 'anarchic' in just the right way; 'disorder' is a virtue and needs to be understood as such; and this positive notion of 'anarchy' – autonomy is perhaps a better word here – shapes local notions of personhood and value" (Scheele 2015: 36). Evidently, the disorder of Tubu anarchy, too, is ordered.

5 Barclay (1982: 13) defines anarchy as "the condition of society in which there is no ruler." Similarly, anthropologist Charles Macdonald (2009: 1) defines anarchic social organization as "a situation where rules of conduct are not enforced by any government apparatus," and Robert Bettinger (2015: 12) uses the term "in its literal sense to mean 'without rulers,' referring more broadly to a system without a publicly enforced government." These anthropological definitions resonate with those of classical anarchist thinkers. Petr Kropotkin (1995: 233), for instance, defined anarchism as "a principle or theory of life and conduct under which society is conceived without government – harmony in such a society being obtained, not by submission

unpredictability may have *looked* to Euro-Canadian observers like "chaos," but it was not; it was simply governed by a radically different set of organizing principles than was the expanding Canadian state. The problem, of course, is that in attempting to characterize non-state forms of social order it is difficult to avoid drawing on analytic terms (including *society* and *social order*) that arise from a statist view of society as a geographically, socially, and temporally bounded social entity.

The other, utopian, sense of the term *anarchy*, too, has long served as a basis for (mis)understanding indigenous peoples. Indeed, the romantic image of anarchy-as-egalitarian freedom underlies the age-old stereotype of the "noble savage" in exactly the same way the regressive image of anarchy props up the stereotype of ignoble savagery. Berkhofer (1978) observes that the noble and ignoble savages are not so much different stereotypes as different evaluations of the same stereotype. After all, both of these mythic figures are "savages" precisely because they live outside the bounds of sovereign society and so lack all of the cultural attributes that sovereignty entails: politics, law, science, history, and so on. Whether one views these savages as noble or ignoble depends entirely on one's evaluation of sovereign society and its sociocultural trappings. Those who accept the Hobbesian view that sovereignty is the precondition for politics and civilized life cannot help but view the figure of the "savage" with fear and contempt. By contrast, those critical of the state and of Euro-American civilization more broadly have long tended to view the figure of the savage in a more positive light. Because they lack all the trappings of sovereign society, savages are also supposedly free of all of the problems and character flaws associated with the state: authoritarianism, political corruption, inequality, alienation from nature, and so on. From this perspective, savagery is stripped of many of its negative connotations and becomes instead a foil for critiquing the shortcomings of state society, and the extra-sovereign savage appears not as bloodthirsty and violent, but rather as the "original democrat," staunch defender of personal liberty and as-yet uncorrupted citizen of a "natural" egalitarian society.

---

to law, or by obedience to any authority, but by free agreements concluded between various groups, territorial and professional, freely constituted for the sake of production and consumption, as also for the satisfaction of the infinite variety of needs and aspirations of a civilized being." Note his assertion, contra Hobbes, that anarchic society is composed of "civilized" beings.

The problem with this seemingly positive stereotype is that it paints indigenous peoples and their societies as one-dimensional caricatures, the straightforward negation of all that is supposedly wrong with life in the sovereign state. In fact, although they may tend more towards the egalitarian end of the political spectrum than do state societies, non-state societies described by anthropologists are never the egalitarian utopias some theorists suppose them to be. On the contrary, violence and (sometimes extreme) social inequality can be found in non-state societies too.[6] It is very difficult for anyone labouring under the image of indigenous people as noble savages to recognize the complexity and variety of indigenous social relations – much less their contemporary relations with the sovereign state (for a full discussion, see Nadasdy 2005a). Many anthropologists have been favourably impressed by the stateless societies they studied and have often defended their research subjects against the charges of "ignoble savagery" levelled against them by state officials, charges often used to justify assimilationist and sometimes even genocidal policies. In so doing, it can be hard not to tap into the noble savage stereotype, always so close at hand, and simply counter one stereotype with another – while taking a satisfying jab at "the state" in the process.[7] Indigenous people themselves often strategically invoke the image of savage nobility (in one guise or another) in their struggles with state officials, although this is a risky strategy that can sometimes backfire (Nadasdy 2005a; see also Conklin and Graham 1995). If we want to understand indigenous peoples and their long and fraught relationships with the territorial states encompassing them, however, we must scrupulously avoid any recourse to either of these pernicious stereotypes and the misconceptions of anarchy that underlie them.

So what would radical indigenous anti-sovereignty actually look like? There can be no single or straightforward answer to this question. The difficulty is that both "anti-sovereignty" and "anarchy" are

6 The most common forms of inequality in non-state societies are based on gender and age set, though other forms are possible too. If Legros (1985) is correct, for example, nineteenth-century Tutchone society in the central Yukon was an anarchic system characterized by extreme levels of inequality. For a comprehensive theory on how principles of northern Athapaskan kinship can lead to socio-economic differentiation in a non-state context, see Ives (1990).

7 Jonsson (2012) has critiqued Scott's (2009) celebration of anarchic social organization in upland southeast Asia on precisely these grounds.

oppositional terms, defined only by what they are not. There is a great variety of possible forms of anarchic social organization; the Nuer, after all, organize their social relations very differently than do northern Athapaskan peoples, yet both can be categorized as anarchic. David Graeber (2004: 40) notes that the range of possible anarchic forms of social organization necessarily includes "an endless variety of communities, associations, networks, projects on every conceivable scale, overlapping and intersecting in any way we could imagine and possibly many that we can't ... There are endless examples of viable anarchism: pretty much any form of organization would count as one, so long as it was not imposed by some higher authority."[8]

Given his critique of sovereignty, it is perhaps not surprising that Taiaiake Alfred, too, has gestured towards what he calls "anarcho-indigenism" (2005a: 45–6) on the grounds that any effective anti-colonial movement must avoid "the institutional-organizational approach to confronting state power, which structures resistance in forms of counter-imperial organizations that mimic the state in order to confront it on its own terms" (ibid.: 56).[9] Rather than build their own state-like

8 Petr Kropotkin (1995: 233–4) painted a similarly broad picture of anarchist society: "In a society developed along these lines, the voluntary associations which already now begin to cover all the fields of human activity would take a still greater extension so as to substitute for the state in all its functions. They would represent an interwoven network, composed of an infinite variety of groups and federations of all sizes and degrees, local, regional, national and international – temporary or more or less permanent – for all possible purposes: production, consumption and exchange, communications, sanitary arrangements, education, mutual protection, defence of the territory and so on; and, on the other side, for the satisfaction of an ever-increasing number of scientific, artistic, literary and sociable needs."

9 Others, too, have argued that because indigenous politics are fundamentally anarchic, any strategy that either reproduces state-like institutions or acknowledges the overarching sovereignty of the capitalist settler state (e.g., the liberal politics of recognition in Canada) necessarily reproduces relations of colonialism (Day 2001). It is worth pointing out that anarchism as political theory arose largely in opposition to capitalism. Indeed, many anarchist thinkers oppose the state precisely because they see it as the chief mechanism enabling capitalist exploitation (see, e.g., Kropotkin 1995: 234–5). Glen Coulthard (2014) has recently made the analogous argument that settler colonialism (i.e., the forcible incorporation of indigenous lands and peoples into settler states) serves primarily to facilitate capitalist exploitation of indigenous lands and peoples. If this is so (and I, at least, am convinced that it is), then it is hard to see how the creation of oppositional First Nations states can solve the fundamental problem of exploitation. This lends additional force to Alfred's argument that the only effective response to colonialism is an anarchist rather than a statist one.

institutions to oppose those of the settler state, he argues, indigenous people should look instead to their own cultures as "the foundation of indigenous resurgence." Only there will they discover the culturally appropriate "tactics of militant non-violence and anti-institutional strategies" for combatting settler colonialism (ibid.; see also Coulthard 2014). Although Alfred himself explores some potential strategies along these lines, it seems clear – given the cultural diversity among indigenous peoples (some of whom had hierarchical – even state-like – forms of social organization prior to contact with Europeans) – that there can be no single anti-colonial strategy that is "culturally appropriate" for all indigenous peoples. After all, "indigeneity," like "anarchy" and "anti-sovereignty," is an oppositional term (vis-à-vis the state) whose positive semantic content is underdetermined. "Anarcho-indigenisms," then, must always be spoken of in the plural (and some "indigenisms" will not be anarchical at all).

Calls for "culturally appropriate" political strategies to combat settler colonialism bring to mind the arguments for cultural sovereignty and the indigenization of the state discussed in chapter 1. Whatever their shortcomings, these arguments do at least acknowledge the constraints imposed on indigenous politics by the settler state. In the current political context, there can be no wholesale rejection of the settler state and restoration of the "ordered anarchies" of the past. For the foreseeable future at least, any anarcho-indigenist practices will necessarily take place inside – and in complex articulation with – existing settler state institutions. I have described some examples of this in the pages of this book; and the Zapatista movement, perhaps the best known "actually existing" anarcho-indigenous movement in the world today, illustrates just how complex relations between such movements and existing settler states can be. Although it has inspired Alfred and other indigenous scholars, Klein (2015) argues that the movement cannot be characterized as either "indigenous" or "anarchical" in any straightforward way. While it has certainly been shaped in important ways by indigenous beliefs and practices, it has also incorporated elements (and people) drawn from Marxist, Maoist, Guevarist, and liberation theology traditions; and the local institutions and practices of Zapatista governance are heavily hybridized forms that show the influence of all these different political approaches. Similarly, Zapatismo cannot be characterized as purely anarchical, since alongside its decentralized and participatory practices of governance it also maintains a centralized and hierarchically structured guerilla army that continues to play an important role in the movement. It seems that whatever else they do, anarcho-indigenous social movements will have to find ways of articulating with the institutions of the settler state – even if only to hold them at bay (witness the Zapatistas' recently announced intentions to field a candidate in Mexico's 2018 presidential elections; see Niembro 2017).

All of this suggests that any attempt to produce a nuanced understanding of indigenous politics in the context of the settler state must begin by rejecting the assumption – widespread in both popular and academic discourse – that there are two radically different types of societies, state and non-state, each characterized by radically different kinds of geographical, social, and temporal relations. Such an assumption creates a binary distinction; any particular society either qualifies as a "state" (or as "state-like") or it does not; it is either ordered by the principles of sovereignty or by those of anarchy. This binary is problematic because it assumes that state formation entails the total eradication and replacement of one way of knowing/relating/being in the world with another. This implies a radical break between "us" (inhabitants of states) and "them" and treats state formation as a completed project rather than as an ongoing process. It also precludes any possibility that non-state forms of knowledge and social relations might survive and even shape ongoing processes of state formation.

As Holly High (2012a: 95) points out, any study that presents the state as "all-pervasive" and "ever-present" is necessarily blind to "those instances where state formation not only falters and fails ... but also those instances [within states] where state formation is either not attempted, or is opposed, or is irrelevant." In fact, nowhere is the "cultural revolution" of state formation complete. Contrary to popular belief, the rise of the territorial state has not consigned all ostensibly non-state forms of social relations, knowledge, and practice to the dust heap of history. Just as nonlinear temporalities continue to govern important social domains within the territorial state (Ingold 2000: 336–8; Richland 2008: 21; Turnbull 2004) so, too, do supposedly "anarchic" principles of socio-political organization, such as kinship and reciprocity. In fact, such principles are already at work in many aspects of life in state societies (Graeber 2000; Ward 1973) – and even at the heart of that quintessentially statist political institution, government bureaucracy (Herzfeld 1992; Lea 2012). As we saw in chapter 4, even supposedly "modern" ideologies such as nationalism, a statist ideology if there ever was one, can be viewed productively as a contemporary way of reckoning kinship (on a large scale) with roots in age-old practices of ancestor worship.[10]

So, while there can be analytic value in separating state and non-state societies as ideal types, as I have done at times in this book, the complex ways in which these forms actually appear and interact within existing societies suggests that rather than thinking of "state"/"sovereignty" and "non-state"/"anarchy" as terms that refer to different *kinds* of societies, we might more productively think of them as organizing principles that can exist to differing degrees – and always in tension with one another – in all societies.[11] Even the term "principle" here is somewhat problematic, because it may imply a more unitary and coherent societal blueprint than I have in mind. Nevertheless, one might plausibly claim that the "principle of sovereignty" consists of something like the relatively coherent and interrelated set of territorial, social, and temporal boundary-making assumptions and processes I examine in this book. Given the endless variety of actually existing and potential anarchical systems, any attempt to articulate a single coherent "principle of anarchy" is necessarily problematic, but I have in mind something like the set of decentralized, anti-institutional, and consensus-based political practices/principles outlined by James Tully in his recent (2014: 33–73) discussions of "civic citizenship."[12] In any case, recent anthropological

10 Graeber (2004: 51–3) is explicitly critical of those who refer to non-state societies as "kin-based," precisely because this incorrectly implies that kinship is irrelevant to the "modern" ways of organizing social relations in state societies: race, class, and gender. There is a long tradition in anthropology, from Lowie (1927) to Graeber (2004), insisting that "the state" is not nearly so quite so new and different from what came before as is often supposed.

11 Similarly, Martin Buber drew a distinction between what he called the "political principle," characterized by "power, authority, hierarchy, and dominion" and the "social principle," which is visible in "all spontaneous human associations built around a common need or common interest" (see Ward 2004: 26).

12 Tully is not generally considered an anarchist thinker, nor I suspect would he consider himself to be one. Indeed, as Shaw (2008: chap. 7) demonstrates, he took sovereignty very much for granted as the precondition for politics in his influential work on constitutionalism in Canada (1995). Yet, even then, his vision of voluntary federalism rooted in (and strengthened by) sociocultural diversity resonated powerfully with similar visions articulated by nineteenth-century anarchist thinkers such as Proudhon and Bakunin (Ward 2004: chap. 9). In his more recent work, Tully has become explicitly critical of sovereignty and the forms of sociality it entails (e.g., 2014: 59–61). At times, taking a cue from Taiaiake Alfred, he even advocates a radical rethinking (indigenization?) of the concept, as for example when he claims that

treatments of anarchy explicitly warn against "attribute[ing] anarchy in blanket terms to entire peoples, societies, or geographic zones," stressing instead that, "when we start exploring state and anarchic forms of social relationship together we will find both in uneven and patchy dispersal wherever we look" (High 2012a: 102, 105; see also Graeber 2004). It follows that there is no such thing as a "pure" state or non-state society. This is certainly the case today, where ostensibly non-state peoples' ways of knowing, relating, and being in the world have been shaped – in some cases for thousands of years now – by their interaction with states (and vice versa).[13] It is possible that no society has ever been entirely free of the categorical boundary-making processes of the "sovereignty principle" – and the legitimized violence, hierarchy, and inequality they authorize – even if the principle of sovereignty is clearly more dominant in some societies than in others. Examining the process of state formation, then, requires a careful analysis of the ways in which principles of social organization that are ostensibly incompatible with

"[indigenous peoples'] prior and continuing 'sovereignty' does not refer to state sovereignty, but, rather, to a stateless, self-governing and autonomous people, equal in status, but not in form, to the Canadian state" (2008: 280). Although sovereignty still colours his view of indigenous–state relations in Canada (see, e.g., Tully 2008: chap. 8), it is significant that he now holds up Gandhi's avowedly anti-state philosophy as an "exemplar" of the kind of politics he has in mind with his notion of "civic citizenship" (Tully 2014: 83, see also pp. 83–4, 96–100). While some might prefer to look to more avowedly anarchist thinkers to elucidate the "principle of anarchy' (see, for example, Ward 2004), Tully's thinking is particularly important in the context of my argument here, because he has come to his increasingly anti-sovereign position in large part through a deep and sustained engagement with indigenous political thought and practice.

13 This is a point stressed by many, even some of those accused of romanticizing non-state peoples. Following Fried (1975) and Clastres (1987), for example, Scott argues that the anarchic societies of highland southeast Asia (and elsewhere) are not merely *non-state* but actively *anti-state*, and that many of their beliefs and practices arose *in opposition to* nearby states. Although area specialists have criticized the empirical basis for both Clastres's and Scott's elaborate claims to this effect (see, respectively, Nugent 2012; Jonsson 2012), there is no doubt that non-state hunting and horticultural peoples have developed a wide range of social mechanisms – chief among them the requirement to share resources widely – that serve, among other things, to minimize social inequality (Lee 1979; Peterson 1993; Sahlins 1972). Indeed, some anarchist thinkers have seized on "the gift" as the key to anarchic social relations (Martin 2012).

those of sovereignty continue to inform social relations, knowledge, and practices within state-like political organizations.[14]

The emerging First Nation states of the Yukon are especially illustrative in this regard, precisely because they are so obviously still works in progress. While the process of First Nation state formation in the Yukon has certainly marginalized many indigenous ways of knowing, relating, and being, it has not eradicated them. On the contrary, they remain important to many – though not all – Yukon Indian people, who continue to use them, at least in some contexts, to structure their interactions with one another, with the land and animals, and sometimes even with Yukon and Canadian state officials. And, as we have seen, Yukon Indian people use them in many different ways. Occasionally they serve as the basis upon which to reject the First Nation state entirely. Recall, for example, some KFN citizens' refusal to obtain firewood permits in chapter 2, Gerald Dickson's rejection of his KFN citizenship in chapter 3, and Yukon Indian people's ongoing refusal to engage in catch-and-release fishing, as discussed in chapter 5. Just as often, however, Yukon Indian people tap into indigenous principles of social organization to subvert statist forms, as for example in the development of the hunting buddy system discussed in chapter 2. Sometimes Yukon Indian people even manage to successfully translate their ideas about proper social relations into terms that are generally compatible with the language and institutions of the state, thus mitigating some of its most disruptive effects. Recall, for instance, the negotiation of First Nation sharing accords (discussed in chapters 2 and 4) and the fact that Kluane and White River elders' refusal to draw a clear territorial boundary between their respective First Nations led to the unusual – though not altogether unprecedented – solution of shared jurisdiction described in chapter 4.

Because Yukon Indian people now deploy indigenous forms of knowing, being, and relating in the context of – and often in direct response to – processes of First Nation state formation, they are intimately shaped by that context. At the same time, because First Nation, Yukon, and Canadian officials must take these indigenous forms into account,

14 Tully, too, suggests (2014: esp. 87–100) that all liberal democratic states are – and should be – composed of a mélange of both civil (sovereign state) and civic (anti-sovereign) citizenship practices, though he clearly believes the latter should predominate.

they help shape the social forms and practices of the always-emerging First Nation and Canadian states. This can result in just the sort of uneven patchwork described by High (2012a), as when, for example, First Nation citizenship coexists uneasily alongside older relativistic forms of political identity. Sometimes, however, even the notion of a patchwork falls short, as brand new hybrid forms emerge. Take, as examples, the rise of the informal hunting buddy system and the negotiation of First Nation sharing accords. Rooted as they are in indigenous norms of sharing and reciprocity, both of these developments can be viewed as strategies that tap into indigenous/anarchic forms to subvert the territorial imperatives of the First Nation state – or at least mitigate the effects of state territoriality. At the same time, however, both sets of practices and the social relations they engender are new and truly hybrid social forms that would never have emerged but for the interplay between sovereign and indigenous/anarchic impulses. It is these new forms and their incorporation into the fabric of the First Nation state, it seems to me, that correspond most closely to what indigenous studies scholars mean when they write about the "indigenization" of the state.

The emergence of such hybrid forms indicates that non-state ways of seeing and being in the world can play a significant role in the process of First Nation state formation and can even mitigate some of its effects – rendering First Nation states more palatable to Yukon Indian people. As I indicated in chapter 1, however, "indigenization" of this sort is a profoundly ambivalent process. Precisely because they render the new First Nation states more palatable to Yukon Indian people, sharing accords and hunting buddies help entrench the sovereign state form – along with all the territorial, social, and temporal assumptions upon which it depends – in the everyday lives of Yukon Indian people. In the Yukon, at least, where there was nothing remotely state-like before the advent of colonialism, even the emergence of fully "indigenized" First Nation states (which Yukon First Nations certainly are not) would represent a cultural imposition with profound and far-reaching consequences. An "indigenized" state is, after all, still a state. And all states – not just indigenized ones – feature practices and institutions that derive in whole or in part from principles other than (and sometimes quite inconsistent with) those of the sovereign ideal; this in and of itself does not make them any less state-like.

In this book, I have examined some of the consequences arising from the gradual imposition of the state form in the Yukon. These include quite dramatic transformations in how Yukon Indian people conceive of and relate to one another, animals, and the land. As I mentioned in the introduction, I try to remain neutral about these changes; and Yukon Indian people themselves are quite mixed in how they perceive them. There are many who view the Yukon agreements and the First Nation states to which they give rise as the best deal they were going to get and have pragmatically set out to use the legal and political tools now at their disposal – indigenized where possible – to build state-like institutions for governing themselves and protecting their lands and resources. They can hardly be faulted for doing so. Cultures are always changing, and the changes ushered in by the Yukon agreements can easily be viewed as more or less successful adaptations to the realities of life in the twenty-first-century Yukon. Yet, there is an irony here. Yukon Indian people first entered into land claim negotiations because they wanted a way to safeguard their way of life in the face of Canadian colonial expansion. But because they are rooted in a set of assumptions about the world that relegate indigenous ways of relating to other humans, the land, animals to the realm of primitive superstition, the resulting agreements actively undermine the very way of life many Yukon Indian people had hoped to protect. So, although Yukon Indian people, like colonized peoples elsewhere, have adopted the discourse and practices of sovereignty and turned them to their own ends in the struggle against colonial domination, the process of First Nation state formation to which this struggle gave rise takes for granted a deeper colonial logic about the modernity of the colonizer and the backwardness of the colonized (Chatterjee 1993). In adopting a "modern" (read: state-like) form of governance, Yukon Indian people are also compelled to adopt state-derived ways of knowing and being in the world. In this way, the Yukon agreements serve as extensions of the colonial project.

Bibliography

Abbott, Andrew. 1995. "Things of Boundaries." *Social Research* 62 (4): 857–82.

Abu-Lughod, Lila. 1990. "The Romance of Resistance: Tracing Transformations of Power through Bedouin Women." *American Ethnologist* 17 (1): 41–55. https://doi.org/10.1525/ae.1990.17.1.02a00030.

Agamben, Giorgio. 2004. *The Open: Man and Animal*. Stanford, CA: Stanford University Press.

Agnew, John. 1994. "The Territorial Trap: The Geographical Assumptions of International Relations Theory." *Review of International Political Economy* 1 (1): 53–80. https://doi.org/10.1080/09692299408434268.

Agnew, John. 2005. "Sovereignty Regimes: Territoriality and State Authority in Contemporary World Politics." *Annals of the Association of American Geographers* 95 (2): 437–61. https://doi.org/10.1111/j.1467-8306.2005.00468.x.

Albers, Patricia. 1996. "Changing Patterns of Ethnicity in the Northeastern Plains, 1780–1870." In *History, Power, and Identity: Ethnogenesis in the Americas, 1492–1992*, ed. Jonathan David Hill, 90–118. Iowa City: University of Iowa Press.

Aleinikoff, Thomas Alexander. 2002. *Semblances of Sovereignty: The Constitution, the State, and American Citizenship*. Cambridge, MA: Harvard University Press.

Alfred, Taiaiake. 1999. *Peace, Power, Righteousness: An Indigenous Manifesto*. Don Mills, ON: Oxford University Press.

Alfred, Taiaiake. 2005a. *Wasáse: Indigenous Pathways of Action and Freedom*. Peterborough, ON: Broadview Press.

Alfred, Taiaiake. 2005b. "Sovereignty." In *Sovereignty Matters: Locations of Contestation and Possibility in Indigenous Struggles for Self-Determination*, ed. Joanne Barker, 33–50. Lincoln: University of Nebraska Press.

Anaya, S. James. 2004. *Indigenous Peoples in International Law*. 2nd ed. New York: Oxford University Press.

Anderson, Benedict. 1990. "The Idea of Power in Javanese Culture." In *Language and Power: Exploring Political Cultures in Indonesia*, 17–77. Ithaca, NY: Cornell University Press.

Anderson, Benedict. 1991. *Imagined Communities: Reflections on the Origin and Spread of Nationalism*. Rev. ed. New York: Verso.

Anderson, James. 1986. "Nationalism and Geography." In *The Rise of the Modern State*, ed. James Anderson, 115–42. Atlantic Highlands, NJ: Humanities Press International.

Anderson, James. 1988. "Nationalist Ideology and Territory." In *Nationalism, Self-Determination and Political Geography*, ed. R.J. Johnston, David B. Knight, and Eleonore Kofman, 18–39. London: Croom Helm.

Anderson, James. 1996. "The Shifting Stage of Politics: New Medieval and Postmodern Territorialities." *Environment and Planning D, Society & Space* 14 (2): 133–53. https://doi.org/10.1068/d140133.

Anderson, Jeffrey. 2011. "The History of Time in the Northern Arapaho Tribe." *Ethnohistory* 58 (2): 229–61. https://doi.org/10.1215/00141801-1163028.

Anderson, Malcolm. 1997. *Frontiers: Territory and State Formation in the Modern World*. Malden, MA: Polity Press.

Appadurai, Arjun. 2003. "Sovereignty without Territory: Notes for a Post-national Geography." In *The Anthropology of Space and Place*, ed. S. Low and D. Lawrence-Zúñiga, 337–49. Oxford: Blackwell.

Ardrey, Robert. 1966. *The Territorial Imperative: A Personal Inquiry into the Animal Origins of Property and Nations*. 1st ed. New York: Atheneum.

Asch, Michael. 1989. "Wildlife: Defining the Animals the Dene Hunt and the Settlement of Aboriginal Rights Claims." *Canadian Public Policy* 15 (2): 205–19. https://doi.org/10.2307/3551163.

Asch, Michael. 1999. "From Calder to Van Der Peet: Aboriginal Rights and Canadian Law, 1973–96." In *Indigenous People's Rights in Australia, Canada, and New Zealand*, ed. P. Havemann, 428–46. New York: Oxford University Press.

Asch, Michael. 2000. "First Nations and the Derivation of Canada's Underlying Title: Comparing Perspectives on Legal Ideology." In *Aboriginal Rights and Self-Government: The Canadian and Mexican Experience in North American Perspective*, ed. Curtis Cook and Juan David Lindau, 148–67. Montreal: McGill-Queen's University Press.

Asch, Michael. 2002. "From Terra Nullius to Affirmation: Reconciling Aboriginal Rights with the Canadian Constitution." *Canadian Journal of Law and Society* 17 (2): 23–39. https://doi.org/10.1017/S0829320100007237.

Asch, Michael. 2013. "On the Land Cession Provisions in Treaty 11." *Ethnohistory* 60 (3): 451–67. https://doi.org/10.1215/00141801-2140713.

Asch, Michael. 2014. *On Being Here to Stay: Treaties and Aboriginal Rights in Canada*. Toronto: University of Toronto Press.

Auditor General of Canada. 2003. "Indian and Northern Affairs Canada: Transferring Federal Responsibilities to the North." In *Report of the Auditor General of Canada to the House of Commons*. Ottawa, Canada: Minister of Public Works and Government Services Canada.

Auditor General of Canada. 2007. "Inuit Final Agreement." In *Report of the Auditor General of Canada to the House of Commons*. Ottawa, Canada: Minister of Public Works and Government Services Canada.

Barclay, Harold B. 1982. *People without Government*. London: Kahn & Averill with Cienfuegos Press.

Barker, Joanne. 2005a. "For Whom Sovereignty Matters." In *Sovereignty Matters: Locations of Contestation and Possibility in Indigenous Struggles for Self-Determination*, ed. Joanne Barker, 1–31. Lincoln: University of Nebraska Press.

Barker, Joanne, ed. 2005b. *Sovereignty Matters: Locations of Contestation and Possibility in Indigenous Struggles for Self-Determination*. Lincoln: University of Nebraska Press.

Barsh, Russel Lawrence. 1993. "The Challenge of Indigenous Self-Determination." *University of Michigan Journal of Law Reform* 26 (2): 277–312.

Barsh, Russel Lawrence, and James Youngblood Henderson. 1980. *The Road: Indian Tribes and Political Liberty*. Berkeley: University of California Press.

Bartelson, Jens. 1995. *A Genealogy of Sovereignty*. Cambridge: Cambridge University Press.

Bartlett, Richard H. 1979. "Citizens Minus: Indians and the Right to Vote." *Saskatchewan Law Review* 44: 163–94.

Basso, Keith. 1996. *Wisdom Sits in Places: Landscape and Language among the Western Apache*. Albuquerque: University of New Mexico Press.

Bavington, Dean. 2010. *Managed Annihilation: An Unnatural History of the Newfoundland Cod Collapse*. Vancouver: UBC Press.

Beinart, William, and Lotte Hughes. 2007. *Environment and Empire*. Oxford History of the British Empire Companion Series. New York: Oxford University Press.

Bender, John B., and David E. Wellbery, eds. 1991. *Chronotypes: The Construction of Time*. Stanford, CA: Stanford University Press.

Benjamin, Walter. 1968. *Illuminations: Essays and Reflections*. Trans. Harry Zohn. New York: Schocken Books.

Bergson, Henri. 1910. *Time and Free Will: An Essay on the Immediate Data of Consciousness*. Trans. F.L. Pogson. New York: The Macmillan Co.

Berkhofer, Robert. 1978. *The White Man's Indian: Images of the American Indian from Columbus to the Present*. 1st ed. New York: Knopf.

Bettinger, Robert. 2015. *Orderly Anarchy: Sociopolitical Evolution in Aboriginal California*. Oakland: University of California Press.

Bhabha, Homi, ed. 1990. *Nation and Narration*. New York: Routledge.

Biersteker, Thomas, and Cynthia Weber, eds. 1996. *State Sovereignty as Social Construct*. Cambridge: Cambridge University Press.

Biolsi, Thomas. 1995. "The Birth of the Reservation: Making the Modern Individual among the Lakota." *American Ethnologist* 22 (1): 28–53. https://doi.org/10.1525/ae.1995.22.1.02a00020.

Biolsi, Thomas. 2005. "Imagined Geographies: Sovereignty, Indigenous Space, and American Indian Struggle." *American Ethnologist* 32 (2): 239–59. https://doi.org/10.1525/ae.2005.32.2.239.

Black-Rogers, Mary. 1986. "Varieties of 'Starving': Semantics and Survival in the Subarctic Fur Trade, 1750–1850." *Ethnohistory* 33 (4): 353–83. https://doi.org/10.2307/482039.

Blackburn, Carole. 2005. "Searching for Guarantees in the Midst of Uncertainty: Negotiating Aboriginal Rights and Title in British Columbia." *American Anthropologist* 107 (4): 586–96. https://doi.org/10.1525/aa.2005.107.4.586.

Blackburn, Carole. 2009. "Differentiating Indigenous Citizenship: Seeking Multiplicity in Rights, Identity, and Sovereignty in Canada." *American Ethnologist* 36 (1): 66–78. https://doi.org/10.1111/j.1548-1425.2008.01103.x.

Bloch, Maurice. 1977. "The Past and the Present in the Present." *Man* 12 (2): 278–92. https://doi.org/10.2307/2800799.

Boelhower, William. 1988. "Inventing America: The Culture of the Map." *Revue Française d'Études Americaines* 36 (1): 211–24. https://doi.org/10.3406/rfea.1988.1311.

Boldt, Menno, and J. Anthony Long. 1984. "Tribal Traditions and European-Western Political Ideologies: The Dilemma of Canada's Native Indians." *Canadian Journal of Political Science / Revue Canadienne de Science Politique* 17 (3): 537–53. https://doi.org/10.1017/S0008423900031905.

Borneman, John. 1992. *Belonging in the Two Berlins: Kin, State, Nation*. New York: Cambridge University Press.

Borrows, John. 2002. *Recovering Canada: The Resurgence of Indigenous Law*. Toronto: University of Toronto Press.

Borrows, John. 2010a. *Canada's Indigenous Constitution*. Toronto: University of Toronto Press.

Borrows, John. 2010b. *Drawing out Law: A Spirit's Guide*. Toronto: University of Toronto Press.

Bourdieu, Pierre. 1977. *Outline of a Theory of Practice*. Trans. Richard Nice. Cambridge: Cambridge University Press.

Bourdieu, Pierre. 1991. *Language and Symbolic Power*. Cambridge: Harvard University Press.

Brightman, Robert. 1987. "Conservation and Resource Depletion: The Case of the Boreal Forest Algonquians." In *The Question of the Commons: The Culture and Ecology of Communal Resources*, ed. B. McCay and M. Acheson, 121–41. Tucson: University of Arizona Press.

Brightman, Robert. 1993. *Grateful Prey: Rock Cree Human–Animal Relationships*. Los Angeles: University of California Press.

Brody, Hugh. 1982. *Maps and Dreams*. New York: Pantheon Books.

Brown, Michael. 2007. "Sovereignty's Betrayals." In *Indigenous Experience Today*, ed. Marisol de la Cadena and Orin Starn, 171–94. Oxford: Berg.

Brubaker, Rogers. 1992. *Citizenship and Nationhood in France and Germany*. Cambridge, MA: Harvard University Press.

Brubaker, Rogers. 2002. "Ethnicity without Groups." *Archives Européennes de Sociologie* 43 (2): 163–89. https://doi.org/10.1017/S0003975602001066.

Brubaker, Rogers, and Frederick Cooper. 2000. "Beyond 'Identity.'" *Theory and Society* 29 (1): 1–47. https://doi.org/10.1023/A:1007068714468.

Bruyneel, Kevin. 2007. *The Third Space of Sovereignty: The Postcolonial Politics of U.S.–Indigenous Relations*. Minneapolis: University of Minnesota Press.

Burman, Rickie. 1981. "Time and Socioeconomic Change on Simbo, Solomon Islands." *Man* 16 (2): 251–67. https://doi.org/10.2307/2801398.

Cairns, Alan. 2000. *Citizens Plus: Aboriginal Peoples and the Canadian State*. Vancouver: UBC Press.

Carens, Joseph. 1987. "Who Belongs? Theoretical and Legal Questions about Birthright Citizenship in the United States." *University of Toronto Law Journal* 37 (4): 413–43. https://doi.org/10.2307/825799.

Carlson, David J. 2016. *Imagining Sovereignty: Self-Determination in American Indian Law and Literature*. University of Oklahoma Press.

Carlson, Hans. 2008. *Home Is the Hunter: The James Bay Cree and Their Land*. Vancouver: UBC Press.

Carlson, Hans. 2017. "'That's the Place Where I Was Born': History, Narrative, Ecology, and Politics in Canada's North." In *Ice Blink: Navigating Northern Environmental History*, ed. Stephen Bocking and Brad Martin, 295–332. Calgary, AB: University of Calgary Press.

Carter, Paul. 1988. *The Road to Botany Bay: An Exploration of Landscape and History*. 1st American ed. New York: Knopf.

Cattelino, Jessica R. 2008. *High Stakes: Florida Seminole Gaming and Sovereignty*. Durham: Duke University Press.

Cattelino, Jessica R. 2010. "The Double Bind of American Indian Need-Based Sovereignty." *Cultural Anthropology* 25 (2): 235–62. https://doi.org/10.1111/j.1548-1360.2010.01058.x.

Chakrabarty, Dipesh. 2000. *Provincializing Europe: Postcolonial Thought and Historical Difference*. Princeton, NJ: Princeton University Press.

Chatterjee, Partha. 1993. *Nationalist Thought and the Colonial World: A Derivative Discourse*. Minneapolis: University of Minnesota Press.

Cheyfitz, Eric. 1991. *The Poetics of Imperialism: Translation and Colonization from The Tempest to Tarzan*. New York: Oxford University Press.

Cheyfitz, Eric. 2000. "The Navajo-Hopi Land Dispute: A Brief History." *Interventions* 2 (2): 248–75. https://doi.org/10.1080/136980100427342.

Clastres, Pierre. 1987. *Society against the State: Essays in Political Anthropology*. New York: Zone Books.

Clinton, Robert N. 2002. "There Is No Federal Supremacy Clause for Indian Tribes." *Arizona State Law Journal* 34: 113–260.

Coates, Kenneth. 1991. *Best Left as Indians: Native–White Relations in the Yukon Territories, 1840–1973*. Montreal: McGill-Queen's University Press.

Coates, Kenneth, and W.R. Morrison. 2008. "From Panacea to Reality: The Practicality of Canadian Aboriginal Self-Government Agreements." In *Aboriginal Self-Government in Canada: Current Trends and Issues*, 3rd ed., ed. Yale Belanger, 105–22. Aboriginal Issues Series. Saskatoon, SK: Purich.

Cobb, Amanda. 2005. "Understanding Tribal Sovereignty: Definitions, Conceptualizations, and Interpretations." *American Studies* 46 (3–4): 115–32.

Coffey, Wallace, and Rebecca A. Tsosie. 2001. "Rethinking the Tribal Sovereignty Doctrine: Cultural Sovereignty and the Collective Future of Indian Nations." *Stanford Law and Policy Review* 12 (2): 191–221.

Cohen, Anthony Paul, ed. 1986. *Symbolising Boundaries: Identity and Diversity in British Cultures*. Manchester University Press.

Conklin, Beth, and Laura Graham. 1995. "The Shifting Middle Ground: Amazonian Indians and Eco-Politics." *American Anthropologist* 97 (4): 695–710. https://doi.org/10.1525/aa.1995.97.4.02a00120.

Cooper, Frederick, and Ann L. Stoler. 1989. "Introduction Tensions of Empire: Colonial Control and Visions of Rule." *American Ethnologist* 16 (4): 609–21. https://doi.org/10.1525/ae.1989.16.4.02a00010.

Corrigan, Philip, and Derek Sayer. 1985. *The Great Arch: English State Formation as Cultural Revolution*. New York: Blackwell.

Coulthard, Glen Sean. 2014. *Red Skin, White Masks: Rejecting the Colonial Politics of Recognition*. Minneapolis: University of Minnesota Press.

Council for Yukon Indians. 1993. Umbrella Final Agreement between the Government of Canada, the Council for Yukon Indians, and the Government of the Yukon. Ottawa, Canada: Minister of Indian Affairs and Northern Development.

Craib, Raymond B. 2004. *Cartographic Mexico: A History of State Fixations and Fugitive Landscapes*. Durham, NC: Duke University Press.

Craib, Raymond B. 2015. "A Foreword." In *No Gods, No Masters, No Peripheries: Global Anarchisms*, ed. Barry Maxwell and Raymond Craib, 1–8. Oakland, CA: PM Press.

Cronon, William. 1983. *Changes in the Land: Indians, Colonists, and the Ecology of New England*. New York: Hill and Wang.

Cruikshank, Julie. 1981. "Legend and Landscape: Convergence of Oral and Scientific Traditions in the Yukon Territory." *Arctic Anthropology* 18 (2): 67–93.

Cruikshank, Julie. 1985. "The Gravel Magnet: Some Social Impacts of the Alaska Highway on Yukon Indians." In *The Alaska Highway: Papers of the 40th Anniversary Symposium*, ed. Kenneth Coates, 172–87. Vancouver: UBC Press.

Cruikshank, Julie. 1990a. "Getting the Words Right: Perspectives on Naming and Places in Athapaskan Oral History." *Arctic Anthropology* 27 (1): 52–65.

Cruikshank, Julie. 1990b. *Life Lived Like a Story: Life Stories of Three Yukon Native Elders*. Lincoln: University of Nebraska Press.

Cruikshank, Julie. 1998. *The Social Life of Stories: Narrative and Knowledge in the Yukon Territory*. Lincoln: University of Nebraska Press.

Culhane, Dara. 1998. *The Pleasure of the Crown: Anthropology, Law, and First Nations*. Vancouver, BC: Talon.

Dacks, Gurston. 2004. "Implementing First Nations Government in Yukon: Lessons for Canada." *Canadian Journal of Political Science / Revue Canadienne de Science Politique* 37 (3): 671–94. https://doi.org/10.1017/S0008423904030367.

Day, Richard. 2001. "Who Is This We That Gives the Gift? Native American Political Theory and the Western Tradition." *Critical Horizons* 2 (2): 173–201. https://doi.org/10.1163/156851601760001300.

Deloria, Sam. 2002. "Commentary on Nation-Building: The Future of Indian Nations." *Arizona State Law Journal* 34 (1): 55–61.

Deloria, Vine. 1974. *Behind the Trail of Broken Treaties: An Indian Declaration of Independence*. New York: Delacorte Press.

Deloria, Vine. 1979. "Self-Determination and the Concept of Sovereignty." In *Economic Development in American Indian Reservations*, ed. R.D. Ortiz, 22–8. University of New Mexico Development Series no. 1. Albuquerque: University of New Mexico Native American Studies.

Deloria, Vine. 1988. *Custer Died for Your Sins: An Indian Manifesto*. Norman: University of Oklahoma Press.

Deloria, Vine. 1992. *God Is Red: A Native View of Religion*. 2nd ed. Golden, CO: North American Press.

Deloria, Vine, and Clifford Lytle. 1984. *The Nations within: The Past and Future of American Indian Sovereignty*. Austin: University of Texas Press.

Den Ouden, Amy E., and Jean M. O'Brien. 2013. "Introduction." In *Recognition, Sovereignty Struggles, and Indigenous Rights in the United States: A Sourcebook*, ed. Amy E. Den Ouden and Jean M. O'Brien, 1–33. Chapel Hill: University of North Carolina Press.

Dobrowolsky, Helene. 1997. White River First Nation Land Use and Occupancy Study. Prepared by Midnight Arts for the White River First Nation. Draft 2. Whitehorse, Yukon.

Donaldson, Sue, and Will Kymlicka. 2011. *Zoopolis: A Political Theory of Animal Rights*. New York: Oxford University Press.

Duara, Prasenjit. 1995. *Rescuing History from the Nation: Questioning Narratives of Modern China*. Chicago: University of Chicago Press.

Durkheim, Emile. 1915. *The Elementary Forms of the Religious Life*. London: Allen & Unwin.

Dussias, Allison M. 1993. "Geographically-based and Membership-based Views of Indian Tribal Sovereignty: The Supreme Court's Changing Vision." *University of Pittsburgh Law Review* (University of Pittsburgh. School of Law) 55: 1–97.

Easton, Norman Alexander. 2001. "Intergenerational Differences in Ethnic Identification in a Northern Athapaskan Community." *American Review of Canadian Studies* 31 (1–2): 105–19. https://doi.org/10.1080/02722010109481585.

Easton, Norman Alexander. 2008. "'It's Hard Enough to Control Yourself; It's Ridiculous to Think You Can Control Animals': Competing Views On 'the Bush' in Contemporary Yukon." *The Northern Review* 29 (Fall): 21–38.

Easton, Norman Alexander. 2005. *An Ethnohistory of the Chisana River Basin. Report to the US National Parks Service*. Whitehorse, Yukon: Northern Research Institute, Yukon College.

Easton, Norman Alexander. 2007. "King George Got Diarrhea: The Yukon-Alaska Boundary Survey, Bill Rupe, and the Scotty Creek Dineh." *Alaska Journal of Anthropology* 5 (1): 95–118.

Easton, Norman Alexander, Dorothy Kennedy, and Randy Bouchard. 2013. WRFN: Consideration of the Northern Boundary. Report Prepared for the White River First Nation. Whitehorse, YT.

Eggan, Fred. 1960. "The Sagada Igorots of Northern Luzon." In *Social Structure in Southeast Asia*, ed. George Murdoch, 24–50. Chicago: Quadrangle Books.

Eisenberg, Avigail. 2014. "Self-Determination versus Recognition: Lessons and Conclusions." In *Recognition versus Self-Determination: Dilemmas of Emancipatory Politics*, ed. Avigail Eisenberg, Jeremy Webber, Glen Sean Coulthard, and Andrée Boisselle, 293–306. Vancouver, BC: UBC Press.

Eisenberg, Avigail, Jeremy Webber, Glen Sean Coulthard, and Andrée Boisselle, eds. 2014. *Recognition versus Self-Determination: Dilemmas of Emancipatory Politics*. Vancouver, BC: UBC Press.

Elias, Norbert. 2000. *The Civilizing Process: Sociogenetic and Psychogenetic Investigations*. Rev. ed. Oxford: Blackwell Publishers.

Evans-Pritchard, E.E. 1940a. *The Nuer*. Oxford: Oxford University Press.

Evans-Pritchard, E.E. 1940b. "The Nuer of the Southern Sudan." In *African Political Systems*, ed. Meyer Fortes and E.E. Evans-Pritchard, 272–96. Oxford: Oxford University Press.

Fabian, Johannes. 1983. *Time and the Other: How Anthropology Makes Its Object*. New York: Columbia University Press.

Farnell, Richard, P. Gregory Hare, Erik Blake, Vandy Bowyer, Charles Schweger, Sheila Greer, and Ruth Gotthardt. 2004. "Multidisciplinary Investigations of Alpine Ice Patches in Southwest Yukon, Canada: Paleoenvironmental and Paleobiological Investigations." *Arctic* 57 (3): 247–59. https://doi.org/10.14430/arctic502.

Feit, Harvey A. 1998. "Reflections on Local Knowledge and Wildlife Resource Management: Differences, Dominance and Decentralization." In *Aboriginal Environmental Knowledge in the North*, ed. Louis-Jacques Dorais, Murielle Nagy, and Ludger Müller-Wille, 123–48. Quebec: GÉTIC.

Feit, Harvey, and Robert Beaulieu. 2001. "Voices from a Disappearing Forest: Government, Corporate, and Cree Participatory Forestry Management Practices." In *Aboriginal Autonomy and Development in Northern Quebec and Labrador*, ed. Colin Scott, 119–48. Vancouver: UBC Press.

Fenge, Terry. 2015. "Negotiation and Implementation of Modern Treaties between Aboriginal Peoples and the Crown in Right of Canada." In *Keeping Promises: The Royal Proclamation of 1763, Aboriginal Rights, and Treaties in Canada*, ed. Terry Fenge and Jim Aldridge, 105–37. Montreal and Kingston, ON: McGill-Queen's University Press.

Ferguson, James, and Akhil Gupta. 2002. "Spatializing States: Toward an Ethnography of Neo-Liberal Governmentality." *American Ethnologist* 29 (4): 981–1002. https://doi.org/10.1525/ae.2002.29.4.981.

Ferry, Elizabeth. 2008. "Rocks of Ages: Temporal Trajectories of Mexican Mined Substances." In *Timely Assets: The Politics of Resources and Their Temporalities*, ed. Elizabeth Ferry and Mandana Limbert, 51–74. Santa Fe, NM: SAR Press.

Fienup-Riordan, Ann. 1990. *Eskimo Essays: Yup'ik Lives and How We See Them*. New Brunswick: Rutgers University Press.

Flanagan, Thomas. 1985. "The Sovereignty and Nationhood of Canadian Indians: A Comment on Boldt and Long." *Canadian Journal of Political Science* 18 (2): 367–74. https://doi.org/10.1017/S0008423900030304.

Flanagan, Thomas. 2000. *First Nations? Second Thoughts*. Montreal: McGill-Queen's University Press.

Fortes, Meyer, and E.E. Evans-Pritchard. 1940. *African Political Systems*. London: Oxford University Press.

Foster, Robert J. 1991. "Making National Cultures in the Global Ecumene." *Annual Review of Anthropology* 20 (1): 235–60. https://doi.org/10.1146/annurev.an.20.100191.001315.

Fraser, Nancy, and Axel Honneth. 2003. *Redistribution or Recognition? A Political Philosophical Exchange*. New York: Verso.

Fried, Morton H. 1966. "On the Concepts of 'Tribe' and 'Tribal Society.'" *Transactions of the New York Academy of Sciences* 28 (4, Series II): 527–40. https://doi.org/10.1111/j.2164-0947.1966.tb02369.x.

Fried, Morton H. 1968. "On the Concept of 'Tribe' and 'Tribal Society.'" In *Essays on the Problem of Tribe*, ed. June Helm, 3–20. Proceedings of the 1967 Annual Spring Meeting of the American Ethnological Society. Seattle: American Ethnological Society.

Fried, Morton H. 1975. *The Notion of Tribe*. Menlo Park, CA: Cummings Pub. Co.

Fujimura, Joan. 1992. "Crafting Science: Standardized Packages, Boundary Objects, and 'Translation.'" In *Science as Practice and Culture*, ed. Andrew Pickering, 168–211. Chicago: University of Chicago Press.

Gallie, W.B. 1956. "Essentially Contested Concepts." *Proceedings of the Aristotelian Society* 56 (1): 167–98. https://doi.org/10.1093/aristotelian/56.1.167.

Galison, Peter. 2004. *Einstein's Clocks, Poincaré's Maps: Empires of Time*. New York: W.W. Norton.

Geertz, Clifford. 1973. "Person, Time and Conduct in Bali." In *The Interpretation of Cultures*, 360–411. New York: Basic Books.

Gell, Alfred. 1992. *The Anthropology of Time: Cultural Constructions of Temporal Maps and Images*. Oxford: Berg.

Gellner, Ernest. 1983. *Nations and Nationalism*. Ithaca: Cornell University Press.

Giddens, Anthony. 1987. *The Nation-State and Violence: Volume Two of A Contemporary Critique of Historical Materialism*. Berkeley: University of California Press.

Glenn, Evelyn Nakano. 2011. "Constructing Citizenship: Exclusion, Subordination, and Resistance." *American Sociological Review* 76 (1): 1–24. https://doi.org/10.1177/0003122411398443.

Goldberg-Hiller, Jonathan, and Noenoe K. Silva. 2011. "Sharks and Pigs: Animating Hawaiian Sovereignty against the Anthropological Machine." *South Atlantic Quarterly* 110 (2): 429–46. https://doi.org/10.1215/00382876-1162525.

Gordillo, Gastón. 2006. "The Crucible of Citizenship: ID Paper Fetishism in the Argentinian Chaco." *American Ethnologist* 33 (2): 162–76. https://doi.org/10.1525/ae.2006.33.2.162.

Gotthardt, Ruth, Sally Robinson, and Greg Skuce. 2004. *Historic Sites in the White River/Donjek River Area*. Whitehorse, YT: Heritage Resources, Government of Yukon.

Goulet, Jean-Guy. 1998. *Ways of Knowing: Experience, Knowledge, and Power among the Dene Tha*. Lincoln: University of Nebraska Press.

Gover, Kirsty. 2010. *Tribal Constitutionalism: States, Tribes, and the Governance of Membership*. New York: Oxford University Press.

Graeber, David. 2000. "Are You an Anarchist? The Answer May Surprise You." *The Anarchist Library*. http://theanarchistlibrary.org/library/david-graeber-are-you-an-anarchist-the-answer-may-surprise-you.

Graeber, David. 2004. *Fragments of an Anarchist Anthropology*. Chicago: Prickly Paradigm Press.

Greenhouse, Carol. 1996. *A Moment's Notice: Time Politics across Cultures*. Ithaca, NY: Cornell University Press.

Grovogui, Siba N'Zatioula. 1996. *Sovereigns, Quasi Sovereigns, and Africans: Race and Self-Determination in International Law*. Minneapolis: University of Minnesota Press.

Grovogui, Siba N'Zatioula. 2002. "Regimes of Sovereignty: International Morality and the African Condition." *European Journal of International Relations* 8 (3): 315–38. https://doi.org/10.1177/1354066102008003001.

Gurvitch, Georges. 1963. "Social Structure and the Multiplicity of Times." In *Sociological Theory, Values, and Sociocultural Change*, ed. A. Tiyakian, 171–84. New York: Free Press.

Gurvitch, Georges. 1964. *The Spectrum of Social Time*. Trans. M. Korenbaum. Dordrecht: D. Reidel.

Hall, Stuart, and David Held. 1990. "Citizens and Citizenship." In *New Times: The Changing Face of Politics in the 1990s*, ed. Stuart Hall and Martin Jacques, 173–88. New York: Verso.

Hallowell, A. Irving. 1937. "Temporal Orientation in Western Civilization and in a Preliterate Society." *American Anthropologist* 39 (4): 647–70. https://doi.org/10.1525/aa.1937.39.4.02a00100.

Hallowell, Irving. 1960. "Ojibwa Ontology, Behavior, and Worldview." In *Culture in History: Essays in Honor of Paul Radin*, ed. Stanley Diamond, 19–52. New York: Columbia University Press.

Hamilton, Alexander, James Madison, John Jay, and J.R. Pole. 2005. *The Federalist*. Indianapolis: Hackett Pub. Co.

Handler, Richard. 1988. *Nationalism and the Politics of Culture in Quebec. New Directions in Anthropological Writing*. Madison: University of Wisconsin Press.

Hannum, Hurst. 1996. *Autonomy, Sovereignty, and Self-Determination: The Accommodation of Conflicting Rights*. Revised. Philadelphia: University of Pennsylvania Press.

Hare, P. Gregory, Sheila Greer, Ruth Gotthardt, Richard Farnell, Vandy Bowyer, Charles Schweger, and Diane Strand. 2004. "Ethnographic and Archaeological Investigations of Alpine Ice Patches in Southwest Yukon, Canada." *Arctic* 57 (3): 260–72. https://doi.org/10.14430/arctic503.

Harley, J.B. 1989. "Deconstructing the Map." *Cartographica* 26 (2): 1–20. https://doi.org/10.3138/E635-7827-1757-9T53.

Harvey, David. 1990. *The Condition of Postmodernity: An Enquiry into the Origins of Cultural Change*. Cambridge, MA: Blackwell.

Hayes, Charles. 1892. "An Expedition through the Yukon District." *National Geographic* 4: 117–62.

Helm, June, ed. 1968. "Essays on the Problem of Tribe." Proceedings of the 1967 Annual Spring Meeting of the American Ethnological Society. Seattle: American Ethnological Society.

Henderson, James (Sákéj) Youngblood. 2002. "Sui Generis and Treaty Citizenship." *Citizenship Studies* 6 (4): 415–40. https://doi.org/10.1080/1362102022000041259.

Hendrix, Burke A. 2008. *Ownership, Authority, and Self-Determination: Moral Principles and Indigenous Rights Claims*. University Park: Pennsylvania State University Press.

Henkel, Heiko, and Roderick Stirrat. 2001. "Participation as Spiritual Duty; Empowerment as Secular Subjection." In *Participation: The New Tyranny?* ed. Bill Cooke and Uma Kothari, 168–84. New York: Zed Books.

Herzfeld, Michael. 1992. *The Social Production of Indifference: Exploring the Symbolic Roots of Western Bureaucracy*. Chicago: University of Chicago Press.

High, Holly. 2012a. "Anthropology and Anarchy: Romance, Horror or Science Fiction?" *Critique of Anthropology* 32 (2): 93–108. https://doi.org/10.1177/0308275X12438426.

High, Holly, ed. 2012b. "Special Issue: Anthropology and Anarchy." *Critique of Anthropology* 32 (2).

Hildebrandt, Walter, Dorothy First Rider, and Sarah Carter. 1996. *The True Spirit and Original Intent of Treaty 7*. Montreal: McGill-Queen's University Press.

Hobbes, Thomas. 1998. *Leviathan or the Matter, Forme, & Power of a Common-Wealth Ecclesiasticall and Civill*. McMaster University Archive of the History of Economic Thought. ProQuest ebrary.

Hobsbawm, Eric. 1992. *Nations and Nationalism since 1780: Programme, Myth, Reality*. 2nd ed. New York: Cambridge University Press.

Hogg, Peter, and Mary Turpel. 1995. "Implementing Aboriginal Self-Government: Constitutional and Jurisdictional Issues." *Canadian Bar Review* 74 (2): 187–224.

Holston, James. 2008. *Insurgent Citizenship: Disjunctions of Democracy and Modernity in Brazil*. Princeton, NJ: Princeton University Press.

Implementation Review Group. 2007. *Yukon First Nation Final and Self-Government Agreement Implementation Reviews*. Whitehorse, YT: Implementation Review Group.

Ingold, Tim. 1996. "Hunting and Gathering as Ways of Perceiving the Environment." In *Redefining Nature: Ecology, Culture, and Domestication*, ed. Roy Ellen and Katsuyoshi Fukui, 117–55. London: Berg.

Ingold, Tim. 2000. *The Perception of the Environment: Essays in Livelihood, Dwelling, and Skill*. New York: Routledge.

Innes, Robert Alexander. 2013. *Elder Brother and the Law of the People: Contemporary Kinship and Cowessess First Nation*. Winnipeg: University of Manitoba Press.

Irlbacher-Fox, Stephanie. 2009. *Finding Dahshaa: Self-Government, Social Suffering, and Aboriginal Policy in Canada*. Vancouver: UBC Press.

Isin, Engin F., and Bryan S. Turner. 2007. "Investigating Citizenship: An Agenda for Citizenship Studies." *Citizenship Studies* 11 (1): 5–17. https://doi.org/10.1080/13621020601099773.

Ives, John W. 1990. *A Theory of Northern Athapaskan Prehistory*. Boulder: Westview Press.

Jackson, Robert. 1992. *Quasi-States: Sovereignty, International Relations, and the Third World*. Cambridge: Cambridge University Press.

Jacoby, Karl. 2001. *Crimes against Nature: Squatters, Poachers, Thieves, and the Hidden History of American Conservation*. Berkeley: University of California Press.

Jaimes, M. Annette. 1992. "Federal Indian Identification Policy: A Usurpation of Indigenous Sovereignty in North America." In *The State of Native America:*

Genocide, Colonization, and Resistance, ed. M.A. Jaimes, 123–38. Boston: South End Press.

Jamieson, Kathleen. 1978. *Indian Women and the Law in Canada: Citizens Minus*. Ottawa, Canada: Advisory Council on the Status of Women, Indian Rights for Indian Women.

Jenson, Jane, and Martin Papillon. 2000. "Challenging the Citizenship Regime: The James Bay Cree and Transnational Action." *Politics & Society* 28 (2): 245–64. https://doi.org/10.1177/0032329200028002005.

Johnson, Frederick, and Hugh Raup. 1964. "Appendix III: Notes on the Ethnology of the Kluane Lake Region." In *Investigations in Southwest Yukon: Geobotanical and Archaeological Reconnaissance*, 159–98. Papers of the Robert S. Peabody Foundation for Archaeology. Andover, MA: Peabody Foundation.

Johnson, Kenneth. 1973. "Sovereignty, Citizenship, and the Indian." *Arizona Law Review* 15: 973–1003.

Johnston, Darlene. 1993. "First Nations and Canadian Citizenship." In *Belonging: The Meaning and Future of Canadian Citizenship*, ed. William Kaplan, 349–67. Montreal: McGill-Queen's University Press.

Jones, Stephen. 1959. "Boundary Concepts in the Setting of Place and Time." *Annals of the Association of American Geographers* 49 (3): 241–55. https://doi.org/10.1111/j.1467-8306.1959.tb01611.x.

Jonsson, Hjorleifur. 2012. "Paths to Freedom: Political Prospecting in the Ethnographic Record." *Critique of Anthropology* 32 (2): 158–72. https://doi.org/10.1177/0308275X12437980.

Kaiser, Robert. 2002. "Homeland Making and the Territorialization of National Identity." In *Ethnonationalism in the Contemporary World: Walker Connor and the Study of Nationalism*, ed. Daniele Conversi, 229–47. New York: Routledge.

Kaska Dena Constitution Working Group. 2008. Gūkēyeh Guk'éh Gūs'ānī K'úgé': Kaska Nation Constitution. http://www.liardaboriginalwomen.ca/images/stories/PDFs/Kaska_Dena_Constitution_2008.pdf.

Kauanui, J. Kēhaulani. 2008. *Hawaiian Blood: Colonialism and the Politics of Sovereignty and Indigeneity*. Durham, NC: Duke University Press.

Kingsley, Jean-Pierre. 2007. *A History of the Vote in Canada*. 2nd ed. Ottawa, Canada: Elections Canada.

Kipnis, Andrew. 2004. "Anthropology and the Theorisation of Citizenship." *Asia Pacific Journal of Anthropology* 5 (3): 257–78. https://doi.org/10.1080/1444221042000299592.

Klein, Hilary. 2015. "The Zapatista Movement: Blending Indigenous Traditions with Revolutionary Praxis." In *No Gods, No Masters, No Peripheries: Global Anarchisms*, ed. Barry Maxwell and Raymond B. Craib, 22–43. Oakland, CA: PM Press.

Kluane First Nation. 1995. *Kluane First Nation Constitution*. Burwash Landing, YT: Kluane First Nation.

Kluane First Nation. 2003a. Kluane First Nation Self-Government Agreement among Kluane First Nation and Her Majesty the Queen in Right of Canada and the Government of the Yukon. Ottawa, Canada: Minister of Public Works and Government Services Canada.

Kluane First Nation. 2003b. Kluane First Nation Final Agreement among the Government of Canada and Kluane First Nation and the Government of the Yukon. Ottawa, Canada: Minister of Public Works and Government Services Canada.

Kluane First Nation. 2003c. Kluane First Nation Final Agreement Implementation Plan. Ottawa, Canada: Minister of Public Works and Services Canada.

Kluane First Nation. 2003d. Kluane First Nation Self-Government Agreement Implementation Plan. Ottawa, Canada: Minister of Public Works and Government Services Canada.

Knight, David. 1982. "Identity and Territory: Geographical Perspectives on Nationalism and Regionalism." *Annals of the Association of American Geographers* 72 (4): 514–31. https://doi.org/10.1111/j.1467-8306.1982.tb01842.x.

Krauss, Michael. 1964. "Review of *Studies in the Athapaskan Languages*, by Harry Hoijer and Others." *International Journal of American Linguistics* 30 (4): 409–15. https://doi.org/10.1086/464800.

Krauss, Michael. 1973. "Na-Dene." In *Linguistics in North America*, Current Trends in Linguistics 10, ed. Thomas Sebeok, 903–78. The Hague: Mouton.

Krech, Shepard. 2006. "Bringing Linear Time Back In." *Ethnohistory* 53 (3): 567–93. https://doi.org/10.1215/00141801-2006-005.

Kropotkin, Petr Alekseevich. 1902. *Mutual Aid: A Factor of Evolution*. New York: McClure, Philips & Co.

Kropotkin, Petr Alekseevich. 1995. *The Conquest of Bread and Other Writings*. Cambridge: Cambridge University Press.

Kuehls, Thom. 2003. "The Environment of Sovereignty." In *A Political Space: Reading the Global through Clayquot Sound*, ed. Warren Magnusson and Karena Shaw, 179–97. Minneapolis: University of Minnesota Press.

Kulchyski, Peter Keith, and Frank J. Tester. 2007. *Kiumajut (Talking Back): Game Management and Inuit Rights, 1900–70*. Vancouver: UBC Press.

Kushniruk, Rose. 2012. Southern Tutchone Tribal Council Update. Dàkwänía: Champagne and Aishihik First Nations Newsletter, February: 14.

Kymlicka, Will. 1995. *Multicultural Citizenship: A Liberal Theory of Minority Rights*. New York: Oxford University Press.

Kymlicka, Will, and Wayne Norman, eds. 2000. *Citizenship in Diverse Societies*. New York: Oxford University Press.

Landes, David. 2000. *Revolution in Time: Clocks and the Making of the Modern World*. 2nd ed. Cambridge: Harvard University Press.

Lawrence, Bonita. 2004. *Indians and Others: Mixed-Blood Urban Native Peoples and Indigenous Nationhood*. Lincoln: University of Nebraska Press.

Le Goff, Jacques. 1980. *Time, Work, and Culture in the Middle Ages*. Chicago: University of Chicago Press.

Lea, Tess. 2012. "When Looking for Anarchy, Look to the State: Fantasies of Regulation in Forcing Disorder within the Australian Indigenous Estate." *Critique of Anthropology* 32 (2): 109–24. https://doi.org/10.1177/0308275X12438251.

Leach, Edmund. 1961. *Rethinking Anthropology*. Vol. 22. London: Athlone Press.

Lee, Richard B. 1979. *The !Kung San: Men, Women, and Work in a Foraging Society*. New York: Cambridge University Press.

Legros, Dominique. 1985. "Wealth, Poverty, and Slavery among 19th-Century Tutchone Athapaskans." *Research in Economic Anthropology* 7: 37–64.

Legros, Dominique. 2007. "Oral History as History: Tutchone Athapaskan in the Period of 1840–1920." Occasional Papers in Yukon History, 3. Whitehorse, YT: Cultural Services Branch, Yukon Government.

Li, Tania M. 2000. "Articulating Indigenous Identity in Indonesia: Resource Politics and the Tribal Slot." *Comparative Studies in Society and History* 42 (1): 149–79. https://doi.org/10.1017/S0010417500002632.

Limbert, Mandana. 2008. "Depleted Futures: Anticipating the End of Oil in Oman." In *Timely Assets: The Politics of Resources and Their Temporalities*, ed. Elizabeth Ferry and Mandana Limbert, 25–50. Santa Fe, NM: SAR Press.

Lowie, Robert. 1927. *The Origin of the State*. New York: Harcourt Brace.

Lukes, Steven. 1977. "Power and Structure." In *Power*, ed. S. Lukes, 3–29. New York: Columbia University Press.

Lurie, Nancy Oestreich. 1999. "Sol Tax and Tribal Sovereignty." *Human Organization* 58 (1): 108–17. https://doi.org/10.17730/humo.58.1.y84xh610402x182u.

Lyons, Scott Richard. 2000. "Rhetorical Sovereignty: What Do American Indians Want from Writing?" *College Composition and Communication* 51 (3): 447–68. https://doi.org/10.2307/358744.

Lyons, Scott Richard. 2010. *X-Marks: Native Signatures of Assent*. Minneapolis: University of Minnesota Press.

Macdonald, Charles. 2009. "The Anthropology of Anarchy." Occasional Papers of the School of Social Science: Paper no. 35, Princeton, NJ.

MacKenzie, John M. 1988. *The Empire of Nature: Hunting, Conservation, and British Imperialism*. Studies in Imperialism. Manchester, UK: Manchester University Press.

Macklem, Patrick. 1993. "Distributing Sovereignty: Indian Nations and Equality of Peoples." *Stanford Law Review* 45 (5): 1311–67. https://doi.org/10.2307/1229071.

Macpherson, C.B. 1962. *The Political Theory of Possessive Individualism: Hobbes to Locke*. Oxford: Clarendon Press.

Malkki, Liisa. 1992. "National Geographic: The Rooting of Peoples and the Territorialization of National Identity among Scholars and Refugees." *Cultural Anthropology* 7 (1): 24–44. https://doi.org/10.1525/can.1992.7.1.02a00030.

Malmberg, Torsten. 1980. *Human Territoriality: Survey of Behavioural Territories in Man with Preliminary Analysis and Discussion of Meaning*. New York: Mouton.

Malotki, Ekkehart. 1983. *Hopi Time: A Linguistic Analysis of the Temporal Concepts in the Hopi Language*. Amsterdam: Mouton.

Marks, Stuart. 1984. *The Imperial Lion: Human Dimensions of Wildlife Management in Central Africa*. Boulder, CO: Westview Press.

Marshall, Thomas Humphrey. 1950. *Citizenship and Social Class and Other Essays*. Cambridge: Cambridge University Press.

Martin, Keir. 2012. "The 'Potlatch of Destruction': Gifting against the State." *Critique of Anthropology* 32 (2): 125–42. https://doi.org/10.1177/0308275X12437861.

Marx, Karl. 1972. "On the Jewish Question." In *The Marx-Engels Reader*, ed. Robert C. Tucker. New York: Norton.

Mathews, Andrew. 2008. "State Making, Knowledge, and Ignorance: Translation and Concealment in Mexican Forestry Institutions." *American Anthropologist* 110 (4): 484–94. https://doi.org/10.1111/j.1548-1433.2008.00080.x.

Maxwell, Barry, and Raymond B. Craib, eds. 2015. *No Gods, No Masters, No Peripheries: Global Anarchisms*. Oakland, CA: PM Press.

McCandless, Robert. 1985. *Yukon Wildlife: A Social History*. Edmonton: University of Alberta Press.

McClellan, Catharine. 1964. "Culture Contacts in the Early Historic Period in Northwestern North America." *Arctic Anthropology* 2 (2): 3–15.

McClellan, Catharine. 1975. *My Old People Say: An Ethnographic Survey of Southern Yukon Territory*. Ottawa, Canada: National Museum of Man.

McClellan, Catharine. 1992. "Before Boundaries: People of Yukon/Alaska." In *Borderlands: A Conference on the Alaska-Yukon Border*, 8–34. Whitehorse, YT: Yukon Historical and Museums Association.

McClellan, Catharine. 2007. *My Old People's Stories: A Legacy for Yukon First Nations*. Vol. 5. Occasional Papers in Yukon History. Whitehorse, YT: Cultural Services Branch, Yukon Government.

McClellan, Catharine, Lucie Birckel, Robert Bringhurst, et al. 1987. *Part of the Land, Part of the Water: A History of the Yukon Indians*. Vancouver, Toronto: Douglas & McIntyre.

McClellan, Catharine, and Glenda Denniston. 1981. "Environment and Culture in the Cordillera." In *Handbook of North American Indians*, vol. 6, ed. J. Helm, 372–86. Washington, DC: Smithsonian Institution Press.

McDonnell, Roger. 1975. "Kasini Society: Some Aspects of the Social Organization of an Athapaskan Culture between 1900–1950." Ph.D. thesis, University of British Columbia.

McDonnell, Roger. 1984. "Symbolic Orientations and Systematic Turmoil: Centering on the Kaska Symbol of Dene." *Canadian Journal of Anthropology* 4 (1): 39–56.

McEachern, Allan. 1991. Reasons for Judgment: Delgamuukw v. B.C. Smithers, BC: Supreme Court of British Columbia.

McKennan, Robert. 1959. *The Upper Tanana Indians*. New Haven: Department of Anthropology, Yale University.

McKennan, Robert. 1981. "Tanana." In *Handbook of North American Indians*, vol. 6, ed. June Helm, 562–76. Washington, DC: Smithsonian Institution.

McNeil, Kent. 1998. "Aboriginal Rights in Canada: From Title to Land to Territorial Jurisdiction." *Tulsa Journal of Comparative and International Law* 5 (2): 253–389.

Meek, Barbra A. 2010. *We Are Our Language: An Ethnography of Language Revitalization in a Northern Athabascan Community*. Tucson: University of Arizona Press.

Meek, Barbra A. 2014. "'She Can Do It in English Too': Acts of Intimacy and Boundary-Making in Language Revitalization." *Language & Communication* 38: 73–82. https://doi.org/10.1016/j.langcom.2014.05.004.

Merchant, Carolyn. 1989. *Ecological Revolutions: Nature, Gender, and Science in New England*. Chapel Hill: University of North Carolina Press.

Miller, J.R. 2009. *Compact, Contract, Covenant: Aboriginal Treaty-Making in Canada*. Toronto: University of Toronto Press.

Minister of Indian Affairs and Northern Development. 1995. "Aboriginal Self-Government: The Government of Canada's Approach to Implementation of the Inherent Right and the Negotiation of Aboriginal Self-Government." Ottawa, Canada: Minister of Public Works and Government Services Canada.

Mitchell, Timothy. 1990. "Everyday Metaphors of Power." *Theory and Society* 19 (5): 545–77. https://doi.org/10.1007/BF00147026.

Mitchell, Timothy. 1991. "The Limits of the State: Beyond Statist Approaches and Their Critics." *American Political Science Review* 85 (1): 77–96.

Mitchell, Timothy. 2002. *Rule of Experts: Egypt, Techno-Politics, Modernity*. Berkeley: University of California Press.

Miyazaki, Hirokazu. 2003. "The Temporalities of the Market." *American Anthropologist* 105 (2): 255–65. https://doi.org/10.1525/aa.2003.105.2.255.

Montsion, Jean Michel. 2015. "Disrupting Canadian Sovereignty? The 'First Nations & China' Strategy Revisited." *Geoforum* 58: 114–21. https://doi.org/10.1016/j.geoforum.2014.11.001.

Moore, Adam. 2016. "Ethno-Territoriality and Ethnic Conflict." *Geographical Review* 106 (1): 92–108. https://doi.org/10.1111/j.1931-0846.2015.12132.x.

Morrow, Phyllis, and Chase Hensel. 1992. "Hidden Dissension: Minority-Majority Relationships and the Use of Contested Terminology." *Arctic Anthropology* 29 (1): 38–53.

Morse, Bradford. 1999. "The Inherent Right of Aboriginal Governance." In *Aboriginal Self-Government in Canada: Current Trends and Issues*, 2nd ed., ed. John Hylton, 16–44. Saskatoon, SK: Purich.

Morse, Bradford. 2008. "Regaining Recognition of the Inherent Right of Aboriginal Governance." In *Aboriginal Self-Government in Canada: Current Trends and Issues*, 3rd ed., ed. Yale Belanger, 39–68. Saskatoon, SK: Purich.

Muckenheim, Stephanie. 1998. *The Importance of Fishing and Fish Harvesting to Yukon First Nations People*. Yukon Fish and Wildlife Management Board Report Series # 1. Whitehorse: Yukon Fish and Wildlife Management Board.

Mumford, Lewis. 1962. *Technics and Civilization*. New York: Harcourt, Brace, and World.

Munasinghe, Viranjini. 2002. "Nationalism in Hybrid Spaces: The Production of Impurity out of Purity." *American Ethnologist* 29 (3): 663–92. https://doi.org/10.1525/ae.2002.29.3.663.

Murphy, Alexander. 1989. "Territorial Policies in Multiethnic States." *Geographical Review* 79 (4): 410–21. https://doi.org/10.2307/215115.

Murphy, Alexander. 1996. "The Sovereign State System as Political-Territorial Ideal: Historical and Contemporary Considerations." In *State Sovereignty as Social Construct*, ed. Thomas J. Biersteker and Cynthia Weber, 81–120. Cambridge: Cambridge University Press.

Nadasdy, Paul. 2002. "'Property' and Aboriginal Land Claims in the Canadian Subarctic: Some Theoretical Considerations." *American Anthropologist* 104 (1): 247–61. https://doi.org/10.1525/aa.2002.104.1.247.

Nadasdy, Paul. 2003. *Hunters and Bureaucrats: Power, Knowledge, and Aboriginal–State Relations in the Southwest Yukon*. Vancouver: UBC Press.

Nadasdy, Paul. 2005a. "Transcending the Debate over the Ecologically Noble Indian: Indigenous Peoples and Environmentalism." *Ethnohistory* 52 (2): 291–331. https://doi.org/10.1215/00141801-52-2-291.

Nadasdy, Paul. 2005b. "The Anti-Politics of TEK: The Institutionalization of Co-Management Discourse and Practice." *Anthropologica* 47 (2): 215–32.

Nadasdy, Paul. 2007a. "Adaptive Co-Management and the Gospel of Resilience." In *Adaptive Co-Management: Collaboration, Learning, and Multilevel Governance*, ed. Derek Armitage, Fikret Berkes, and Nancy Doubleday, 208–27. Vancouver: UBC Press.

Nadasdy, Paul. 2007b. "The Gift in the Animal: The Ontology of Hunting and Human-Animal Sociality." *American Ethnologist* 34 (1): 25–43.

Nadasdy, Paul. 2008. "The Antithesis of Restitution? A Note on the Dynamics of Land Negotiations in the Yukon, Canada." In *The Rights and Wrongs of Land Restitution: Restoring What Was Ours*, ed. D. Fay and D. James, 85–97. London: Routledge.

Nadasdy, Paul. 2010. "Resilience and Truth: A Response to Berkes." *Maritime Studies (MAST)* 9 (1): 40–5.

Nadasdy, Paul. 2011. "'We Don't Harvest Animals; We Kill Them': Agricultural Metaphors and the Politics of Wildlife Management in the Yukon." In *Knowing Nature: Conversations at the Intersection of Political Ecology and Science Studies*, ed. M. Goldman, P. Nadasdy, and M. Turner, 135–51. Chicago: University of Chicago Press.

Nadasdy, Paul. 2012. "Boundaries among Kin: Sovereignty, the Modern Treaty Process, and the Rise of Ethno-Territorial Nationalism among Yukon First Nations." *Comparative Studies in Society and History* 54 (3): 499–532. https://doi.org/10.1017/S0010417512000217.

Nadasdy, Paul. 2016. "First Nations, Citizenship and Animals, or Why Northern Indigenous People Might Not Want to Live in Zoopolis." *Canadian Journal of Political Science* 49 (1): 1–20. https://doi.org/10.1017/S0008423915001079.

Nadasdy, Paul. 2017. "Imposing Territoriality: First Nation Land Claims and the Transformation of Human-Environmental Relations in the Yukon." In *Ice Blink: Navigating Northern Environmental History*, ed. Stephen Bocking and Brad Martin, 333–76. Calgary, AB: University of Calgary Press.

Natcher, David, Susan Davis, and Clifford Hickey. 2005. "Co-Management: Managing Relationships, Not Resources." *Human Organization* 64 (3): 240–50. https://doi.org/10.17730/humo.64.3.23yfnkrl2ylapjxw.

Nelson, Richard K. 1983. *Make Prayers to the Raven: A Koyukon View of the Northern Forest*. Chicago: University of Chicago Press.

Nesper, Larry. 2007. "Negotiating Jurisprudence in Tribal Court and the Emergence of a Tribal State: The Lac Du Flambeau Ojibwe." *Current Anthropology* 48 (5): 675–99. https://doi.org/10.1086/520132.

Neu, Dean. 2000. "'Presents' for the 'Indians': Land, Colonialism, and Accounting in Canada." *Accounting, Organizations and Society* 25 (2): 163–84. https://doi.org/10.1016/S0361-3682(99)00030-6.

Neumann, Roderick P. 1998. *Imposing Wilderness: Struggles over Livelihood and Nature Preservation in Africa*. California Studies in Critical Human Geography, 4. Berkeley: University of California Press.

Niembro, Rasec. 2017. *The Zapatista Candidate*. Jacobin.

Niezen, Ronald. 2000. "Recognizing Indigenism: Canadian Unity and the International Movement of Indigenous Peoples." *Comparative Studies in Society and History* 42 (1): 119–48. https://doi.org/10.1017/S0010417500002620.

Notzke, Claudia. 1994. *Aboriginal Peoples and Natural Resources in Canada*. North York, ON: Captus University Publications.

Nugent, Stephen. 2012. "Anarchism out West: Some Reflections on Sources." *Critique of Anthropology* 32 (2): 206–16. https://doi.org/10.1177/0308275X12437860.

Omura, Keiichi. 2013. "The Ontology of Sociality: 'Sharing' and Subsistence Mechanisms." In *Groups: The Evolution of Human Sociality*, ed. Kaori Kawai, 123–42. Kyoto, Japan: Kyoto University Press.

Ong, Aihwa. 1999. *Flexible Citizenship: The Cultural Logics of Transnationality*. Durham: Duke University Press.

Ong, Aihwa. 2003. *Buddha Is Hiding: Refugees, Citizenship, the New America*. Berkeley: University of California Press.

Ong, Aihwa. 1996. "Cultural Citizenship as Subject-Making: Immigrants Negotiate Racial and Cultural Boundaries in the United States." *Current Anthropology* 37 (5): 737–62. https://doi.org/10.1086/204560.

Osgood, Cornelius. 1936. *The Distribution of the Northern Athapaskan Indians*. Yale University Publications in Anthropology, 7. New Haven: Yale University Press.

Osiander, A. 2001. "Sovereignty, International Relations, and the Westphalian Myth." *International Organization* 55 (2): 251–87. https://doi.org/10.1162/00208180151140577.

Paasi, Anssi. 1996. *Territories, Boundaries, and Consciousness: The Changing Geographies of the Finnish-Russian Border*. New York: J. Wiley & Sons.

Penrose, Jan. 2002. "Nations, States, and Homelands: Territory and Territoriality in Nationalist Thought." *Nations and Nationalism* 8 (3): 277–97. https://doi.org/10.1111/1469-8219.00051.

Peterson, Nicolas. 1993. "Demand Sharing: Reciprocity and the Pressure for Generosity among Foragers." *American Anthropologist* 95 (4): 860–74. https://doi.org/10.1525/aa.1993.95.4.02a00050.

Pickering, Kathleen. 2004. "Decolonizing Time Regimes: Lakota Conceptions of Work, Economy, and Society." *American Anthropologist* 106 (1): 85–97. https://doi.org/10.1525/aa.2004.106.1.85.

Porter, Robert. 1999. "The Demise of the Ongwehoweh and the Rise of the Native Americans: Redressing the Genocidal Act of Forcing American Citizenship upon Indigenous Peoples." *Harvard Blackletter Law Journal* 15: 107–83.

Porter, Robert B. 2002. "The Meaning of Indigenous Nation Sovereignty." *Arizona State Law Journal* 34: 75–112.

Povinelli, Elizabeth. 1995. "Do Rocks Listen? The Cultural Politics of Apprehending Australian Aboriginal Labor." *American Anthropologist* 97 (3): 505–18. https://doi.org/10.1525/aa.1995.97.3.02a00090.

Povinelli, Elizabeth A. 2002. *The Cunning of Recognition: Indigenous Alterities and the Making of Australian Multiculturalism*. Durham, NC: Duke University Press. https://doi.org/10.1215/9780822383673.

Power, Michael. 1997. *The Audit Society: Rituals of Verification*. Oxford: Oxford University Press.

Price, Richard. 1999. *The Spirit of the Alberta Indian Treaties*. 3rd ed. Edmonton: University of Alberta Press.

Prucha, Francis. 1994. *American Indian Treaties: The History of a Political Anomaly*. Berkeley: University of California Press.

Rappaport, Roy A. 1984. *Pigs for the Ancestors: Ritual in the Ecology of a New Guinea People*. New Haven: Yale University Press.

Raustiala, Kal. 2009. *Does the Constitution Follow the Flag? The Evolution of Territoriality in American Law*. New York: Oxford University Press.

Rée, Jonathan. 1992. "Internationality." *Radical Philosophy* 60: 3–11.

Renan, Ernest. 1990. "What Is a Nation?" In *Nation and Narration*, ed. Homi Bhabha, 8–22. New York: Routledge.

Richland, Justin. 2008. "Sovereign Time, Storied Moments: The Temporalities of Law, Tradition, and Ethnography in Hopi Tribal Court." *Political and Legal Anthropology Review* 31 (1): 8–27. https://doi.org/10.1111/j.1555-2934.2008.00004.x.

Richland, Justin. 2011. "Hopi Tradition as Jurisdiction: On the Potentializing Limits of Hopi Sovereignty." *Law & Social Inquiry* 36 (1): 201–34. https://doi.org/10.1111/j.1747-4469.2010.01229.x.

Richland, Justin B., and Sarah Deer. 2016. *Introduction to Tribal Legal Studies*. 3rd ed. New York: Rowman & Littlefield.

Rickard, Jolene. 2011. "Visualizing Sovereignty in the Time of Biometric Sensors." *South Atlantic Quarterly* 110 (2): 465–86. https://doi.org/10.1215/00382876-1162543.

Rifkin, Mark. 2009. "Indigenizing Agamben: Rethinking Sovereignty in Light of the 'Peculiar' Status of Native Peoples." *Cultural Critique* 73 (1): 88–124. https://doi.org/10.1353/cul.0.0049.

Robinson, Andrew, and Simon Tormey. 2012. "Beyond the State: Anthropology and 'Actually-Existing-Anarchism.'" *Critique of Anthropology* 32 (2): 143–57. https://doi.org/10.1177/0308275X12438779.

Rosen, Lawrence. 1984. *Bargaining for Reality: The Construction of Social Relations in a Muslim Community*. Chicago: University of Chicago Press.

Rotenberg, Robert. 1992. "The Power to Time and the Time to Power." In *The Politics of Time*, ed. Henry Rutz, 18–36. American Ethnological Society Monograph Series. Washington, DC: American Anthropological Association.

Royal Commission on Aboriginal Peoples. 1992. *The Right of Aboriginal Self-Government and the Constitution: A Commentary*. Ottawa, Canada: Royal Commission on Aboriginal Peoples.

Ruggie, John. 1993. "Territoriality and Beyond: Problematizing Modernity in International Relations." *International Organization* 47 (1): 139–74. https://doi.org/10.1017/S0020818300004732.

Rutz, Henry, ed. 1992. *The Politics of Time*. American Ethnological Society Monograph Series. Washington, DC: American Anthropological Association.

Rynard, Paul. 2000. "Welcome In, but Check Your Rights at the Door: The James Bay and Nisga'a Agreements in Canada." *Canadian Journal of Political Science* 33 (2): 211–43. https://doi.org/10.1017/S0008423900000081.

Rynard, Paul. 2001. "Ally or Colonizer?: The Federal State, the Cree Nation and the James Bay Agreement." *Journal of Canadian Studies. Revue d'Études Canadiennes* 36 (2): 8–48. https://doi.org/10.3138/jcs.36.2.8.

Sack, Robert. 1986. *Human Territoriality: Its Theory and History*. New York: Cambridge University Press.

Sahlins, Marshall. 1972. *Stone Age Economics*. London: Tavistock.

Sahlins, Peter. 1989. *Boundaries: The Making of France and Spain in the Pyrenees*. Berkeley: University of California Press.

Samson, Colin, and Elizabeth Cassell. 2013. "The Long Reach of Frontier Justice: Canadian Land Claims 'Negotiation' Strategies as Human Rights Violations." *International Journal of Human Rights* 17 (1): 35–55. https://doi.org/10.1080/13642987.2012.695860.

Sandlos, John. 2007. *Hunters at the Margin: Native People and Wildlife Conservation in the Northwest Territories*. Vancouver: UBC Press.

Sassen, Saskia. 1999. *Guests and Aliens*. New York: New Press.

Sayer, Derek. 1991. *Capitalism and Modernity: An Excursus on Marx and Weber*. New York: Routledge.

Scheele, Judith. 2015. "The Values of 'Anarchy': Moral Autonomy among Tubu-Speakers in Northern Chad." *Journal of the Royal Anthropological Institute* 21 (1): 32–48. https://doi.org/10.1111/1467-9655.12141.

Schieffelin, Bambi. 2002. "Marking Time: The Dichotomizing Discourse of Multiple Temporalities." *Current Anthropology* 43 (S4 Supplement): S5–17. https://doi.org/10.1086/341107.

Schneider, David. 1977. "Kinship, Nationality, and Religion in American Culture: Toward a Definition of Kinship." In *Symbolic Anthropology*, ed. Janet Doglin, David Kemnitzer, and David Schneider, 63–71. New York: Columbia University Press.

Schuck, Peter H., and Rogers M. Smith. 1985. *Citizenship without Consent: Illegal Aliens in the American Polity*. New Haven: Yale University Press.

Scott, Colin. 1988. "Property, Practice, and Aboriginal Rights among Quebec Cree Hunters." In *Hunters and Gatherers: Property, Power, and Ideology*, ed. Tim Ingold, David Riches, and James Woodburn, 35–51. New York: St Martin's Press.

Scott, James C. 1998. *Seeing like a State: How Certain Schemes to Improve the Human Condition Have Failed*. New Haven: Yale University Press.

Scott, James C. 2009. *The Art of Not Being Governed: An Anarchist History of Upland Southeast Asia*. Yale Agrarian Studies Series. New Haven: Yale University Press.

Seed, Patricia. 1995. *Ceremonies of Possession in Europe's Conquest of the New World, 1492–1640*. Cambridge: Cambridge University Press.

Segal, Daniel, and Richard Handler. 1992. "How European Is Nationalism?" *Social Analysis* 32: 1–15.

Seton-Watson, Hugh. 1977. *Nations and States: An Enquiry into the Origins of Nations and the Politics of Nationalism*. Boulder, CO: Westview Press.

Sharp, Henry. 1988. *The Transformation of Bigfoot: Maleness, Power, and Belief among the Chipewyan*. Washington, DC: Smithsonian Institution Press.

Sharp, Henry S. 2001. *Loon: Memory, Meaning, and Reality in a Northern Dene Community*. Lincoln: University of Nebraska Press.

Shaw, Karena. 2008. *Indigeneity and Political Theory: Sovereignty and the Limits of the Political*. New York: Routledge.

Simpson, Audra. 2008. "Subjects of Sovereignty: Indigeneity, the Revenue Rule, and Juridics of Failed Consent." *Law and Contemporary Problems* 71: 191–215.

Simpson, Audra. 2014. *Mohawk Interruptus: Political Life across the Borders of Settler States*. Durham, NC: Duke University Press.

Simpson, Leanne. 2008. "Looking after Gdoo-Naaganinaa: Precolonial Nishnaabeg Diplomatic and Treaty Relationships." *Wicazo Sa Review* 23 (2): 29–42. https://doi.org/10.1353/wic.0.0001.

Slattery, Brian. 1992. "First Nations and the Constitution: A Question of Trust." *Canadian Bar Review* 71: 261–93.

Smith, Adam T. 2003. *The Political Landscape: Constellations of Authority in Early Complex Polities*. Berkeley: University of California Press.

Smith, Anthony. 1979. *Nationalism in the Twentieth Century*. London: Martin Robertson.

Smith, Anthony. 1981. "States and Homelands: The Social and Geopolitical Implications of National Territory." *Millennium: Journal of International Studies* 10 (3): 187–202. https://doi.org/10.1177/03058298810100030201.

Smith, David. 2002. "The Flesh and the Word: Stories and Other Gifts of the Animals in Chipewyan Cosmology." *Anthropology and Humanism* 27 (1): 60–79. https://doi.org/10.1525/anhu.2002.27.1.60.

Soja, Edward. 1971. *The Political Organization of Space*. Washington: Association of American Geographers.

Southall, Aiden. 1970. "The Illusion of Tribe." *Journal of Asian and African Studies* 5 (1): 28–50. https://doi.org/10.1177/002190967000500104.

Steinman, Erich. 2011. "Sovereigns and Citizens? The Contested Status of American Indian Tribal Nations and Their Members." *Citizenship Studies* 15 (1): 57–74. https://doi.org/10.1080/13621025.2011.534927.

Stevenson, Marc. 2006. "The Possibility of Difference: Rethinking Co-Management." *Human Organization* 65 (2): 167–80. https://doi.org/10.17730/humo.65.2.b2dm8thgb7wa4m53.

Strang, David. 1996. "Contested Sovereignty: The Social Construction of Colonial Imperialism." In *State Sovereignty as Social Construct*, ed. Thomas J. Biersteker and Cynthia Weber, 22–49. Cambridge: Cambridge University Press.

Strathern, Marilyn, ed. 2000. *Audit Cultures: Anthropological Studies in Accountability, Ethics, and the Academy*. New York: Routledge.

Strayer, Joseph. 1970. *On the Medieval Origins of the Modern State*. Princeton, NJ: Princeton University Press.

Sturm, Circe. 2002. *Blood Politics: Race, Culture, and Identity in the Cherokee Nation of Oklahoma*. Berkeley: University of California Press.

Sweetman, John. 1984. *War and Administration: The Significance of the Crimean War for the British Army*. Edinburgh: Scottish Academy Press.

Tanner, Adrian. 1979. *Bringing Home Animals: Religious Ideology and Mode of Production of the Mistassini Cree Hunters*. New York: St Martin's Press.

Taylor, Peter. 1994. "The State as Container: Territoriality in the Modern World System." *Progress in Human Geography* 18 (2): 151–62. https://doi.org/10.1177/030913259401800202.

Teschke, Benno. 2003. *The Myth of 1648: Class, Geopolitics, and the Making of Modern International Relations*. London: Verso.

Thom, Brian. 2009. "The Paradox of Boundaries in Coast Salish Territories." *Cultural Geographies* 16 (2): 179–205. https://doi.org/10.1177/1474474008101516.

Thompson, E.P. 1967. "Time, Work Discipline, and Industrial Capitalism." *Past & Present* 38 (1): 56–97. https://doi.org/10.1093/past/38.1.56.

Thongchai Winichakul. 1994. *Siam Mapped: A History of the Geo-Body of a Nation*. Honolulu: University of Hawaii Press.

Tocqueville, Alexis de. 1945. *Democracy in America*. New York: A.A. Knopf.

Torpey, John. 2000. *The Invention of the Passport: Surveillance, Citizenship, and the State*. New York: Cambridge University Press.

Traweek, Sharon. 1988. *Beamtimes and Lifetimes: The World of High Energy Physicists*. Cambridge, MA: Harvard University Press.

Tully, James. 1993. "Rediscovering America: The Two Treatises and Aboriginal Rights." In *An Approach to Political Philosophy: Locke in Contexts*, 137–76. New York: Cambridge University Press.

Tully, James. 1995. *Strange Multiplicity: Constitutionalism in an Age of Diversity*. New York: Cambridge University Press.

Tully, James. 2008. *Public Philosophy in a New Key*. Cambridge: Cambridge University Press.

Tully, James. 2014. *On Global Citizenship: James Tully in Dialogue*. London: Bloomsbury Academic.

Tully, James. 2016. On Gaia Citizenship, The Mastermind Lecture. University of Victoria, Victoria, Canada, 20 April. http://www.uvic.ca/socialsciences/politicalscience/assets/docs/faculty/tully/tully-on-gaia-citizenship.pdf.

Turnbull, David. 2004. "Narrative Traditions of Space, Time, and Trust in Court: Terra nullius, 'Wandering,' the Yorta Yorta Native Title Claim, and the Hindmarsh Island Bridge Controversy." In *Expertise in Regulation and Law*, ed. Gary Edmond, 166–83. Ashgate.

Turner, Bryan. 1990. "Outline of a Theory of Citizenship." *Sociology* 24 (2): 189–217. https://doi.org/10.1177/0038038590024002002.

Usher, Peter. 1986. *The Devolution of Wildlife Management and the Prospects for Wildlife Conservation in the Northwest Territories*. Ottawa, Canada: Canadian Arctic Resources Committee.

Vail, Leroy, ed. 1991. *The Creation of Tribalism in Southern Africa*. Berkeley: University of California Press.

Vandergeest, Peter, and Nancy Peluso. 1995. "Territorialization and State Power in Thailand." *Theory and Society* 24 (3): 385–426. https://doi.org/10.1007/BF00993352.

Verdery, Katherine. 1992. "The 'Etatization' of Time in Ceausescu's Romania." In *The Politics of Time*, ed. Henry Rutz, 37–61. American Ethnological Society Monograph Series. Washington, DC: American Anthropological Association.

Verdery, Katherine. 1993a. "Whither 'Nation' and 'Nationalism'?" *Daedalus* 122 (3): 37–46.

Verdery, Katherine. 1993b. "Nationalism and National Sentiment in Post-Socialist Romania." *Slavic Review* 52 (2): 179–203. https://doi.org/10.2307/2499919.

Verdery, Katherine. 1994a. "From Parent-State to Family Patriarchs: Gender and Nation in Contemporary Eastern Europe." *Eastern European Politics and Societies* 8 (2): 225–55. https://doi.org/10.1177/0888325494008002002.

Verdery, Katherine. 1994b. "Ethnicity, Nationalism, and State-Making." In *The Anthropology of Ethnicity: Beyond "Ethnic Groups and Boundaries,"* ed. Hans Vermuelen and Cora Govers, 33–58. Amsterdam: Het Spinhuis.

Verdery, Katherine. 1996. "Nationalism, Postsocialism, and Space in Eastern Europe." *Social Research* 63 (1): 77–95.

Verdery, Katherine. 1999. *The Political Lives of Dead Bodies: Reburial and Post-socialist Change*. New York: Columbia University Press.

Walker, Robert B.J. 1993. *Inside/Outside: International Relations as Political Theory*. Cambridge: Cambridge University Press.

Wallerstein, Immanuel. 2003. "Citizens All? Citizens Some! The Making of the Citizen." *Comparative Studies in Society and History* 45 (4): 650–79. https://doi.org/10.1017/S0010417503000318.

Ward, Colin. 1973. *Anarchy in Action*. London: Allen and Unwin.

Ward, Colin. 2004. *Anarchism: A Very Short Introduction*. Oxford: Oxford University Press.

Warrior, Robert Allen. 1995. *Tribal Secrets: Recovering American Indian Intellectual Traditions*. Minneapolis: University of Minnesota Press.

Watkins, Mel. 1977. *Dene Nation: The Colony within*. Toronto: University of Toronto Press.

Weber, Cynthia, and Thomas Biersteker. 1996. "The Social Construction of State Sovereignty." In *State Sovereignty as Social Construct*, ed. Thomas J. Biersteker and Cynthia Weber, 1–21. Cambridge: Cambridge University Press.

Weber, Max. 1946a. "Politics as a Vocation." In *From Max Weber: Essays in Sociology*, ed. H.H. Gerth and C.W. Mills, 77–128. New York: Oxford University Press.

Weber, Max. 1946b. "Bureaucracy." In *From Max Weber: Essays in Sociology*, ed. H.H. Gerth and C. Wright Mills, 196–244. New York: Oxford University Press.

Weitz, Morris. 1977. *The Opening Mind: A Philosophical Study of Humanistic Concepts*. Chicago: University of Chicago Press.

Wenzel, George. 1991. *Animal Rights, Human Rights: Ecology, Economy, and Ideology in the Canadian Arctic*. Toronto: University of Toronto Press.

White, Graham. 2009. "Governance in Nunavut: Capacity vs. Culture?" *Journal of Canadian Studies. Revue d'Études Canadiennes* 43 (2): 57–81. https://doi.org/10.3138/jcs.43.2.57.

Whorf, Benjamin. 1956. "An American Indian Model of the Universe." In *Language, Thought, and Reality: Selected Writings of Benjamin Lee Whorf*, ed. John Carroll, 57–64. Cambridge, MA: MIT Press.

Wilkins, David E. 1997. *American Indian Sovereignty and the U.S. Supreme Court: The Masking of Justice*. Austin: University of Texas Press.

Wilkins, David, and Tsianina Lomawaima. 2001. *Uneven Ground: American Indian Sovereignty and Federal Law*. Norman: University of Oklahoma Press.

Wilkinson, Charles. 1987. *American Indians, Time, and the Law: Native Societies in a Modern Constitutional Democracy*. New Haven, CT: Yale University Press.

Williams, Brackette. 1989. "A Class Act: Anthropology and the Race to Nation across Ethnic Terrain." *Annual Review of Anthropology* 18 (1): 401–44. https://doi.org/10.1146/annurev.an.18.100189.002153.

Williams, Colin, and Anthony Smith. 1983. "The National Construction of Social Space." *Progress in Human Geography* 7 (4): 502–18.

Williams, Nancy M. 1986. *The Yolngu and Their Land: A System of Land Tenure and the Fight for Its Recognition*. Stanford, CA: Stanford University Press.

Williams, Robert A. 2005. *Like a Loaded Weapon: The Rehnquist Court, Indian Rights, and the Legal History of Racism in America*. Minneapolis: University of Minnesota Press.

Willow, Anna J. 2013. "Doing Sovereignty in Native North America: Anishinaabe Counter-Mapping and the Struggle for Land-Based Self-Determination." *Human Ecology* 41 (6): 871–84. https://doi.org/10.1007/s10745-013-9593-9.

Witkin, Alexandra. 1995. "To Silence a Drum: The Imposition of United States Citizenship on Native Peoples." *Historical Reflections. Réflexions Historiques* 21 (2): 353–83.

Wolf, Eric. 1982. *Europe and the People without History*. Berkeley: University of California Press.

Wolfe, Patrick. 2006. "Settler Colonialism and the Elimination of the Native." *Journal of Genocide Research* 8 (4): 387–409. https://doi.org/10.1080/14623520601056240.

Wood, Denis. 1992. *The Power of Maps*. New York: Guilford Press.

Woolford, Andrew. 2005. *Between Justice and Certainty: Treaty Making in British Columbia*. Vancouver: UBC Press.

Young, Iris Marion. 1989. "Polity and Group Difference: A Critique of the Ideal of Universal Citizenship." *Ethics* 99 (2): 250–74. https://doi.org/10.1086/293065.

Young, Iris Marion. 1990. *Justice and the Politics of Difference*. Princeton, NJ: Princeton University Press.

Yukon Department of Renewable Resources. 1997. Sport Fishing Regulations Summary 1997–8. Whitehorse, Yukon: Yukon Territorial Government.

Yukon Fish and Wildlife Management Board. 2000. Fifth Annual Report. Whitehorse, Yukon: Yukon Fish and Wildlife Management Board.

Yukon Native Brotherhood. 1973. *Together Today for Our Children Tomorrow*. Whitehorse: Yukon Native Brotherhood.

Zerubavel, Eviatar. 1981. *Hidden Rhythms: Schedules and Calendars in Social Life*. Berkeley: University of California Press.

Index

Page numbers in italics indicate illustrations.

www.ingramcontent.com/pod-product-compliance
Lightning Source LLC
LaVergne TN
LVHW090802070826
844660LV00022B/1056